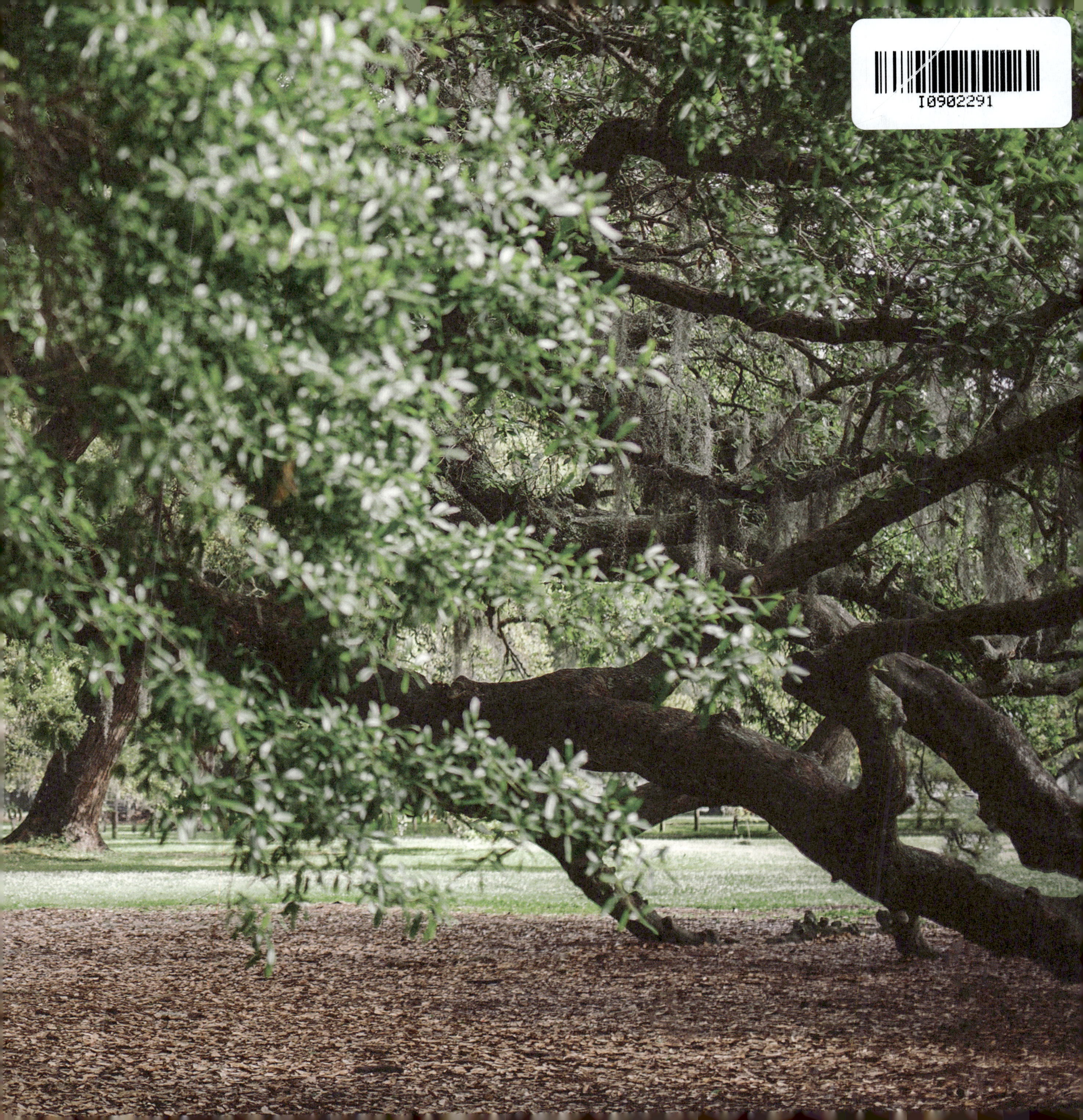

The Incomparable *Magazine* Street

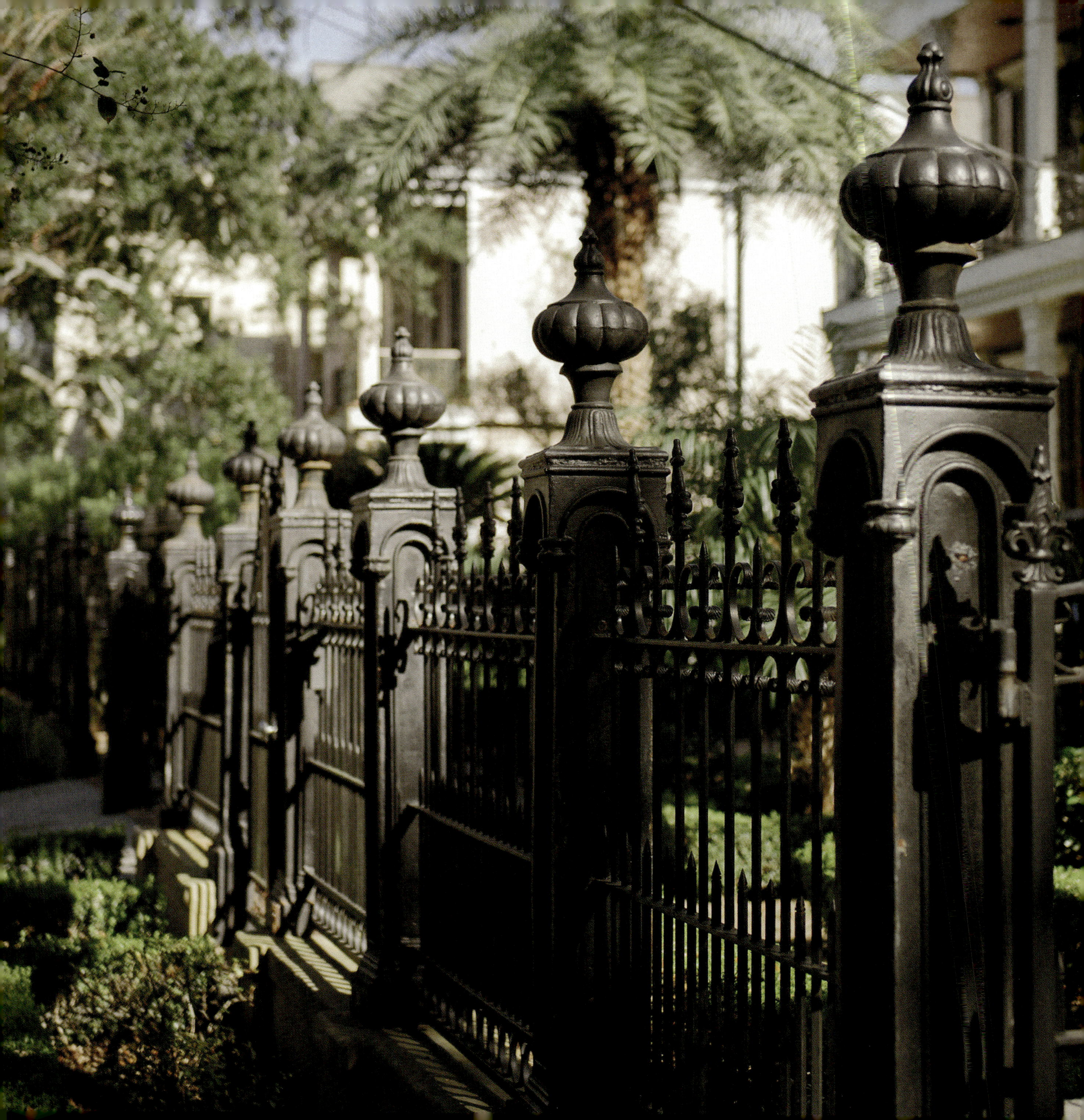

The Incomparable *Magazine* Street

John Magill

Photography by
Margot Landen

RIVER
ROAD
PRESS
New Orleans 2017

To the memories of my dear father and mother, Franklin and Alison Magill. Sorely missed.—JM

The completion of this book could not have been possible without the love and encouragement of my family and friends.

I would like to thank my mom for being my biggest cheerleader and for her endless support as I follow my dreams.

To my dad for teaching me to be bold, to be strong, and to follow what inspires me.

To Charles for always holding the tripod and endlessly giving without question.

To my brother for showing me the heartbeat and soul of New Orleans.

Lastly, to the people of New Orleans, thank you for constantly reminding me what home feels like.—ML

ISBN: 9781941879108

For information on other River Road Press titles, please visit www.riverroadpress.com.

Printed in Korea

Published by River Road Press
PO Box 125
Metairie, LA 70004

Contents

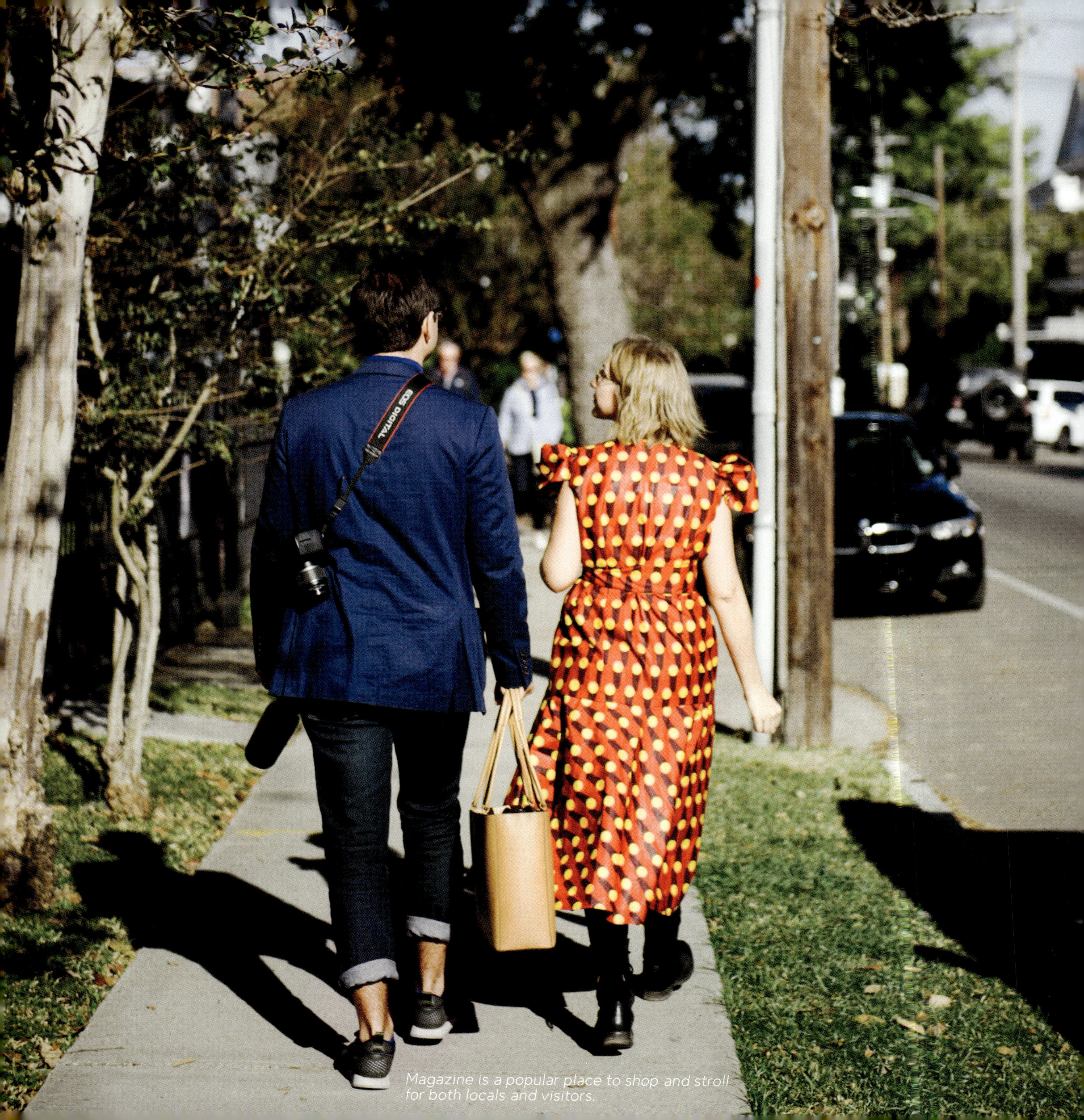

Magazine is a popular place to shop and stroll for both locals and visitors.

Chapter One

An "Incomparable" Street

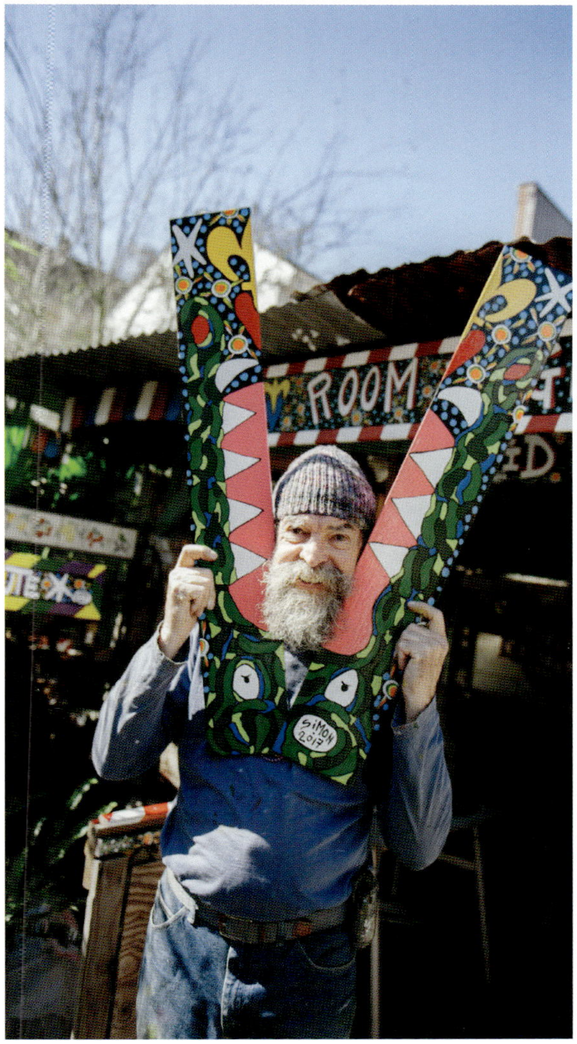

Signs painted by French folk artist Simon Hardeveld can be found along Magazine Street.

Today for the residents of metropolitan New Orleans, as well as for its many visitors, Magazine Street conjures up happy thoughts of shops, eateries, taverns, and other attractions along its six-mile route.

Once upon a time, Magazine did not have such a good reputation. It was considered rough and unsavory, especially in the area downriver from Jackson Avenue. Magazine was the dividing line between working-class neighborhoods toward the Mississippi River and grander areas toward the mansions of St. Charles Avenue. It has been said that if a person living on the "wrong" side of Magazine got written up in the newspaper, they would find themselves in the police reports, while those on the "right" side of Magazine would end up in the society section.

Now, Magazine is trendy, chic, and the place to go. For some people it also signifies something else: gentrification. This once blue-collar street has become a shopping Mecca. In the 1960s, Magazine was mostly working-class residences and apartments interspersed with several shopping strips that served

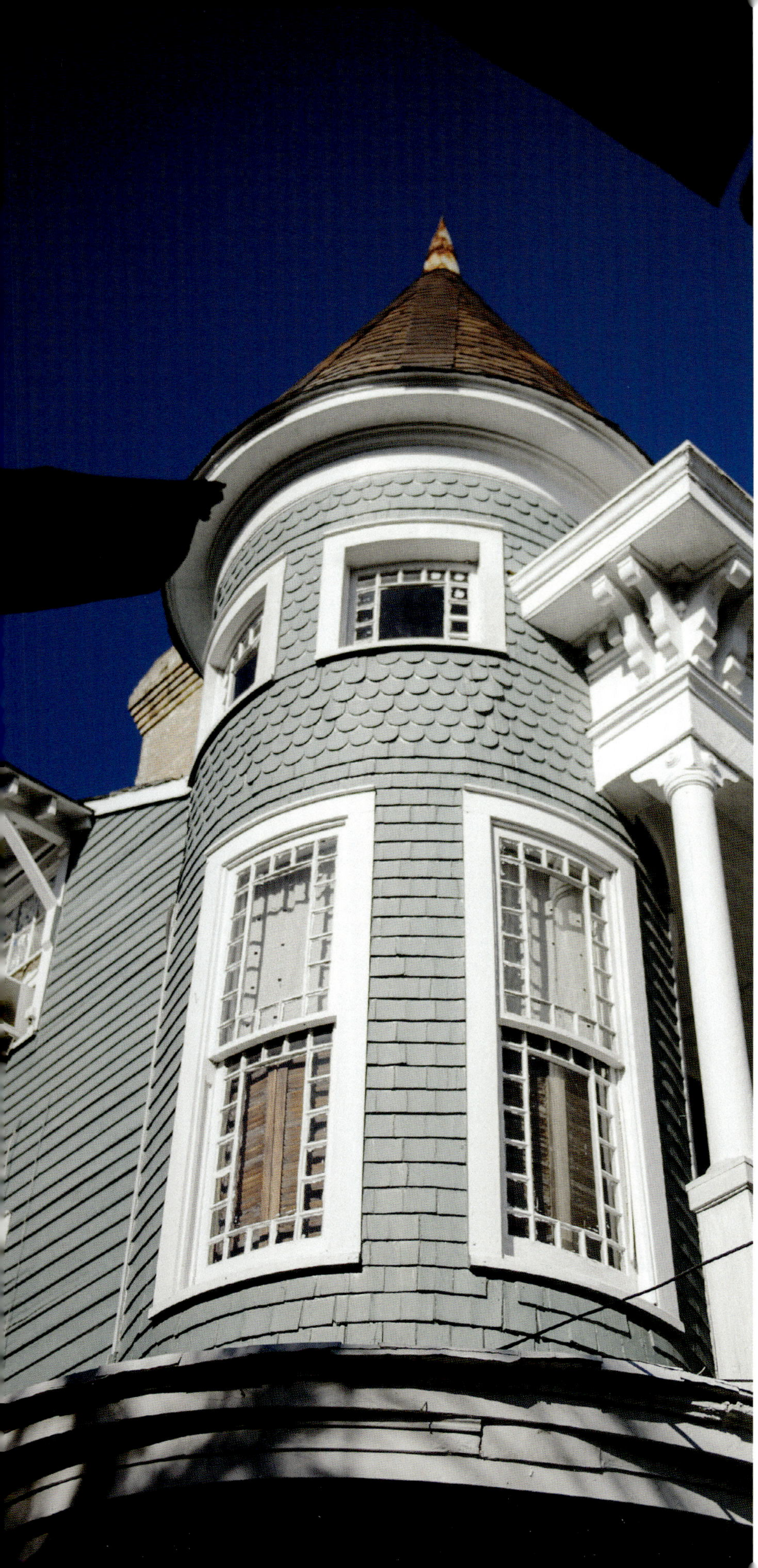

neighborhood needs like groceries and drugstores. Today shoppers jockey for parking space on nearby streets to experience what has become a metropolitan destination with its many amenities. Few people realize that this long thoroughfare is not just a land for disposable income, but an integral part of Crescent City urban development.

Magazine's commercial districts are centered in areas that evolved around four publicly owned markets that were once anchors for surrounding businesses. The Magazine Market, in the triangle at Sophie Wright Place; the Ninth Street Market, between Eighth and Ninth Streets; and the Jefferson Market, at General Pershing, date from the middle of the nineteenth century, while the fourth, Ewing at Octavia, dates from the early twentieth century.

New Orleans spread upriver much like a carpet being unrolled, and these markets and surrounding business districts became established as this expansion was occurring. The prototype was the French Market, which dates from the 1780s, and by 1911, when the last one was built, there were thirty-four public markets throughout New Orleans. Each market was owned by the city, and vendors rented stalls from

A stately Queen Anne-style home towers over Magazine Street.

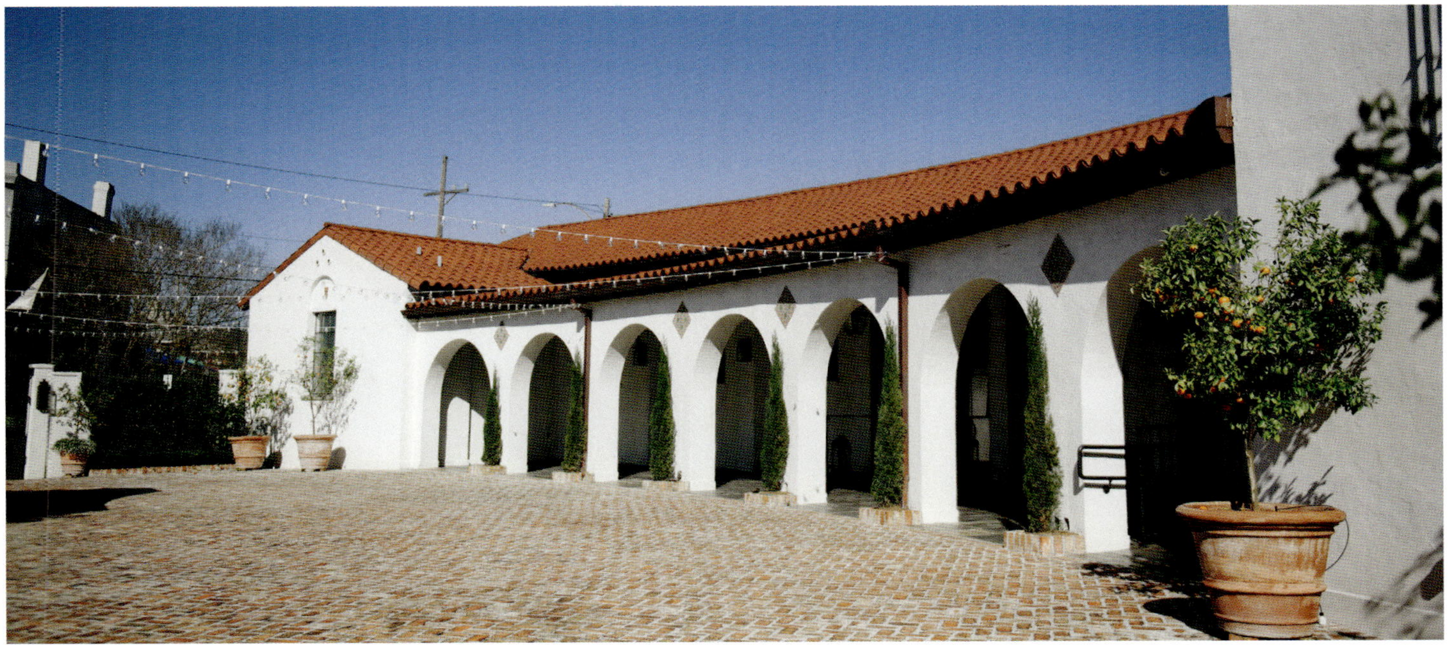

Magazine Market, now Il Mercato event venue.

which they dispensed all variety of food, prepared meals, flowers and plants, and even dry goods. And there were the fabled coffee stands, where one could get coffee, *café au lait,* or coffee and chicory. Patrons could also enjoy calas, beignets, doughnuts, or bread and butter. The markets were gathering places that encouraged the construction of other businesses nearby, just as twentieth-century businesses flocked around big regional malls which serve as hubs for myriad other commercial enterprises. The four markets of Magazine Street may be closed and readapted to other uses, but the business districts that they helped create are still there—only much expanded—and thriving.

Magazine Street has grown and evolved during a period of over two centuries and stretches from its oldest part at Canal Street, just outside the original city in the French Quarter, to the Mississippi River levee at Leake Avenue. It curves along a huge crescent of the river and is never more than about half a mile away from the river's wharves.

As New Orleans boomed and sprawled out during the nineteenth century,

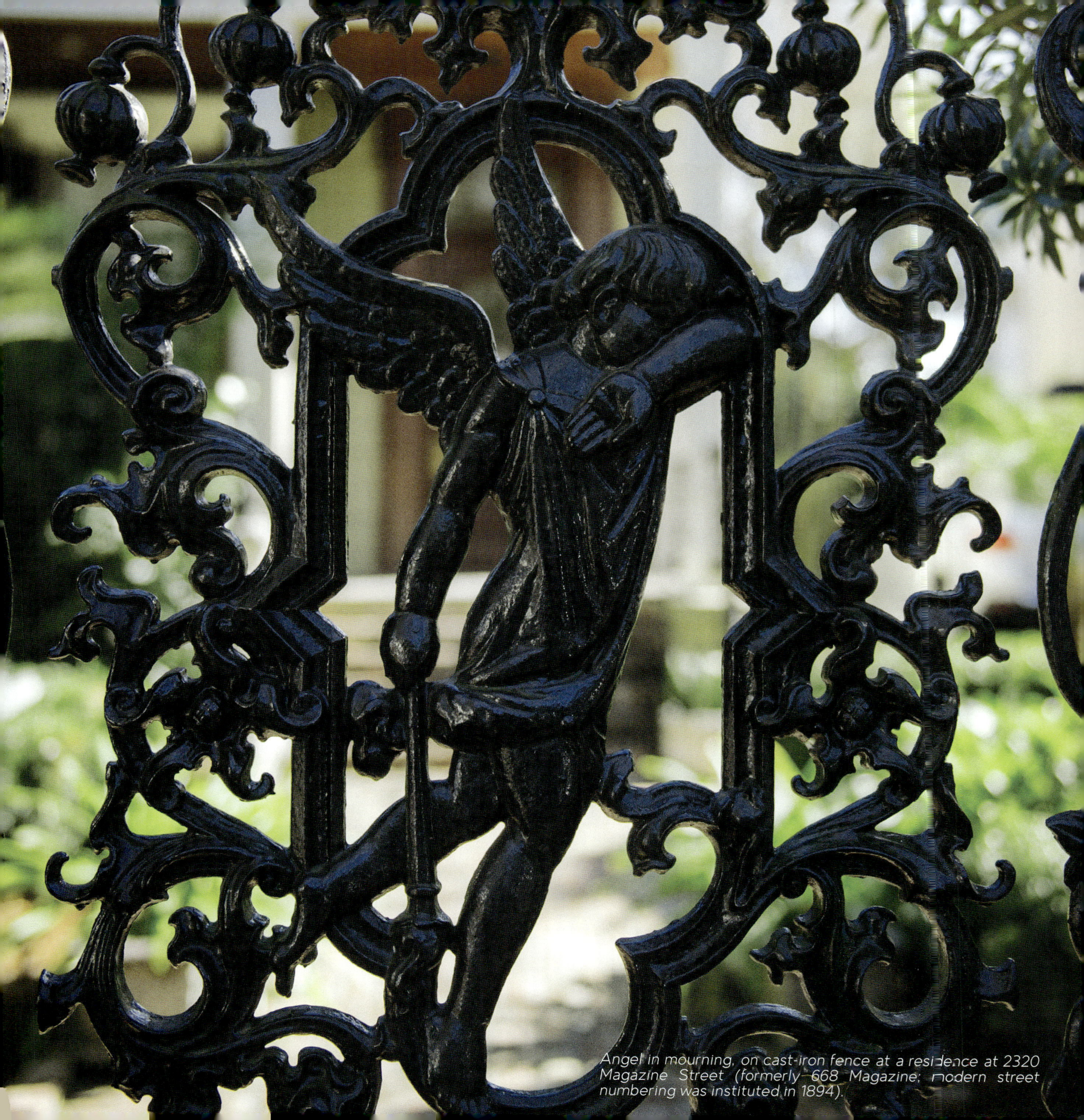

Angel in mourning, on cast-iron fence at a residence at 2320 Magazine Street (formerly 668 Magazine; modern street numbering was instituted in 1894).

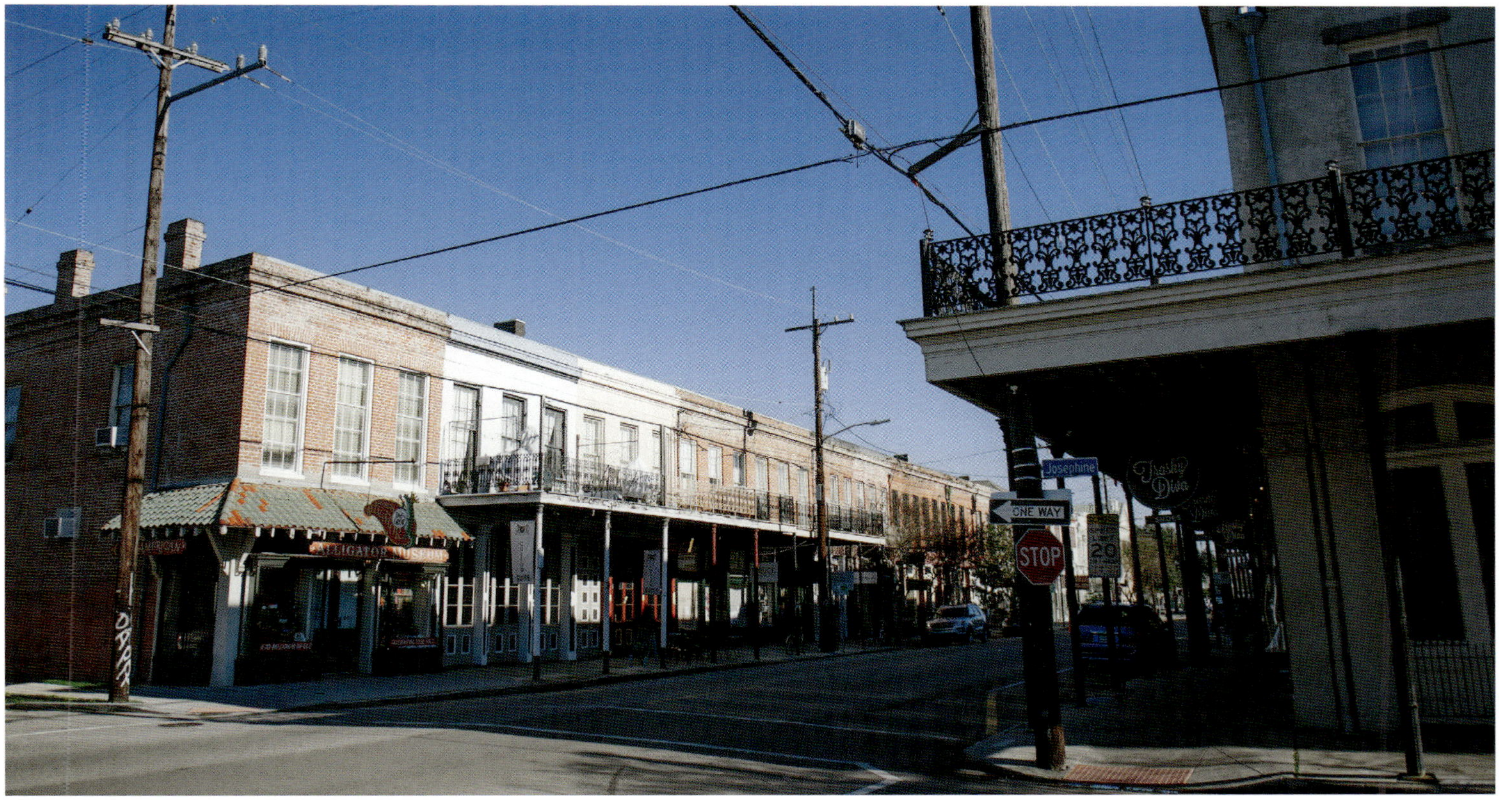

The 1900 block of Magazine is lined with buildings dating from the 1850s and '60s.

plantations that lined the river were subdivided into streets. Magazine carved through twenty plantations upriver from the French Quarter. Surveyors aligned streets such as Levee (now Tchoupitoulas), Magazine, Prytania, and Nyades (St. Charles) to parallel and gently curve along with the river. These early plantations-turned-subdivisions are on the highest ground in New Orleans (about twelve feet above sea level at the river and about seven feet above sea level along Magazine), formed by silt deposits left by the Mississippi when it overflowed during spring floods before levees helped keep it within its banks.

With the exception of Uptown, where most of Magazine Street is located, and other riverfront neighborhoods, much of New Orleans is below sea level. Uptown's higher ground is where most of New Orleans' expansion was centered prior to the introduction of drainage and flood control after 1900. It is this higher elevation that helped spare Magazine Street and most of Uptown between St. Charles and the river from inundation when inadequately designed levees failed during Hurricane Katrina in 2005, putting eighty

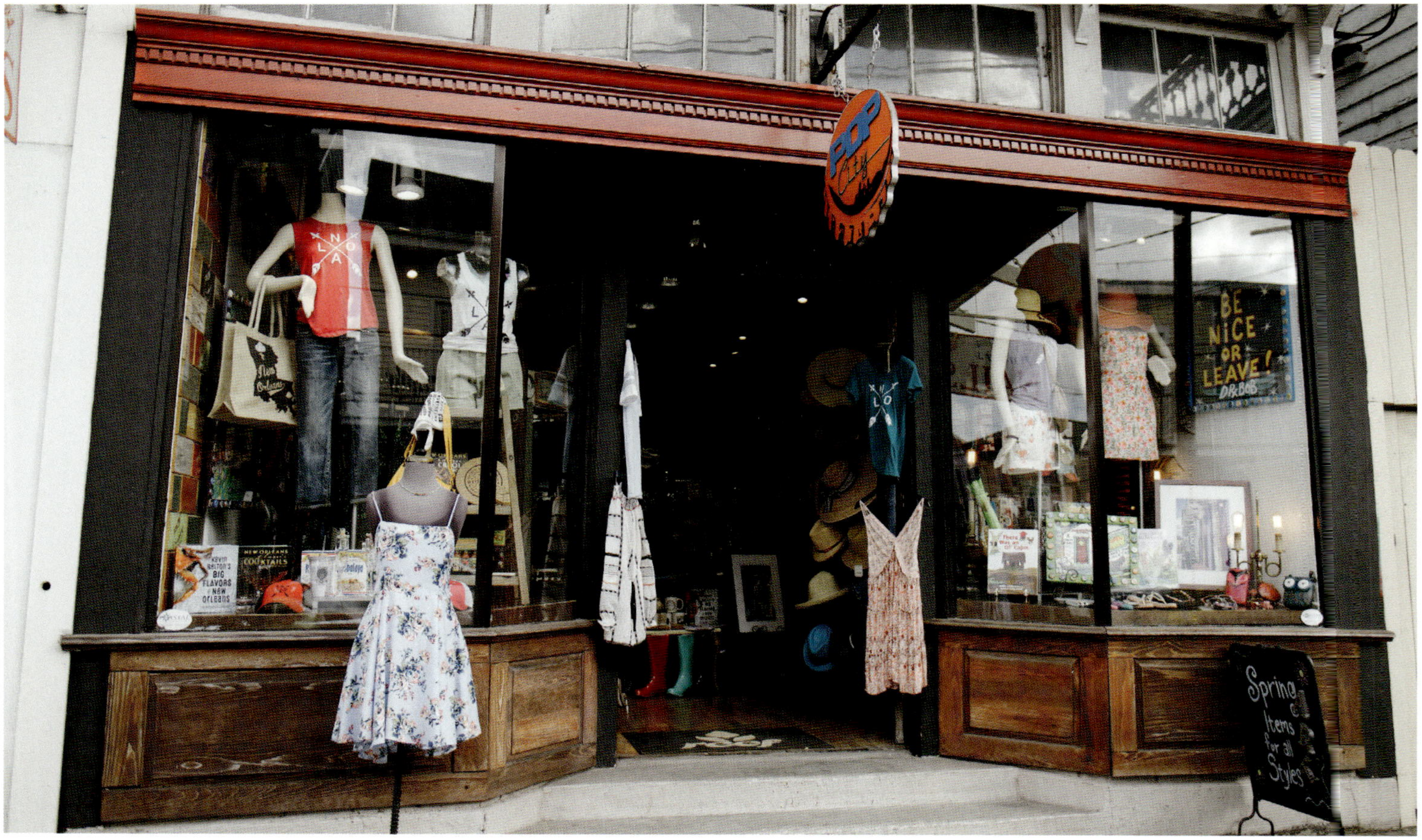

While antiques are associated with Magazine, today boutiques and trendy shops like Pop City line the street.

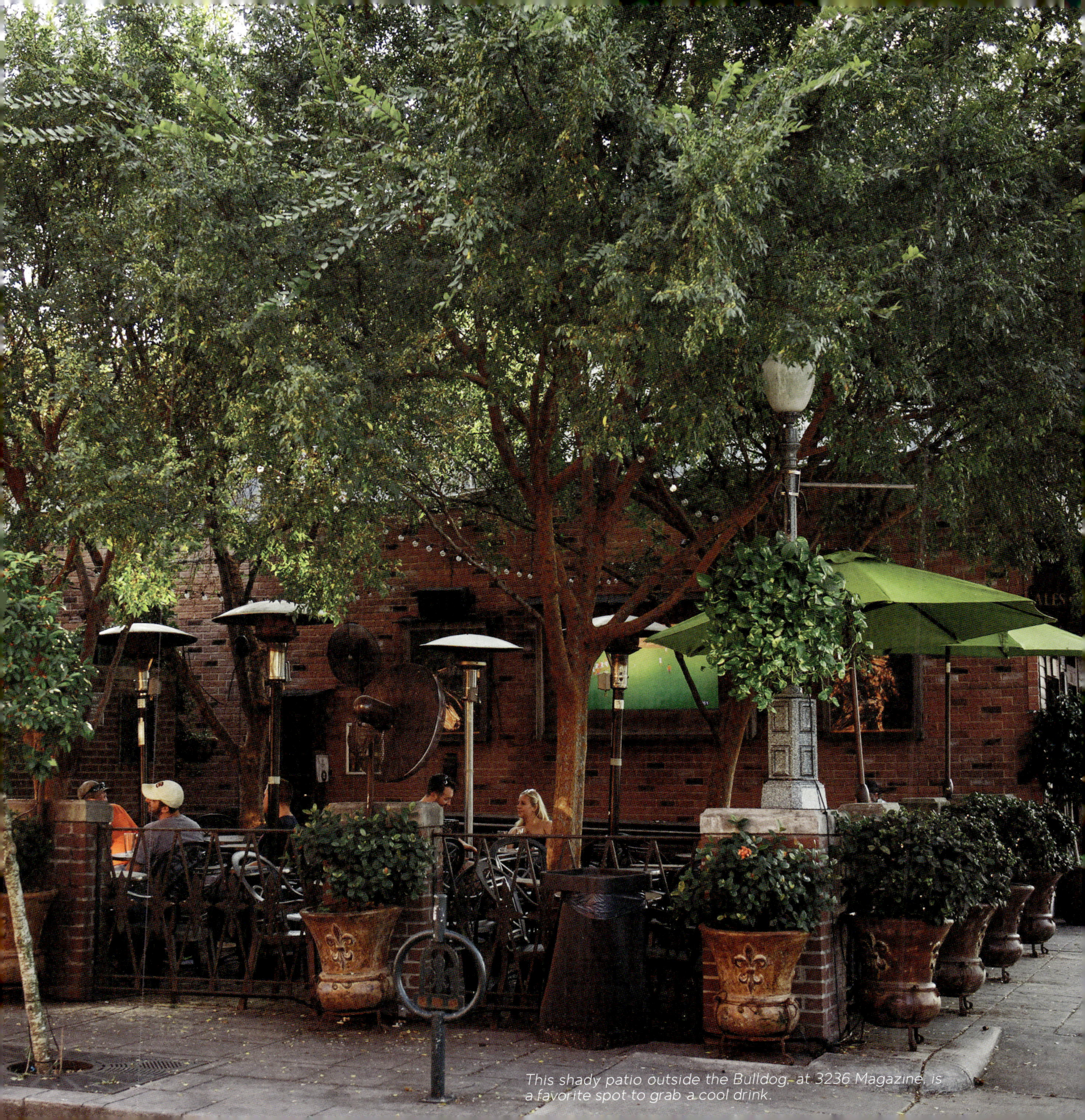

This shady patio outside the Bulldog, at 3236 Magazine, is a favorite spot to grab a cool drink.

percent of the city under water. This dry riverfront land has since been dubbed "the sliver by the river."

In the months after Katrina—especially during the 2005 holiday season—Magazine Street was one of the few shopping areas open for business. Already an emerging shopping destination, Magazine Street blossomed like never before. Many New Orleanians also chose to spend their money at local business during those hard times. Those who had never visited Magazine before soon discovered what it was all about and many were pleasantly surprised and continue to return.

Libby Bonner, manager since 1988 of British Antiques at 5415 Magazine, recalled how during this time people really came through to support the small Magazine businesses. British Antiques was among the first to reopen on the block, although only on Fridays and Saturdays, but was quickly followed by other shops.

Mrs. Bonner fondly remembers a gentleman who came in and bought a "slew of Christmas gifts and ornaments." He made a point of loudly saying that he wanted to help by spending his money in New Orleans. The store was filled with other buyers at the time, and they laughingly said that they were there to do the same thing.

In the months after the storm, as the city was repopulating post-Katrina, Mrs. Bonner said that during weekends Magazine was clogged with traffic, as people came to do their Christmas gift buying. She witnessed instances where displaced residents who had just returned would actually walk into traffic when they saw people they knew but from whom they had not heard since the devastating storm. It was also a sad time, she recalled, since many of her beloved customers from as distant as the Mississippi Gulf Coast came in to say their

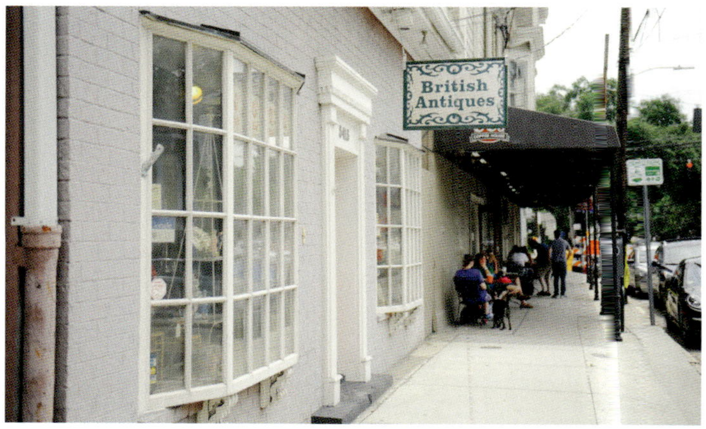

British Antiques and CC's Coffee House, 5400 block.

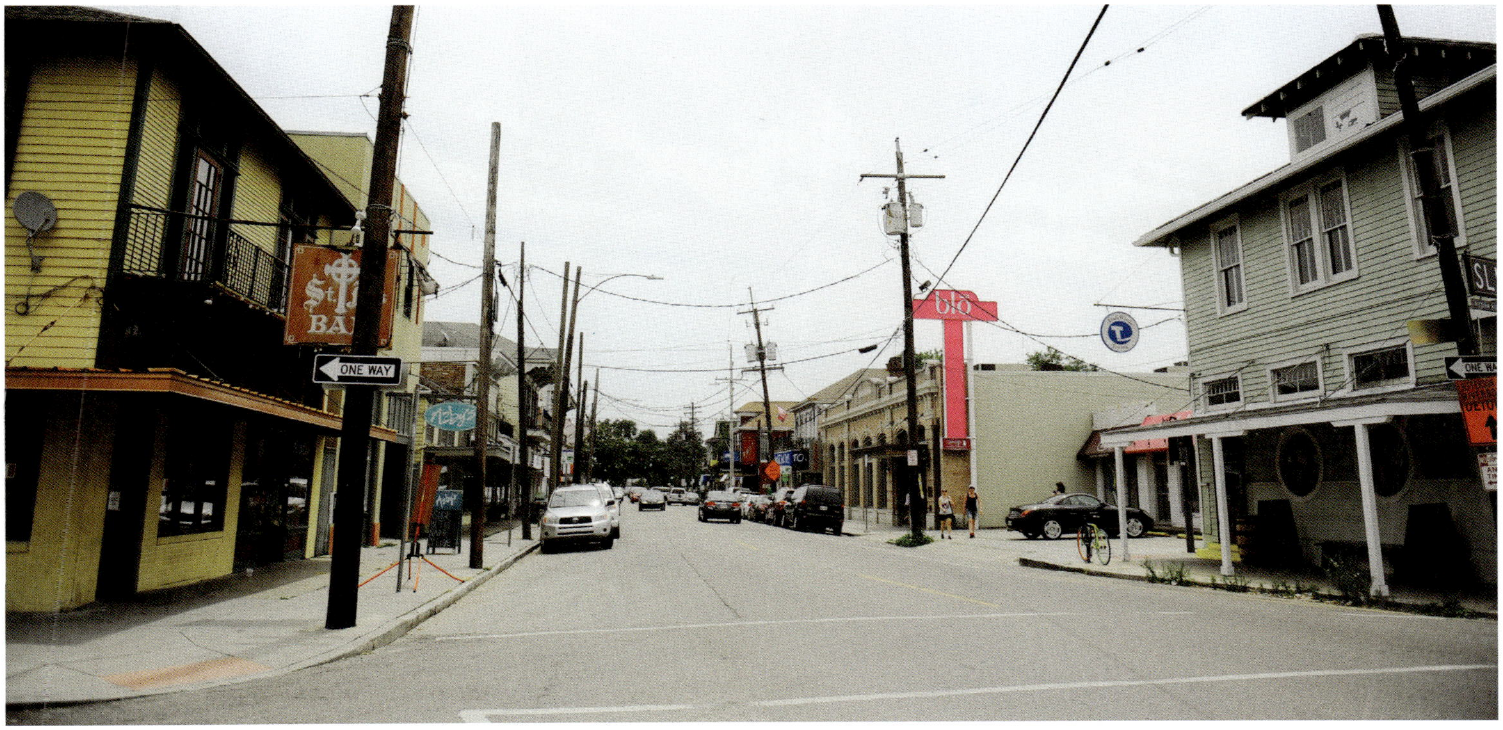

The intersection at Magazine and Joseph today (above) and in 1948 (below).

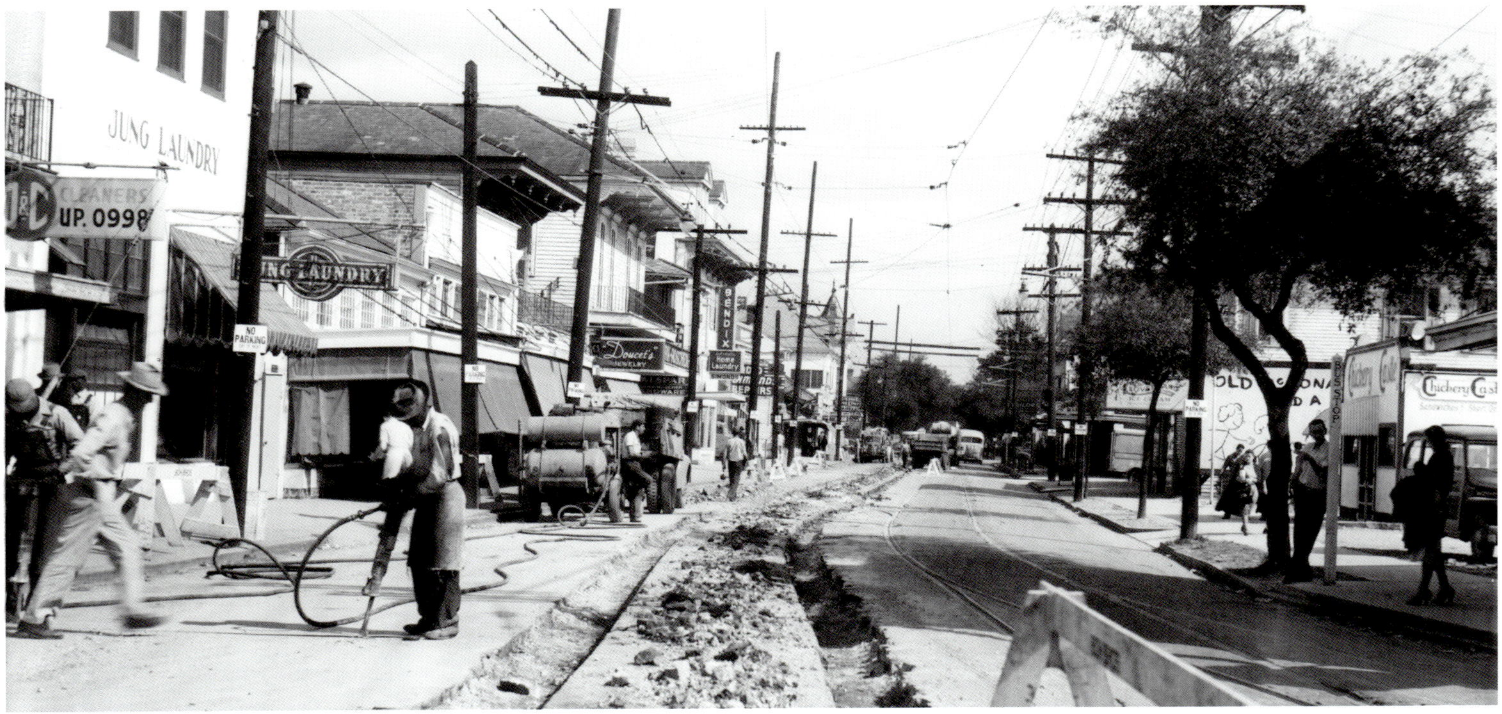

(Courtesy The Historic New Orleans Collection, 1979.325.5401.)

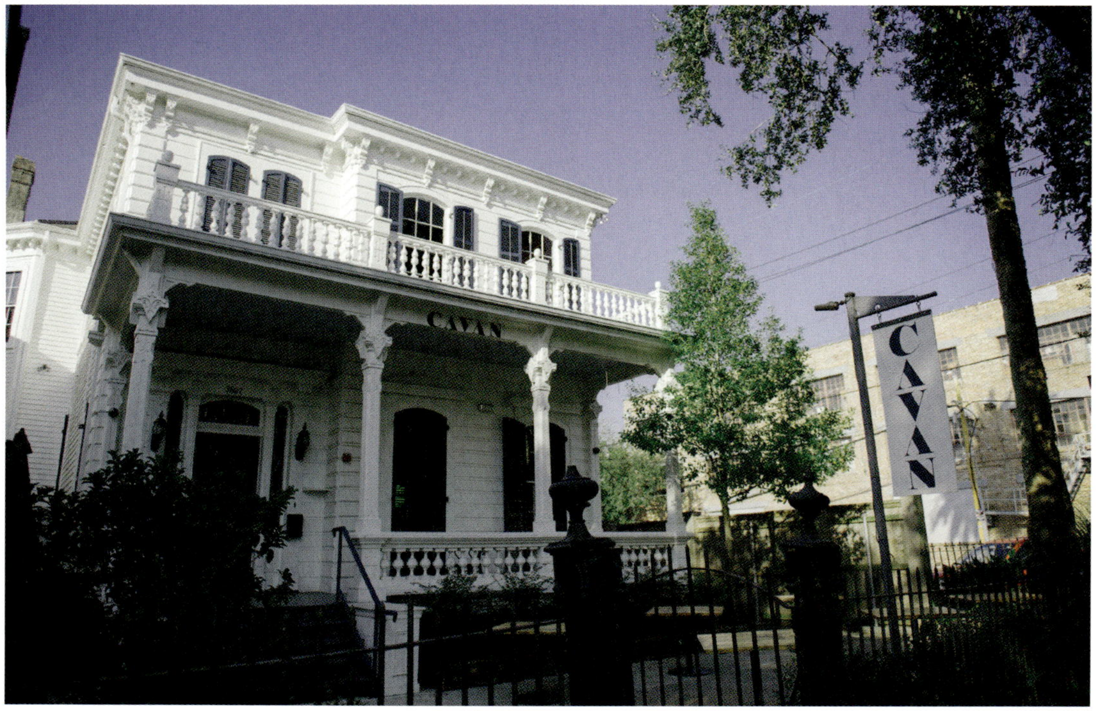

Cavan Restaurant, built as a residence in 1883.

farewells; they had lost their homes and were moving away with no plans to return.

Dannal Perry, owner of Plum, across Magazine at 5430, and then only a year in business, saw her business return dramatically. "Everyone was so enthusiastic—wanted to do something normal—so bought something."

Bryan Batt, co-owner of Hazelnut, at that time in the next block at 5515, said that after Katrina business was "through the roof . . . People wanted to spend." Mr. Batt remembered fitness guru and New Orleans native Richard Simmons shopping at the store during the holidays for his brother, whose house had flooded. While there, Mr. Simmons paid for another customer's purchase when he overheard that that person could not afford the price, and then he helped pay for other people's purchases.

Katrina not only spared Magazine Street, it also gave it a mighty boost, as the street had already been going through decades of change. Through much of its history it was primarily a residential street with houses ranging from a few grand mansions to working-class doubles and bungalows. Many of these houses still stand as treasures of New Orleans' architectural past, and there are still many residents living along the street—some who have lived there for decades—but the street has become considerably more commercial. Indeed, scores of remaining dwellings have

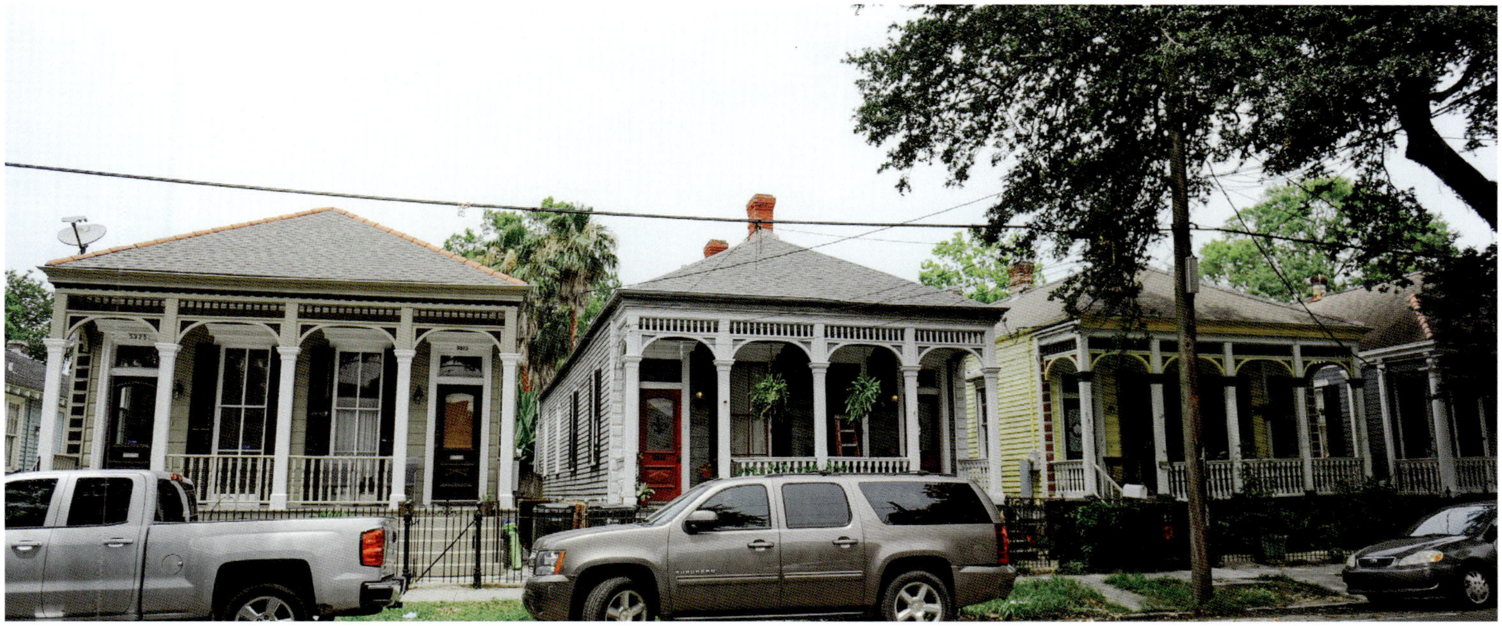

Typical early 1890s residential doubles (5300 block).

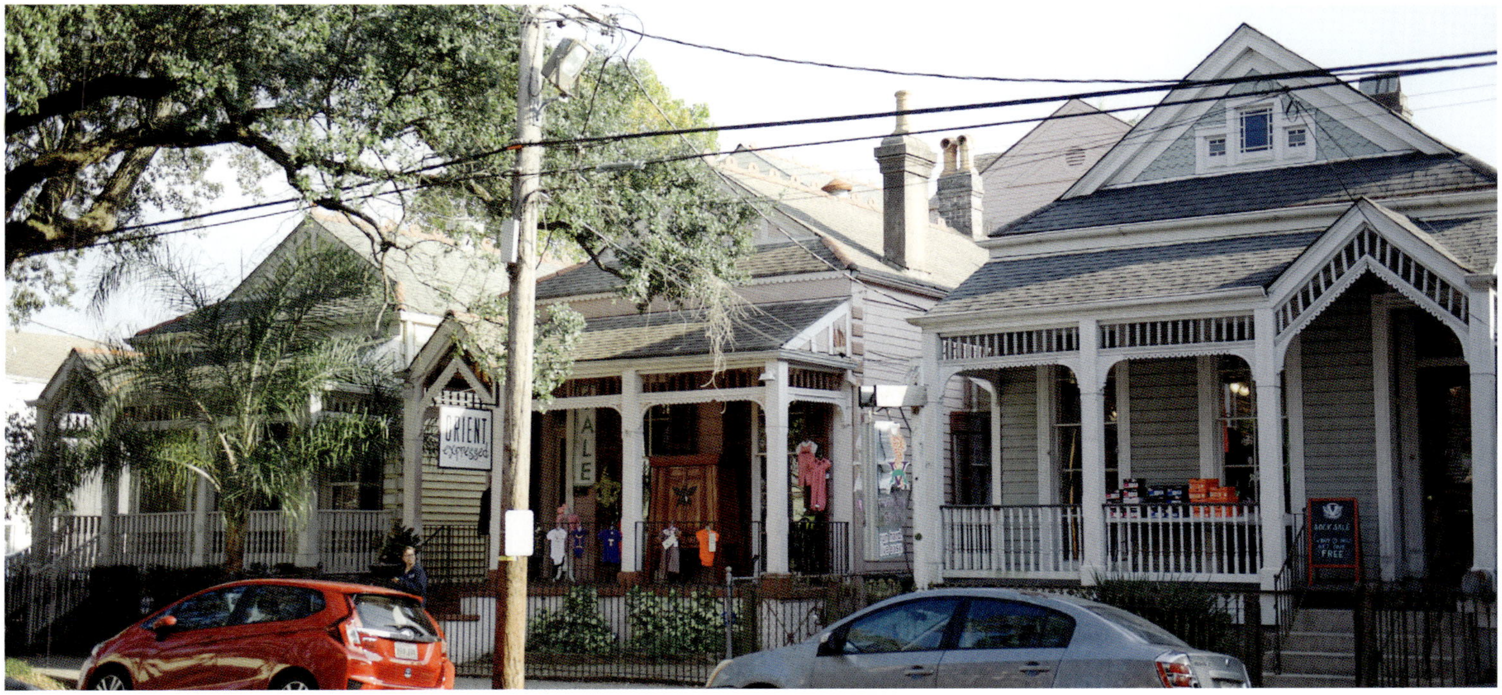

The shops at 3444-3450 Magazine Street were originally built as private residences.

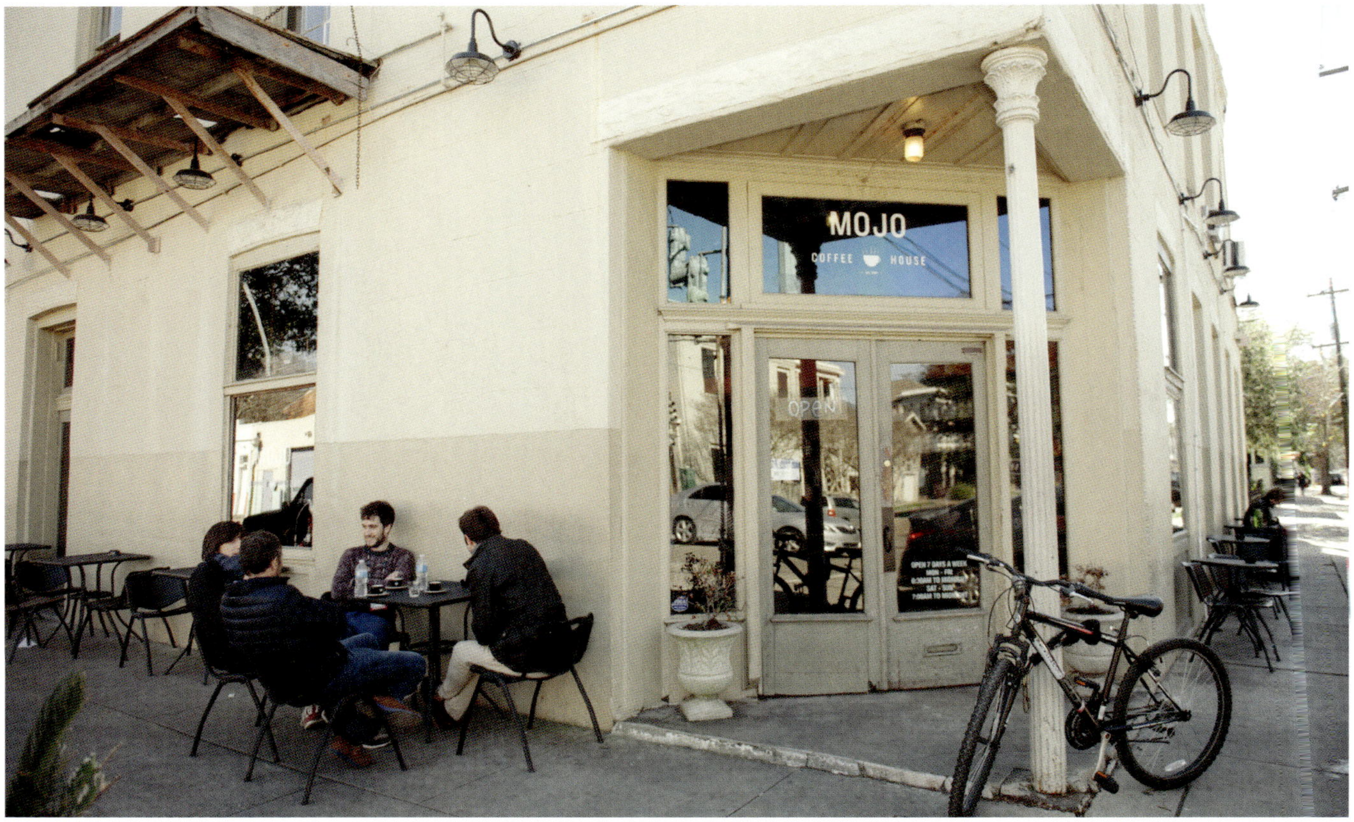

Coffee houses are popular meeting places.

been readapted for business purposes.

While Magazine Street's rents and property values are high today, just a few short decades ago, the street was popular for its reasonable rents. Many of the old-time, family-run stores, whose owners lived upstairs above the shops, had moved out to the suburbs, leaving empty storefronts. They wouldn't stay empty for long. They were soon taken over by antiques shops, boutiques, and art galleries, and this eclectic mix began giving the street its reputation for being "cool."

A respite on a pedestrian-friendly street.

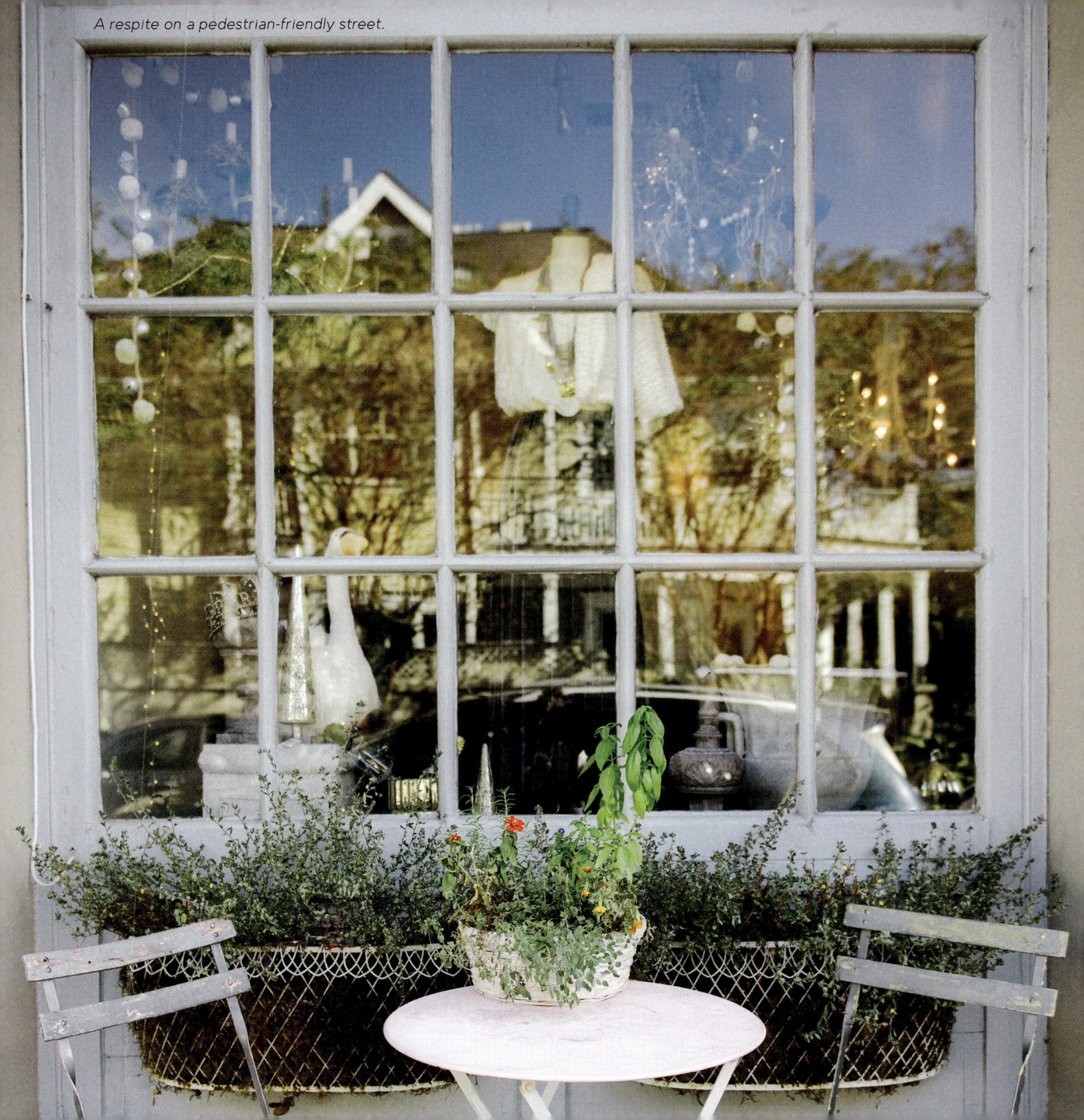

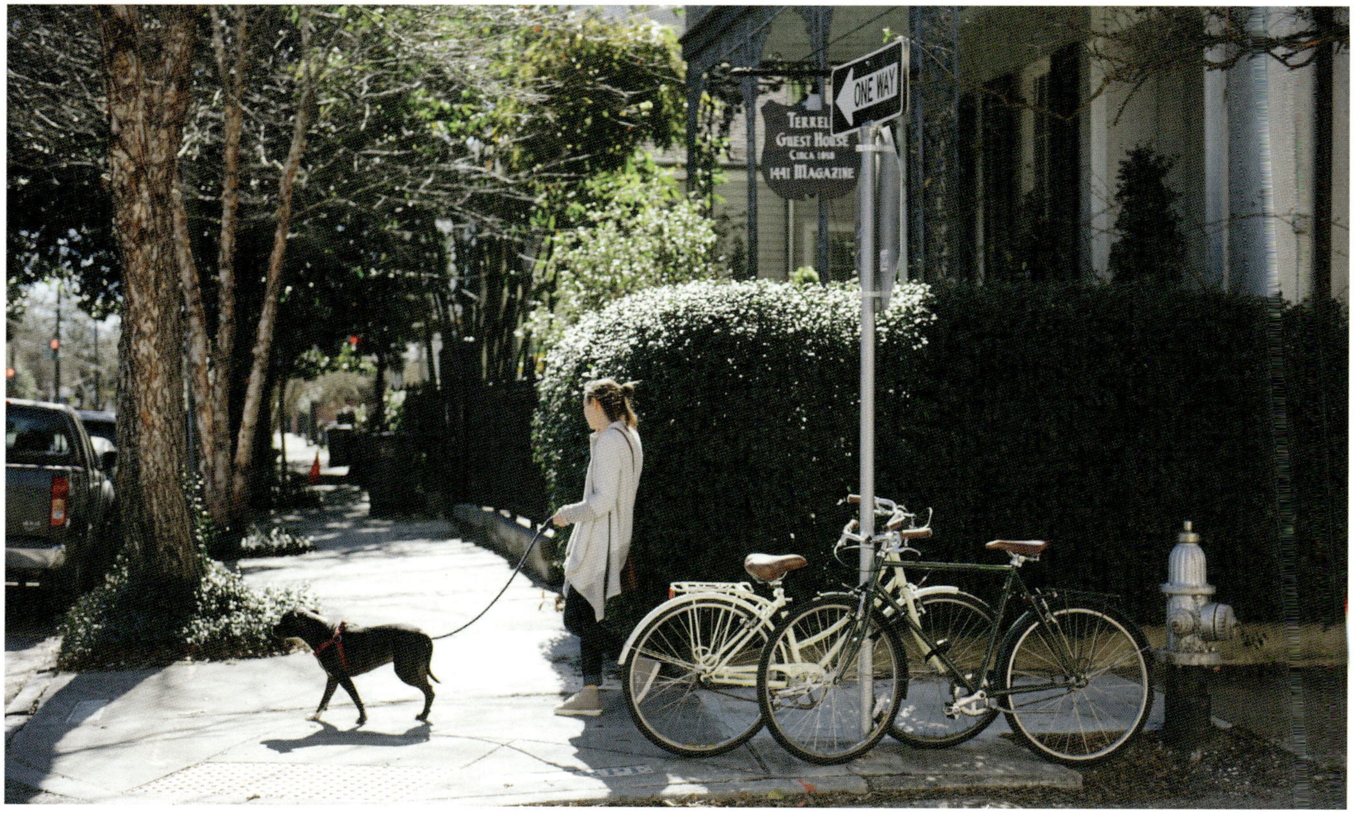

Pedestrian-friendly Magazine Street, in front of the Terrell Guest House.

In more recent years high-end fashion stores have added to this mix, increasing foot traffic and property values. With higher rents there is concern about national stores moving in since their deeper pockets can better meet the rent, but so far this has not proven to be a problem. Preservation groups are working to protect the old buildings which, with lack of parking, do not suit the needs of big box retailers. Some national retailers, like Lush Cosmetics at 3121 Magazine and West Elm at 2929 Magazine, have opened, but many business owners along Magazine feel that they fit

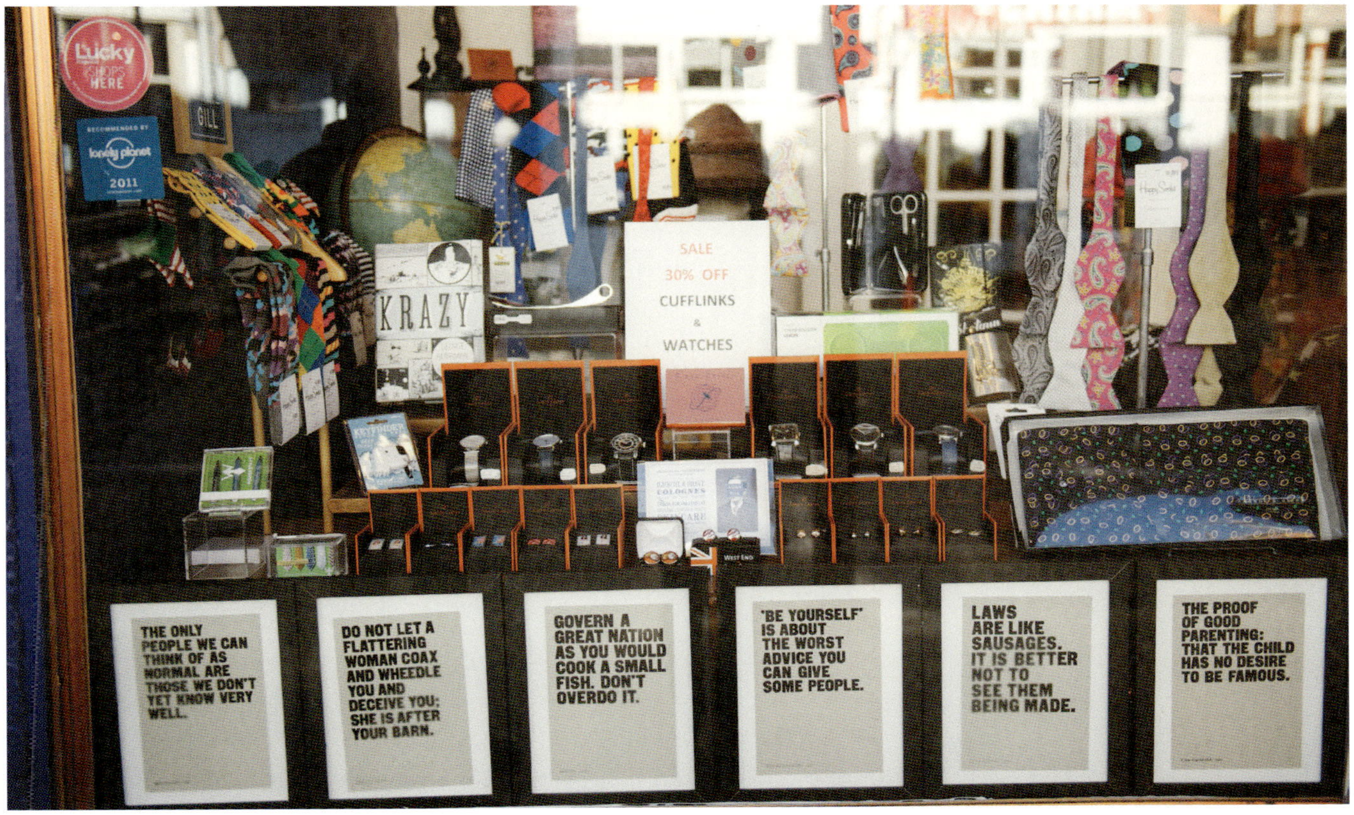

Aidan Gill's barber shop and gentleman's emporium.

into the mix and have acted as anchors, helping to attract new shoppers to other stores on Magazine Street. Wal-Mart on Tchoupitoulas Street was also initially a source of concern for retailers and residents alike. However, Wal-Mart, in improving its own neighborhood, helped spark the renaissance of lower Magazine between Felicity and Jackson, which had been mostly empty storefronts before the national retailer moved in.

It is a far cry from the days when businesses were concentrated around the public markets serving the needs

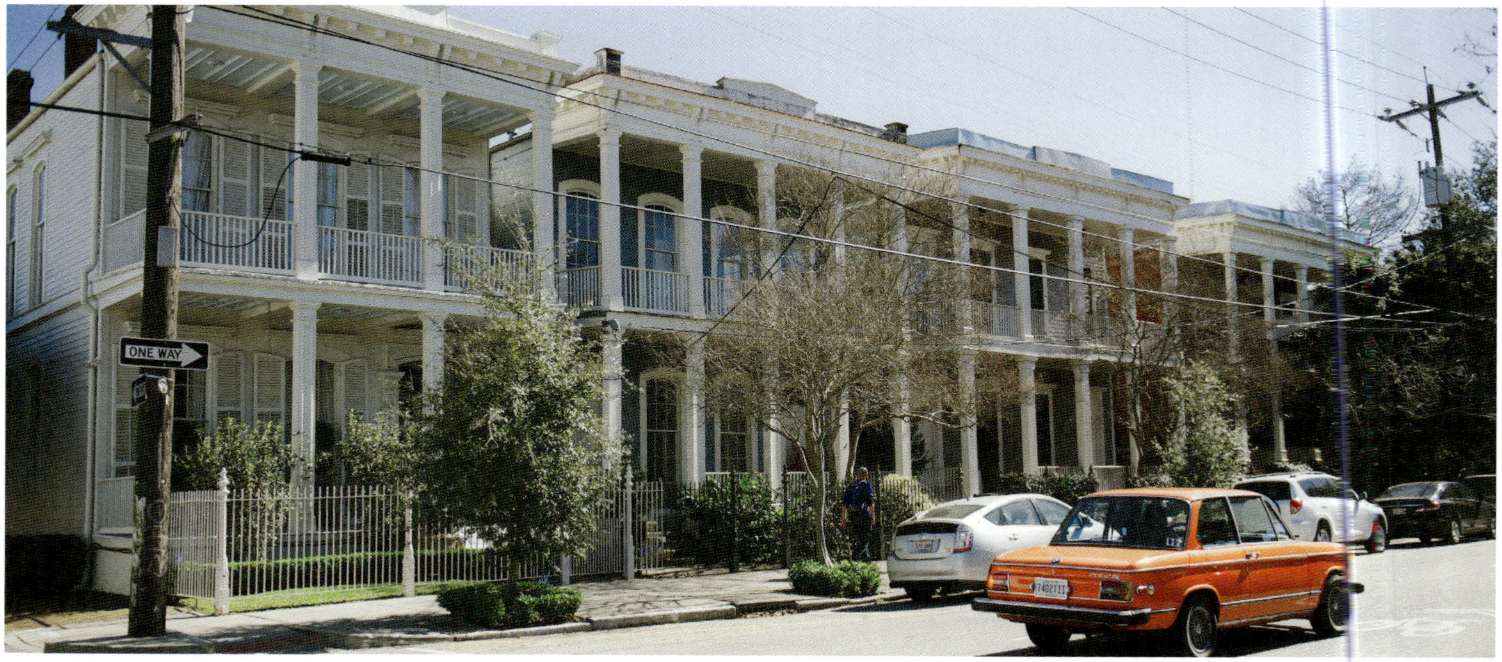

Rows of mid-nineteenth-century Greek Revival columns can be found along lower Magazine Street.

of neighborhood families who usually walked just a few blocks to "make their groceries." Magazine has become a popular—and now fashionable—destination for people from across greater New Orleans, along with out-of-town visitors. Less frequently are grocery bags carried, unless they say Whole Foods, Breaux Mart, or Chez Nous, as they have been replaced by an array of upscale shopping bags emblazoned with boutique store names.

Many current-day city planners criticize the rise of the shopping mall, big box stores, and the dependence on automobiles. They frequently promote the importance of urban environments where shops and business are in close proximity to residential neighborhoods. The features of this "New Urbanism" allow residents ideally to walk, bike, or use public transit for shopping rather than rely on cars. It is pointed out that nineteenth-century American cities grew in this manner—nineteenth-century Magazine Street is a prime example—until cars allowed businesses to relocate to suburbs and necessitated access to freeways. This both depopulated old neighborhoods and brought the closure of old businesses.

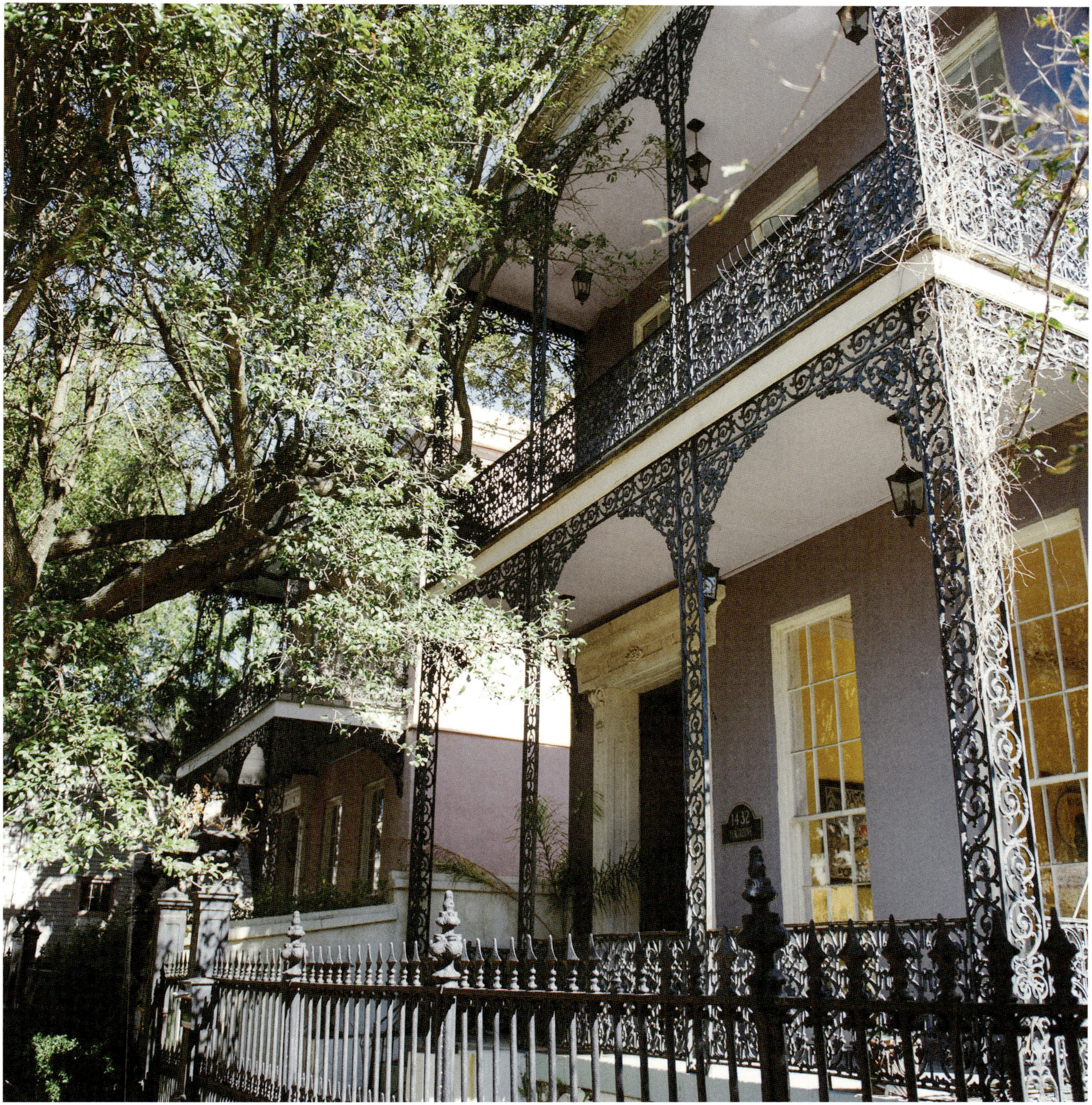

Beautiful 1850s ironwork galleries grace Magazine Street.

In some spots of the United States, real estate developers have built upscale towns designed along these lines with open-air business centers containing a variety of different storefronts. These "lifestyle centers" oppose covered shopping malls and attempt to mimic nineteenth-century neighborhood business districts. This is just such the lifestyle that Magazine Street has successfully evolved into on its own, being of an earlier time and without much modern planning.

The street pattern above Canal Street was actually not unplanned but rather laid out by surveyors between 1788 and the 1870s. Public markets—lifestyle centers of their day—were planned and built to serve the city's outwardly moving population. In spite of these conceptual aspects of Uptown's urban growth, Magazine as we have come to know it did not really grow as part of an overall master plan. Nevertheless, Magazine is a successful example of what today's urban planners argue cities should be all about and are attempting to emulate. Every city should have a street like Magazine. But Magazine may be said to have just been in the right place at the right time.

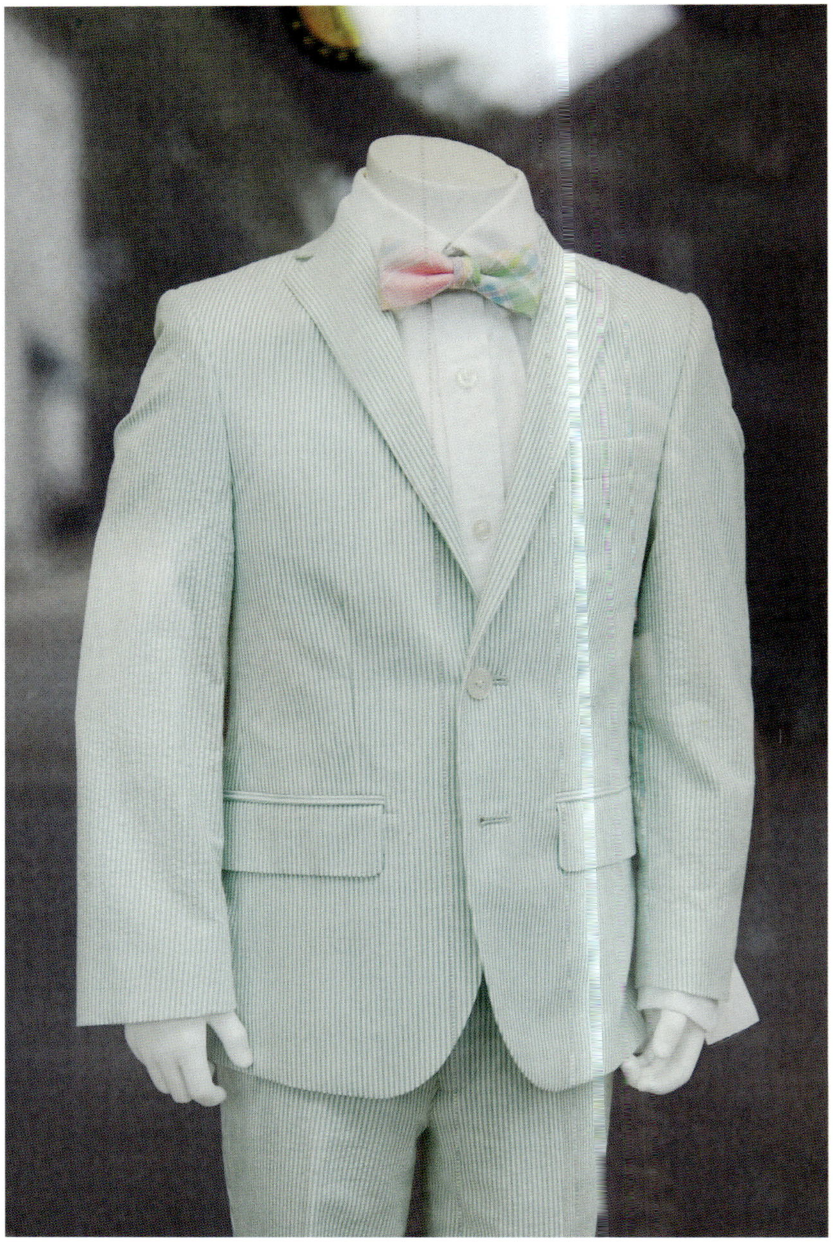

Perlis shop windows let locals know when it's spring and time for seersucker suits.

Pulitzer Prize-winning architectural critic, preservationist, and all-around respecter of urban spaces Ada Louise Huxtable (1921-2013) included an essay about New Orleans in *Goodbye History, Hello Hamburger: An Anthology of Architectural Delights and Disasters*, published in 1986 by The Preservation Press. She is critical of changes in New Orleans, especially in the Central Business District, where a building boom at the time was replacing early human-scale commercial buildings with office towers and parking lots. On a bright note for the Crescent City, she writes, "Curiously, while this tragic destruction takes place, other New Orleans neighborhoods are being spontaneously salvaged. . . . [T]here are the long avenues such as the incomparable Magazine Street, with its vital commercial mix in modest structures sometimes arcaded or galleried for the length of a block or more."

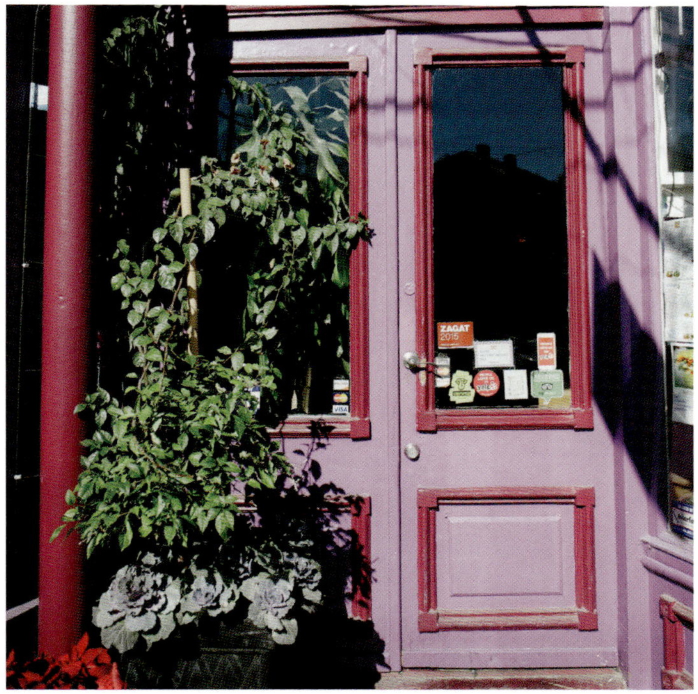

Character and color brighten Magazine Street facades.

This is indeed still Magazine Street, although the observation was made some twenty years before Hurricane Katrina devastated most of New Orleans. Huxtable could have never imagined that as Katrina's floodwaters spared Magazine Street, they would dramatically boost its drawing power and commercial importance, turning Magazine into a regional shopping destination that both retains its historical architectural mix and boasts that most of its businesses are locally owned.

The evolution of modern Magazine Street began well before the hurricane struck. As far back as 1948, there was a turning point in the street's fortunes. It might be said that this was when Magazine Street began to come of age and even foresaw the distant future.

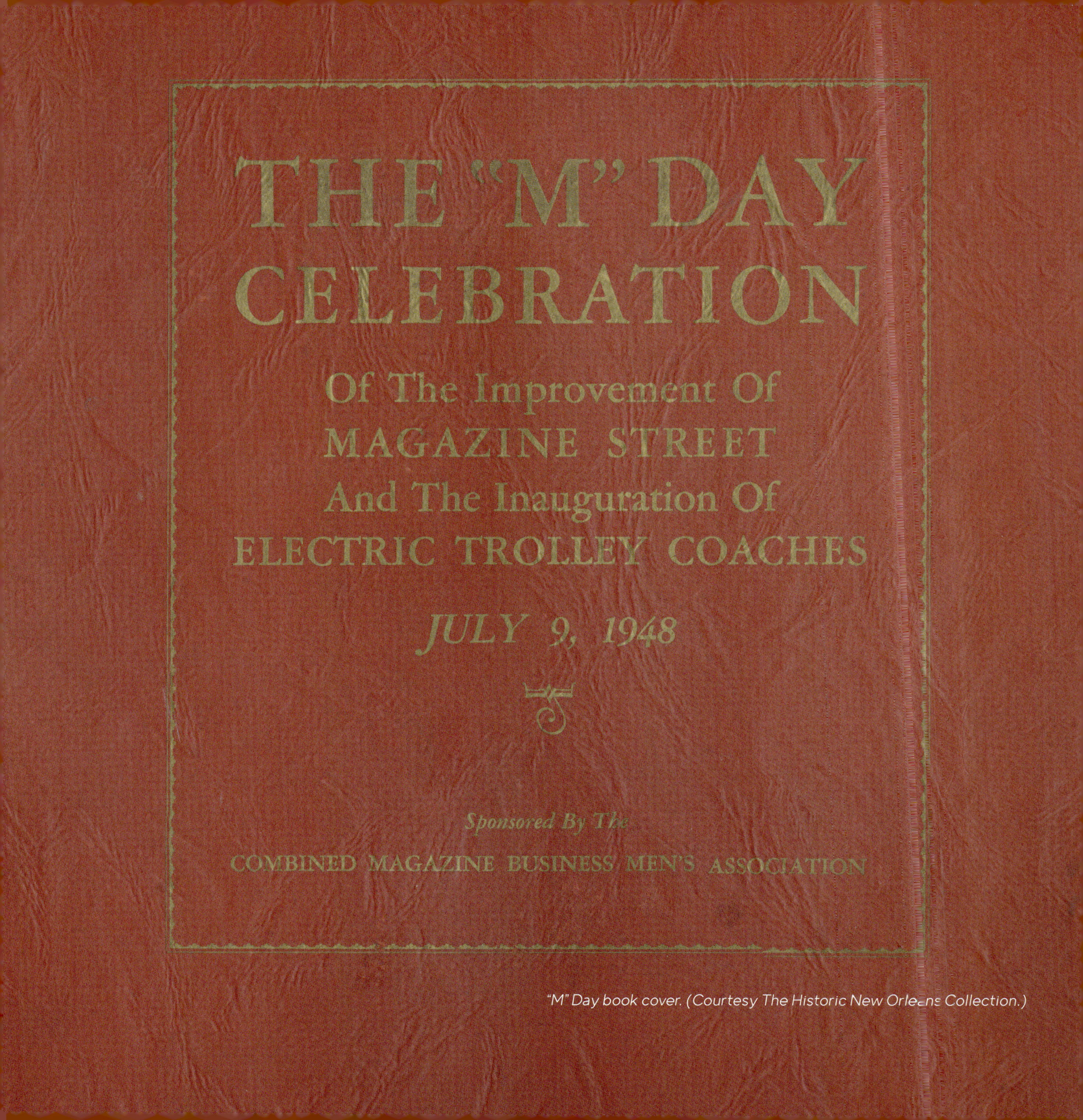

"M" Day book cover. (Courtesy The Historic New Orleans Collection.)

Chapter Two

"M" Day, 1948: A Pivotal Moment

Friday, July 9, 1948, was declared "M" Day in New Orleans by Mayor deLesseps S. Morrison. "M" stood for Magazine Street, and that day a parade was held to inaugurate the completion of new asphalt paving along with the introduction of trolleybuses. This new form of public transportation was being heralded across the United States as a replacement for streetcars. More flexible than streetcars, trolleybuses were trackless but still electrically powered through two spring-loaded trolley poles connecting the bus to overhead wires.

These changes on Magazine would have passed with little fanfare had it not been for the efforts of more than two hundred of the street's businessmen who were intent on showing off the comfortable new buses and smooth street paving. They saw the "M" Day festivities as a way of increasing their customer base by turning Magazine into not just a place for neighborhood shopping, but also—and more importantly—a destination for the whole city.

Prior to this event, there were four business associations serving Magazine: the Uptown Businessmen's Club, the Jefferson Businessmen's Club, the Ninth Street Association,

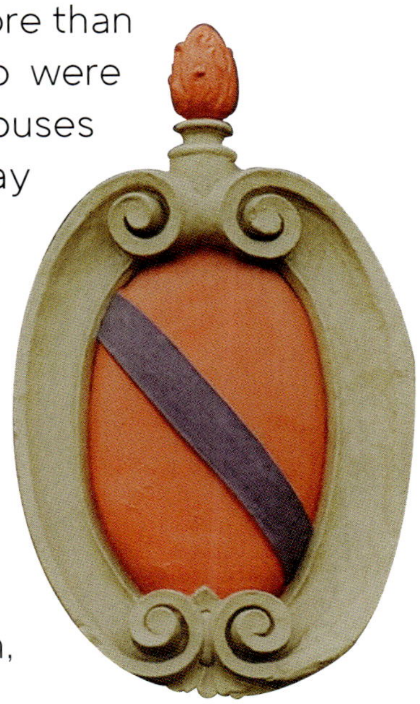

Architectural detail, Uptown Delivery Pharmacy (Magazine at Nashville).

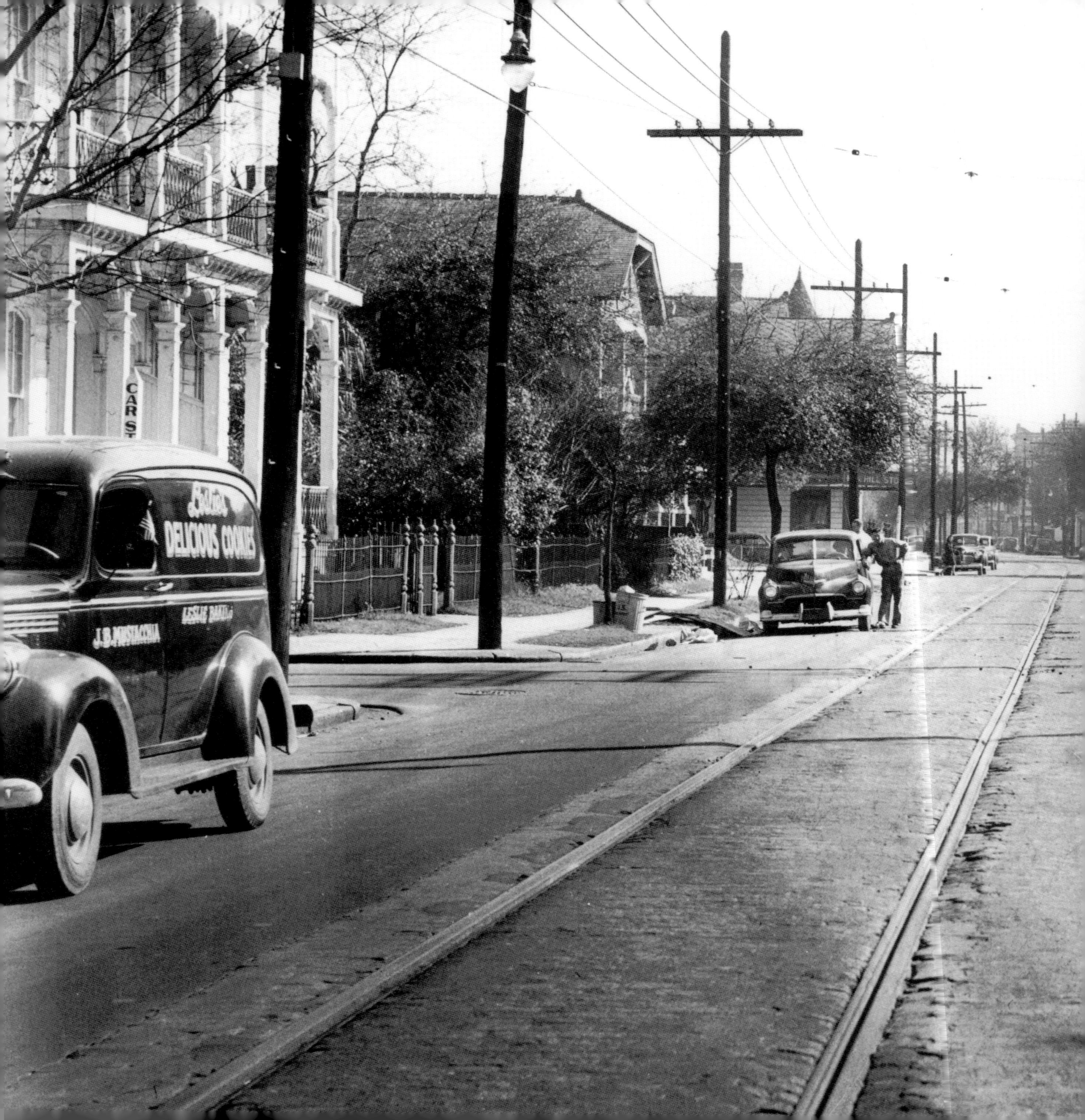
DELICIOUS COOKIES
J.B. MUSTACCHIA

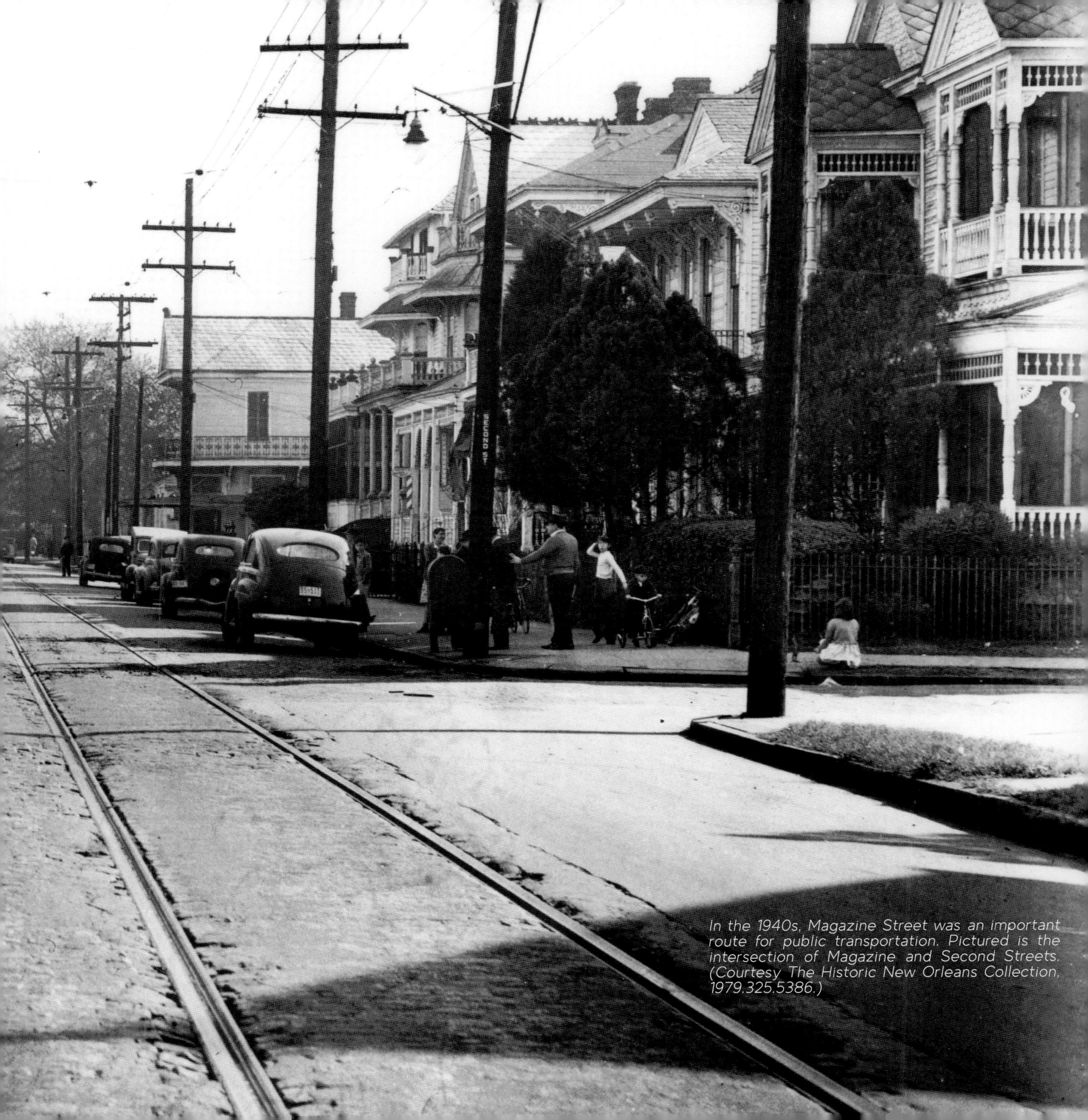

In the 1940s, Magazine Street was an important route for public transportation. Pictured is the intersection of Magazine and Second Streets. (Courtesy The Historic New Orleans Collection, 1979.325.5386.)

Firms Who Participated in The "M" Day Celebration

A. & P. Super Food Stores	*3017-19 Magazine St.*
Adams Laundry & Machinery Repair Serv.	*6108 Magazine St.*
Allan Shops	*2010 Magazine St.*
All Day Meat Market	*3138 Magazine St.*
Don Allen Shop	*4234 Magazine St.*
American Drug Store No. 2	*1800 Magazine St.*
American Drug Store No. 5	*3218 Magazine St.*
I. J. April Co., Inc., Upholsterers	*2904 Magazine St.*
Arabella Cleaners	*5419 Magazine St.*
Arabella Shoe Service	*5432 Magazine St.*
Audubon Radio Shop	*6054 Magazine St.*
Frank Baehr Bakery	*2028 Magazine St.*
Bazile Super Service	*3401 Magazine St.*
Behrman and Company	*2026 Magazine St.*
Warren Bernadas Auto Painting	*4727 Magazine St.*
Berlot Shoe Store	*2124 Magazine St.*
Better Class Cleaners	*1922 Magazine St.*
Betty Lou Shoe Store	*2022 Magazine St.*
Bienvenu's Crab Boil Shop	*3244 Magazine St.*
Broverman Bros., Cabinet Makers	*2027 Magazine St.*
Brown Appliance and Furniture Co.	*4112 Magazine St.*
Jos. Bruno, Antique Furniture Reproducer	*3923 Magazine St.*
Bungalow Furniture Company	*4800 Magazine St.*
Buras Variety Store	*5435 Magazine St.*
Burgess Barber Shop	*803 Arabella St.*
Capitol Food Stores, Inc.	*3131 Magazine St.*
M. Caronna Restaurant and Bar	*2032 Magazine St.*
Carter's Hardware Store	*4228 Magazine St.*
Jos. Casamento Restaurant	*4330 Magazine St.*
Chickery Castle Restaurant	*5526 Magazine St.*
Chong Wah Laundry	*1814 Magazine St.*
City Furniture Exchange	*2116 Magazine St.*
Clark-Roscher Hardware Store	*4209 Magazine St.*
Clark-Roscher Hardware Store	*2103 Magazine St.*
Clark-Roscher Hardware Store	*5513 Magazine St.*
Coakley's Place — Beer	*3101 Magazine St.*
Compagno Bar	*1601 Magazine St.*
Compagno Restaurant	*4605 Magazine St.*
Comus Cleaners & Laundry	*3806 Magazine St.*
Constantine Pharmacy	*3121 Magazine St.*
Corona's Auto Elect. & Appliance Store	*2924 Magazine St.*
Cortese's Grocery	*5259 Magazine St.*
Crane's Barber Shop	*4225 Magazine St.*
Crone's Bar	*5101 Magazine St.*
D & C Cleaners	*5533 Magazine St.*
D'Angelo's Shoe Service	*1808 Magazine St.*
De Lange Flower Shop	*4132 Magazine St.*
De Luxe Package Liquor Store	*5418 Magazine St.*
DeRowen Pharmacy	*2051 Magazine St.*
Dixie Baking Co., Inc.	*3212 Magazine St.*
Dixie Department Store	*3201 Magazine St.*
Dixie Sales	*3300 Magazine St.*
Dorian's Radio and Record Shop	*5405 Magazine St.*
Dud's Bar	*5535 Magazine St.*
Dupeire's Esso Service Station	*5800 Magazine St.*
Duvalle Decorator	*4219 Magazine St.*
Eddie's Service and Auto Repair	*4532 Constance St.*
Ellzey Store No. 2	*2050 Magazine St.*
Engelbracht's Bar	*4336 Magazine St.*
Musette Farish School of Dancing	*3416 Constance St.*
Fisher's Department Store	*2108 Magazine St.*
Freidman's Department Store	*4310 Magazine St.*
Friendly House Restaurant and Bar	*5538 Magazine St.*
W. T. Fripp 5 and 10 Store	*3340 Magazine St.*
Fuhr's Bakery	*3336 Magazine St.*
Gambino's Food Store	*5206 Magazine St.*
Garden Theatre	*3312 Magazine St.*
George's Hardware & Paint Store	*3215 Magazine St.*
Greiner's Auto Parts Co.	*2929 Magazine St.*
J. & L. Grosz Hardware Store	*3100 Magazine St.*
Mrs. Charles Guillie	*5201 Magazine St.*
P. H. Guilliot Barber Shop	*2127 Magazine St.*
Edw. L. Hagardon & Son	*3811 Magazine St.*
Half Moon Restaurant & Bar	*1121 St. Mary St.*
Happy Hour Theatre	*2015-19 Magazine St.*
Harmony Furniture Store	*3205 Magazine St.*
Harold's Shoe Repair	*4217 Magazine St.*
Heller's Department Store	*5414 Magazine St.*
J. Herman, Antiques	*2031 Magazine St.*
Hibernia National Bank, Jefferson Branch	*4300 Magazine St.*
H. G. Hill Stores, Inc.	*Magazine St.*
Holliday's Food Store	*4000 Annunciation St.*
Home Finance Service	*2140 Magazine St.*
Hood Furniture Company	*2038 Magazine St.*
Hooper Stove House	*3242 Magazine St.*
H. Hopfensitz & Bros., Jewelers	*2109 Magazine St.*
Howell's Pharmacy	*State and Magazine Sts.*
Hubble's Barber Shop	*5404 Magazine St.*
Industrial Electric, Inc.	*3227 Magazine St.*
Irwin Service and Auto Repair	*4041 Magazine St.*
Itzkovitch Furniture Co., Inc.	*4119 Magazine St.*
Jack's Repair Shop	*3827 Magazine St.*
Jefferson Accessory Store	*4238 Magazine St.*
Jefferson Drug Store	*4316 Magazine St.*
Jerry's Auction Exchange	*3117 Magazine St.*
W. H. Johnson, Painting Contractor	*4437-39 Magazine St.*
Hugh T. Jones	*628 Arabella St.*
Jung Laundry	*5529 Magazine St.*
Dave Katz	*1119 St. Mary St.*
Kay Cake Shop	*4130 Magazine St.*
Keystone Cleaners	*3500 Magazine St.*
Kirby's Auto Repair	*2240 Magazine St.*
Knobloch Pharmacy	*4138 Magazine St.*
Kollin Service Station	*5023 Magazine St.*
Kottemann Furniture Company	*4032-38 Magazine St.*
Lafayette Fire Insurance Company	*2123 Magazine St.*
Joseph Laughlin Company	*4500 Magazine St.*
Laundermatic Self-Service Laundry	*1921 Sophie Wright Pl.*
George Lawrence & Sons	*4111 Magazine St.*
W. M. Lear's Pharmacy	*3341 Magazine St.*
Le Corgne Hardware Store	*2035 Magazine St.*
Fred Leitz Insurance Company	*2115 Magazine St.*
Leslie's Baking Company	*1021 Pleasant St.*
Leslie's Shell Service Station	*2133 Magazine St.*
Locque & Doerflein Service Station	*2931 Magazine St.*
Louisiana Food Store	*1914 Magazine St.*
Loyola Cleaners	*915 Gen. Pershing St.*
Magazine Appliance Company	*4107 Magazine St.*
Magazine Furniture Store	*2043 Magazine St.*
Magazine Grocery	*4937 Magazine St.*
Magazine Leader	*3228 Magazine St.*
Manuel's Sandwich Shop	*4501 Magazine St.*
Martiny and Son	*2824 Magazine St.*
Maxwell Cleaners	*3823 Magazine St.*
Benny Mayer's Garage	*5023 Magazine St.*
Mayeux Bros. Pharmacy	*900 Jefferson Ave.*
May's Poultry House	*3137 Magazine St.*
McGovern's Service Station	*6001 Magazine St.*
McKinnis Spring and Brake Service	*2850 Magazine St.*
Meisel's Upholstering and Fabric Co.	*2018 Magazine St.*
Merlin's Dry Goods Store	*5523 Magazine St.*
Messina's Restaurant	*2104 Magazine St.*
Phil Miller	*4203 Magazine St.*
Miller's Jewelry Store	*4214 Magazine St.*
Mother's Home Made Bakery Products	*3523 Magazine St.*
Motto's Restaurant and Bar	*2049 Magazine St.*
Myown Beauty Salon	*2112 Magazine St.*
National Bank of Comerce, 9th Street Market Branch	*3200 Magazine St.*
National Craft and Hobby Shop	*5835 Magazine St.*
New Kitchen Restaurant	*3301 Magazine St.*
New Orleans Ass'n. for the Blind	*1809 Magazine St.*
New Orleans Woodware Company	*3105 Magazine St.*
Oldenburg's Shoe Store	*5525 Magazine St.*
Old Famous Bar & Package Liquor Store	*2600 Magazine St.*
Original Wallace's Carmel Crisp Co.	*1825 Magazine St.*
Orleans Insurance Company	*2001 Magazine St.*
Outlet Store	*3031 Magazine St.*
Pauli's Bicycle Shop	*3118 Magazine St.*
Pelman Jewelry Store	*4222 Magazine St.*
Perlis' Men's Store	*6070 Magazine St.*
Pete's Place	*4207 Magazine St.*
Pinero's Food Store	*4600 Magazine St.*
Plaza Department Store	*4320 Magazine St.*
Probst Bros. Heater Service	*4610 Magazine St.*
Prytania Pharmacy	*3942 Prytania St.*
H. Rault, Locksmith	*3027 Magazine St.*
Red Bird Inn	*1931 Sophie Wright Pl.*
Wm. Rednour Transfer & Storage Co.	*1024-34 Louisiana Ave.*
Regina Cleaners	*3964 Magazine St.*
H. Reuther Bakery	*5434 Magazine St.*
Richard's Grocery	*5241 Magazine St.*
A. Rodi's Confectionery	*3316 Magazine St.*
Royal Cleaners	*6112 Magazine St.*
Royal Plating & Polishing Works	*3944 Magazine St.*
Ruddock Bakery	*4229 Magazine St.*
Russo's Used Furniture Store	*3112 Magazine St.*
Samuels Printing House	*2009 Magazine St.*
Semel Dry Cleaners	*1943 Sophie Wright Pl.*
Sharp's Department Store	*3033 Magazine St.*
Shipley Esso Service Station	*1600 Magazine St.*
Silverman's Hardware & Paint Store	*6008 Magazine St.*
Simplex Electric	*5214 Magazine St.*
Southern States Electronics	*2025 Magazine St.*
Spano's Barber Shop	*2033 Magazine St.*
Square Deal Service Saving Store	*1916 Magazine St.*
Square Deal Shoe Repair	*4204 Magazine St.*
Steve Tailor & Cleaner	*2044 Magazine St.*
Stillwell Furniture & Pianos	*1821 Magazine St.*
Superior Cleaners	*6117 Magazine St.*
Sureway Cleaners	*4538 Magazine St.*
Suttle's Restaurant	*3206 Magazine St.*
Sutton's Service Station	*4100 Magazine St.*
Tac and Automatic Coin Machine Co.	*1900 Magazine St.*
Tam's Fine Foods	*1001 St. Mary St.*
Tate's Beauty Parlor	*4115 Magazine St.*
Taylor Furniture Company	*4933 Magazine St.*
R. Theriot Liquor Stores, Inc.	*4200 Magazine St.*
H. Toll's Bakery & Confectionery	*2800 Magazine St.*
Top Cleaners	*5508 Magazine St.*
Tramontana's Poultry House	*4428 Magazine St.*
Tranchina's Restaurant	*5605 Magazine St.*
Triple "S" Radio Service	*2013 Magazine St.*
Try's Cleaning & Dyeing Service	*3224 Magazine St.*
Uncle Bill's Bar	*4133 Magazine St.*
Unique Cleaners	*6010 Magazine St.*
U. S. Cleaners	*3412 Constance St.*
Usner Bros., Sheet Metal & Roofing	*2845 Magazine St.*
Valor Store	*1930 Magazine St.*
Van Vranken Beer Parlor	*3400 Magazine St.*
Varenholt Studio	*4218 Magazine St.*
Veith Plumbing Supply Co.	*1810 Magazine St.*
Verde Printing Shop	*3207 Magazine St.*
Weaver's Fresh Meats	*4303 Magazine St.*
Weinstein Department Store	*4101 Magazine St.*
Chas. Wendell Hardware & Paint Store	*2901 Magazine St.*
Wendt's Pharmacy	*3005 Magazine St.*
Wexler Shoe Store	*3342 Magazine St.*
Wexler's Poultry House	*3222 Magazine St.*
Roy Wilson, Printing	*4125 Magazine St.*
Winsberg Wearing Apparel	*4304 Magazine St.*
Winston's Printing Shop	*4226 Camp St.*
F. W. Woolworth Co.	*2014 Magazine St.*
F. W. Woolworth Co.	*4308 Magazine St.*
Young's Furniture Store	*2011 Magazine St.*
T. Zoller	*5422 Magazine St.*

Firms who participated in "M" Day are memorialized in a commemorative booklet. (Courtesy The Historic New Orleans Collection.)

and the Magazine Market Association. They represented the four chief business districts of the street. One was between Felicity and Jackson; the next from Washington to Louisiana; then between Marengo and Napoleon; and finally the blocks between Jefferson and Webster. These areas are still focuses of commercial Magazine, although much expanded since the 1940s. The four business groups were separate entities, but in 1948 they joined forces to better represent the whole street and to enhance its competitiveness with the city's other leading retail districts by becoming the Combined Magazine Business Men's Association.

This was around the same time that the first modest shopping centers began to open for business in New Orleans in the late 1940s and 1950s—Gentilly, Gentilly Woods, Carrollton, Airline Village, and Westside Shopping Center—followed by Lakeside Mall, which opened in 1960, changing shopping patterns forever. In 1948, New Orleans' most upscale shopping district was Canal Street with its big department stores like Maison Blanche, D.H. Holmes, Godchaux's, Krauss, Marks Issacs, and Gus Mayer. Now most of these sites have been converted to hotels or apartments. The city's longest shopping strip—and most frequented by African American shoppers—was South Rampart and Dryades (now Oretha Castle Haley Boulevard). The big anchors here were Kaufman's and Handleman's, both on Dryades. During the next half-century Canal, South Rampart, and Dryades saw

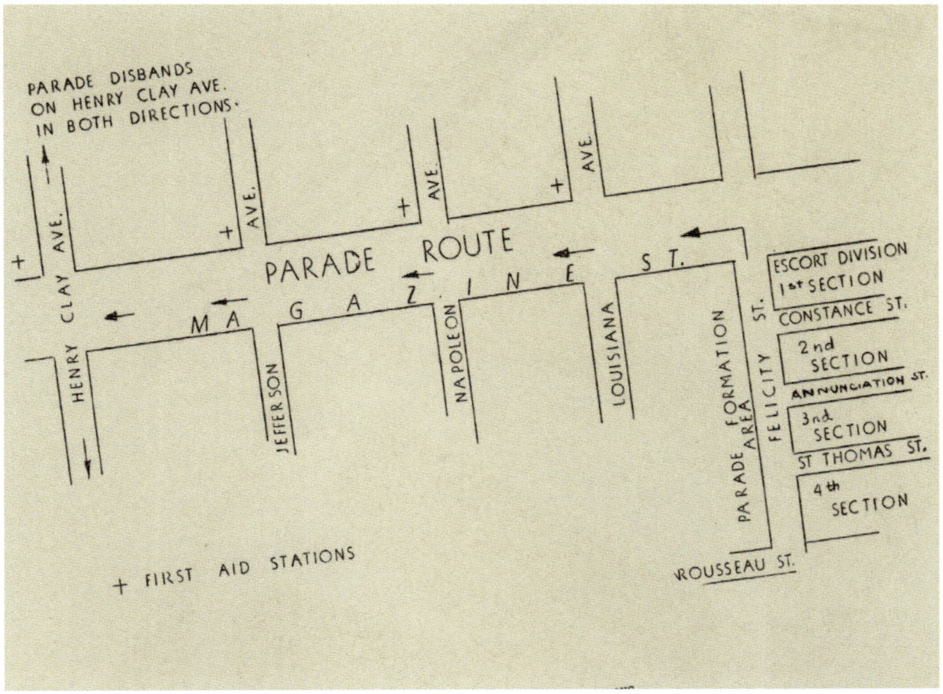

Mimeographed copies of the parade route were given to all individuals and organizations participating in the "M" Day parade. (Courtesy The Historic New Orleans Collection.)

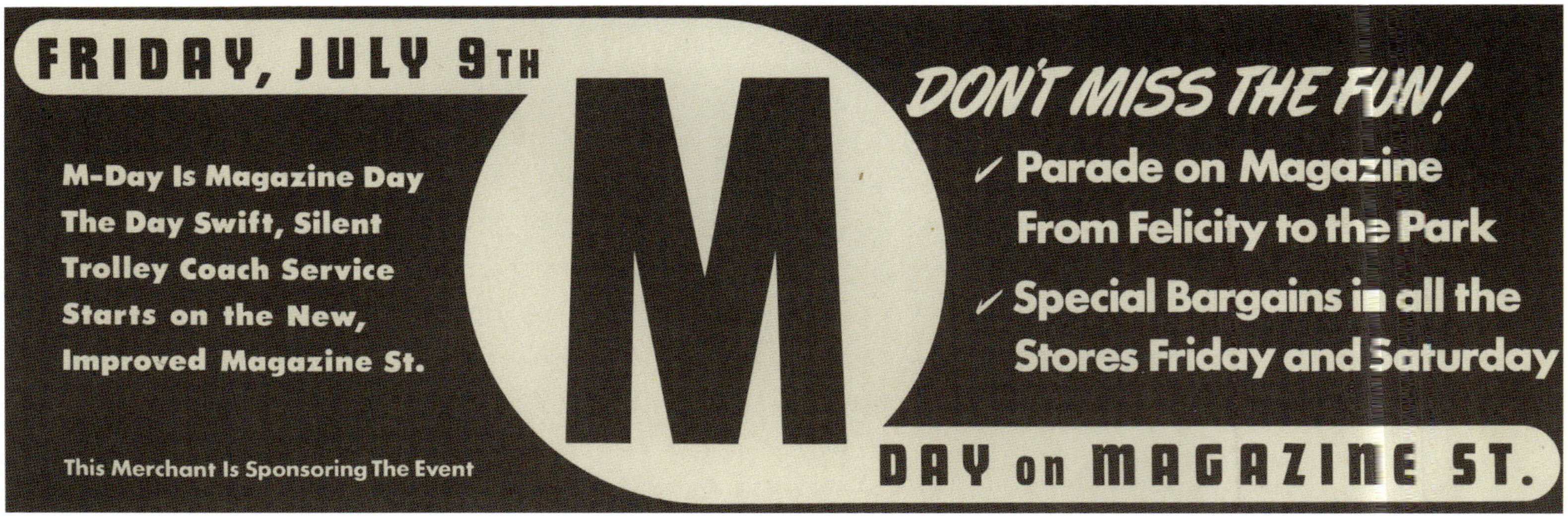

These window streamers announcing the big "M" Day celebration were given to all participating merchants to be placed in windows, on counters, and on their trucks about ten days before the celebration took place. (Courtesy The Historic New Orleans Collection.)

their retail fortunes dwindle as shoppers flocked to the malls. Magazine, however, managed to hang on.

In 1948, Magazine had two F.W. Woolworth's five-and-dime stores, at 2014 (now Razzle Dazzle Home) and 4308 (now Peaches), complete with soda fountain. There were assorted dry goods, clothing retailers, shoe stores, and jewelers, but the street's businesses were heavily made up of small, family-owned neighborhood necessity shops like grocers, pharmacies, hardware stores, laundries, cobblers, and quite a few bars. The Combined Magazine Business Men's Association was determined through "M" Day to put all eyes of the Crescent City on Magazine as never before. This is possibly the first little step toward Magazine Street's evolution into today's shopping hot spot.

Aside from the parade, merchants enticed new customers with big sales and displays of the widest range of merchandise available on Magazine. The sales lasted through Saturday, July 10, and merchants promoted the new, modern Magazine as being not just a friendly neighborhood shopping street, but a destination for the entire city. Shops all along Magazine were decorated with red and white bunting and banners, and matching window streamers fluttered in the breeze.

There was considerable preliminary advertising for "M" Day events. Double-page advertising spreads were placed in the *Times-Picayune* morning paper and in the afternoon papers, the *States* and the *Item*, highlighting both the parade and the convenience of Magazine. There were special-interest stories in the papers as well, telling not only about the bargains but historical tidbits and memories of Magazine from old-timers. The Business Men's Association purchased time at Magazine movie shows where scripted announcements with background music were used to build up excitement. The Coca-Cola Bottling Company, then located near the foot of Canal Street, sponsored a short film about "M" Day for presentation in theaters all over town.

Several radio stations aired delayed broadcasts recounting all the "M" Day events, while WWL-AM sent out popular local personalities Henry Dupre and Jill Jackson for live coverage of the day's excitement. This was still a bit before television, since WDSU-TV, the city's first television station, did not go on the air until

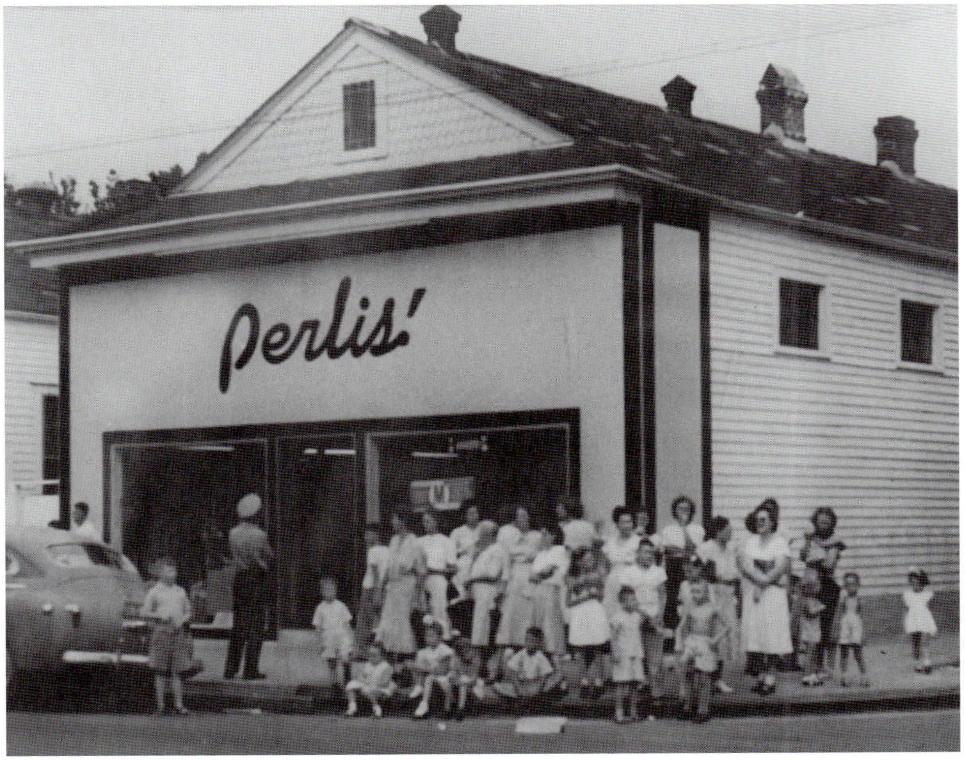

"M" Day crowds gather in front of Perlis, 1948. (Courtesy David George Perlis.)

five months later, on December 18, 1948.

The official parade route started at Felicity Street at 2:00 P.M. and reached Henry Clay before disbanding at Audubon Park. The parade itself was divided into four sections. Each section had a float replicating full-size streetcars from different historic periods, tracing the advancement of public transportation on Magazine. The parade was logically called "The Dramatization of the Four Periods of Public Transportation on Magazine Street."

The first float was of a horse-drawn car from 1835. The Business Men's Association proudly boasted that the first horse-drawn streetcar in New Orleans traversed Magazine. While the St. Charles streetcar line also dated to 1835—and is now the country's oldest one still operating—at its inception it was drawn by steam engines, not horses or mules.

The Magazine line was chartered by the New Orleans and Carrollton Railway, the same company that started the line on St. Charles, and initially approved by the city council in 1833. It had a single track that ran up Magazine from Poydras to Robert, where it turned toward the river. It returned on the same track. Two horses pulled the car at a rate of four miles per hour, a speed designed so as not to be a noisy nuisance for households living along the route.

Accompanying this section of the parade was a grand marshal and Mayor Morrison himself. There were also motorcycle and mounted divisions of the New Orleans Police Department along with the police department band.

The second float was a replica of an 1895 streetcar, the first electric cars on Magazine. This was two years after the first electric line was inaugurated on the St. Charles line. Electric lines had been an instant success, and the city's many independent streetcar companies (they would not merge until 1922 under New Orleans Public Service, Inc.) quickly electrified their cars, making trips much faster than the plodding, old-fashioned mule-drawn cars.

Leading this section of the parade was the Jefferson City Buzzards, the city's oldest Carnival marching group, accompanied by troops of Boy Scouts. There was also a 1903 fire engine and a "Black Maria" police paddy wagon of the same period. Adding a comic touch was a "Toonerville Trolley." This overcrowded, broken-down, old streetcar was based on the popular newspaper comic strip *Toonerville Folk*, which ran from 1908 to 1955.

Float three was a replica of one of the longer, faster 1926 streetcar models—the kind being replaced by trolleybuses and still operating on St. Charles today. Prominent marchers in this section were the American Legion band accompanied by members of several veterans' organizations, including the Veterans of Foreign Wars. Their participation recalls the fact that 1948 was only three years after the end of World War II and thirty years after the end of World War I. There were also several civic and school marching groups and more Boy Scouts.

The final float represented the new 1948 trolleybuses and was led by the Lyons Carnival Club. The accompanying city dignitaries were chauffeured in 1948 car models, taking advantage of the smooth new asphalt paving.

Throughout the parade there were horse-drawn carriages, high wheel bicycles, and vintage automobiles—though at the time the oldest cars were not even sixty years old yet. There were four pieces of firefighting equipment, two dating from 1926 and two from 1948. Men and women were costumed in fashions from each of the four periods represented. In all there were nine marching bands and two additional Carnival marching groups, the Eleonore and Garden District Clubs. Riding onboard the floats were children from the five orphanages located in the vicinity of Magazine Street, two of which were located directly on Magazine itself: St. Vincent de Paul's Orphans' Asylum, a Catholic orphanage (opened in 1865) at 1507, and St. John's Protestant Orphans' Home (opened in 1887-88) at 3000 Magazine. Excitement was added when fighter planes from the New Orleans Naval

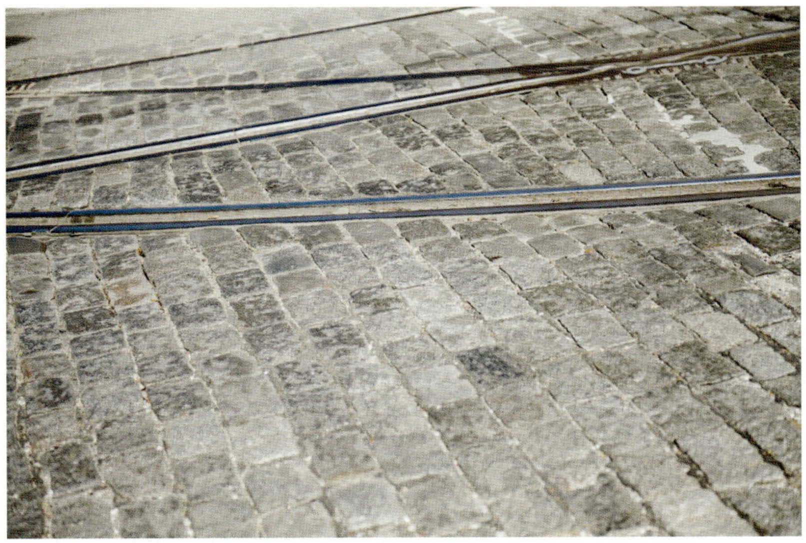

Bricks and remnants of the streetcar tracks on present-day Magazine.

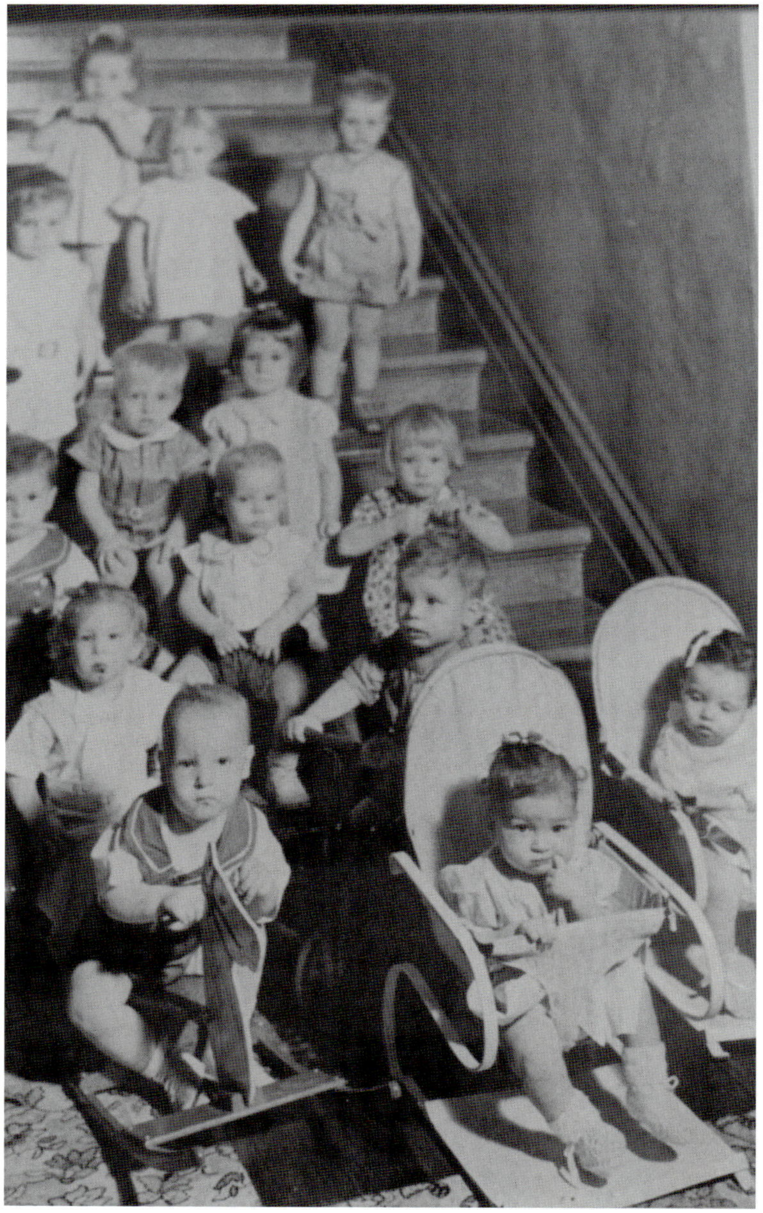

This photograph of orphans at St. Vincent de Paul's Orphans' Asylum is currently displayed on the wall at St. Vincent Guest House.

Air Station on the lakefront—the site of the University of New Orleans since 1958—flew in formation over the parade.

It was a usual hot, sticky New Orleans summer day, but the crowds along the street were thick for the parade and extended several people deep along sections of the route. Since schools were out for the summer, there were plenty of children running around and following the parade. Unlike virtually every parade in New Orleans today, there were no screams of "Throw me something, Mister!" because there were no throws tossed in this parade. In the late '40s there were very few throws tossed from even the biggest Mardi Gras parades—far from the extravagance of today's Carnival throws, which can now be seen decorating trees along upper Magazine Street.

On November 3, 1947, work had begun to remove the old Magazine streetcar tracks to allow for the new pavement. Even as late as the 1940s parts of Magazine were unpaved, while paved parts varied from granite stones in the commercial districts to wooden planks and even wooden blocks that had the tendency to become buoyant and float in rainstorms.

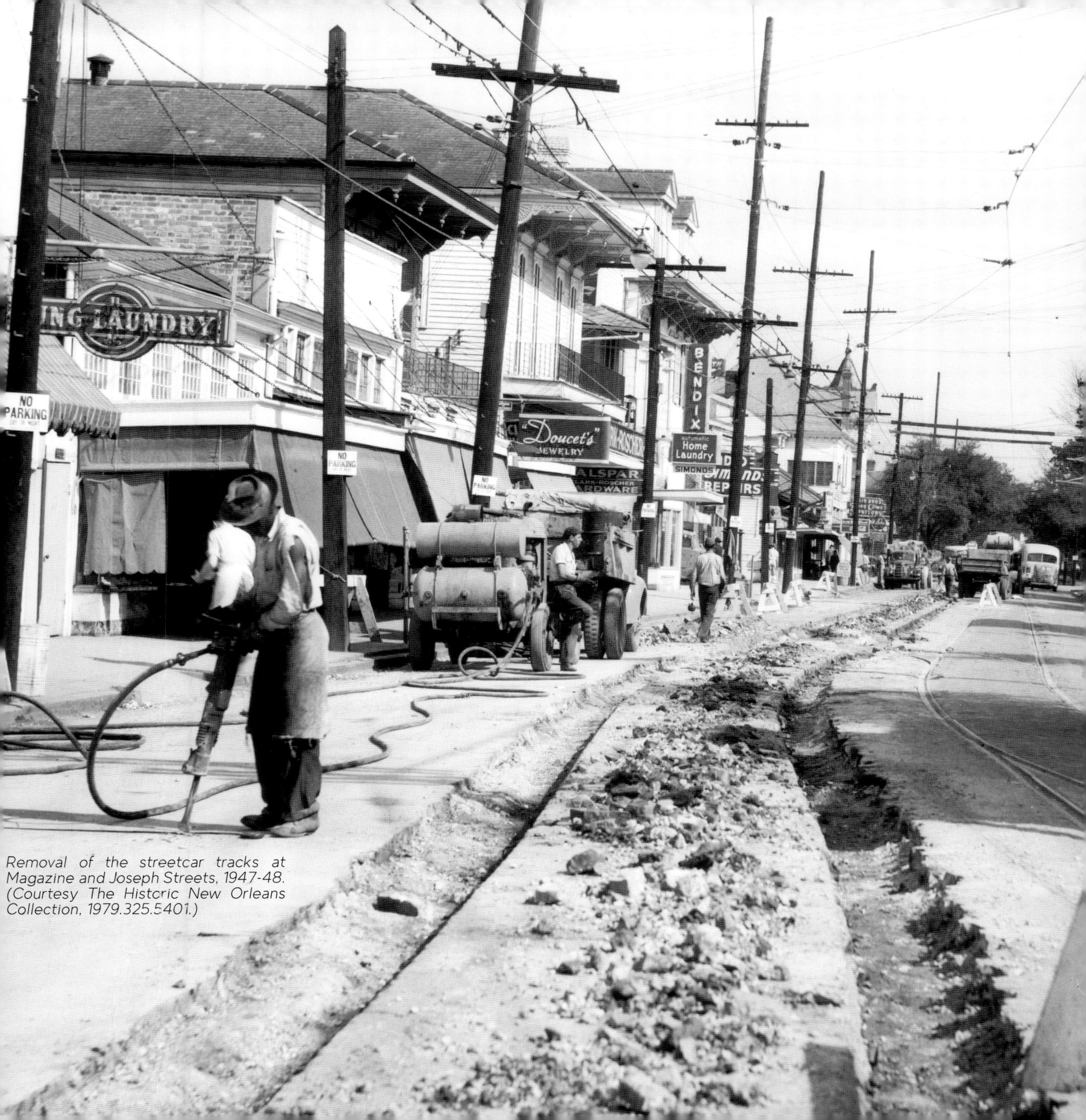

Removal of the streetcar tracks at Magazine and Joseph Streets, 1947-48. (Courtesy The Historic New Orleans Collection, 1979.325.5401.)

It took only six months to complete the entire paving project, and as the tracks were pulled up, the old streetcars were retired and temporarily replaced with small diesel buses. Beginning in February 1948, New Orleans Public Service began distributing leaflets to businesses and homes in the neighborhood informing people of the improvements that would include "Swift, Convenient, Low Cost Transit Service."

Following the parade, the last diesel buses were replaced by sixty new trolleybuses that would serve Magazine Street. This number was nearly double the thirty-five streetcars that had previously rumbled along Magazine. Passengers riding on the buses were ceremoniously invited to step down and transfer onto the new vehicles. The number of trolleybuses in operation at the time indicates the importance of public transit in 1948. It seems difficult today to imagine narrow Magazine Street clogged with so many streetcars then even more buses. Of course there were far fewer automobiles in that day, and waiting for a bus would have been a matter of only a few minutes. And it cost only seven cents with free transfers. This was just what the Business Men's Association hoped to promote.

This was also the growing automobile age. The new, smooth Magazine pavement was far superior to the bumpy streetcar tracks, bricks, and planks surfacing the street prior to 1948. The association also let it be known that there was plenty of free parking on or near Magazine.

Magazine Street was already a principle traffic artery in New Orleans and did serve a large and important segment of the city's nearly six hundred thousand residents. With "M" Day it was proclaimed that "The merchants and residents along Magazine Street and all citizens of New Orleans will enjoy the benefits of the forward step in community progress." This was indeed the birth of what was being called "Modern Magazine Street."

"M" Day is commemorated in a large, richly illustrated souvenir booklet in the holdings of The Historic New Orleans Collection with the lengthy title, *The "M" Day Celebration: Of the Improvement of Magazine Street and the Inauguration of Electric Trolley Coaches, July 9, 1948; Sponsored by the Combined Magazine Business Men's Associations.*

The great bulk of the buildings along Magazine Street in 1948 are still standing,

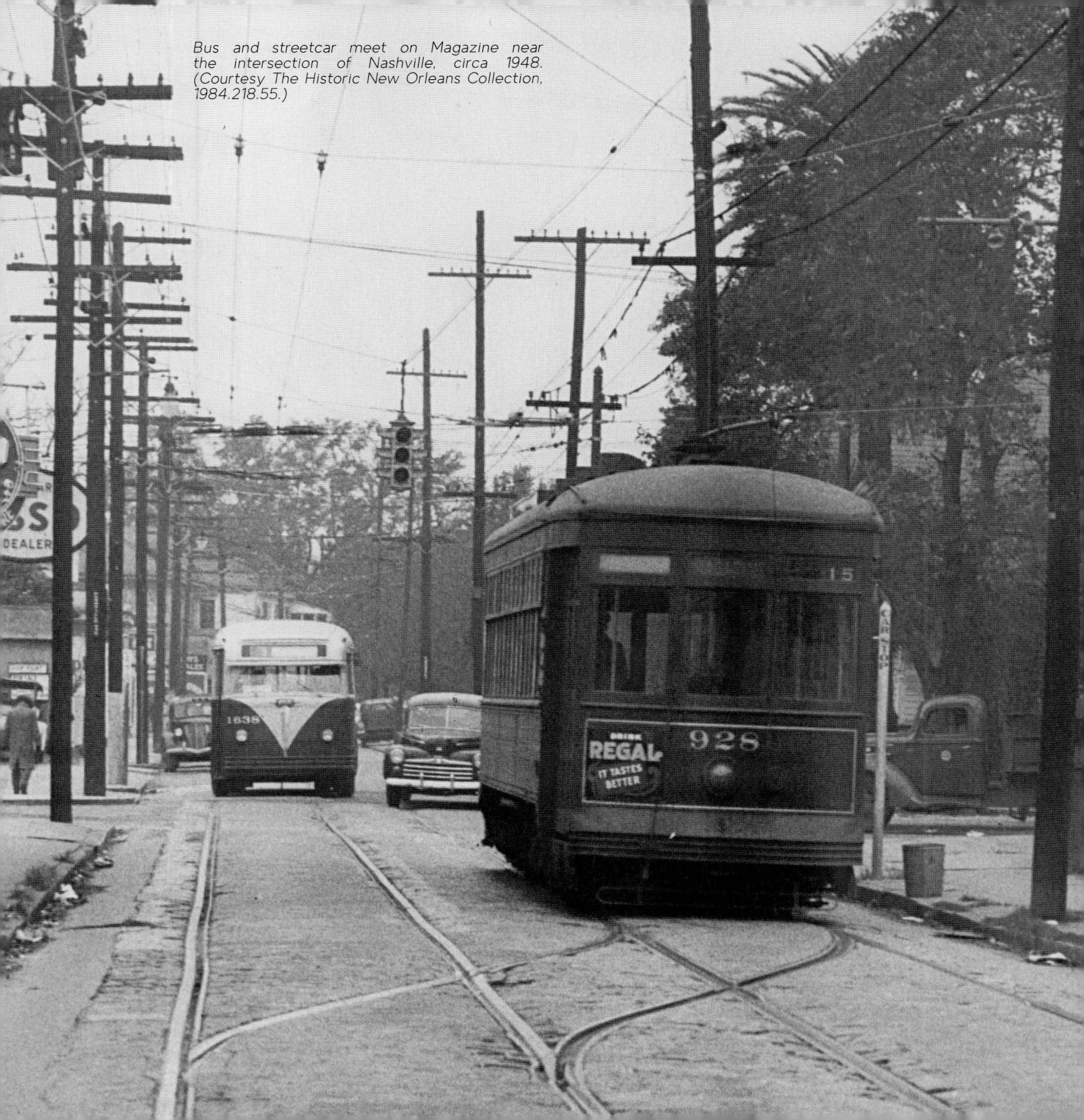

Bus and streetcar meet on Magazine near the intersection of Nashville, circa 1948. (Courtesy The Historic New Orleans Collection, 1984.218.55.)

although many have been altered, some considerably. Virtually all of the businesses that took part in "M" Day events are now long gone, but a few familiar establishments are still in operation, including Casamento's Restaurant, Henry's Uptown Bar, Perlis, H. Rault Locksmiths, and Usner Brothers—all part of that continuity that adds to the charm and history of Magazine Street.

Today the support group on Magazine is not the Combined Magazine Business Men's Association, but the Magazine Street Merchants Association. The goals of the two groups are similar, but today the mission statement of the MSMA is not just the goal of promoting the street as a regional destination; it has a much farther reach: "To establish an image of Magazine Street as a charming, unique and easily accessible commercial area with strong appeal to the local market as well as tourists and conventioneers." Tourism is a much bigger, international business than it was in 1948.

The current logo of the Magazine Street Merchants Association. (Courtesy Magazine Street Merchants Association.)

According to Stan Levy, the MSMA's third president, who served in the early 1980s, the association began as a group of antiques dealers. Mr. Levy, a retired antiques dealer whose store was located on Magazine at Louisiana until about 2005, said that the antiques dealers initially joined together to issue a brochure promoting Magazine as a destination for antiques. These stores were in their infancy along Magazine at the time. According to Mr. Levy such businesses are not as prevalent today because the collecting of antiques has gone out of fashion. It is less desirable among today's younger buyers.

The current MSMA president is Keith Andrews, owner of Apolline Restaurant at 4729 Magazine, and the previous president is Sam Farnet, owner of Joey K's Restaurant & Bar at 3001 Magazine. They estimate that in 2017 the membership of the MSMA is approaching two hundred and there are nearly five hundred businesses along Magazine Street.

Many members of the MSMA have roots on Magazine Street. Mr. Andrews' grandparents lived in the 5200 block during the early twentieth century, while Mr. Farnet's great-uncle owned a pharmacy at 3218, which in 1948 was the American Drug Store. Amici Ristorante and Bar is now located there.

Mr. Farnet recalled that a man named Cotman Parkerson owned a small, narrow shop near Joey K's that specialized in Civil War tems. The shop had a second floor to which many customers made their way. Mr. Parkerson would lock the shop when he went out to lunch and on several occasions unintentionally locked people inside the store. Eventually he began putting a sign on the inside of the door telling people that if they got locked in, they should call Joey K's across the street.

Just as neighbors and businesspeople once looked out for each other's interests, today the MSMA serves a complementary purpose. "M" Day was designed by the Business Men's Association to entice people to Magazine Street, and today's MSMA entices people to visit the locally owned retailers with annual events like the Champagne Stroll on the Saturday before Mother's Day, Art for Art's Sake on the first Saturday in October, and the holiday season's Merriment on Magazine.

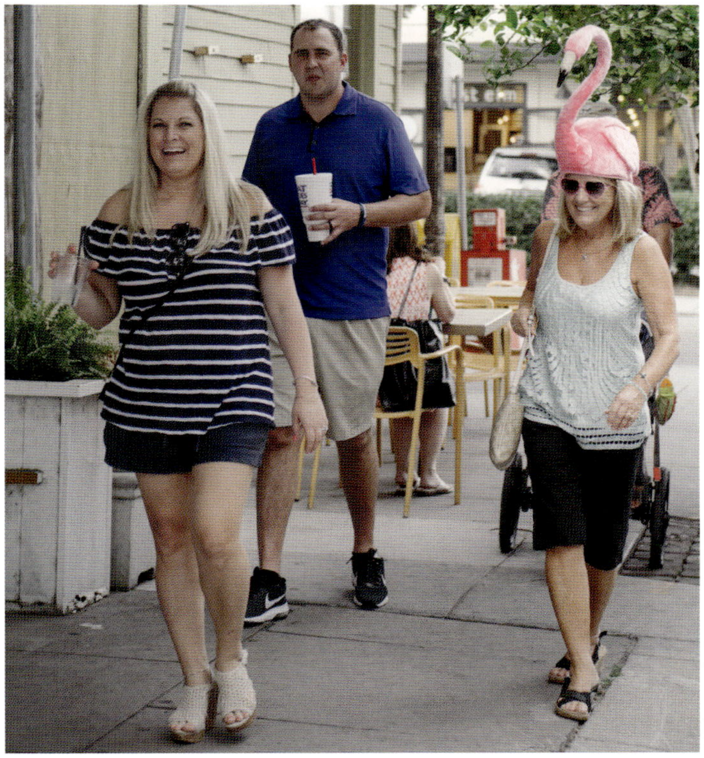

Revelers enjoy shopping and events year-round on Magazine Street.

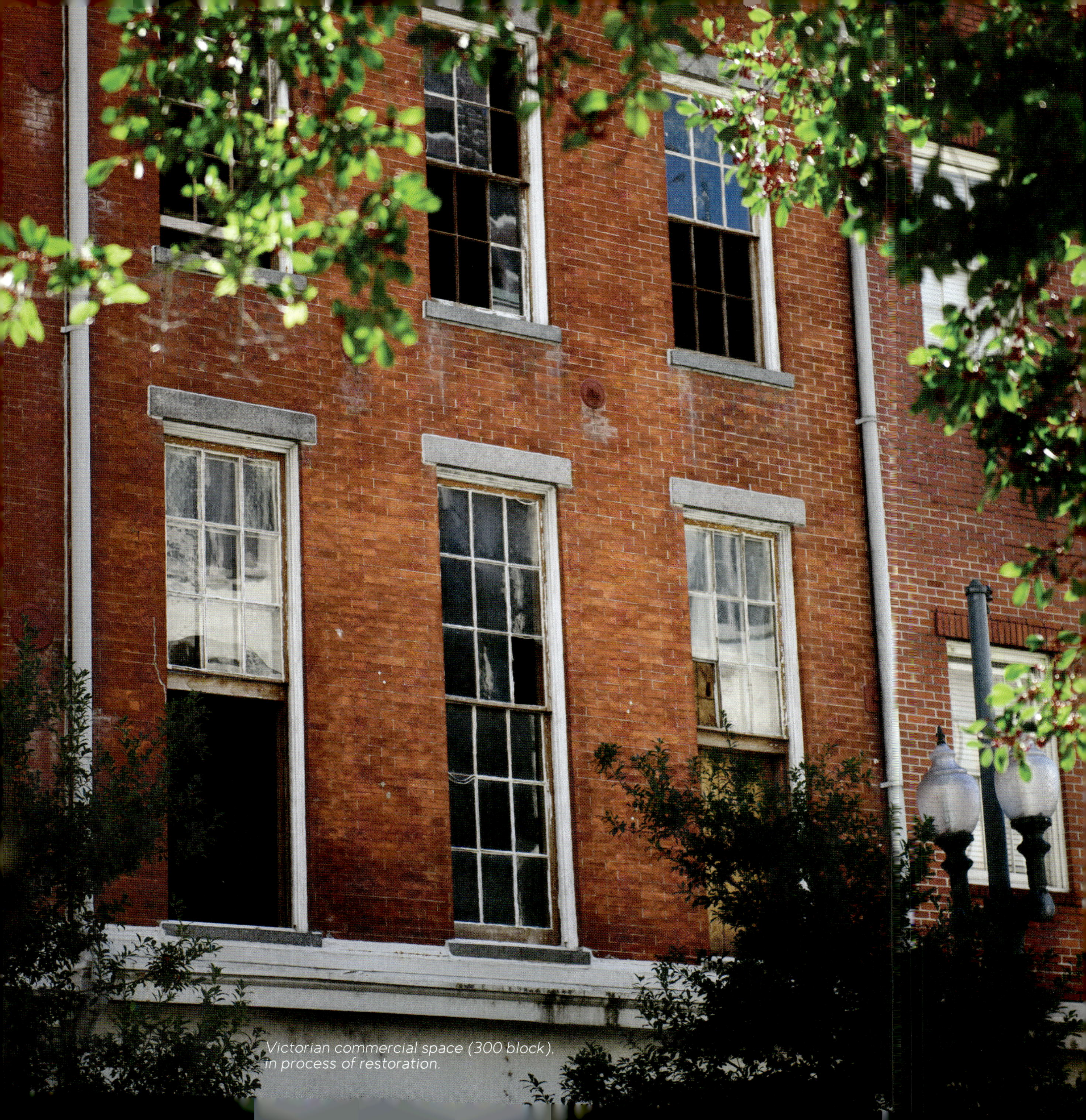

Victorian commercial space (300 block),
in process of restoration.

Chapter Three

From Spanish Warehouses to World War II

The oldest and most historic part of Magazine Street is its first mile, where there is an array of buildings tracing the business history of the Crescent City from the early nineteenth century to the present. During the last half-century the area, like all of Magazine, has changed dramatically.

In the 1960s, Magazine downtown had the reputation of being little better than a run-down secondary business district. It was a place to be avoided, except by those who worked there, and they went home at 5:00 P.M. The section above Poydras centering on Julia was considered part of skid row. Today it has become a center of tourism and inner-city apartment living. The changes were beginning around the time of the 1984 Louisiana World Exposition, as manufacturing and warehousing were moving to the suburbs to take advantage

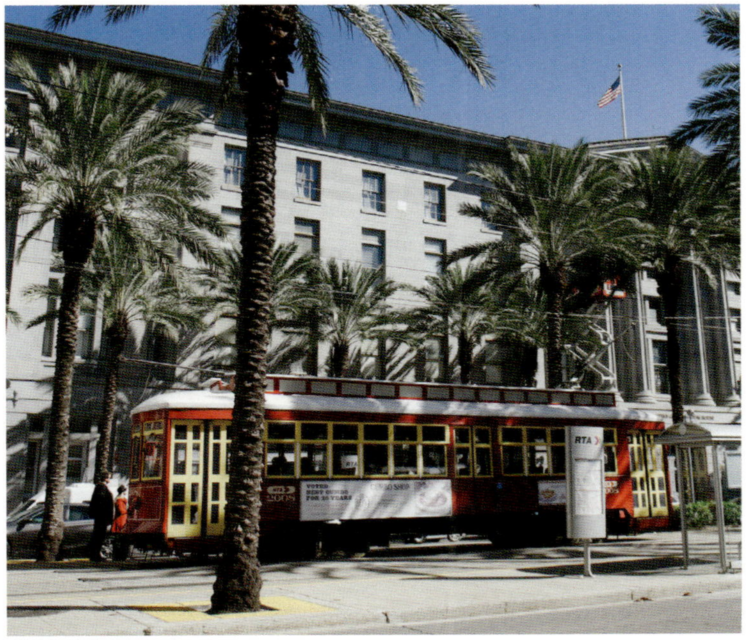

The view toward Decatur Street and site of the former Spanish warehouse that may have lent Magazine Street its name.

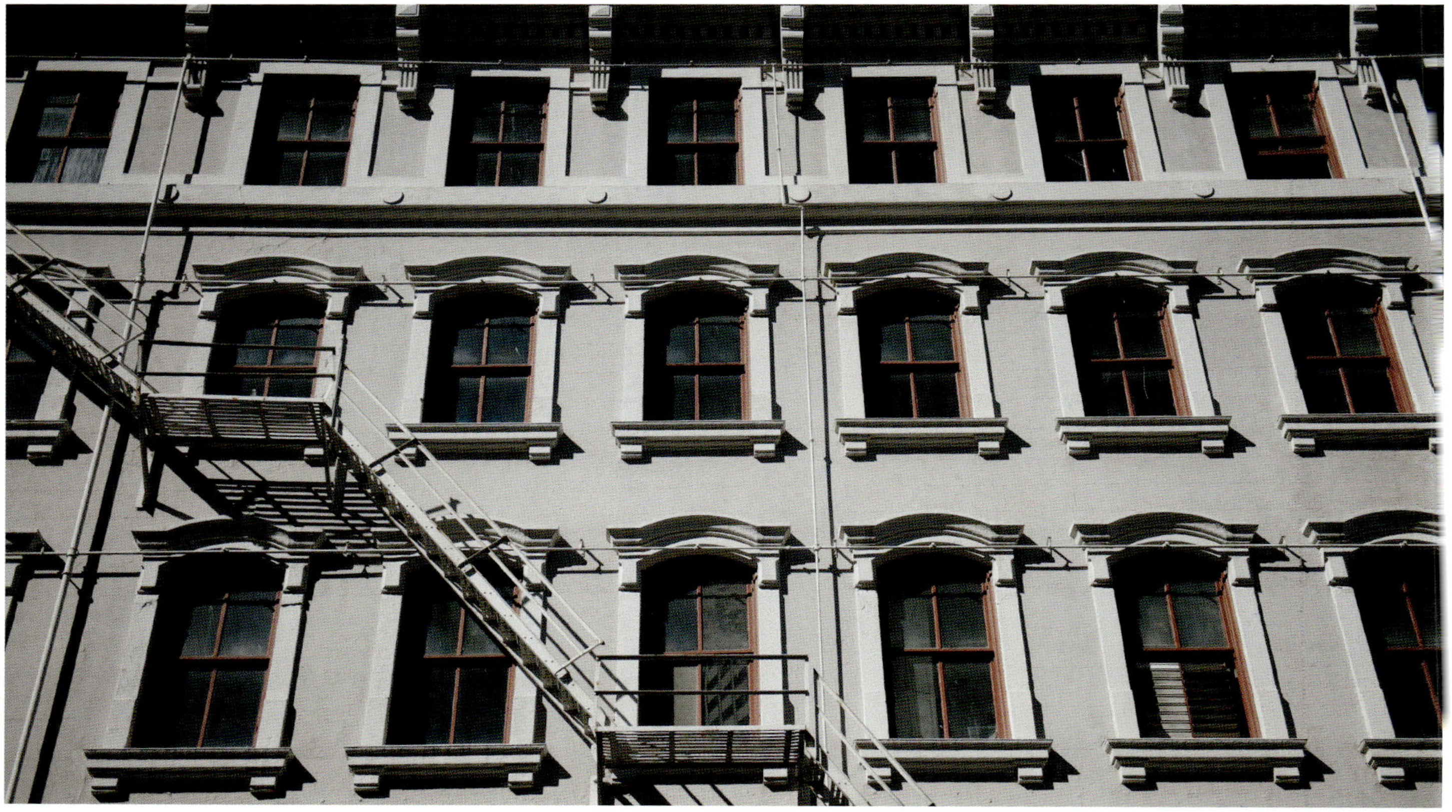

Canal at Magazine. Once a warehouse, now a museum.

of business parks with better trucking access. Accelerated by the World's Fair, warehouses were converted into apartments and condominiums, while restaurants, night spots, and shops sprang up, turning the Warehouse District into a popular residential neighborhood. Near Canal Street, nineteenth-century brick loft buildings were converted into hotels for the city's booming tourist trade.

Magazine's history goes back a long way. Originally its six-mile site was on the vast land grant given to New Orleans founder Jean Baptiste Le Moyne Sieur de Bienville by the Superior Council of Louisiana in 1719. The city was a year old. Bienville sold part of this grant, a tract extending to about today's Felicity Street, to the Jesuits as a plantation. In 1762 when French Louisiana was given by France's King Louis XV to his cousin King Carlos III of Spain—to prevent the colony from falling into the hands of

Great Britain, which was defeating France in war—the Jesuits were expelled and their land confiscated and sold. After several transfers the portion of land extending to about modern St. Joseph Street was acquired by Andres Reynard. Upon his death in 1785 this plantation was left to his widow, Dona Marie Josefa Deslonde, who remarried Don Bertrand Gravier. It was through this marriage that Magazine Street was born.

On Good Friday, March 21, 1788, about ninety percent of New Orleans—then just the French Quarter—was consumed by fire. On April 1 of that year Gravier hired surveyor Carlos Laveau Trudeau to subdivide the plantation, and it was called Faubourg St. Marie in honor of his late wife. There were initially just four streets paralleling the river: El Camino Real, or Levee Street (today's Tchoupitoulas),

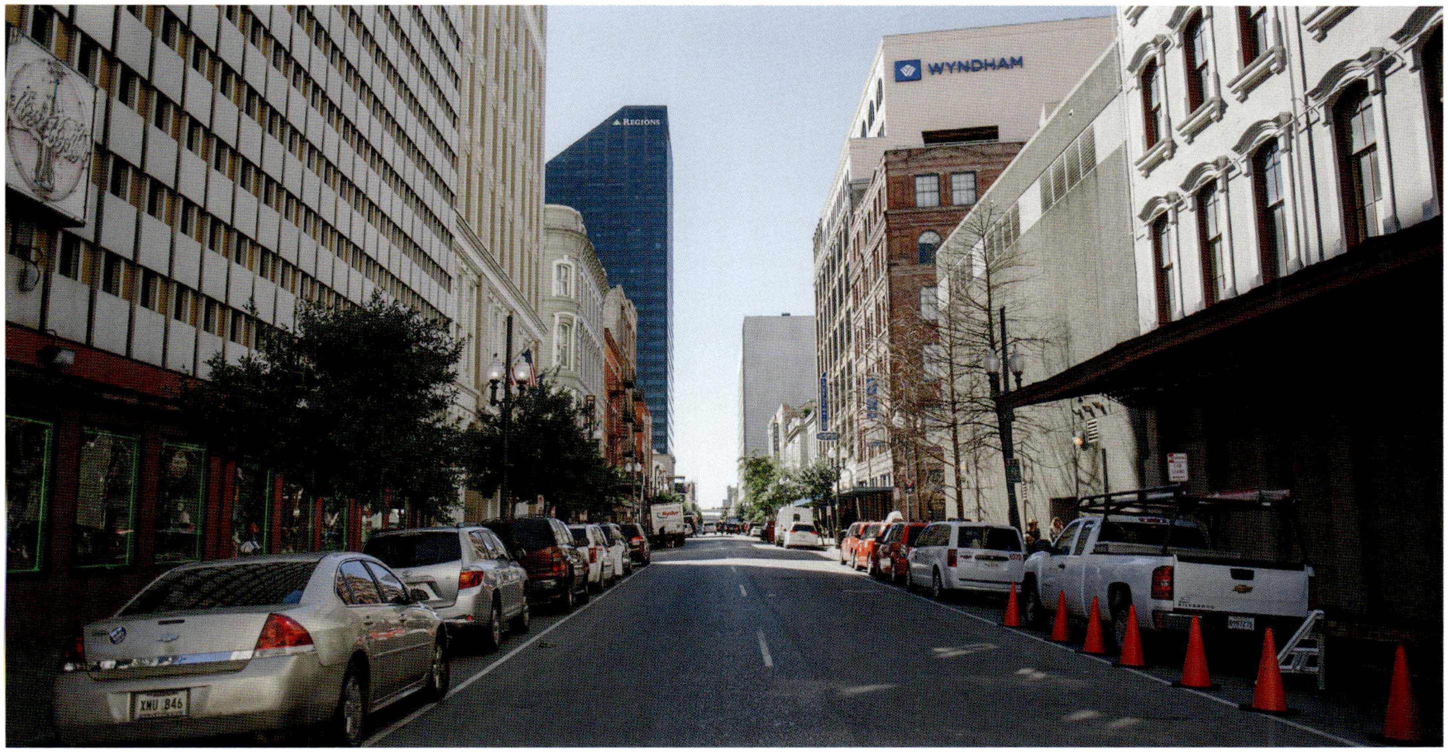

Looking up Magazine from Canal Street.

followed by Magazine, Camp, and San Carlos, for Spain's King Carlos (now known as St. Charles).

The name Magazine Street is generally believed to have been derived from a powder magazine which stood near modern Decatur and Iberville. This facility dates from the city's earliest days, and on French maps it is called simply *poudrière*. A British map of the same period calls it a powder magazine. During the Spanish period a warehouse was set up across Decatur from the magazine on the site of the U.S. Custom House for storage of goods—primarily tobacco—coming downriver from the United States. Spanish for warehouse is *almacén*, and on Spanish-era maps Magazine Street is called *Almacén*. No matter which storage facility Magazine Street is named for—perhaps both—initially the street looked directly toward both of them.

The *almacén* was just across the City Commons from Magazine. The Commons was land containing a protective palisade surrounding the French Quarter and five small forts, essentially forming a ring around the French Quarter. The fort at Magazine was Fort St. Louis. The Commons extended to modern Common Street and was Crown property that became U.S. government property with the Louisiana Purchase of 1803. In 1810, Congress gave the Commons to New Orleans with the stipulation that a navigation canal be dug. Although the name Canal Street stuck, the canal was never dug. The Commons was subdivided, and Magazine was extended a block to intersect with Canal Street, where it begins today.

Prior to the 1820s, there were only scattered cottages plus a few larger houses along a very countrified Magazine. Some of the dwellings were Creole cottages, which was the standard early-nineteenth-century working-class house all over New Orleans. Built of brick between wood posts and covered with plaster, these houses were generally two rooms wide and two deep with heavily shuttered doors and windows. They once lined the streets of the French Quarter and surrounding suburbs but only one such example survives on Magazine, where the 900 block meets St. Joseph. The small hip-roofed building, now an urgent care center, may date to the 1820s. It was during the 1820s that the faubourg began to grow dramatically, and

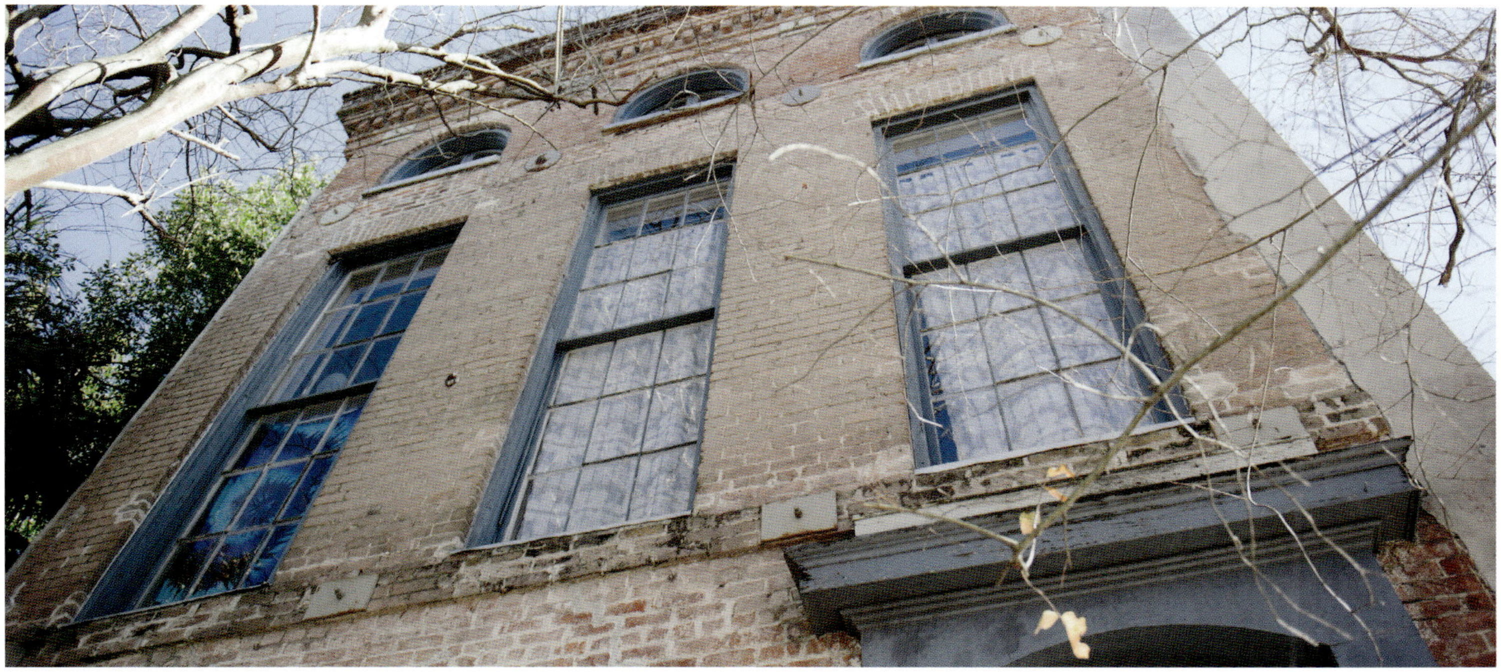

Vestiges of an elegant townhouse on Magazine.

within a decade it was becoming the city's business heart. Magazine was in the thick of this growth.

By the 1880s, Magazine between Canal and Poydras was part of the city's old warehouse district—not to be confused with today's Warehouse District on the other side of Poydras, which at the time was predominantly manufacturing.

The building on the lake corner of Canal and Magazine is a fine warehouse from 1869, with a fifth floor added later. In 1900, Kohn, Weil & Co., Inc., a manufacturer and exporter of hats, caps, gloves, and waterproof clothing, was located here and specialized in "ladies [*sic*] fancy trimmed and walking hats," per a 1903 business listing. By the 1960s it was a furniture store painted yellow and called the "Big Yellow Warehouse." Befitting New Orleans' reputation as a party town, the long empty building is becoming Sazerac House, the Sazerac liquor company's cocktail museum.

Across Magazine from this warehouse-turned-museum is a series of circa 1840 warehouse buildings that in the early twentieth century housed Marx, Weil and

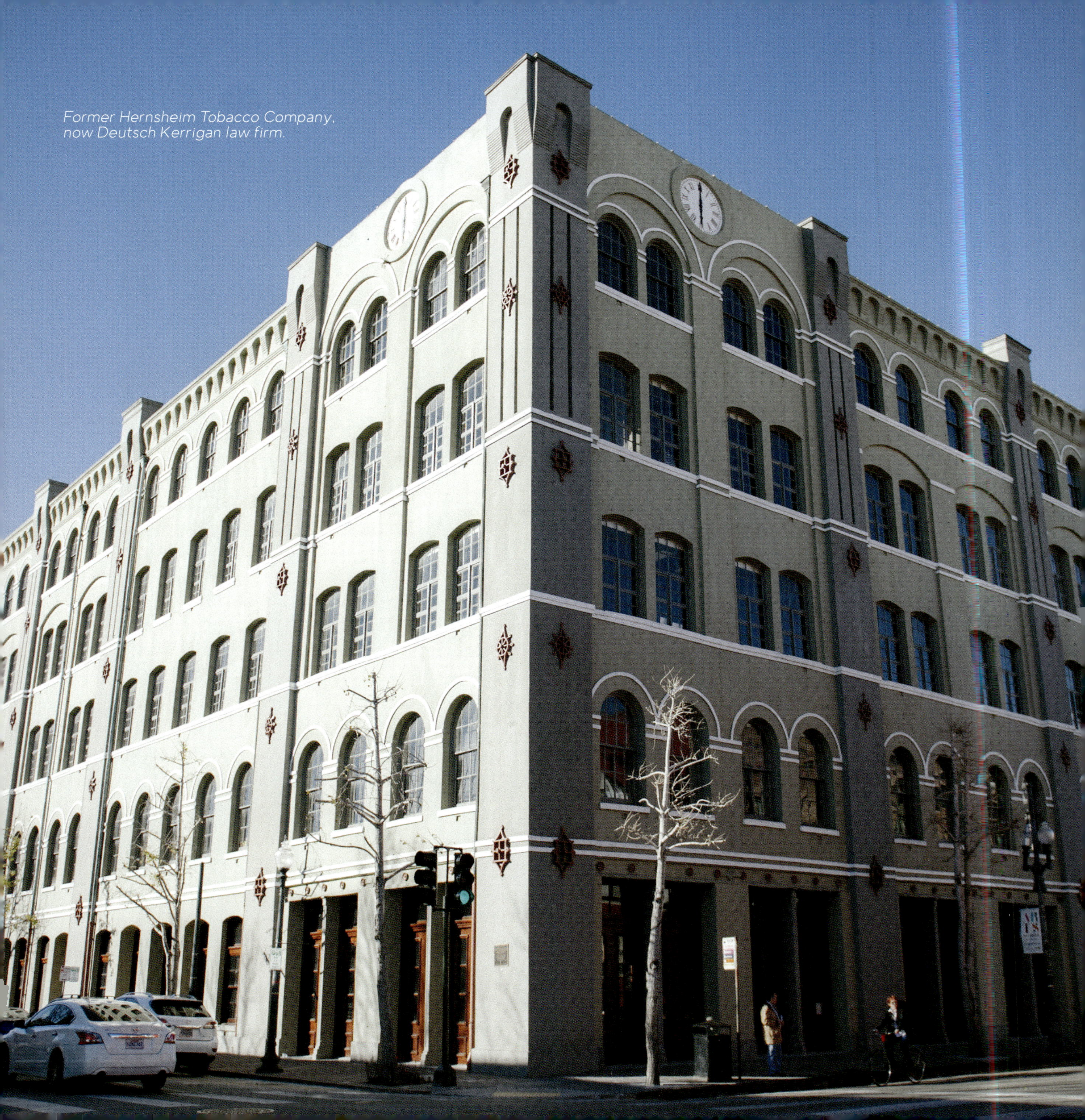

Former Hernsheim Tobacco Company,
now Deutsch Kerrigan law firm.

Sons, dealers in crockery, glassware, tinware, and cutlery. In the early 1960s they were covered with a "modern" facade and the complex was named the Sanlin Building for the owners' two children, Sandy and Lynn. For decades preservationists have cringed at this sight, calling for the buildings to be returned to their original appearance.

A block up Magazine, at the corner of Common, the eight-story Best Western Plus St. Christopher Hotel is in a loft warehouse building dating from the early 1890s and one of the earliest "skyscrapers" in the city. Originally built for the printing company Dwyer Brothers, by the early twentieth century it housed Finley Dicks Company, a dealer in wholesale drugs, druggist supplies, and sundries. By the 1930s it was the dry goods warehouse for Jaubert Brothers and was connected by a passageway across Common Street to the building that now houses the Pelham Hotel, another former dry goods warehouse dating from 1881. It was on the Pelham site that Bienville built his house in the 1720s. The Pelham shares this block of Magazine with several 1840s business buildings. These four-story brick structures with street-level granite posts are typical of

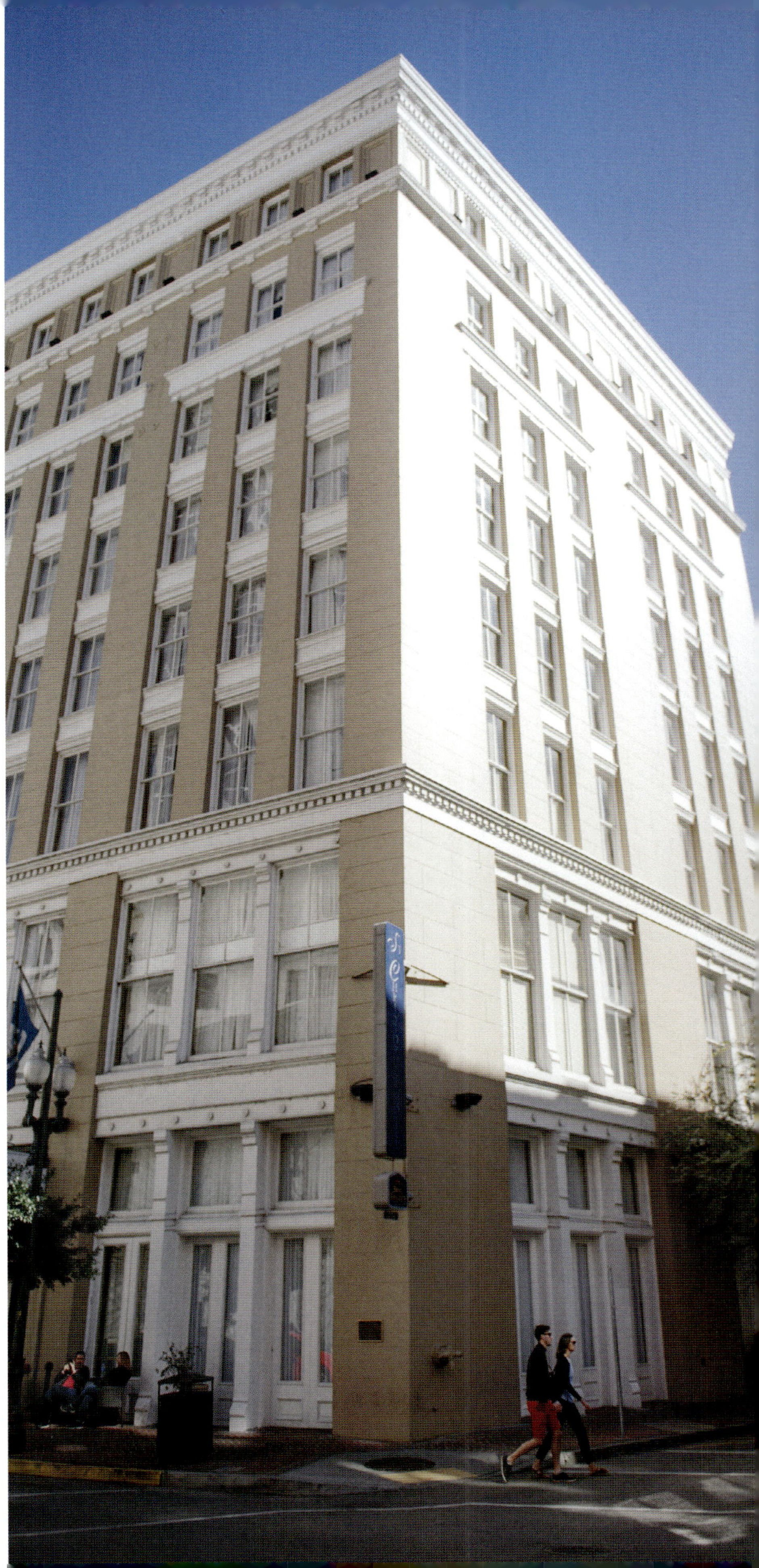

Magazine Street's first "skyscraper," now a hotel.

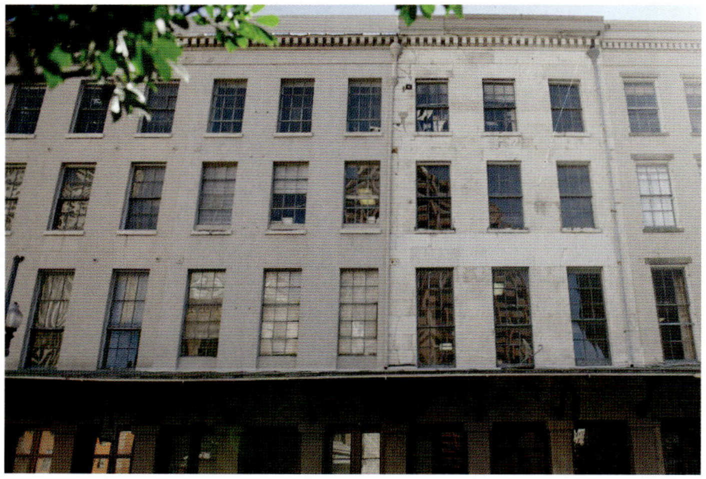

The striking 1850s commercial buildings at 400-12 Magazine Street.

New Orleans' business buildings of that time. A few are left on Magazine, but in the mid-nineteenth century, downtown streets were lined with block after block of these.

The other side of Magazine in this block reveals the more solid and large-scale business architecture of the late nineteenth and early twentieth centuries. The Merchants Lofts Apartments on the corner at 201 and Common was built about 1900 for a dry goods wholesaler, while the larger building to its left, Wyndham La Belle Maison hotel, was built in the 1880s as the Louis P. Price harness and saddlery factory. It was reputedly the largest and most complete "house of this line in the country." For decades after that it housed the Franklin Printing Company before conversion to a hotel.

In the first half of the nineteenth century, the Crescent City's chief financial district shifted from Royal Street in the French Quarter to American Magazine Street. The 1820s and '30s was a period of freewheeling, relatively unregulated banking expansion, and New Orleans, already booming, was able to take advantage of this growth, as its bank clearings often outpaced those of New York City. Banking at the time was centered on Magazine Street. The Canal Bank Apartments at 301 at the corner of Gravier are in the 1843 building of the New Orleans Canal and Banking Company. Granite stonework and the entrance columns were incorporated from an earlier Canal Bank building on the site. In the 1830s on this block between Gravier and Perdido, there were three separate banks designed like Greek temples—one on each corner and one in the middle. Greek Revival was becoming very popular, and the architectural style gave banks a solid, permanent look. Most of the existing buildings along the block—now the Country Inn & Suites—were built in 1854 for retail stores. Their ground-floor posts are cast iron, new building technology of the 1850s, which was replacing granite posts of a decade earlier.

Across Magazine is the site of Banks Arcade, built by Englishman Thomas Banks. Constructed in 1833, this office building was a symbol of the city's rich financial and business trade. It served as a gathering place for merchants and businessmen, and it was here that plans for the Texas Revolution of 1835-36 were hatched. Only part of the block-long building remains and it now hosts the St. James Hotel at 330 Magazine. The other half of the building was destroyed by a fire in 1851, and the fine cast-iron gallery circling the St. James Hotel was added in the late 1860s.

Several brick buildings on the block at the corner of Gravier are typical of the mid-nineteenth century, while Board of Trade Plaza—the attractive pocket park in the center of the block—was the site of an 1870s hotel that was demolished to make way for the park in 1967. The building behind the park was built in 1883 as the Produce Exchange and for many years was the Board of Trade, but it is now a popular events venue.

The next block up at 400-12, between

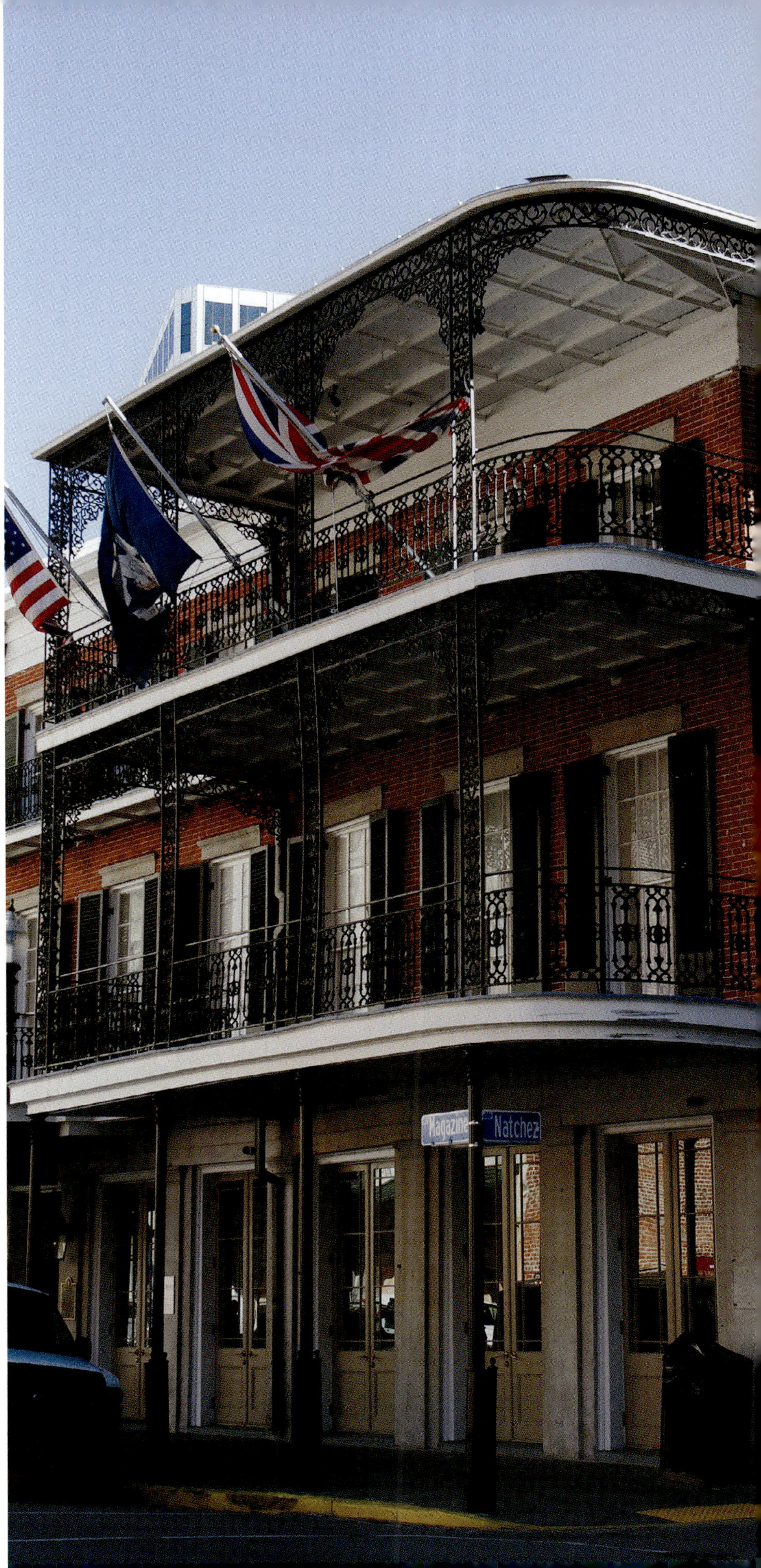

The former Banks Arcade, now site of the St. James Hotel.

Country Inn & Suites, viewed from Board of Trade Plaza.

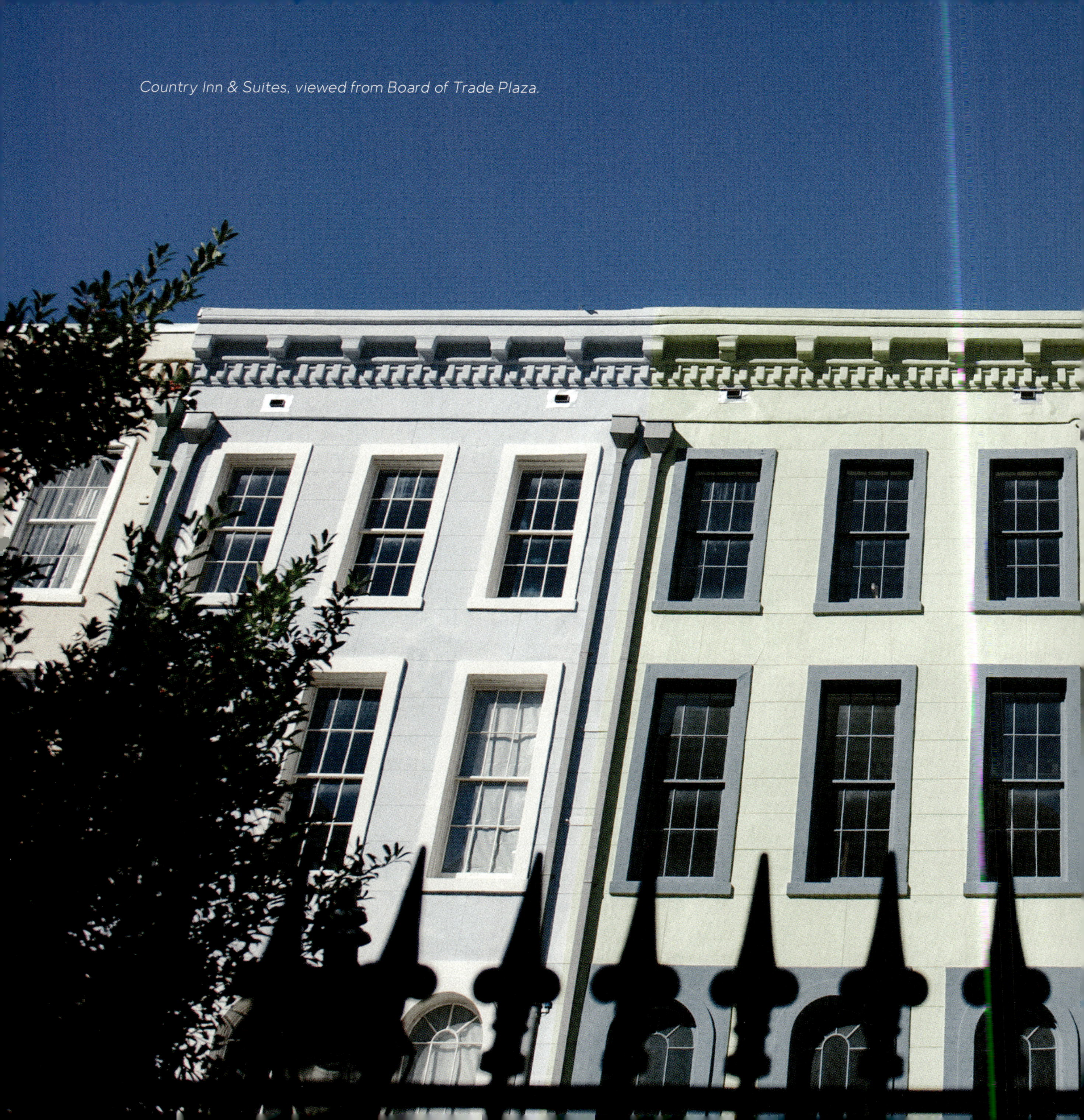

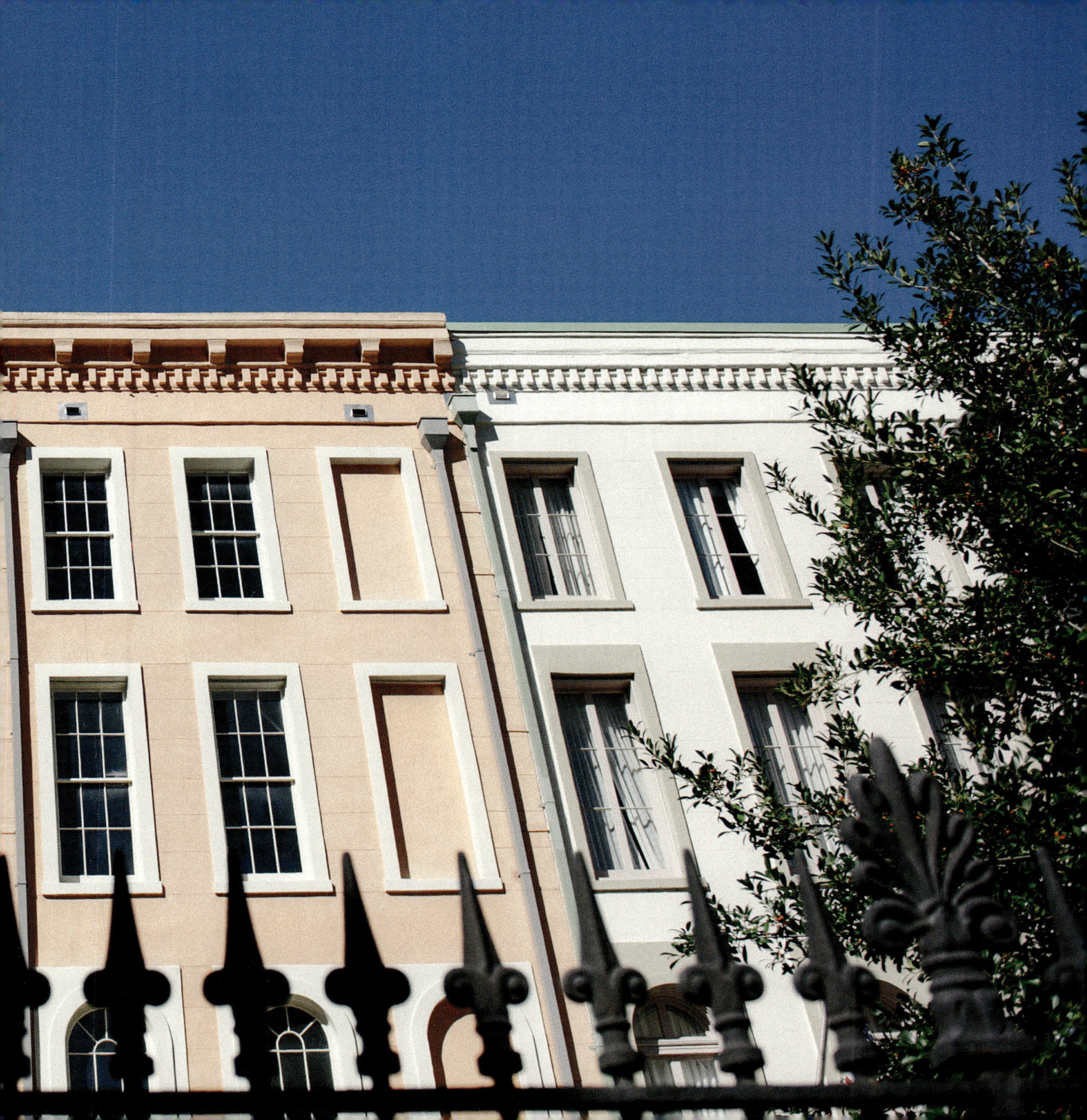

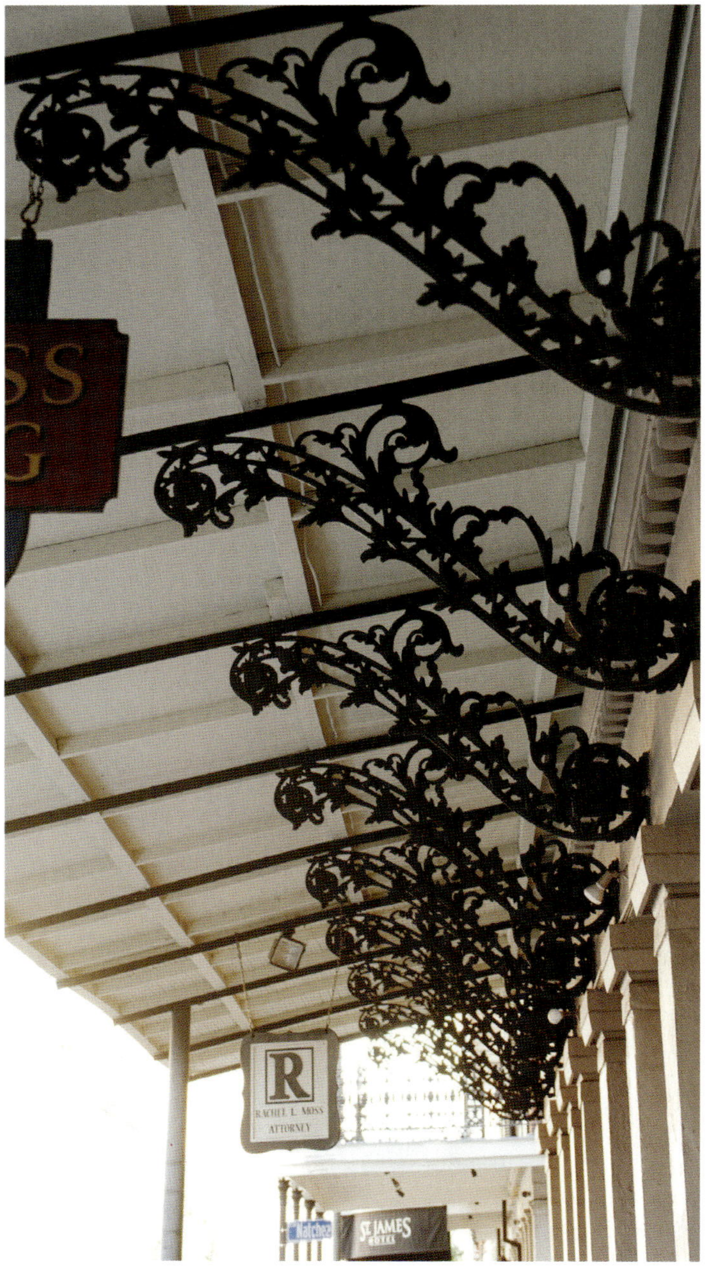

Cast-iron brackets at 400-12 Magazine.

Natchez and Poydras, contains a strikingly pristine row of circa 1850 commercial buildings with granite posts. This series of individual buildings was built with common facades, a style widespread throughout downtown at the time. The overhang is supported by cast-iron brackets, also typical of the time, and since a cast-iron gallery was never added, this fine row offers an interesting glimpse of what most New Orleans business streets would have once looked like.

Magazine prior to the Civil War was a center of banking, insurance, finance, and general wheeling and dealing not just for New Orleans and Louisiana, but the entire South. This was at a time when New Orleans was by far the biggest and richest city south of the Ohio River. While Magazine played an important role in this maneuvering of wealth, its days in that role were numbered. By the 1880s finance was moving a block away to Camp Street, and during the roaring 1920s the city's financial district shifted farther yet to tall buildings on Carondelet and Baronne. By the '20s, Magazine had become a gritty wholesale and manufacturing district.

Today's Magazine changes abruptly after

it crosses Poydras Street, but Poydras was not always as wide as it is now. It was a major wholesale, retail, and warehousing district from the 1850s to the 1960s. It was widened in the mid-1960s, requiring the removal of rows of old buildings along the downriver side of Poydras Street, and this is why there are still a number of narrow parking lots along that side of the thoroughfare. Beginning in the '60s and '70s, Poydras began turning into the city's chief canyon of modern skyscrapers.

In the 1830s and '40s, townhouses were appearing block after block along Magazine above Poydras, but by the 1860s they were being replaced by manufacturing buildings. Among these were rice mills, sugar refineries, and coffee and cotton concerns: four of the city's most important products. While a few townhouses remain in this part of Magazine, they are few and far between. Camp Street, a block away, has more examples.

Where the tall black 1983 Regions Bank—formerly Texaco Center—and the stark white 1970s Hale Boggs Federal Building now stand there had long been small businesses including liquor dealers, machinery supply companies, and building

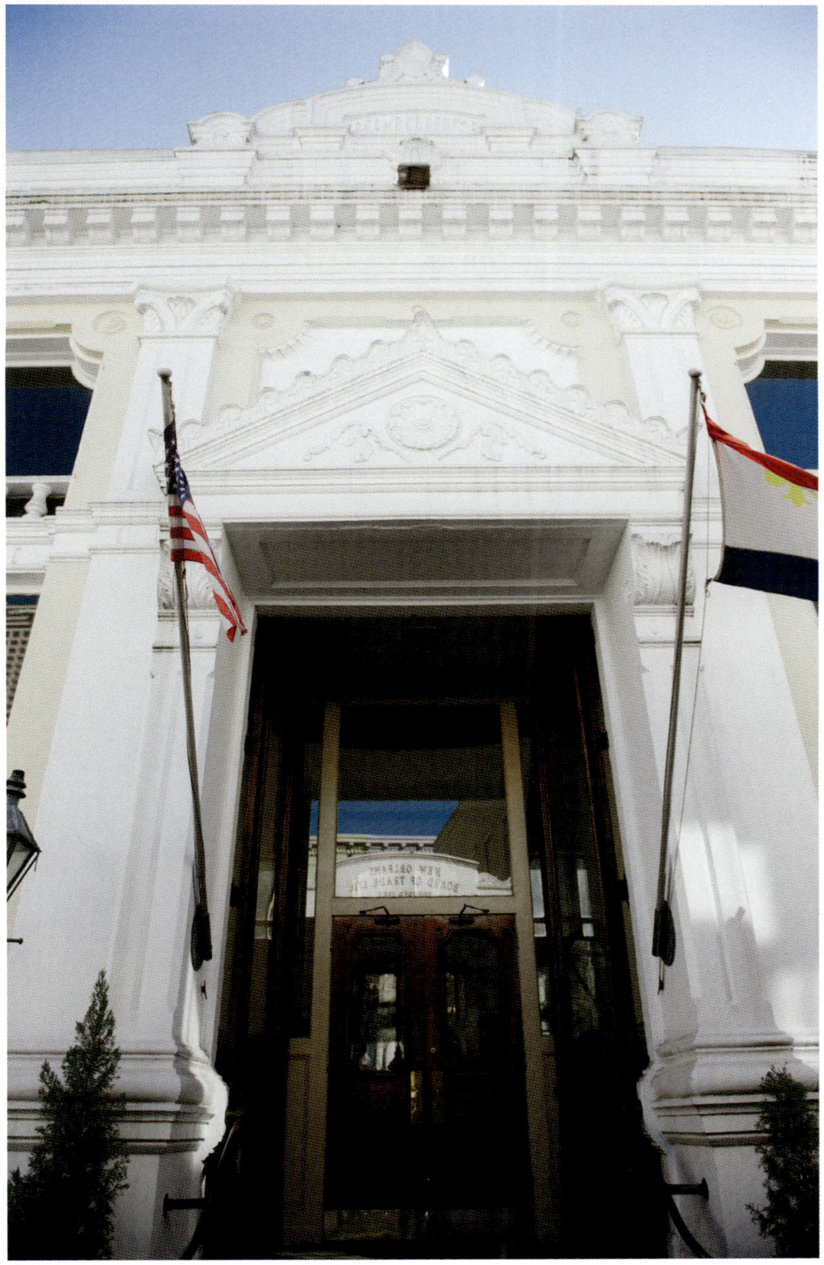

The Board of Trade.

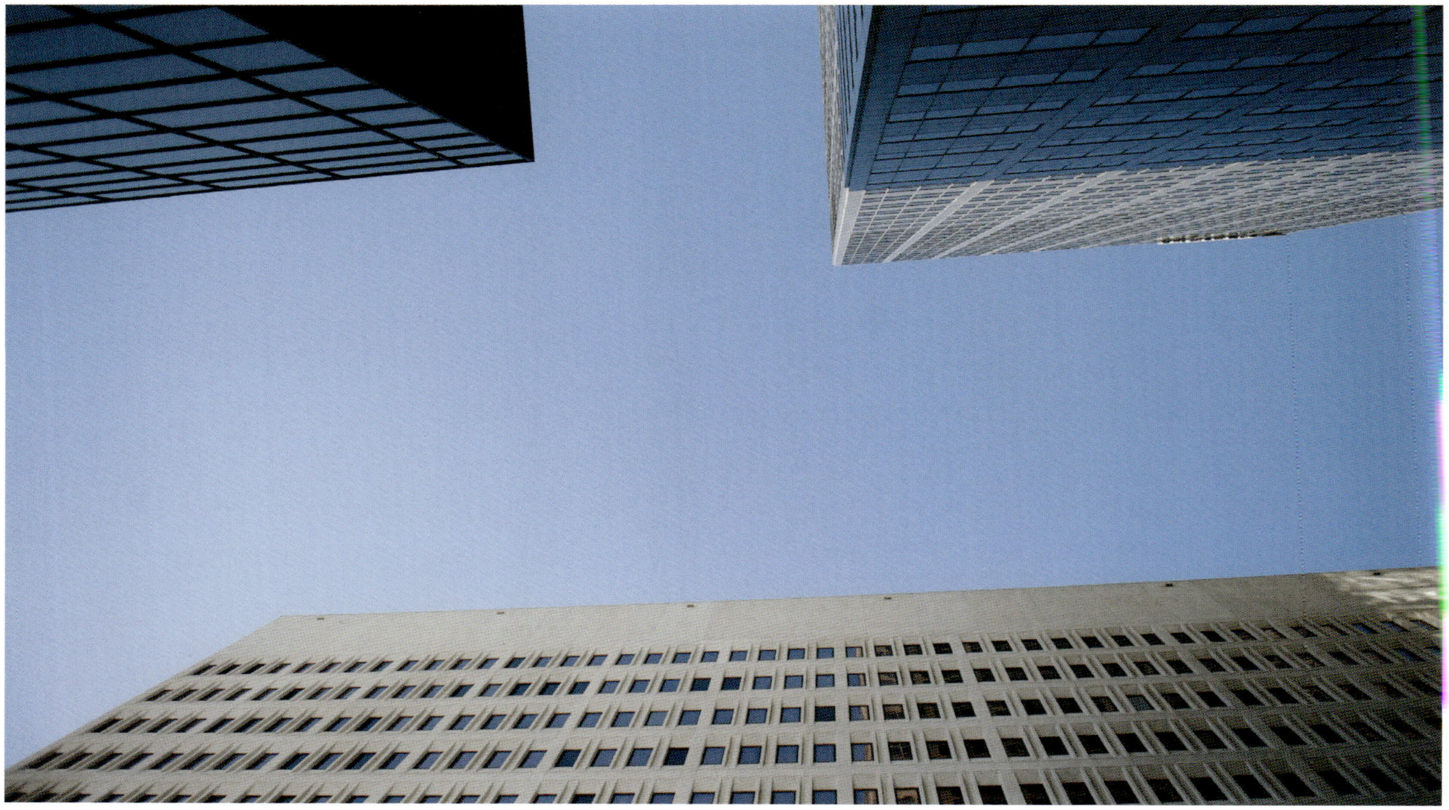

The tallest buildings on Magazine Street.

suppliers as well as small manufacturers like Elmer's Candy Company—now in Ponchatoula, Louisiana—as late as the 1960s. Elmer's had been at 534-36 Magazine in a building that in 1903 had been the Ong-Hiller Company, a dealer in cements, bricks, paints, and other building supplies. At 520, another business on the block at the turn of the twentieth century was John Black and Company, a wholesale liquor dealer, but by the 1920s Charles Dennery and Company had taken possession of the building for their bakers' supplies. This block is Magazine

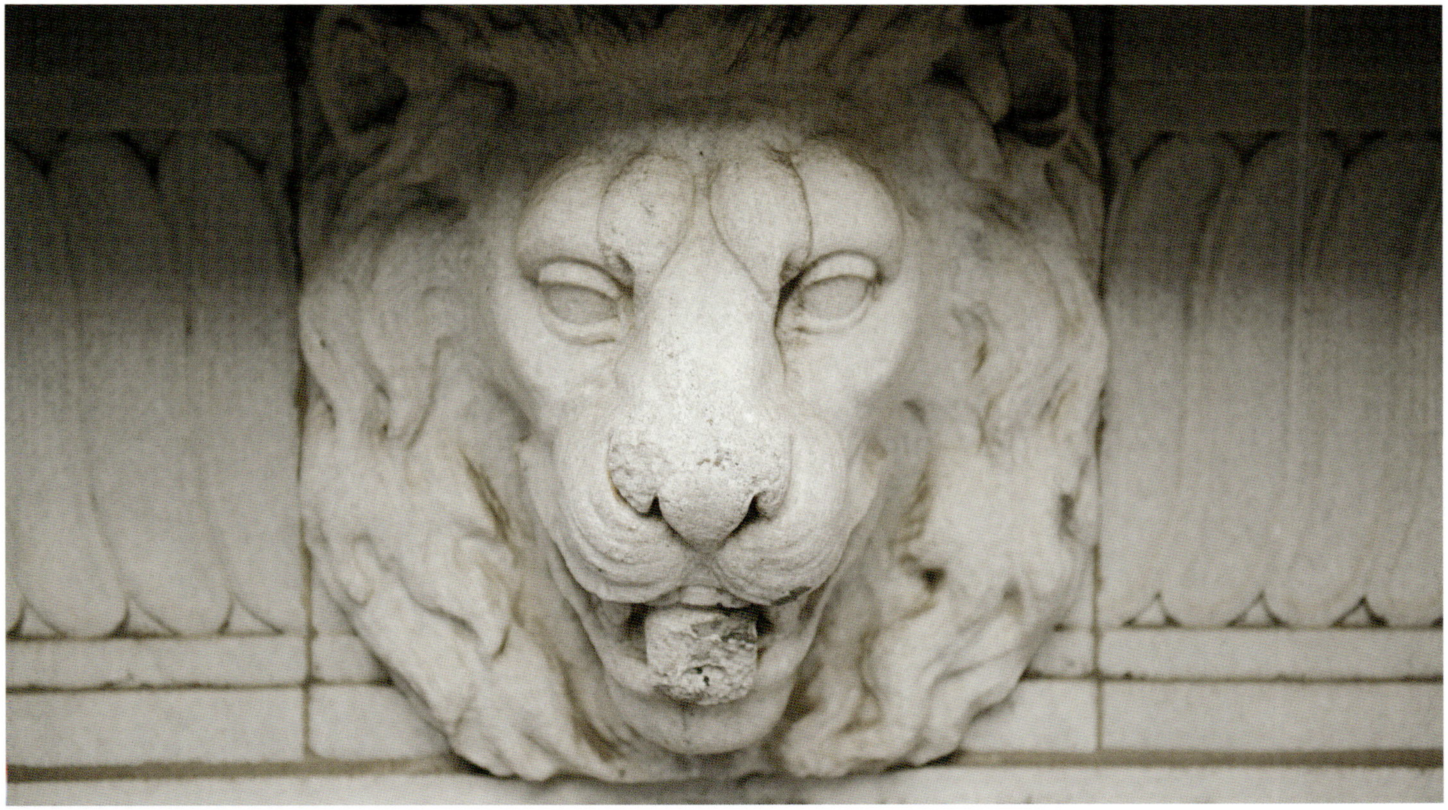

Federal lion at the old post office.

Street's entrance to today's Warehouse District.

Across Lafayette Street from the Federal Building is the Fifth Circuit Court of Appeals building. Until the early 1960s this building housed the main New Orleans post office along with the Court of Appeals and Federal District Court. Completed in 1915, it is typical of the many large and impressive U.S. government buildings built throughout the country in the early twentieth century. In 1961 the post office relocated to Loyola Avenue, and soon afterward the two courts were moved to the current Louisiana

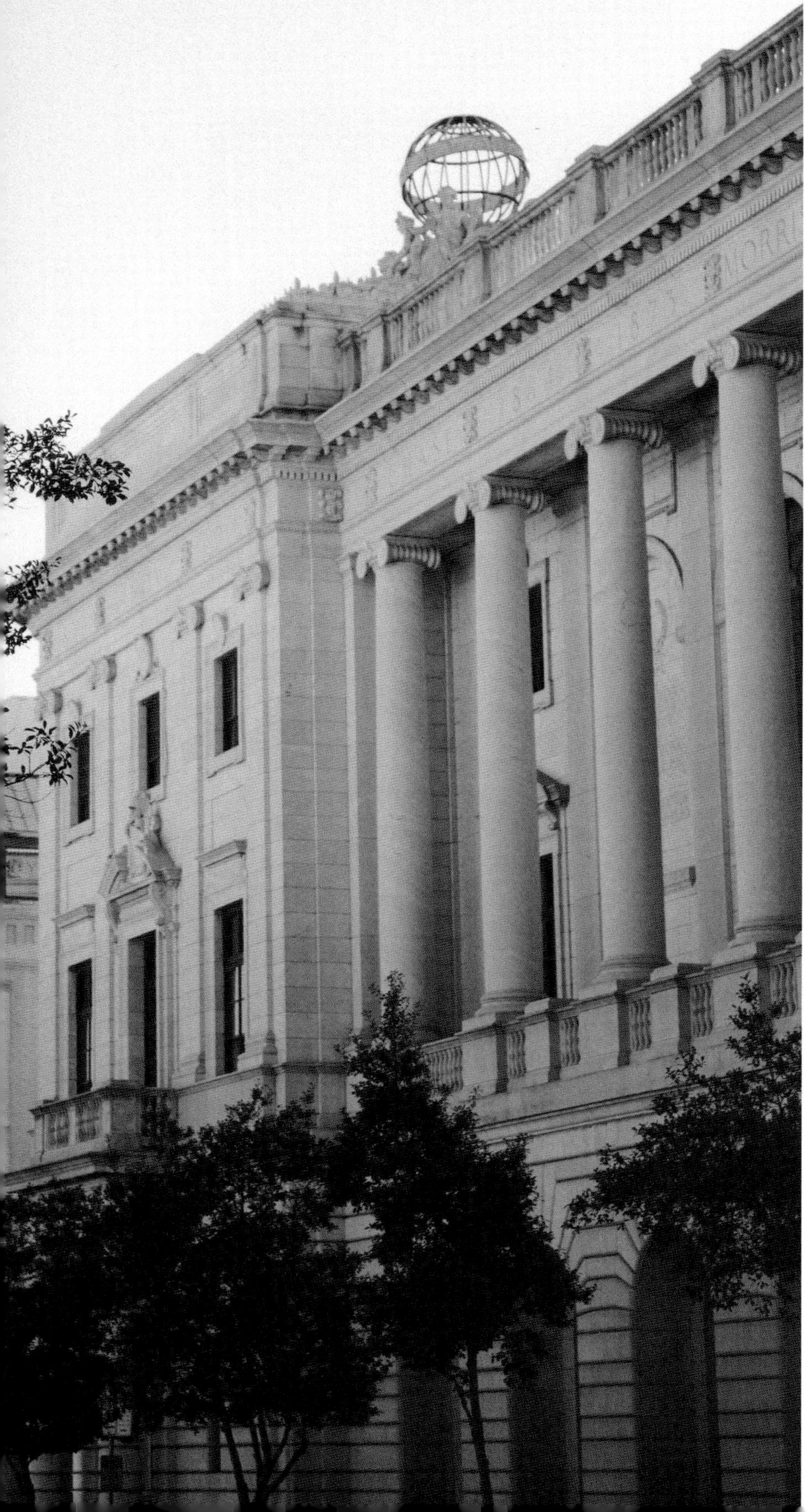

State Supreme Courthouse in the French Quarter. Following 1965's Hurricane Betsy, McDonogh #35 Senior High School, which had been destroyed by the storm, moved into the old post office. In the early 1970s the Court of Appeals returned to the building, while the Federal District Court moved into the Hales Boggs Federal Building. The former post office is one of the few government buildings of that period that is still used for government purposes.

Just across Capdeville Street from the old post office at 643 is the home of iSeatz, a modern computer design firm, and several other businesses. This handsomely readapted mid-nineteenth-century building was not built for offices, but rather housed John H. Murphy and Company, a manufacturer of sugar machinery, boilers, engines, evaporating apparatus, and all sorts of copper, brass, and sheet-iron work. The plant covered most of the block and was a beehive of activity, typical of this part of Magazine in the late nineteenth and early twentieth centuries. By the 1930s it was the Interstate Electrical Supply Company, while in the late 1940s it housed Burglass Bargain Annex, a furniture store.

Many of New Orleans' manufacturing

The United States Fifth Circuit Court of Appeals building, formerly the main post office.

buildings, like this one, are architecturally attractive. The Crescent City was not a major industrial center, but rather one of small manufacturing plants. This lent itself to architectural designs that differed from giant smokestack mills in big industrial cities.

Across Magazine is the longtime headquarters of Reily Foods at 640 Magazine. William B. Reily came to New Orleans in 1902 to build a booming coffee business—famous for the Luzianne brand—and take advantage of New Orleans as one of the greatest coffee ports in the United States. From this was born what is now a company producing over a hundred brands of food products in addition to its ever-important coffee. The Reily Foods building is being readapted for company uses, incorporating retail as well as residential in keeping with the changing character of Magazine in the Warehouse District.

Diagonally across Girod, at 701 Magazine, is another manufacturing building. Made of cast iron, it dates from about 1860. In the 1940s it was a Fairchild auto showroom, but it is now the Lambert Law Firm.

By the 1860s ever-increasing commercial encroachment was dramatically robbing Magazine of its residential character. However, today along the 700 block are some recent businesses that reflect the current character change of Magazine, as apartments and condos make the district residential once again and encourage the development of retail, rather than mills and warehouses. Reyn Yoga Studio and Bittersweet Confections at 725 share an address in a building where the Tropical Printing Company operated in the late 1920s and then the Standard Coffee Company roasted coffee in the 1940s, while next door at 727 is New Orleans Glassworks & Printmaking Studio in a distinctive 1910s or '20s building. In the late 1920s it was the Ferry Stamp Works. Opened in 1992, the studio has a gallery in front, holds classes, conducts demonstrations, and is a destination for school field trips. Farther up at 747 the Sherwin-Williams paint company was located in the 1930s, and by the late '40s the Universal Merchandise Company wholesale drugs and chemicals had taken its place. Today the building houses the George Rodrigue Foundation of the Arts, established by the late artist famous for his Blue Dog paintings.

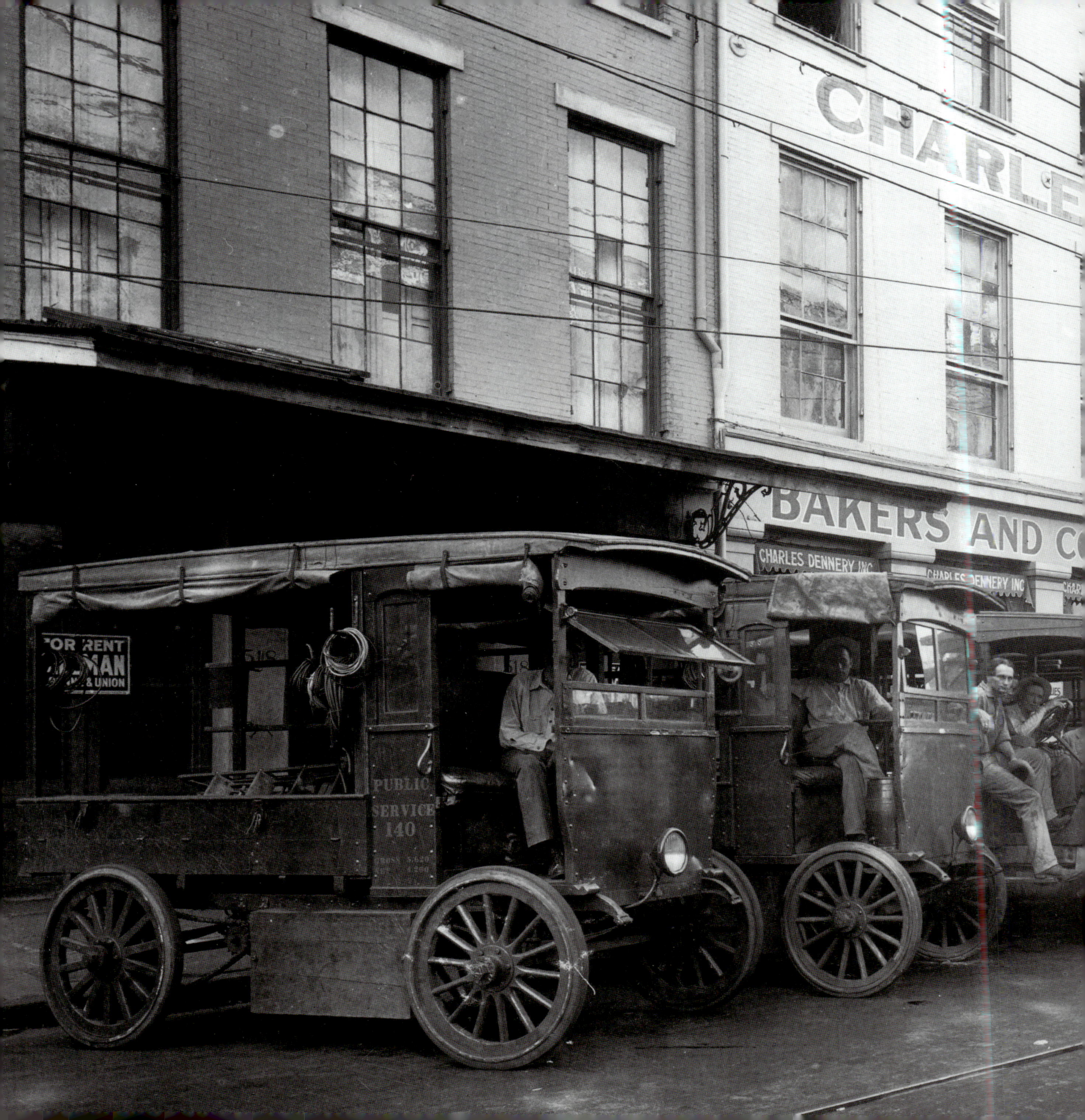
CHARLE
BAKERS AND CO
CHARLES DENNERY INC
CHARLES DENNERY INC
FOR RENT
PUBLIC
SERVICE
140

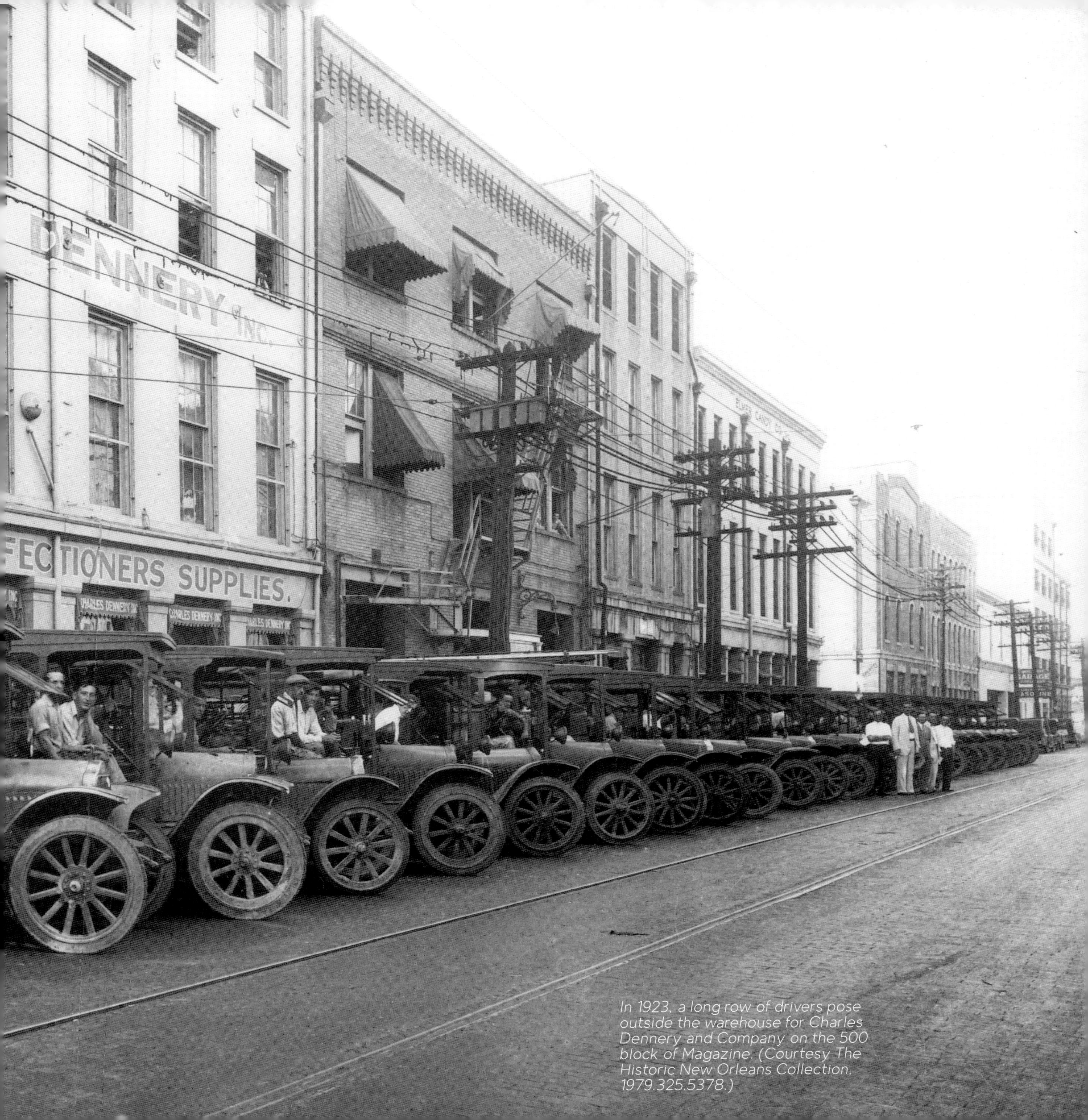

In 1923, a long row of drivers pose outside the warehouse for Charles Dennery and Company on the 500 block of Magazine. (Courtesy The Historic New Orleans Collection, 1979.325.5378.)

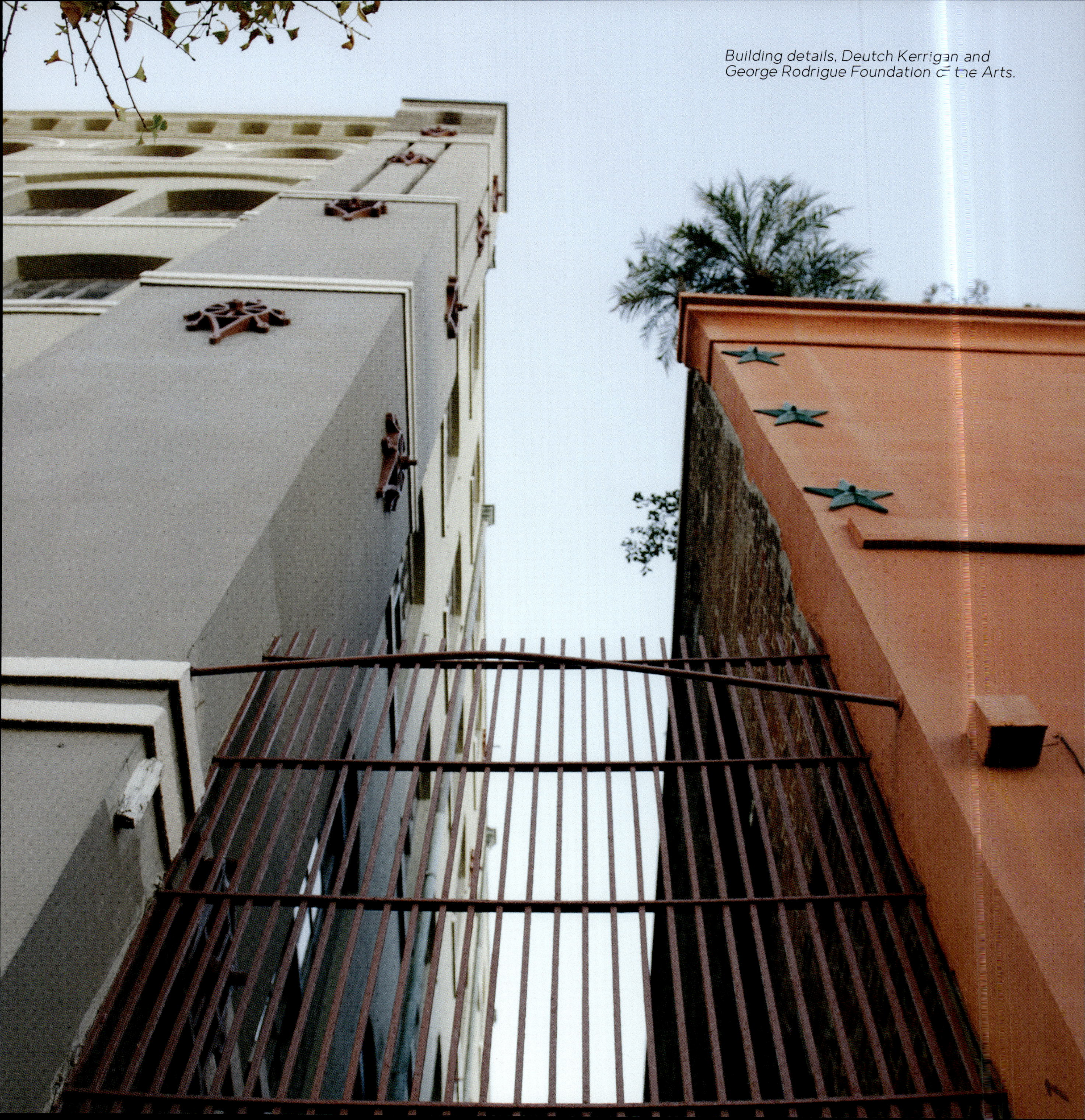

Building details, Deutch Kerrigan and George Rodrigue Foundation of the Arts.

The huge building at the end of the block on the corner of Julia is the home of Deutsch Kerrigan law firm. The building dates to 1882 and was the La Belle Creole cigar plant owned by Simon Hernsheim, an enterprise that dated back to 1857. New Orleans was an important tobacco and cigar manufacturing center, and in the early 1890s this building, with its twelve hundred employees, reputedly produced more cigars than anywhere else in the United States. (Simon Hernsheim's lavish home is what is now known as the Columns Hotel, at 3811 St. Charles Avenue.) By the 1920s the cigar plant had been purchased by William Ratcliffe Irby—a noted early-twentieth-century New Orleans preservationist and philanthropist—and converted into his own cigar company. A decade later it housed the wholesale druggist McKesson, Parker and Blake.

Across Magazine from the cigar plant, at 760 Magazine, was Ernst and Company, a large rice mill established in 1878. By the 1930s it was replaced by a coffee warehouse operated by Blue Plate (a division of Reily Foods Company). Since the 1980s it has been Magazine Place Apartments.

Julia Street in the nineteenth and early twentieth centuries was a busy commercial street and the main route between wharves on the Mississippi and the New

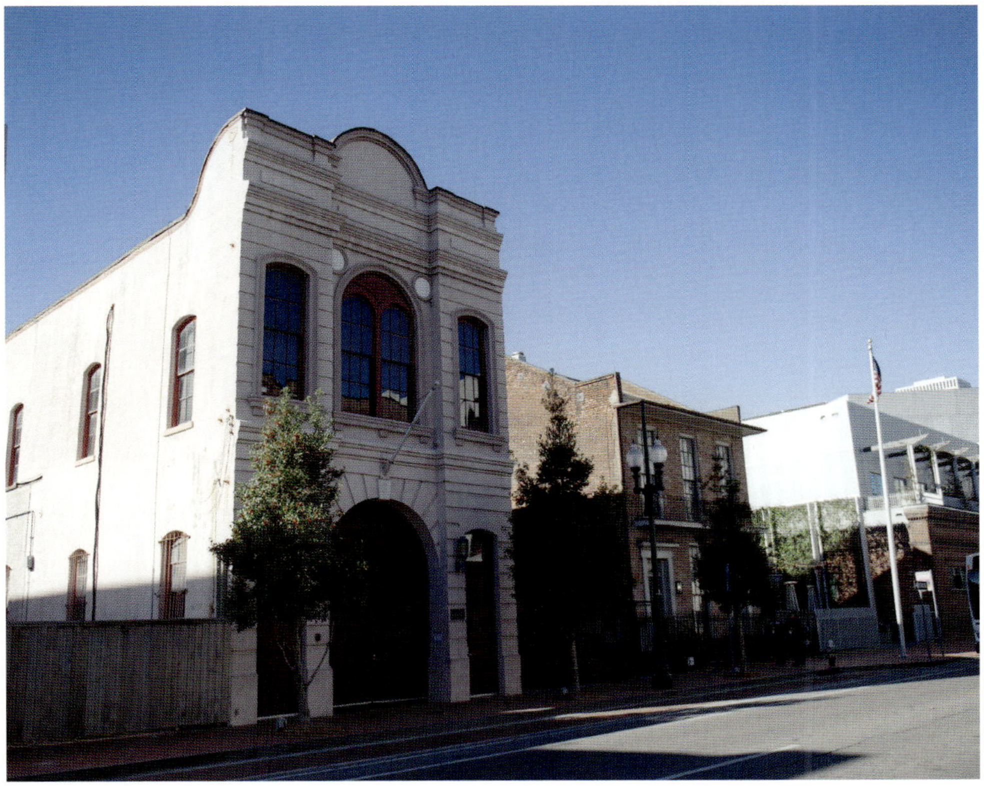

Julia Street Arts District.

Basin Canal dug in the 1830s and leading to Lake Pontchartrain. The Pontchartrain Expressway is on the canal route now. Julia crosses Camp and St. Charles a block down from Magazine, and between these two streets stand the brick townhouses of Julia Row, built in 1832. These homes were once among the most desirable addresses in New Orleans, but as commerce crept in, their desirability declined. Julia Row was considered part of skid row until preservation efforts, initiated in the 1970s, began to turn the neighborhood around. Now these properties are highly valued. As a result, the area has become more gentrified. This is reflected not only in the higher property values, but in higher rents throughout the Magazine Street corridor.

Today Julia Street for several blocks on either side of Magazine is the center of the Arts District with its many art galleries. Not only are there periodic gallery openings, but annual White Linen Night on the first Saturday in August brings crowds of people to the vicinity.

Although Mardi Gras parades do not take place along this part of Magazine, its intersection with Julia is arguably the most important spot in the history of Mardi Gras. By the mid-1850s the festival had become rough and rowdy, causing city authorities to threaten its very existence. Attempting to save it, a group of individuals met and planned the first organized public parade followed by a private ball. The Mistick Krewe of Comus came to life Mardi Gras night February 24, 1857, at the intersection of Magazine and Julia. About 9:00 P.M. bands began playing and torches illuminated the shadowy gas-lit streets. Crowds were ecstatic at the sight of masked marchers and two floats with the theme "The Demon Actors of Milton's Paradise Lost." The parade then moved along Julia to turn down St. Charles. Mardi Gras was never the same. Organized parades and balls have become the standard of the Carnival season—and it all began on Magazine Street.

Just across Julia from the cigar factory at 801 Magazine is another typical manufacturing building from the mid-nineteenth century that has been redeveloped into mixed residential and commercial space, while across the street at 800 Magazine is a more lavish structure built about 1880. Now Pêche Seafood Grill, the building was restored to its ornate

Victorian splendor with the addition of a gallery over the entrance. In the 1890s it was F. Johnson and Son Company, a funeral home and carriage rental concern that advertised "the finest of modern carriages for hire at all times." Funeral homes were common on Magazine Street and dotted the entire length of the thoroughfare. Like many other buildings here, it later became a coffee roasting plant sometime in the 1940s.

Near St. Joseph Street are a few vestiges of Magazine's early residential past. Next to the old Creole cottage at 900 Magazine, which was Johnson's restaurant and bar in the 1940s and is now an urgent care center, is a townhouse at 468 St. Joseph. This townhouse typifies the area in the 1830s or '40s. While derelict, it still shows the style of the many townhouses that once lined Magazine and surrounding streets. Across Magazine at 913 and 917 are two more townhouses that provide a glimpse into the far distant residential past of the street.

At the end of the block at 945 is the Louisiana Brewery of the New Orleans Brewing Association, built in 1887. For much of the twentieth century the building

The Robert E. Lee monument, as once seen from the National WWII Museum.

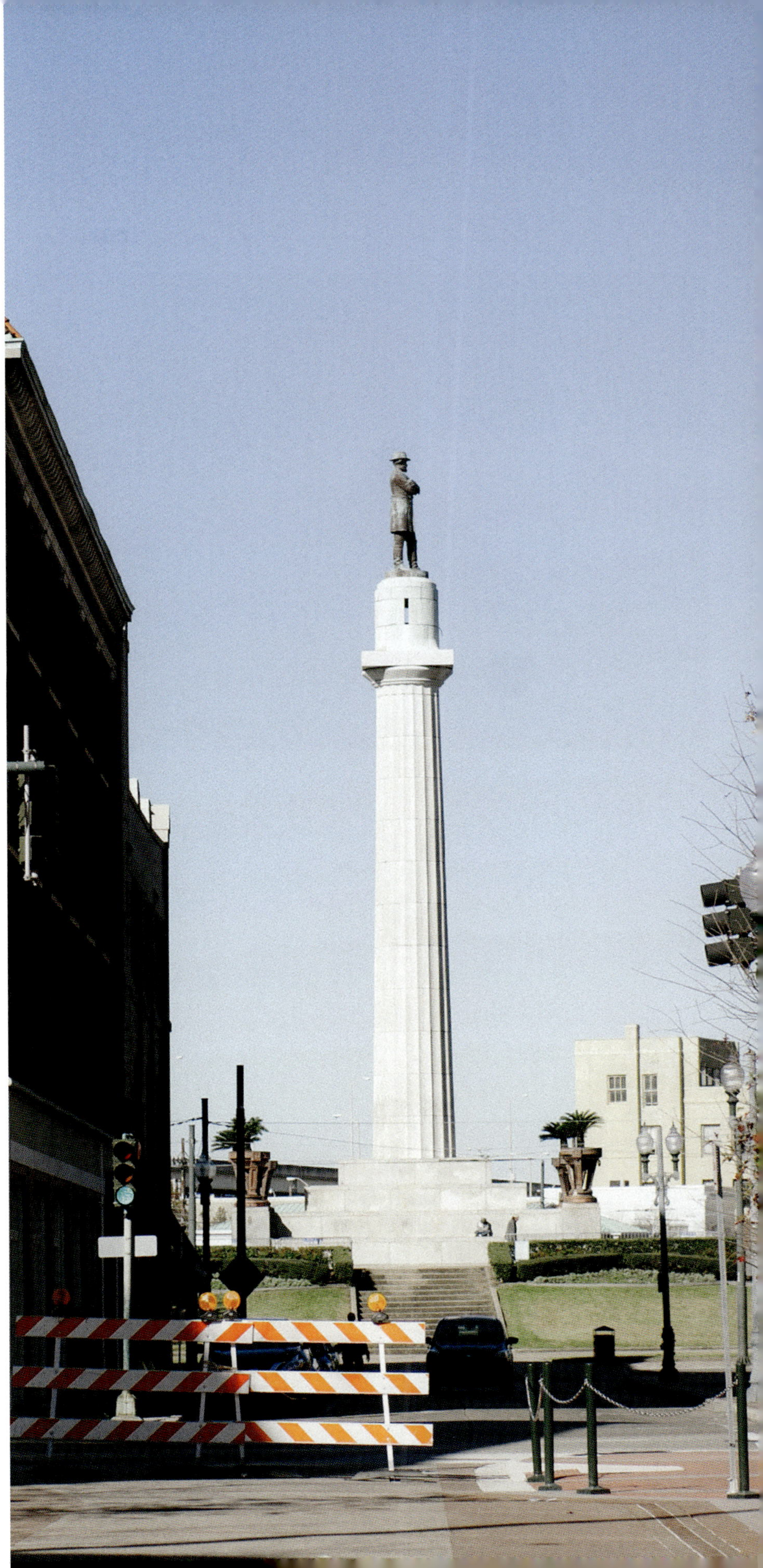

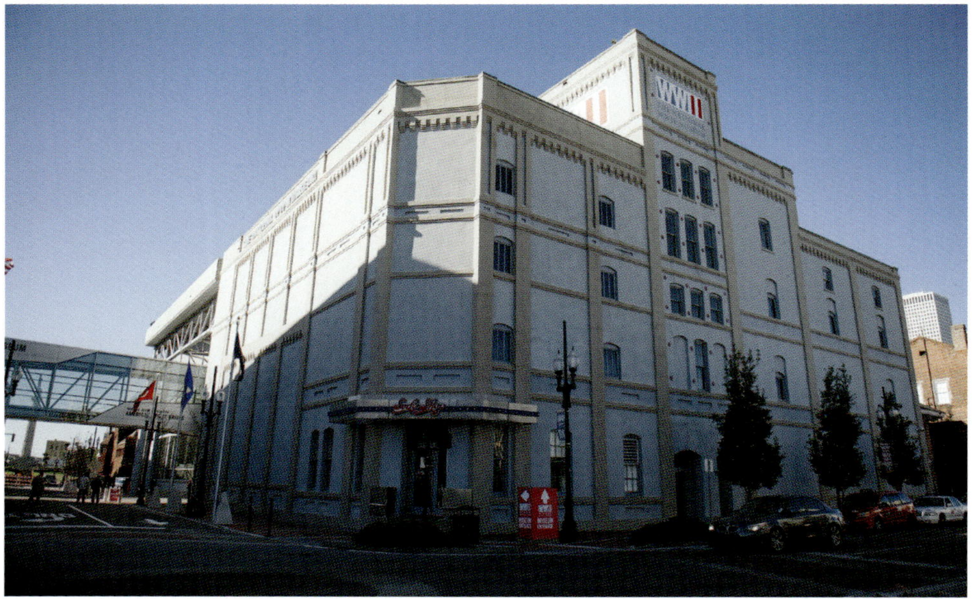

Former Louisiana Brewery, now the National WWII Museum.

served the Gallagher Transfer and Storage Co., now Gallagher International, with roots going back to 1893. In the modern age, it became the first building to house what was formerly known as the D-Day Museum. The museum opened on June 6, 2000, the fifty-sixth anniversary of the D-Day invasion, and the event was marked by a parade of war veterans which crossed Magazine Street and was viewed by two hundred thousand people. The museum is now much expanded, and in 2003 it was designated by the U. S. Congress as the National WWII Museum.

This renowned museum has become one of the most successful in the country and one of the city's leading visitor destinations. From the brewery, which is now the Louisiana Memorial Pavilion, the museum complex has expanded to cover all or part of four city blocks, many of which focus on Magazine Street. Aside from the Louisiana Memorial Pavilion, there are the Solomon Victory Theater, U.S. Freedom Pavilion, The Boeing Center, Campaigns of Courage: European and Pacific Theaters, and the John E. Kushner Restoration Pavilion.

According to Dr. Gordon "Nick" Mueller, board member and CEO from the institution's earliest days, the museum's Magazine Street location was happenstance prompted by the need to spend a million-dollar federal grant before it was lost. While Dr. Stephen E. Ambrose (1936-2002)— the driving force behind the museum—wanted it to be built in the UNO Research Park on the site of Pontchartrain Beach at the end of Elysian Fields, board member John Kushner felt that the museum should be built downtown, because that is

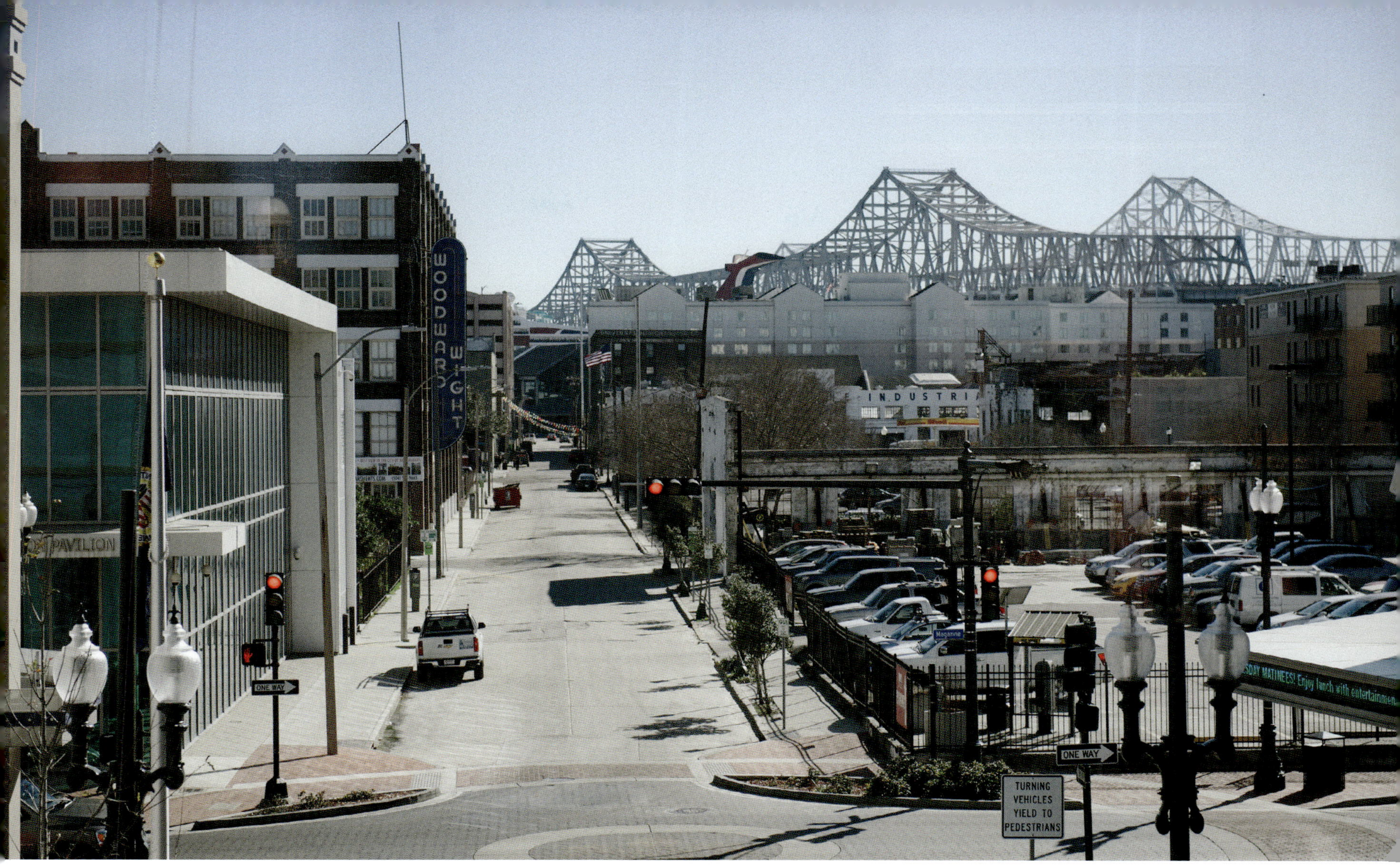

The view from the National WWII Museum, looking toward the Crescent City Connection.

where tourists are concentrated. Although a building had already been designed for the lakefront site, Mr. Kushner found the old, empty Gallagher building and was able to purchase the rundown 1880s brewery. Built without pilings and settling unevenly, it was leaning into Magazine Street. With a state grant of three million dollars, an interior stairwell was restructured to strengthen the building and secure the facade. Had the museum not purchased it, the building would most likely have been demolished.

The museum's master plan was approved in 2003 and by 2020, it will come to full fruition. The last buildings of the complex include the Hall of Democracy, which is designed to hold offices, exhibit and retail space, a library, and the Institute

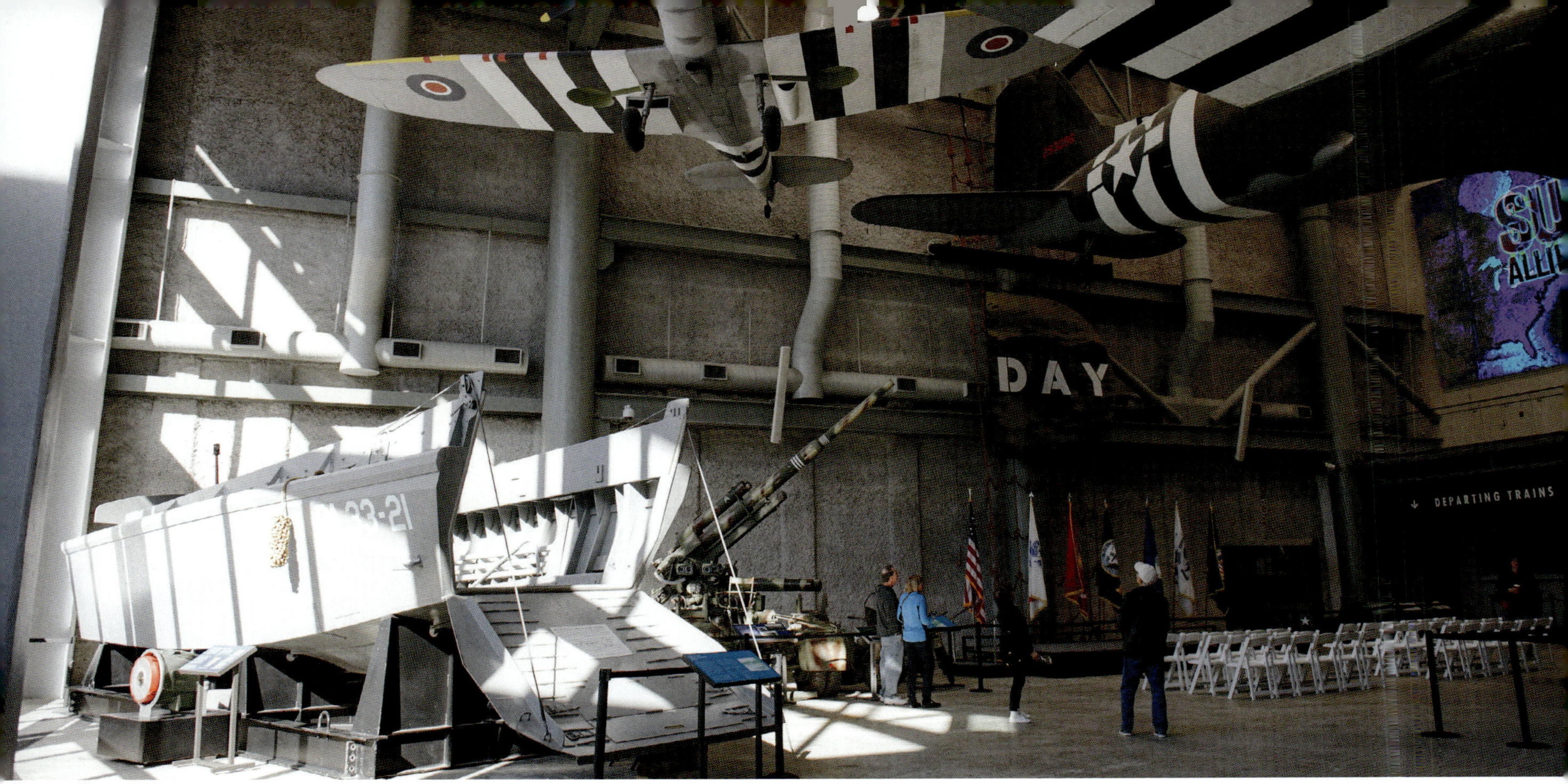

Reproduction of Higgins Boat at the National WWII Museum.

for the Study of War and Democracy; the Liberation Pavilion, which focuses on what World War II means today; and the seven-story Higgins Hotel, with its 20,000-square-foot conference center at the corner of Andrew Higgins Drive on the site of a demolished warehouse. A massive, iconic visual fixture of the campus will be the Bollinger Canopy of Peace. This is designed to sweep over Andrew Higgins Drive between Magazine and Camp Streets and will be a visible symbol of the museum.

A street focus of the museum is a redesigned intersection at Magazine and Andrew Higgins Drive, originally called Delord then later Howard Street. The new street name is for Nebraska-born Andrew Jackson Higgins (1886-1952), who came to New Orleans in the early 1920s and established boat builder Higgins Industries. The company designed and constructed the Landing Craft Vehicle Personnel (LCVP), better known as the Higgins Boat, a flat-bottomed, plywood, amphibious landing craft with a lowered bow ramp used during World War II and during the D-Day invasion. So critical were these boats that the Supreme

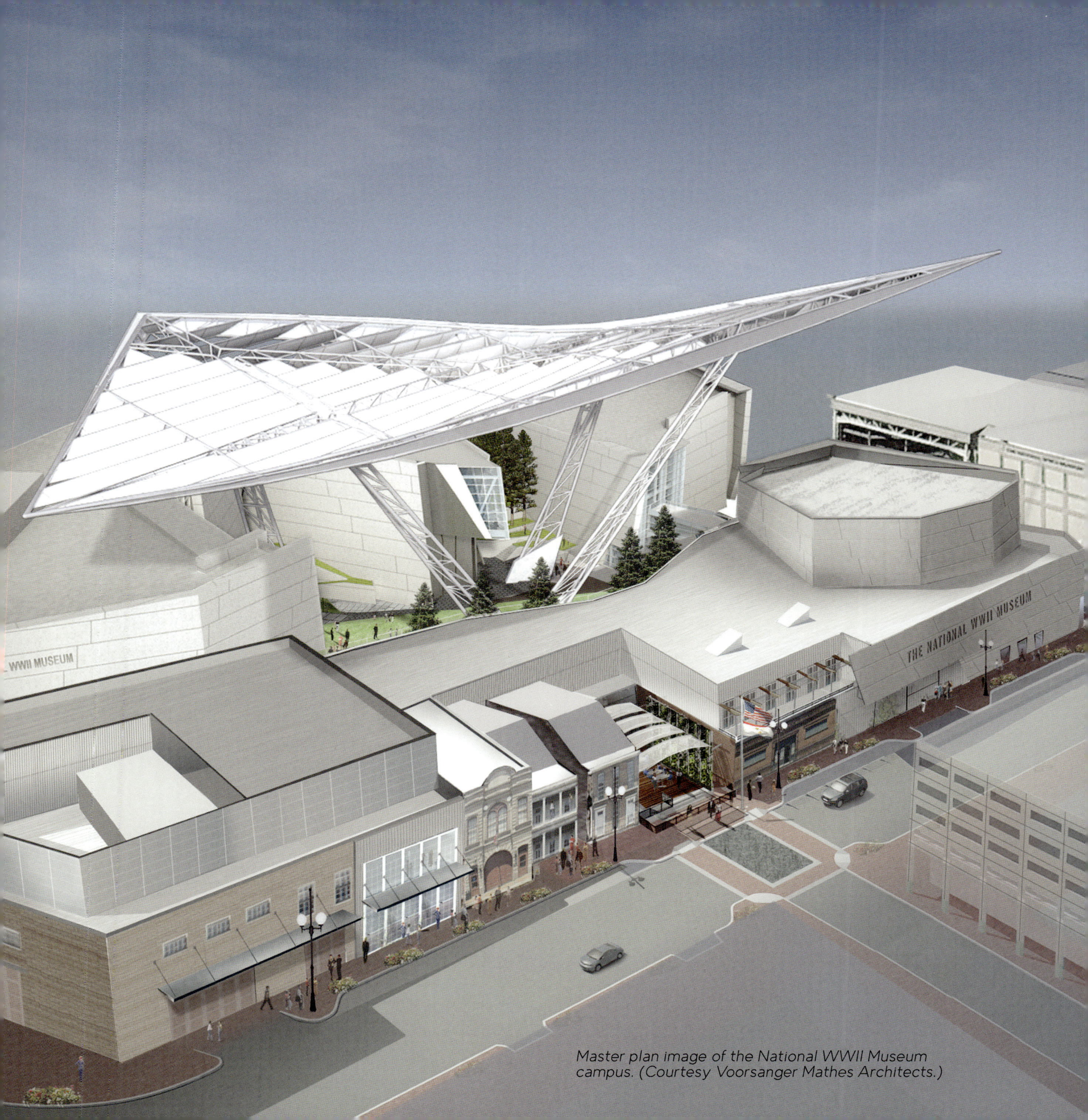

Master plan image of the National WWII Museum campus. (Courtesy Voorsanger Mathes Architects.)

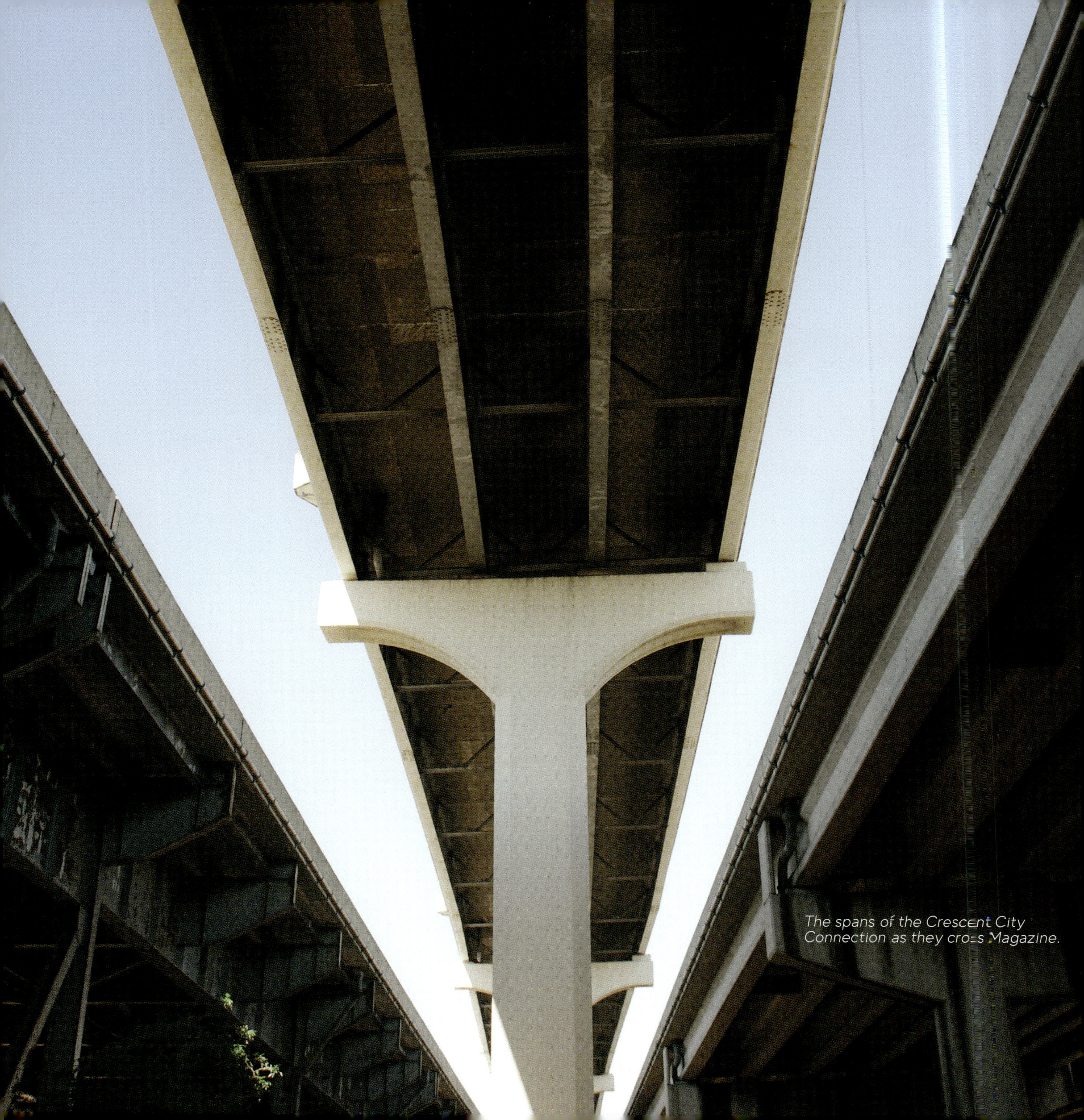

The spans of the Crescent City Connection as they cross Magazine.

Allied Commander, General Dwight D. Eisenhower, is credited with saying that Higgins "is the man who won the war for us." Few original Higgins Boats survive, but the National WWII Museum has a replica built from the original specifications. By the end of the war, ninety-six percent of the Navy's landing craft fleet came from the Higgins shipyards.

The WWII Museum is an anchor for the surrounding Museum District. While the other institutions are not located on Magazine, they are found a block away on Camp and include the Contemporary Arts Center, the Ogden Museum of Southern Art, and Confederate Memorial Hall Museum, a Civil War museum.

Bordering the National WWII Museum is the Pontchartrain Expressway with approaches to the Crescent City Connection crossing the Mississippi River. Officially U.S. Highway 90 Business, the first span was completed in 1958 and called the Greater New Orleans Mississippi River Bridge. The second span opened in 1989, and a contest was held to rename the two bridges. The winner was Jennifer Grodsky, a student from St. Clement of Rome School in Metairie, Louisiana.

Row upon row of nineteenth-century buildings—mostly houses—were leveled for construction of the bridge approaches. One of these was the Delord-Sarpy House. It was located on Andrew Higgins a half-block off Magazine, where the Solomon Victory Theater now stands. Built as a country house between 1814 and 1818, by the 1830s it was surrounded by the burgeoning city. In the way of a bridge off-ramp, and in spite of attempts to save it, it was pulled down in 1957. It was the oldest building in the city above Canal Street at the time. After the initial museum opening in 2000, the off-ramp was reconfigured for construction of the National WWII Museum.

Because of this museum—ranked fourth in the United States and eleventh in the world by TripAdvisor's Travelers' Choice awards, as well as topping the list of local attractions in New Orleans with eighty-five percent of its visitors coming from outside of Louisiana—Magazine Street is now among the most visited streets in New Orleans, as World War II veterans and their families, war buffs, and school groups make their way to this popular destination.

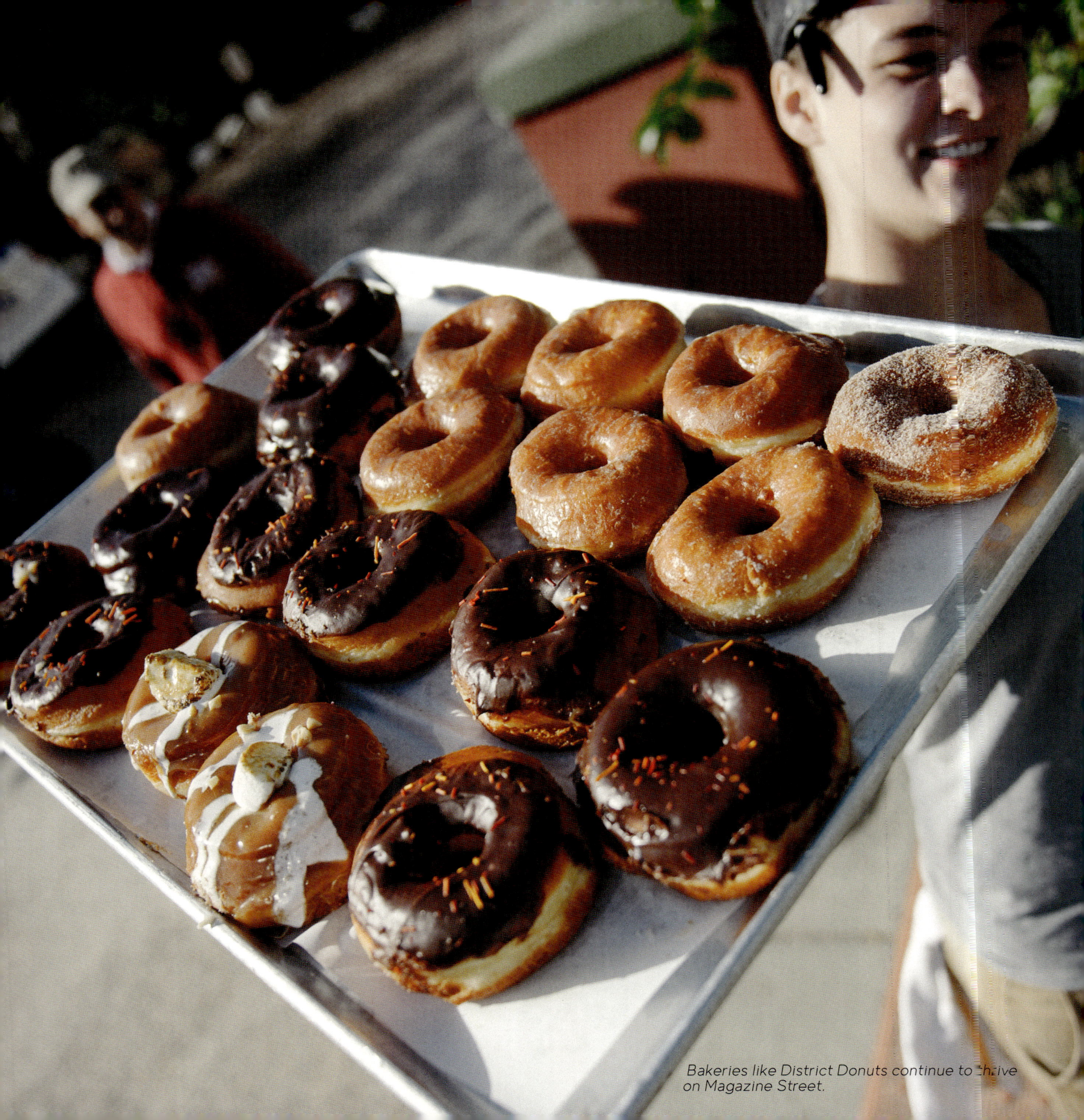

Bakeries like District Donuts continue to thrive on Magazine Street.

Chapter Four

The National WWII Museum to Jackson Avenue

The land on which the National WWII Museum now stands was part of the plantation owned by Marguerite Foucher, widow of Sylvester Delord-Sarpy. Like all of the plantations forming Uptown, it was a long, narrow property known as a long lot, giving each property frontage on the river. In 1806, Foucher employed Barthélémy Lafon to subdivide the land and then sold it to Armand Duplantier, who named it Faubourg Duplantier. He went bankrupt in 1814, and the subdivision reverted back to Madame Delord who renamed it Faubourg Delord. Immediately above this was Thomas Solet's plantation, subdivided in 1810 by Lafon and called Faubourg Saulet. A large, modern apartment complex called The Saulet is on part of this site, a block off Magazine. Next to this was the plantation of Jacques Livaudais, who sold a portion of his land to Robin Delogny, and in 1807 the two had Lafon

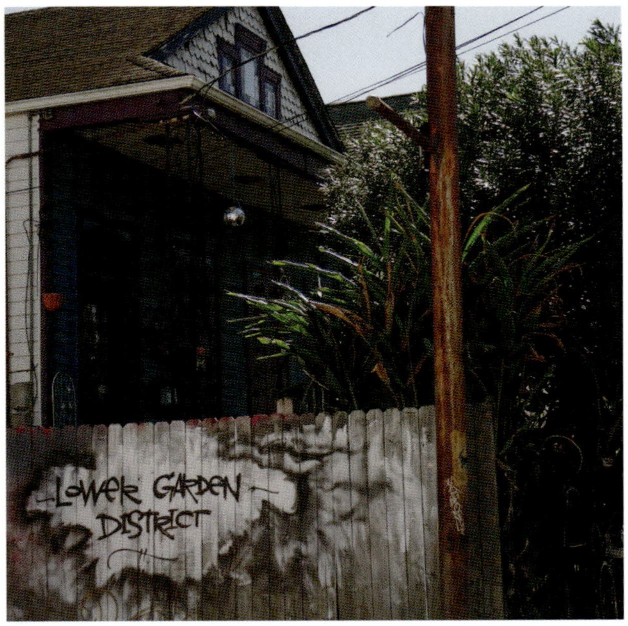

Once the Irish Channel, these homes are now considered part of the Lower Garden District.

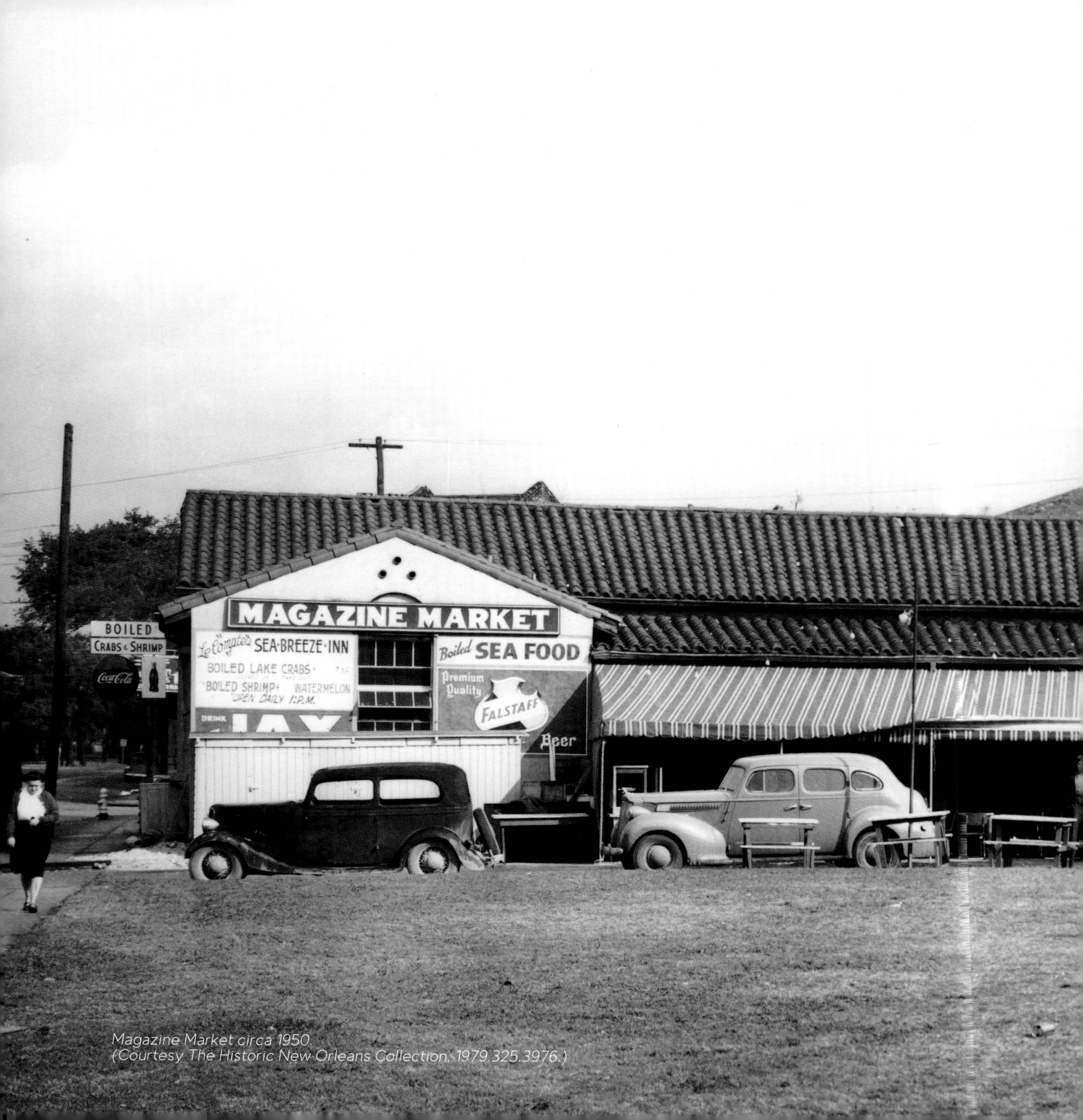

Magazine Market circa 1950.
(Courtesy The Historic New Orleans Collection, 1979.325.3976.)

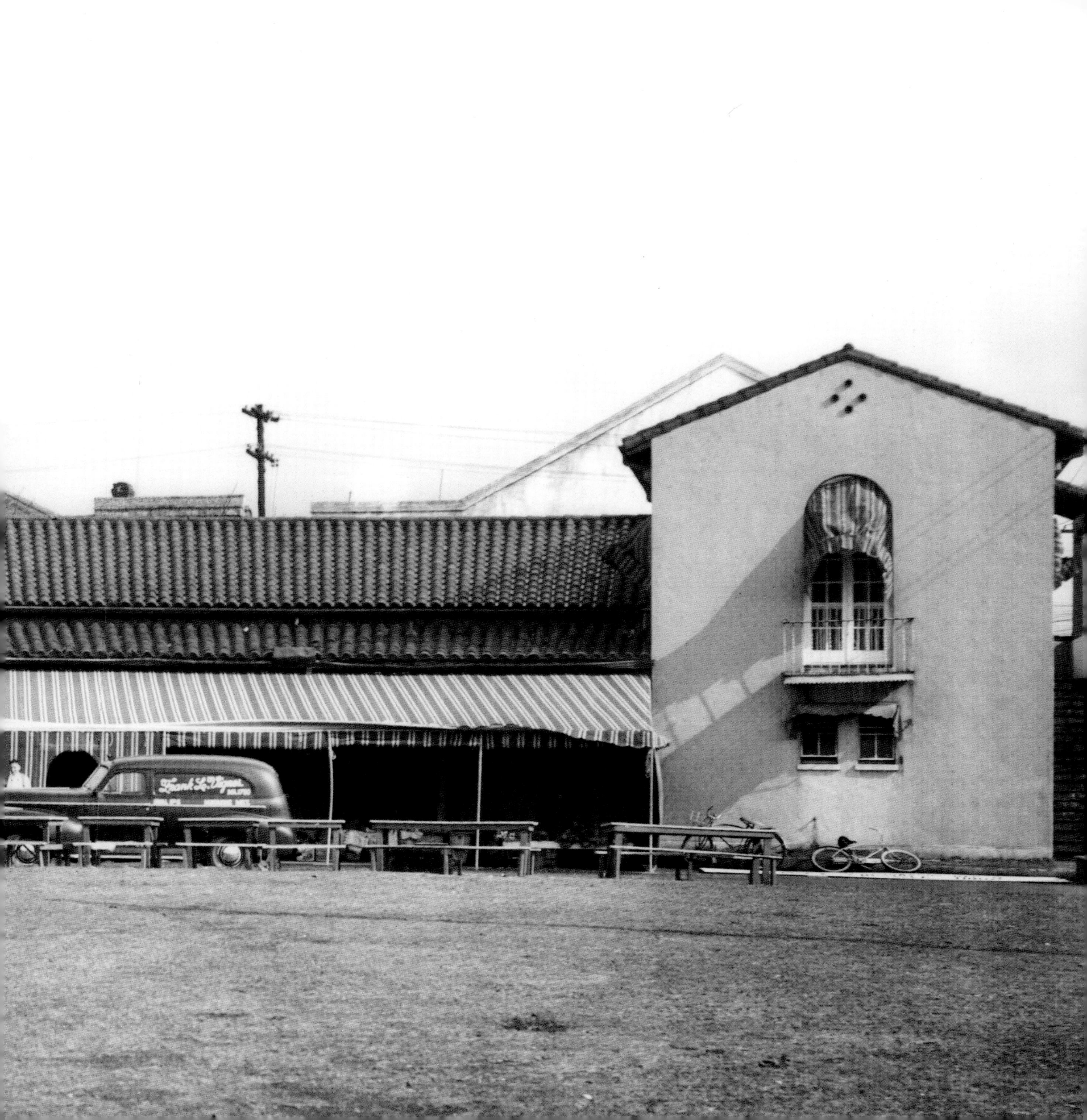

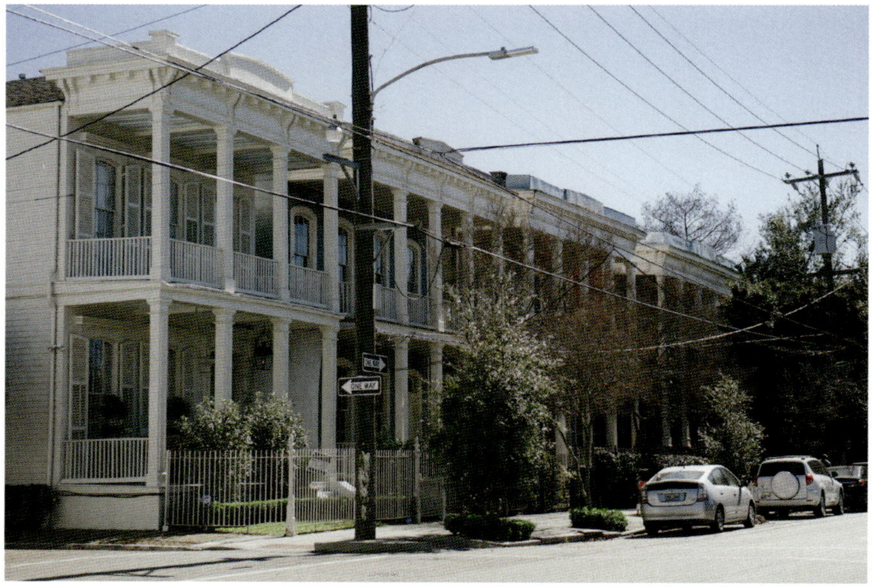

Rows of Greek Revival columns.

subdivide their properties into Faubourg Lacourse and Faubourg Annunciation. The upriver boundary of Annunciation was Felicity Street, which in 1825 was set by the state legislature as the boundary between the city of New Orleans and the newly formed Jefferson Parish. Above this point was a plantation owned by the Ursuline nuns, who had it subdivided by Lafon in 1809 as Faubourg Religieuses, later Americanized to Faubourg Nuns. Directly above Nuns was the plantation of Margarite Wiltz, which was laid out in 1813 by F. V. Potier. Its main street was Cours Panis, named for Wiltz's late husband, but the street was later renamed Jackson.

Through each successive subdivision Magazine was extended farther Uptown, although in the early nineteenth century it was little better than a country road. The overall street layout of the subdivisions was uniform, and streets were aligned to follow the crescent of the Mississippi. This accounts for Magazine's curve at Felicity Street and subsequent curves as the city grew farther upriver.

The subdivisions, although they were connected, did not have a single unifying name until the large neighborhood generally between Jackson and the Crescent City Connection, which includes Magazine Street, was named the Lower Garden District by architectural historian Samuel Wilson, Jr. in the early 1960s. Until then Magazine Street in this area was considered part of the Irish Channel (this name was in use by the 1850s), named for the many Irish immigrants who settled there, although German and Italian immigrants were also heavily represented.

Lafon's subdivision plan shows his taste for classical design, which extended to his naming eight streets, all of which intersect

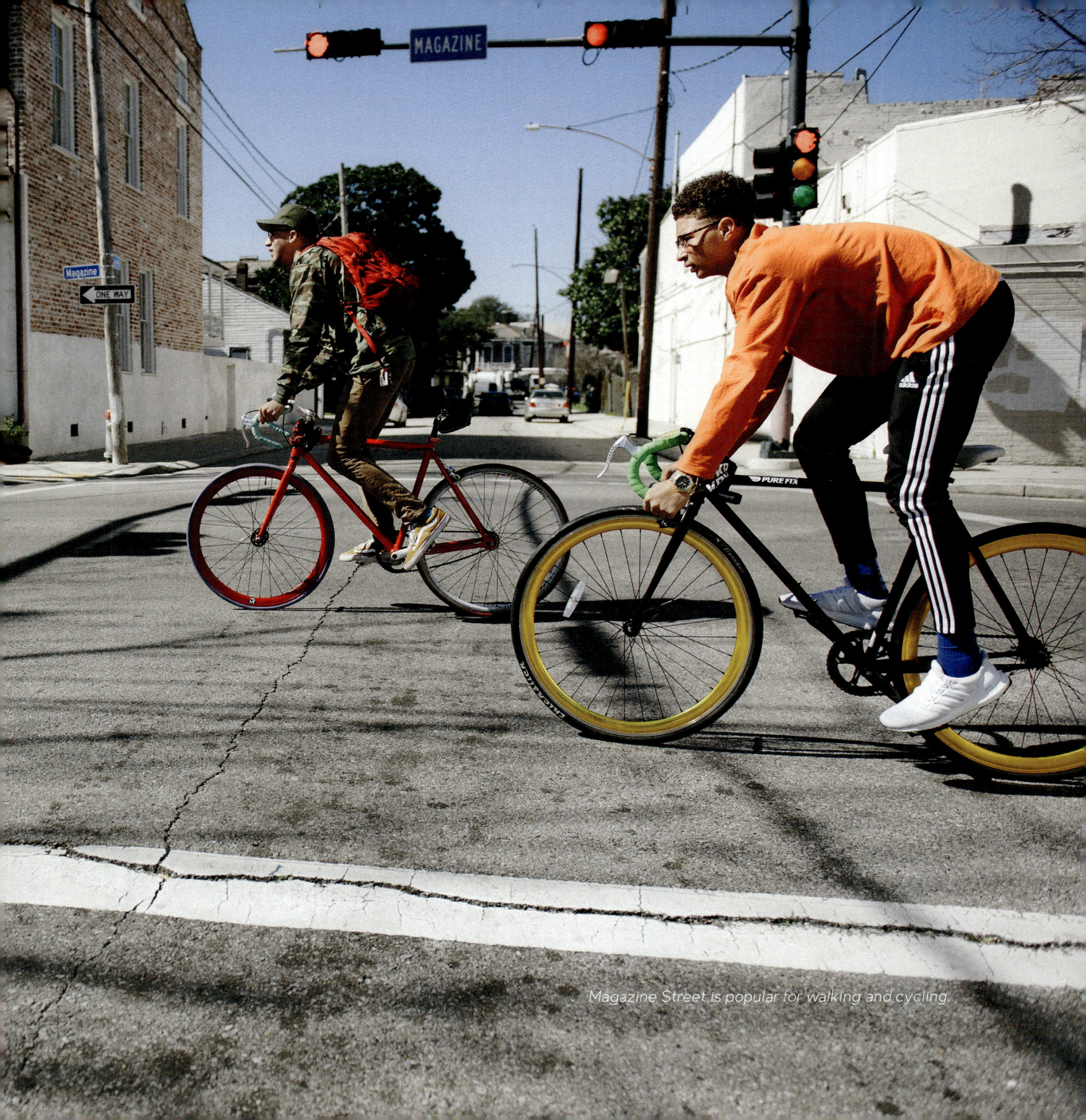

Magazine Street is popular for walking and cycling.

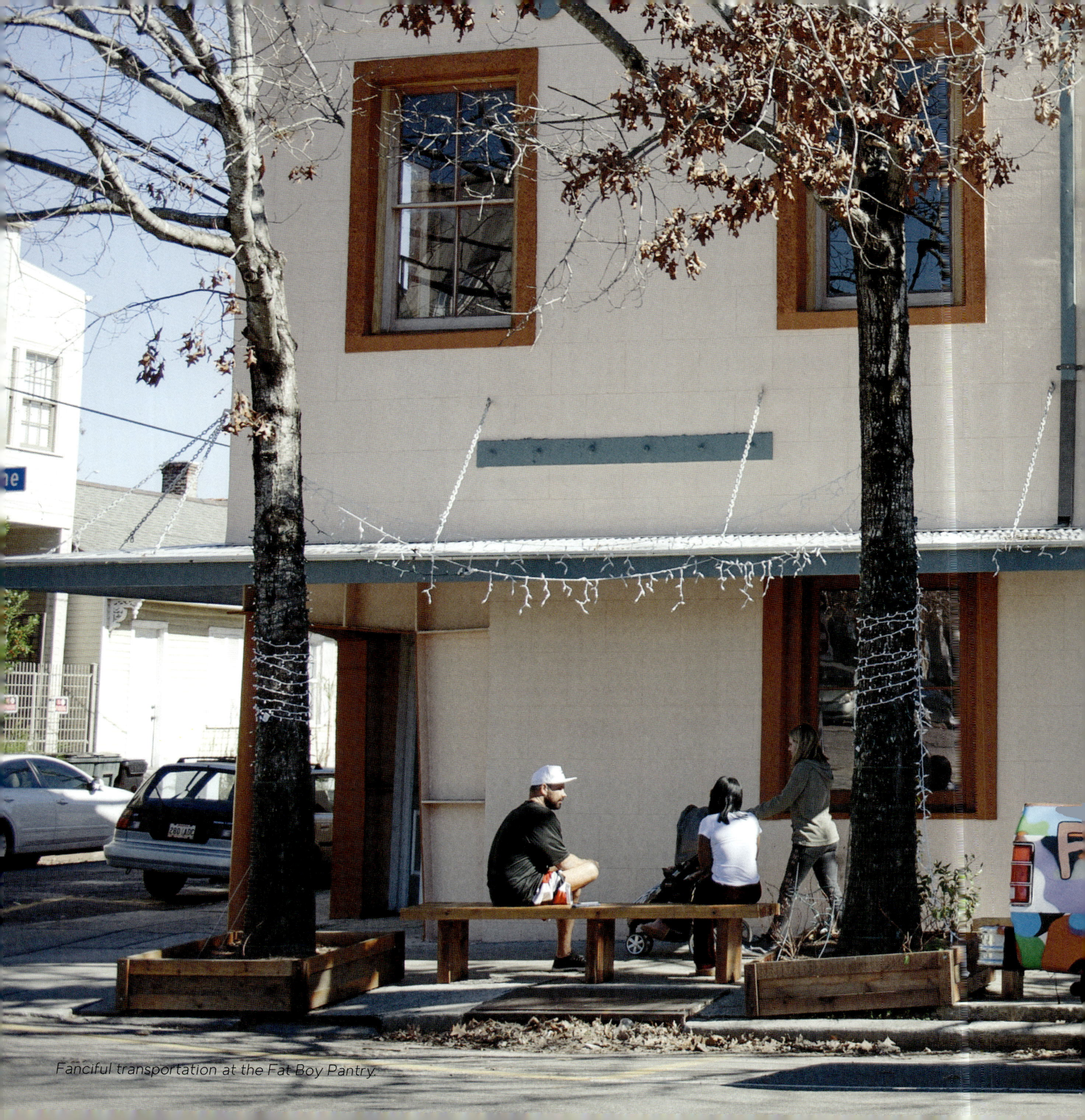

Fanciful transportation at the Fat Boy Pantry.

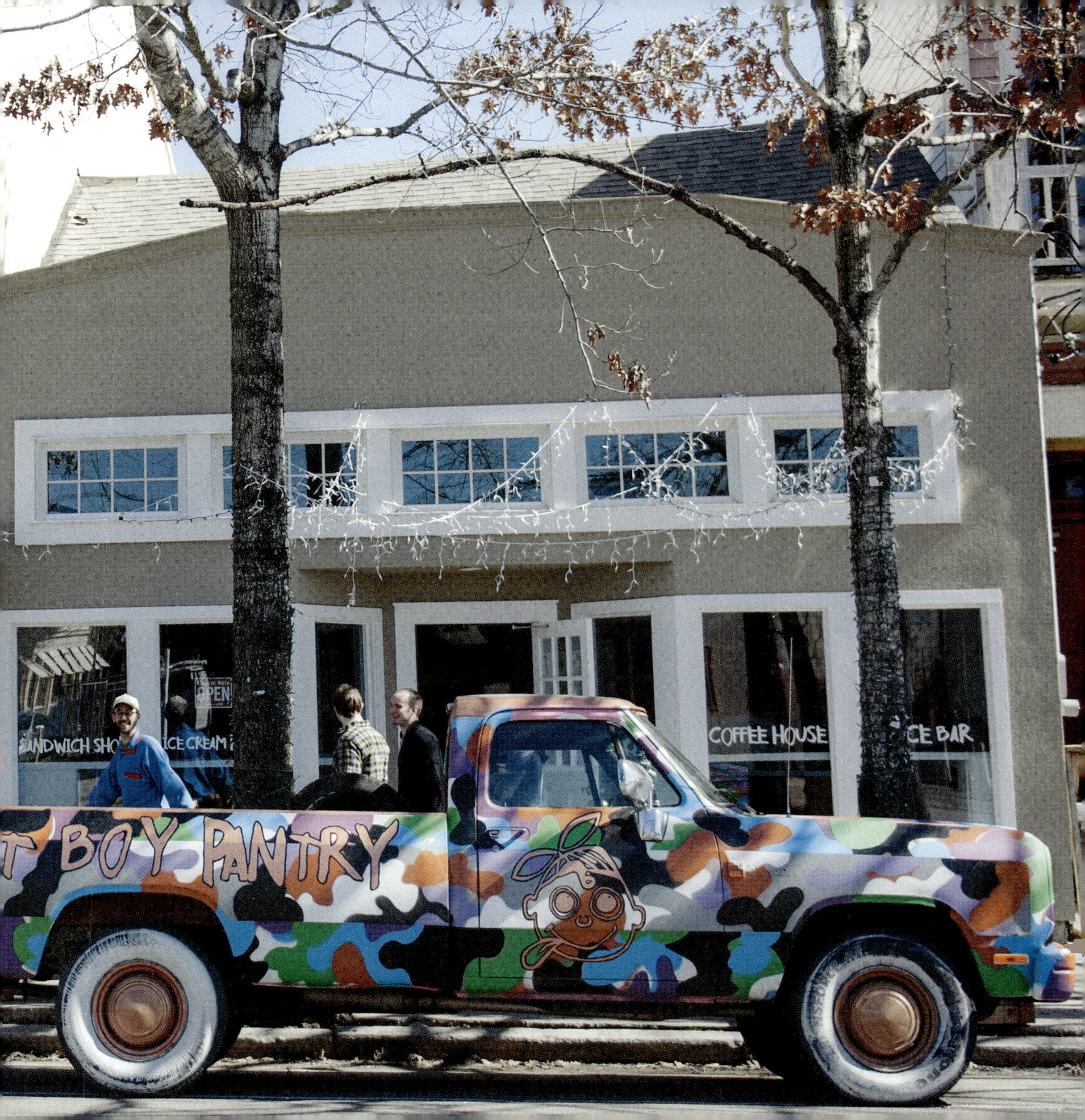
OPEN
ICE CREAM
COFFEE HOUSE
BOY PANTRY

with Magazine, for eight of the nine Muses of Greek mythology. These include Calliope (eloquence and lyric poetry), Clio (lyre playing), Erato (lyric poetry), Thalia (comedy and idyllic poetry), Melpomene (tragedy), Terpsichore (dance and chorus), Euterpe (music), and Polymnia (sacred poetry). The only Muse missing is Urania (astronomy).

New Orleans was expanding dramatically in the first half of the nineteenth century. At the time of the Louisiana Purchase in 1803, New Orleans had about 8,000 residents. By 1840 the city had grown to more than 100,000 and had swollen to 168,000 in 1860. The city spread upriver and downriver from the original settlement in the French Quarter, but at the time most of the growth was upriver, where the land is higher. Magazine was in the center of this growth.

The still predominately residential section of Magazine between the Crescent City Connection and Felicity is marked by vestiges of the 1840s and '50s with wooden Greek Revival houses having rows of square columns. There was once row upon row of similar buildings all over the neighborhood, along with a few substantial and elegant brick townhouses. There are also assorted Victorian structures with ornate wooden millwork. Built later in the 1880s to around 1920, they add to the varied, architecturally diverse landscape. Some tree-shaded blocks create almost country-like walks and vistas.

The 1100 through 1300 blocks of Magazine, although scruffy and commercial in places, provide a glimpse into the street's early residential past. While there are a few examples of late-nineteenth and early-twentieth-century houses, the brick townhouses at 1175 and 1223 are reminders of the 1840s. The building at 1243-45, on the corner of Thalia—now housing Spa Isbell—is another example of an 1840s townhouse. These dwellings are not unlike the brick row houses that would have once lined Magazine at the site of the National WWII Museum.

On the river side corner of Magazine and Melpomene, at 1336 Magazine, is a row of 1856 townhouses. Diagonally across Magazine is a pair of townhouses dating from 1852, while a few doors up, at 1359, is another large brick Greek Revival townhouse of the 1850s. Farther up the street on the river side are several more

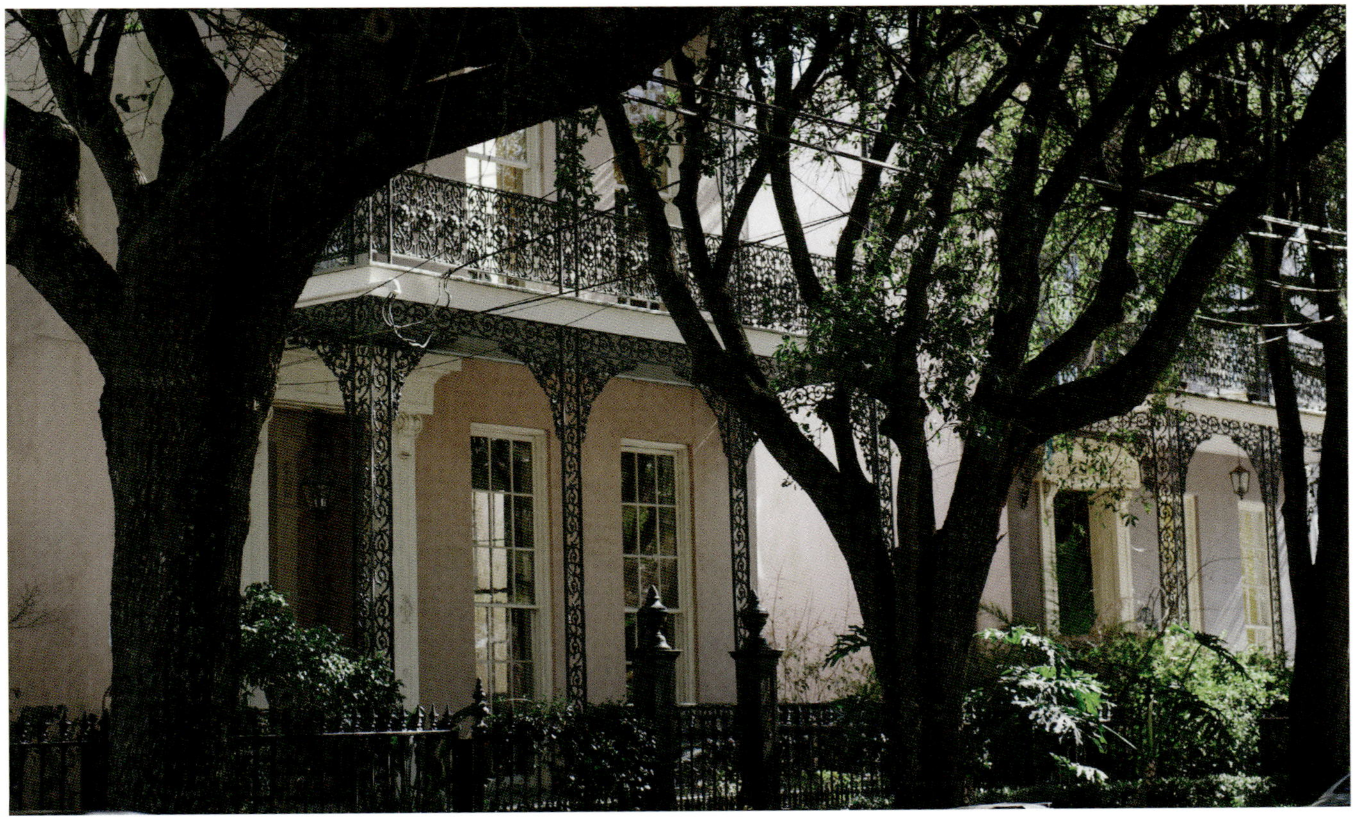

Verdant live oaks and cast iron from the 1850s grace this stretch of Magazine.

detached Greek Revival houses, while on the lake side single-story houses built later in the century are joined by a decidedly twenty-first century house. Such juxtapositions of buildings from divergent periods can be found throughout Magazine but are especially evident in this older section.

Greek Revival continues spectacularly in the 1400 block of Magazine. On the river side four handsome detached buildings from the late 1860s stand side by side with their line of wooden columns. Just beyond a later building housing Surrey's Cafe and Juice Bar are two identical,

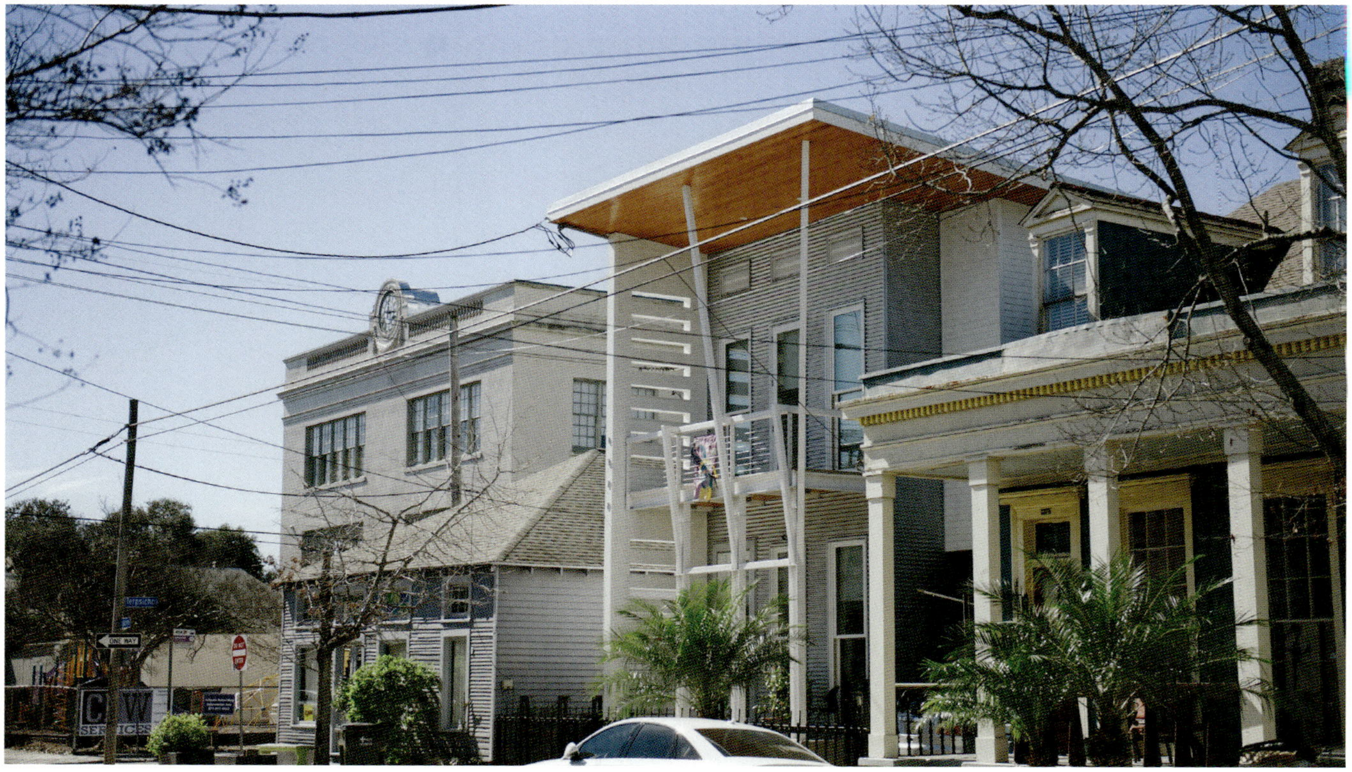

Modern architecture on Magazine. Close by to the left, the International School of Louisiana faces Magazine at the corner of Terpsichore.

very elegant upscale brick houses, at 1426 and 1432, with cast-iron galleries and bay windows dating from the 1860s. Adding to the charm of this block, as with others in the area, are wide-spreading trees and gardens that evoke nineteenth-century Magazine. The green canopy gives a sense of fresh air, although these homes are only a few blocks away from the densely built center of the city. At one time the opposite side of the 1400 block would have been similar, but since 1926 it has been the site of the former Andrew Jackson Elementary School with its distinctive rooftop clock. The building is now home to the Uptown campus of the International School of Louisiana, a charter public school specializing in immersion foreign-language academic programs.

The next block up from the school, Euterpe crosses Magazine, and beyond this for a block the street becomes even more tree lined and bucolic in character. Houses along both sides of this 1400 block provide examples ranging from Greek Revival (circa 1840-1850) to later nineteenth-century homes with ornamental brackets. This latter taste for often lavish wooden millwork, or gingerbread, replaced the simpler mid-century classical lines by the 1870s.

At the 1441 corner of Euterpe is an elegant Greek Revival mansion built by Richard Terrell in 1857, now the Terrell House Bed and Breakfast. Farther up Magazine on the opposite side at 1474, near the corner of Race, is a large, imposing brick townhouse of the 1850s. This was originally one of three that stood on this block. Across Magazine on the corner is another attractive example of columned Greek Revival architecture.

On the river side of Magazine after Race Street, at 1500, are two attached 1848 buildings now housing the Mojo Coffee House. This is all that is left of a row of matching dwellings that would have extended the length of the block. These were speculative buildings, and

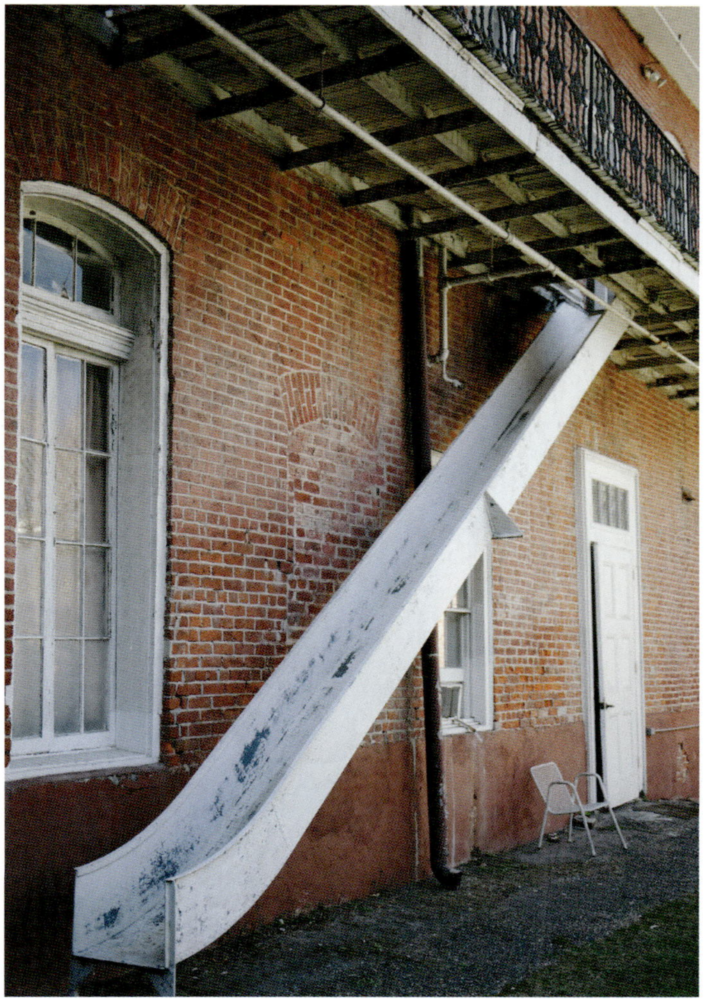

The old children's fire escape at St. Vincent's Guest House is a reminder of the hotel's history as an orphanage.

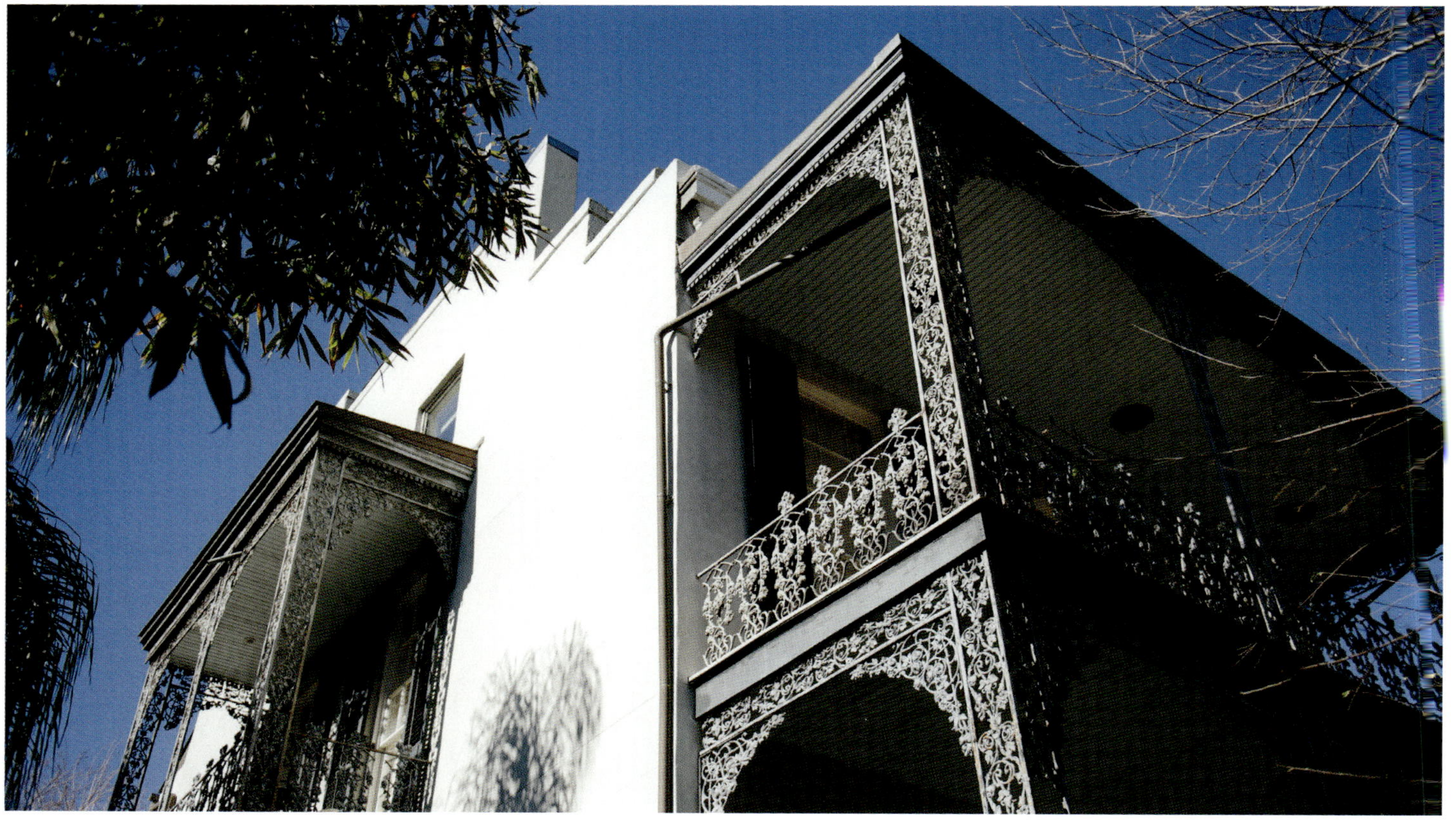

The side of Terrell House, 1441 Magazine Street.

many such structures, both residential and commercial, were put up by developers all over New Orleans. Several such rows remain standing along Magazine.

Across Magazine at this point is one of the street's most distinctive anchors. St. Vincent Infant Asylum was begun in 1864 and finished a year later. It remained in operation for nearly a century. Some years after it was built, the exquisite Italian ironwork was added to the entrance.

High death rates from epidemics like yellow fever left many children without parents, and fathers killed in the Civil War left families destitute. As a result poor children's homes were common around New Orleans and several were built on Magazine. Most orphanages

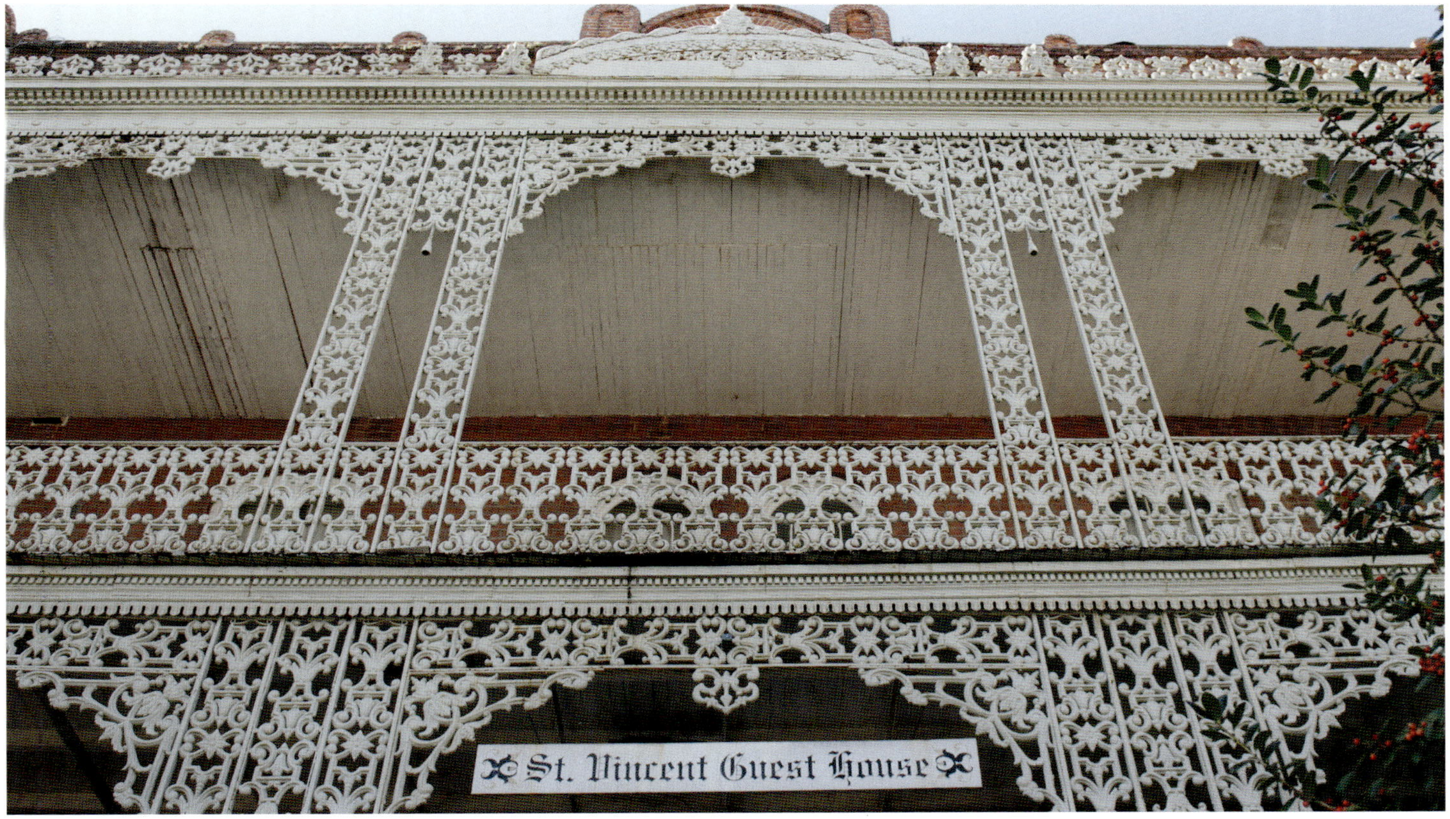

Italian cast iron embellishes St. Vincent's Guest House.

were administered by different church denominations, and in the case of St. Vincent's it was the Sisters of Charity under the auspices of the Catholic Church.

St. Vincent's was the first orphanage financed by Margaret Gaffney Haughery (1813-1882). She was an Irish immigrant who became rich as a baker in New Orleans and donated her fortune for the care of poor orphans. A monument to her memory rests in a small, tree-shaded park at Camp and Prytania Streets, just a block off Magazine next to the approaches to the Crescent City Connection. St. Vincent's is now St. Vincent's Guest House and is noted for its reasonably priced accommodation. Some of its interior public areas are little changed from the nineteenth century.

The next block up between Orange and Richard on the river side showcases another row of columned Greek Revival residential buildings. The matching buildings near the corner of Orange incorporate double-brackets near the roofline. This Italianate addition to the classic was a style growing in popularity about 1860 and would become more common during the rest of the decade.

After Richard Street the commercial section of Magazine starts to take over. The retail history of this section began about 1850 when the Magazine Market, bounded by Magazine, Sophie Wright Place, and St. Mary, was established in the block. This was one of many New Orleans markets similar to the French Market. Prior to construction of the Magazine Market, "making groceries" in the neighborhood meant going to a shed on the riverfront. Improvised stalls dotted the riverfront parallel to Magazine Street. With the new market's proximity to wealthy neighborhoods in the Garden District, and to take advantage of the market as a customer draw, other businesses were quickly established on Magazine, which soon blossomed into a major shopping district. Speculators put up rows of commercial buildings along Magazine, and by 1870 the stretch between Felicity and just beyond Jackson was solid commerce along the ground floor with shop owners living upstairs. It looked then much as we see it today, with some buildings dating from as early as the 1850s. It is undoubtedly among the most significant intact historic shopping districts remaining in the United States.

The Magazine Market was a covered, open-air structure with large brick arches and ornamental pillars that went through several expansion phases over the course of its life. With competition increasing from growing national grocery store chains in the twentieth century, the market was replaced in 1931 by a modern, fully enclosed building in a Spanish Colonial style reminiscent of 1920s and '30s Southern California. No longer publicly owned, it has not been a public market since the mid-1950s, and is now home to Il Mercato, an events venue. The small park in front, which was once part of the market, contains a monument to noted early-twentieth-century New Orleans educator Sophie B. Wright (1866-1912).

The triangular nineteenth-century building housing Harkins the Florist leads into the

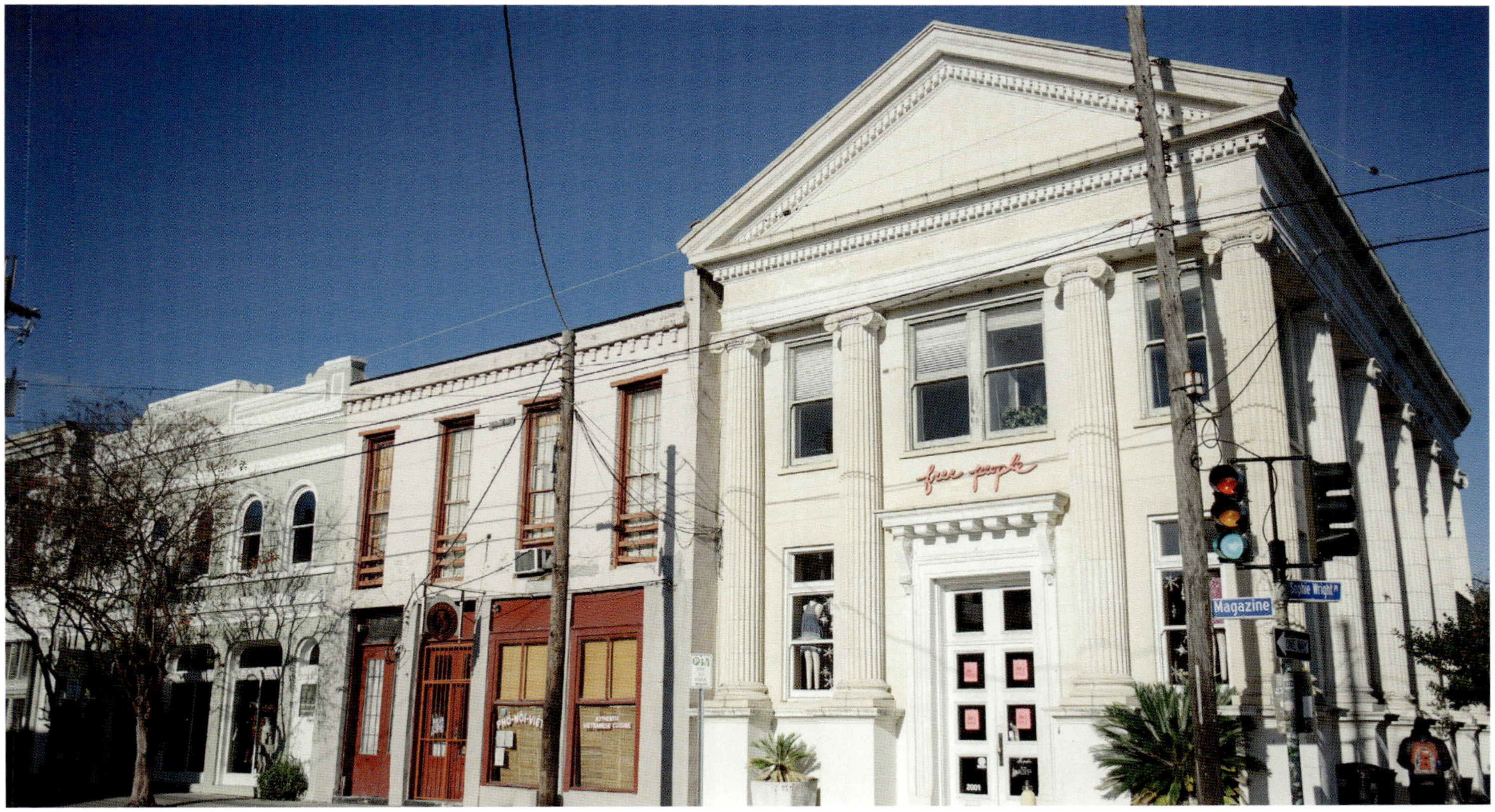

The corner of St. Andrew and Magazine was once home to the Orleans Insurance Company.

shopping area as Magazine curves along the course of the nearby Mississippi River. Just beyond Harkins on the lake side of the 1800 block is the feline mural of The Cat Practice, a cat hospital at the start of a block-long row of speculative commercial buildings with a common facade dating as early as 1851. At the end of the block was the legendary Jim Russell Rare Records, beloved by collectors of vintage discs, in business from 1969 to 2016. This business block was once ringed by a unifying ironwork gallery put up in 1860, and some galleries still remain. Across Magazine is another

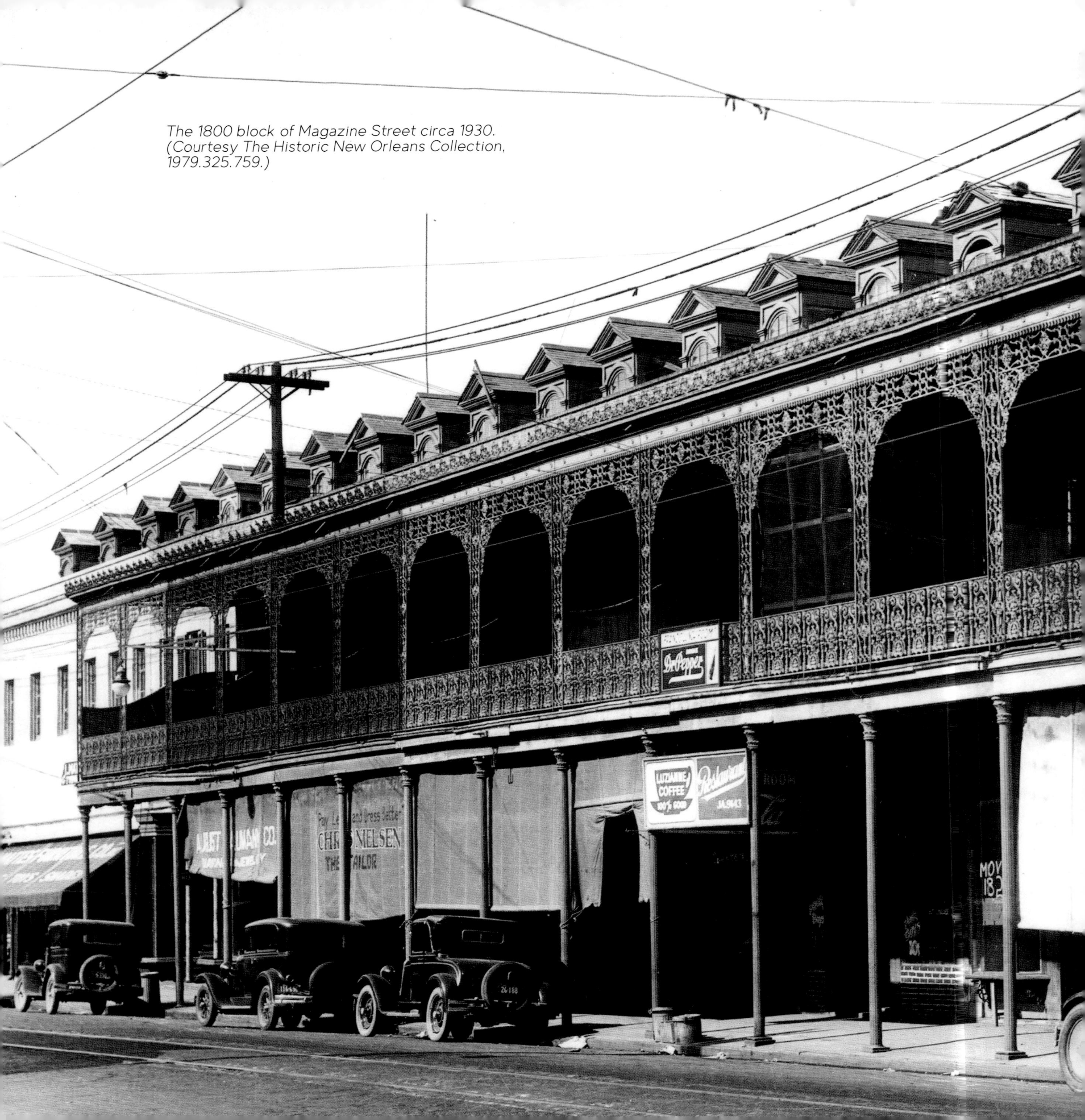

The 1800 block of Magazine Street circa 1930. (Courtesy The Historic New Orleans Collection, 1979.325.759.)

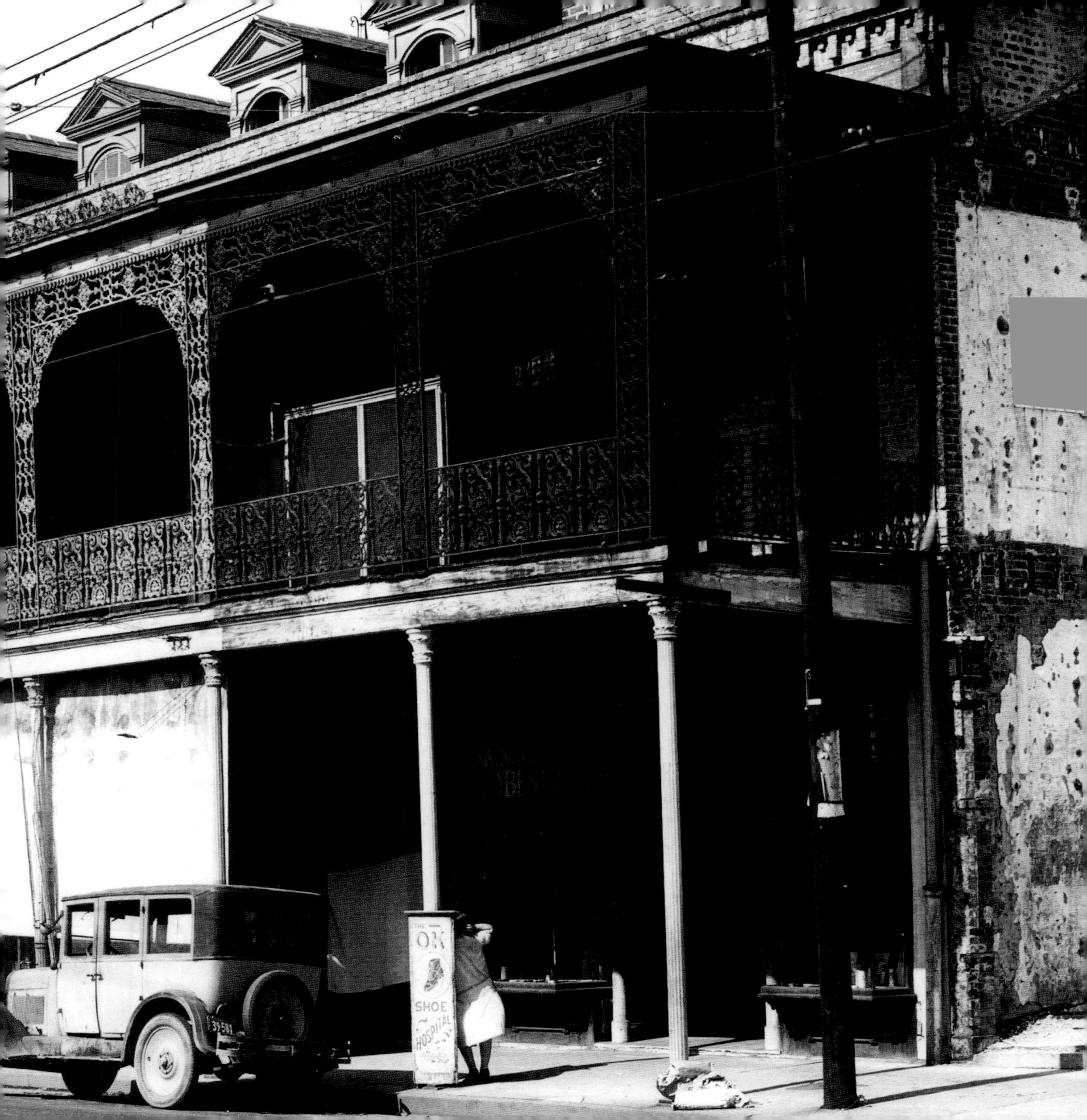
THE
OK
SHOE
HOSPITAL

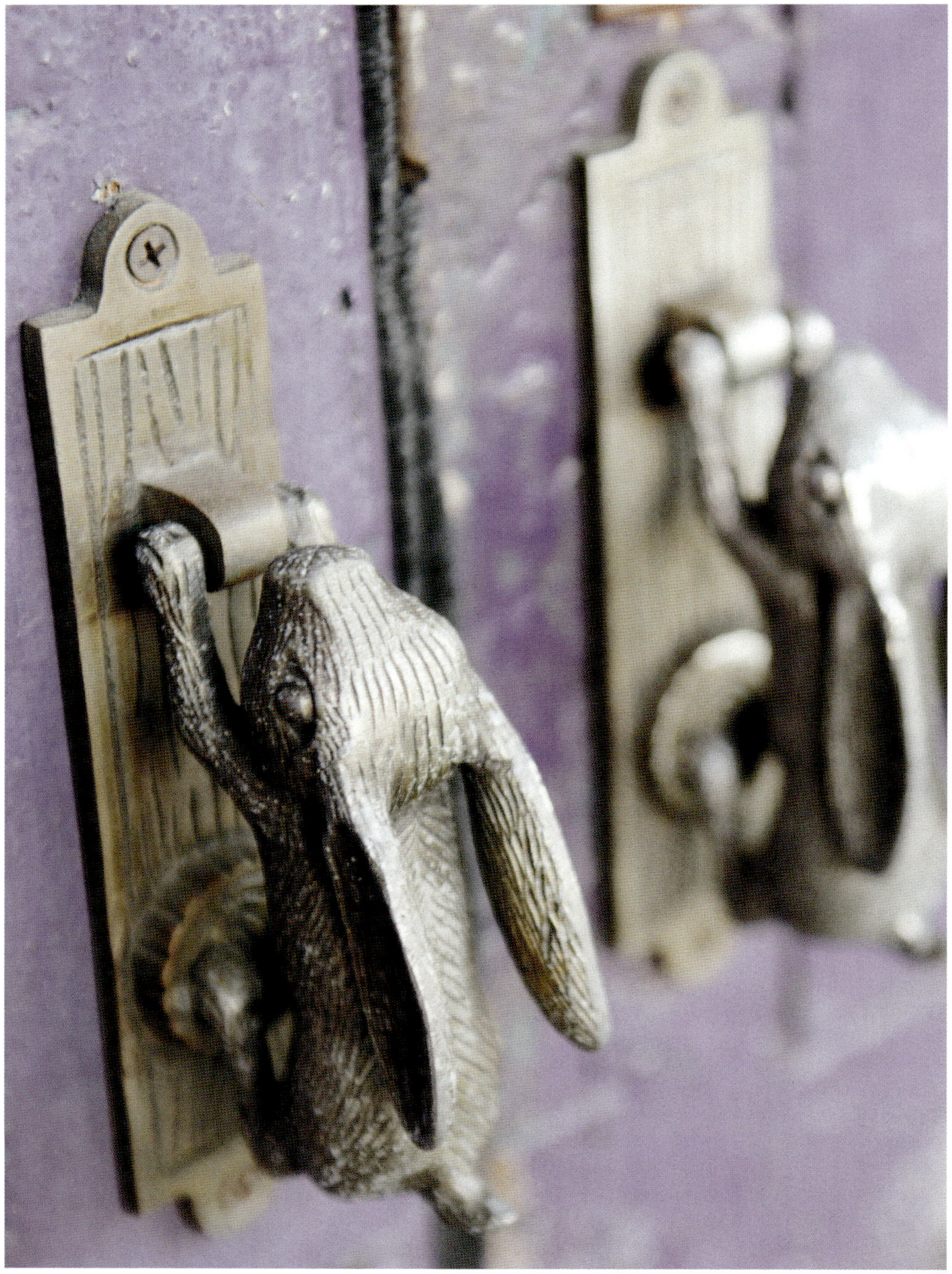

Whimsy at Miette boutique, 2038 Magazine Street.

row of similar 1850s commercial buildings.

Rows of independent buildings behind a common facade was a very popular form of commercial building at the time, and several similar examples still exist downtown, including along the 400 block of Magazine. Shops were on the ground floor, while the owner's family lived above the shop. Shopkeepers living either upstairs or behind their stores remained a common practice throughout Magazine well into the twentieth century.

The next block up, which runs across from the old market site, is another row of 1850s and '60s structures. Although similar to one another, each building has its own varying design. Many of the display windows along here were added later, but as with most of the Shops along Magazine, they represent retail architecture from as far back as the late nineteenth century.

One shop in this block is Plum.

at 1914, where owner Dannal Perry sells an eclectic assortment of "unique" merchandise not readily found elsewhere. Plum began way Uptown at 5430 Magazine, but she prefers the current location because it's "a little hipper and a little funkier." She likes old things and this is an old neighborhood, and as a trained historian of Southern studies, she enjoys being able to talk about the historic neighborhood and the city with tourists. She says that Plum gets lots of tourists, many of whom walk from Downtown. When she was farther Uptown she got mostly locals, but when she moved they continued to come to the new location. Like many people, she says, "I love Magazine Street—love not being in a mall—love being on a street with character."

On the river side of the next block up, between St. Andrew and Josephine, buildings date from 1872. This was the site of the St. Alphonsus Convent, but after the convent's second destruction by fire, the church decided to replace it with speculative commercial development.

In 1948, Buddy LaRocca was interviewed when the new electric trolleybuses were inaugurated. He was age fifty-seven at the time and manager of Caronna's Bar at 2030-32. His family had long been a part of Magazine Street, and his brother was jazz musician Dominick "Nick" LaRocca. A plaque commemorating Nick is high up on the building at 2022 Magazine, where he was born. He was the cornet player and leader of the Original Dixieland Jazz Band, credited with the first jazz recording in 1917, *Livery Stable Blues,* noted for the barnyard sounds the instruments mimic. He also wrote the famous *Tiger Rag,* which is the longtime fight song for Louisiana State University. Buddy recalled that his brother and his band would play at the Magazine Market to entertain shoppers there.

Buddy felt that when he was a boy around the year 1900, Magazine's merchants did as much business as Canal Street. "But," he reasoned, "the number of residences increased, and well the bottom just sort of fell out." He added, "We're over the slump now. This street is growing in importance. More businesses are coming. That new pavement out there is helping bring them back too. There's a great future for our merchants."

LaRocca family members still own the building where Caronna's Bar was located.

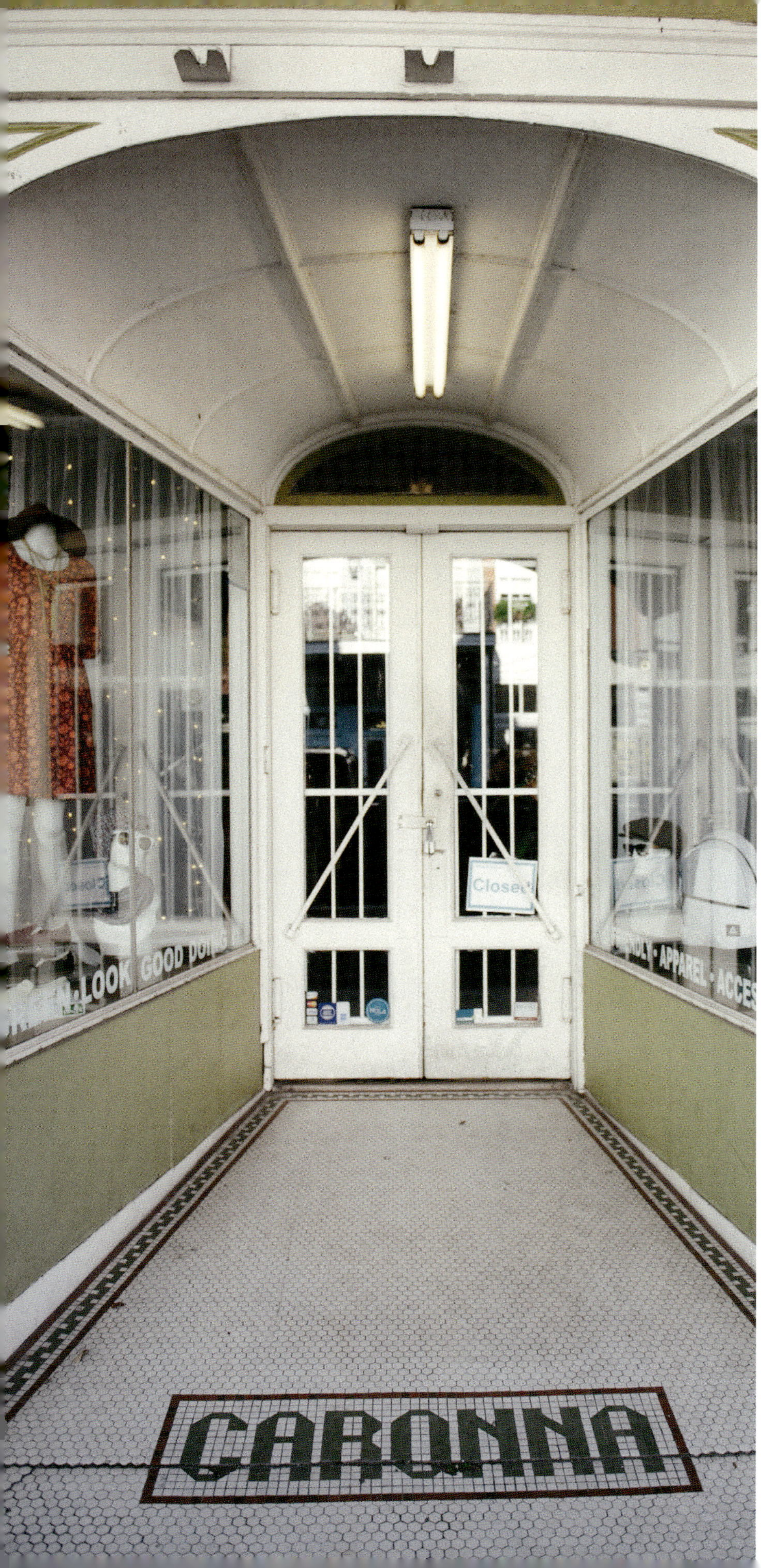

The current owner is Leonard C. Palmisano, whose mother, Mary, was Nick's niece. While Mr. Palmisano's paternal side of the family originated from the island of Ustica near Sicily, his mom's family came from Sicily itself. The latter side arrived in the late nineteenth century and the Palmisanos settled on Magazine Street, where they bought the building at 2022, which by the 1890s was Caronna's Bar. Its handsome tile sign is still imbedded in the concrete at the entrance.

In the early 1920s during Prohibition the bar was closed and the family opened a shoe store here. By 1948 it was called Betty Lou Shoe Store. At the same time they bought the building at 2032, where they opened an ice cream shop. The beautiful original mahogany counter and decorative mirror back remain intact. When Prohibition ended in 1933, Caronna's Bar and Restaurant reopened in this building. The bar remained in operation until around the turn of the twenty-first century, when it was replaced by a boutique more in keeping with today's Magazine Street.

Mr. Palmisano was brought up at 2032 in the 1950s and '60s. He echoes the memories of many who lived in the area

Site of Caronna's Bar.

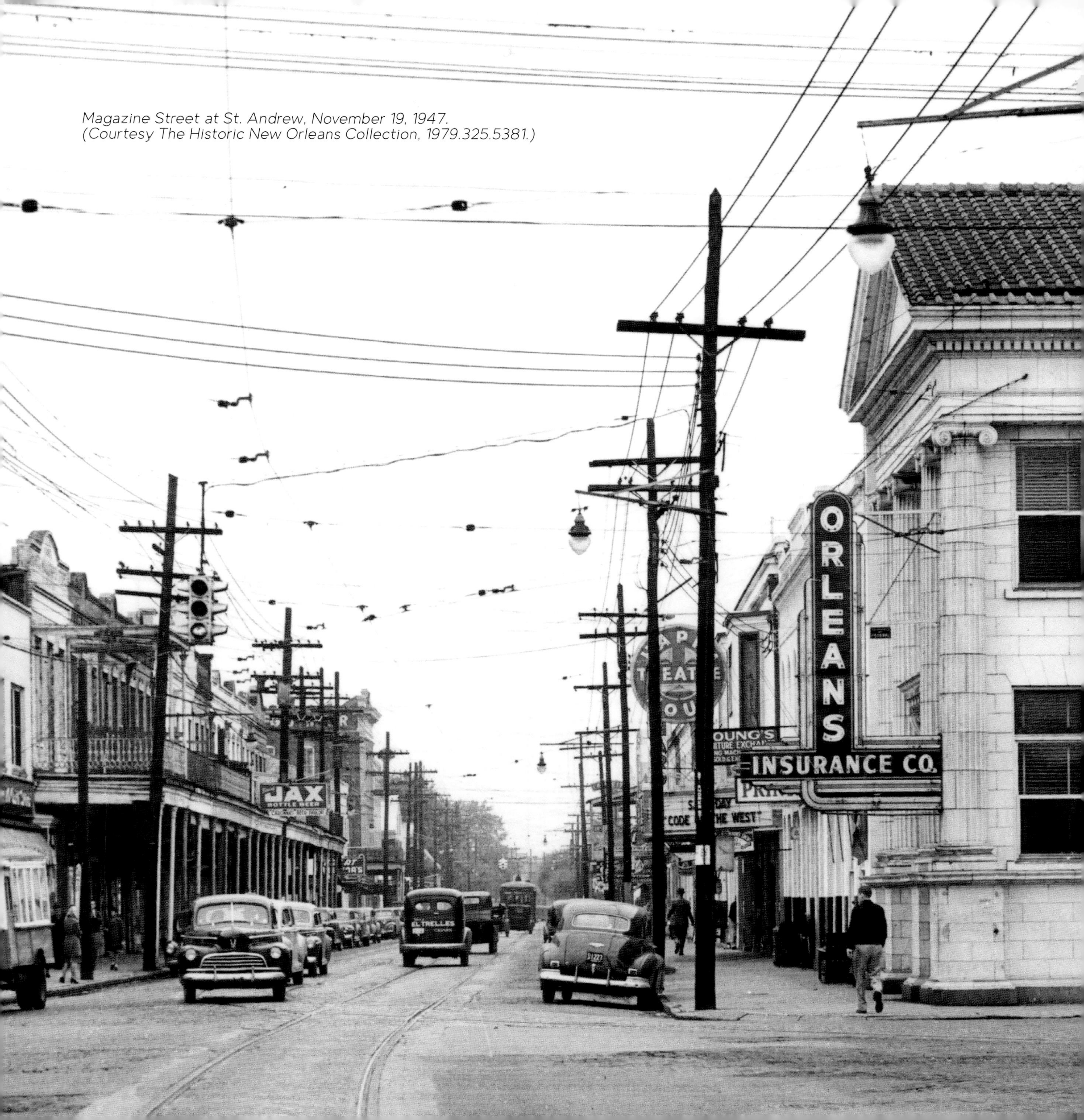

Magazine Street at St. Andrew, November 19, 1947.
(Courtesy The Historic New Orleans Collection, 1979.325.5381.)

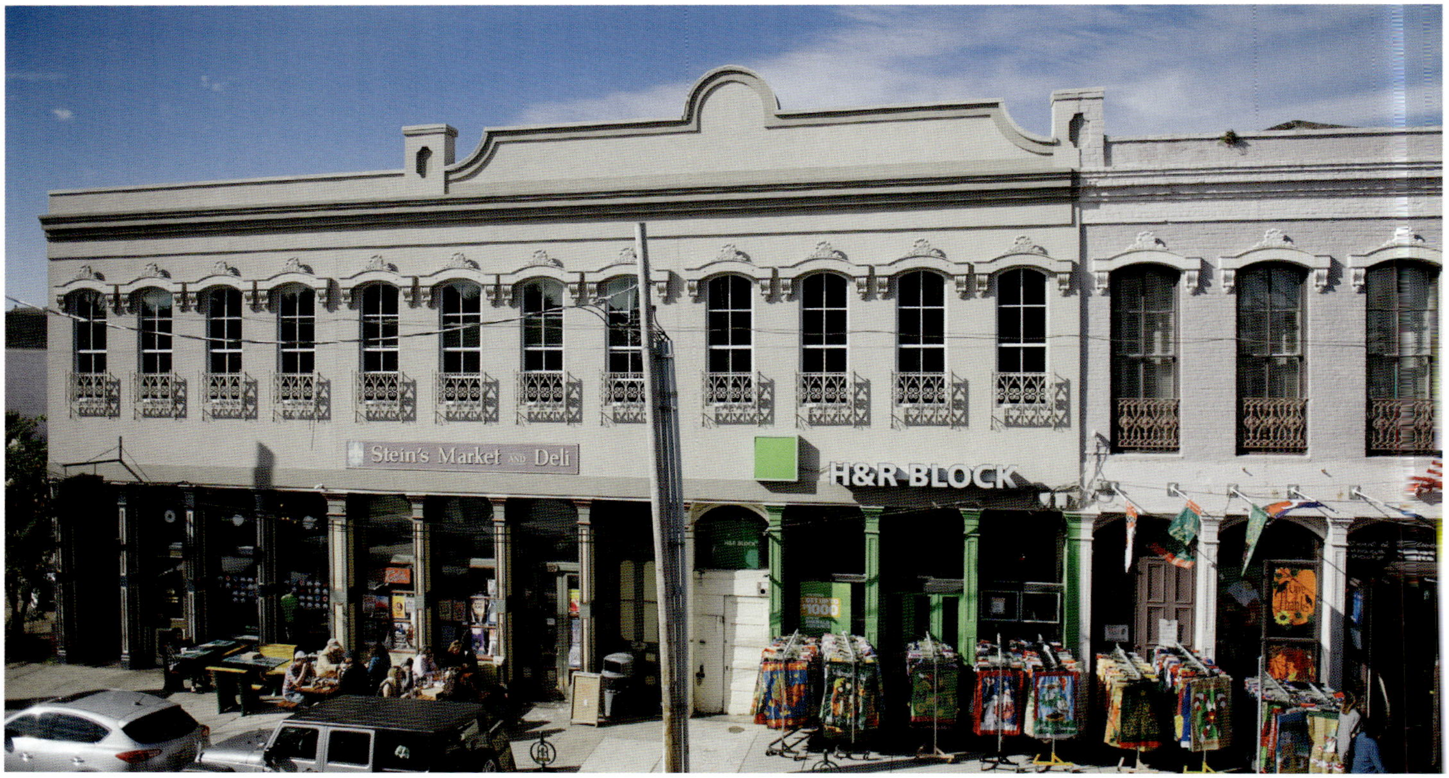

A thriving business community, located in 1850s commercial buildings, on the corner of Jackson.

by recalling that everybody looked after each other. Even then, in most cases shop owners lived upstairs over their stores, continuing the long tradition of Magazine Street. He was an altar boy at St. Alphonsus Church, which stands just behind their home. Every type of business one needed was on Magazine, and he remembers the smell of fresh doughnuts at Frank Baehr's Bakery next door at 2028.

People began selling out in the 1960s and '70s to move to the suburbs. Things were getting rougher in the neighborhood. Gangs were beginning to become active. While drive-by shootings and drugs would not come until the 1980s, the gangs of the 1970s were knife wielding and would occasionally have knife fights.

Mr. Palmisano recalled that growing up with the bar and restaurant, he met a l kinds of people. Caronna's, a music venue, was a popular place for musicians, and political types were regulars. On Mardi Gras morning it was one of the stops for Pete Fountain's Half-Fast Walking Club. He said it was like the bar on the television show *Cheers*, where "everybody knows your name." He also met people from around the world, since seamen passing through the nearby port would stop in. Over the years the bar, along with the entire 2000 block of Magazine, has been used for movies such as *Hard Times*, *Angel Heart*, and *Miller's Crossing*, as well as some television shows.

Mr. Palmisano considers Magazine Street to be one of the "gems" of the city of New Orleans. He still owns some of the old family property, including the building at 2032, and remains involved in what he calls "a rich environment to all that visit it."

Across the street from the old Caronna's Bar, on the lake side of the 2000 block, a number of buildings survive from a block-long row of 1850s buildings once called the Union Block (named such because it was a block of buildings with a unified façade). A more modern addition is the temple-like structure on the corner of St. Andrew, built as a branch of the Canal-Commercial Trust and Savings Bank (now J.P. Morgan Chase) prior to 1909. From the 1940s it is recalled as the Orleans Insurance Company, but it now houses Free People, a women's clothing store.

Several other solid-looking bank structures were built along different parts of Magazine in the early twentieth century. The Ninth Street Market branch of Canal-Commercial at 3200 and the corner of Harmony also dates from before 1909. Recently it housed a branch of African American-owned Liberty Bank but is now a branch of Gulf Coast Bank and Trust. Canal-Commercial also had a branch at Ewing Market, at the 5435 corner of Octavia, which dated from about 1920. In the 1970s the building was The Bank, a shop specializing in salvaged architectural items like shutters, doors, and stained glass, but it has since returned to its original purpose as a branch of Home Bank. The Hibernia Bank and Trust Company (now Capital One) had its circa 1920 Jefferson Market branch at 4300 and the corner of General Pershing. Since 1997 the building has been owned by jewelry designer Mignon Faget as her headquarters and research and development facility.

Two doors up from the bank, at 2011 Magazine, is another twentieth-century

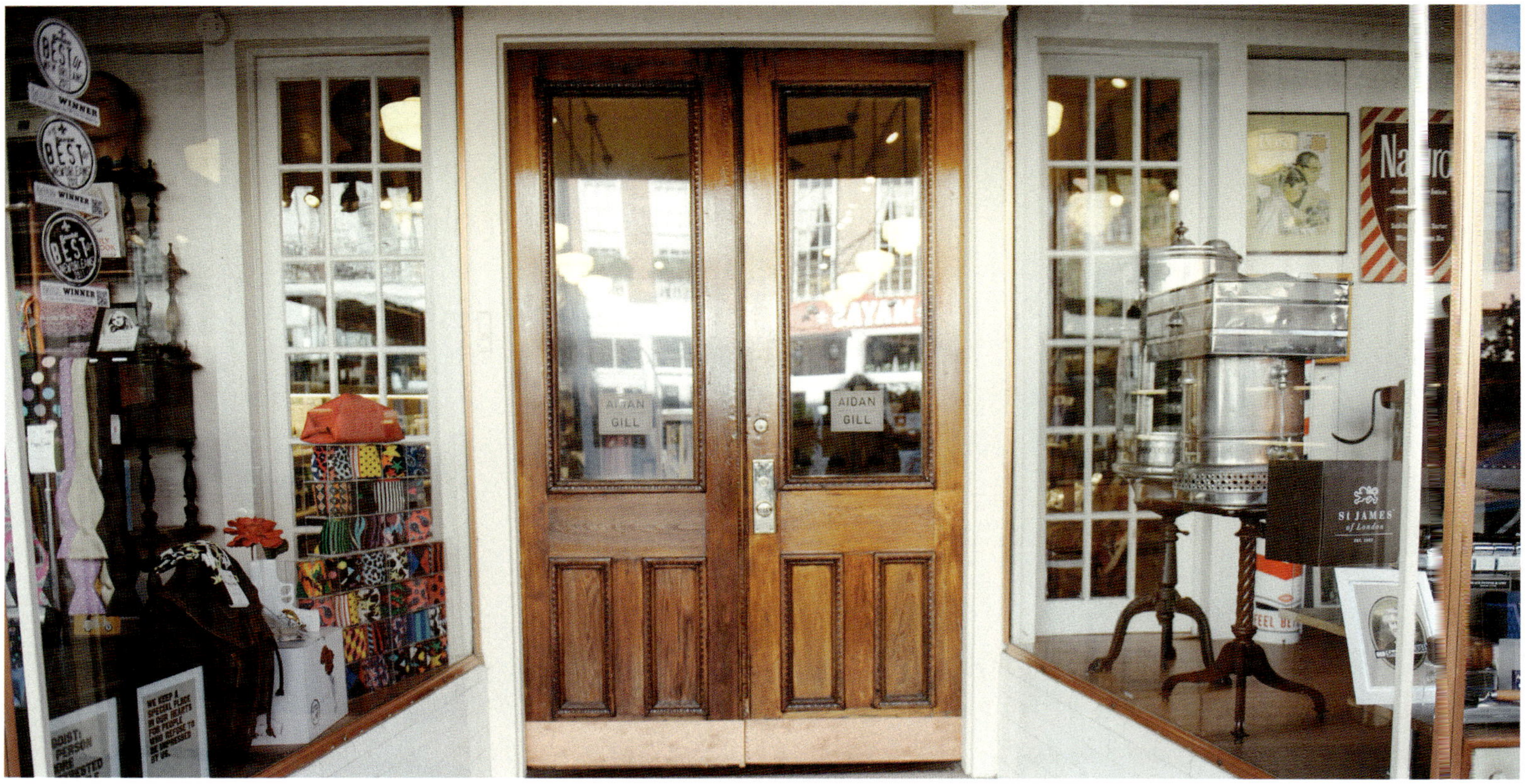

Old-fashioned shop fronts are still a part of Magazine Street.

building that is now The Shops at 2011, an arcade of antiques and design dealers. The original 1850s building was likely destroyed by fire, and according to gallery owner George Saucier, a new building was built in 1905 for a funeral home. This was H. Young's, and the name is set in tiles in the sidewalk in front of the building. The structure still has an extra-wide front entrance and slanted floor to accommodate hearses. Large showrooms at the front of the building were once funeral viewing parlors, while at the back of the building is a two-story atrium with a skylight.

From the upper floor hay could be pitched down to feed the horses below. In the early 1920s the business changed to H. Young's furniture and appliance store. Young's was still around in 1978, and the *Underground Shopping Guide* says it was then "Strictly a used furniture and appliance store."

Another more recent building in Magazine's 2000 block is the former Happy Hour Theater, which opened in 1908 in an old warehouse and offered vaudeville shows and movies. It expanded in the 1920s, and in 1932 a canopy marquee with a big circular sign was added. The popular neighborhood house became a Spanish-language theater in the late 1960s but closed in the 1980s, after which it became an antique shop and is now Talebloo Oriental Rugs. About 1996 a freakish rainstorm collapsed its well-known marquee.

The 2100 block reaches Jackson Avenue and nears the end of Magazine's first and oldest commercial strip. The block contains several buildings from the nineteenth century, the most notable being the Wegmann Building at 2123, which was built as the Lafayette Fire Insurance Company in 1877 and now contains part of Goorin Bros., a nationally owned fine hat shop. The building to the left of Wegmann was once part of the Wade Block, an 1850s row of buildings that extended to Jackson Avenue, but most have been replaced by a service station. Almost directly across the street from the Wade site, at 2134, is another late-nineteenth-century building which for more than half a century was Jacob Young's jewelry store. Now Jewel's Food Store, J. Young's name can still be seen in floor tile at the entrance and painted on the outside wall of the building.

The nineteenth-century building next door to the grocery store, at 2138-40 Magazine on the corner of Jackson, once had an ironwork gallery that curved around the second floor. In the early twentieth century it was Julius Groetsch Restaurant and Wine Vaults, touted as "a favorite uptown resort." At the same Jackson Avenue intersection at the time was A.W. Scardon & Sons Grocery. Now long gone, this store opened in 1869 and dealt in the "fancy grocery trade" doing "handsome business with the fashionable people in the vicinity." Both of these establishments testify to the proximity of the wealthy Garden District.

The neighborhood was not all business

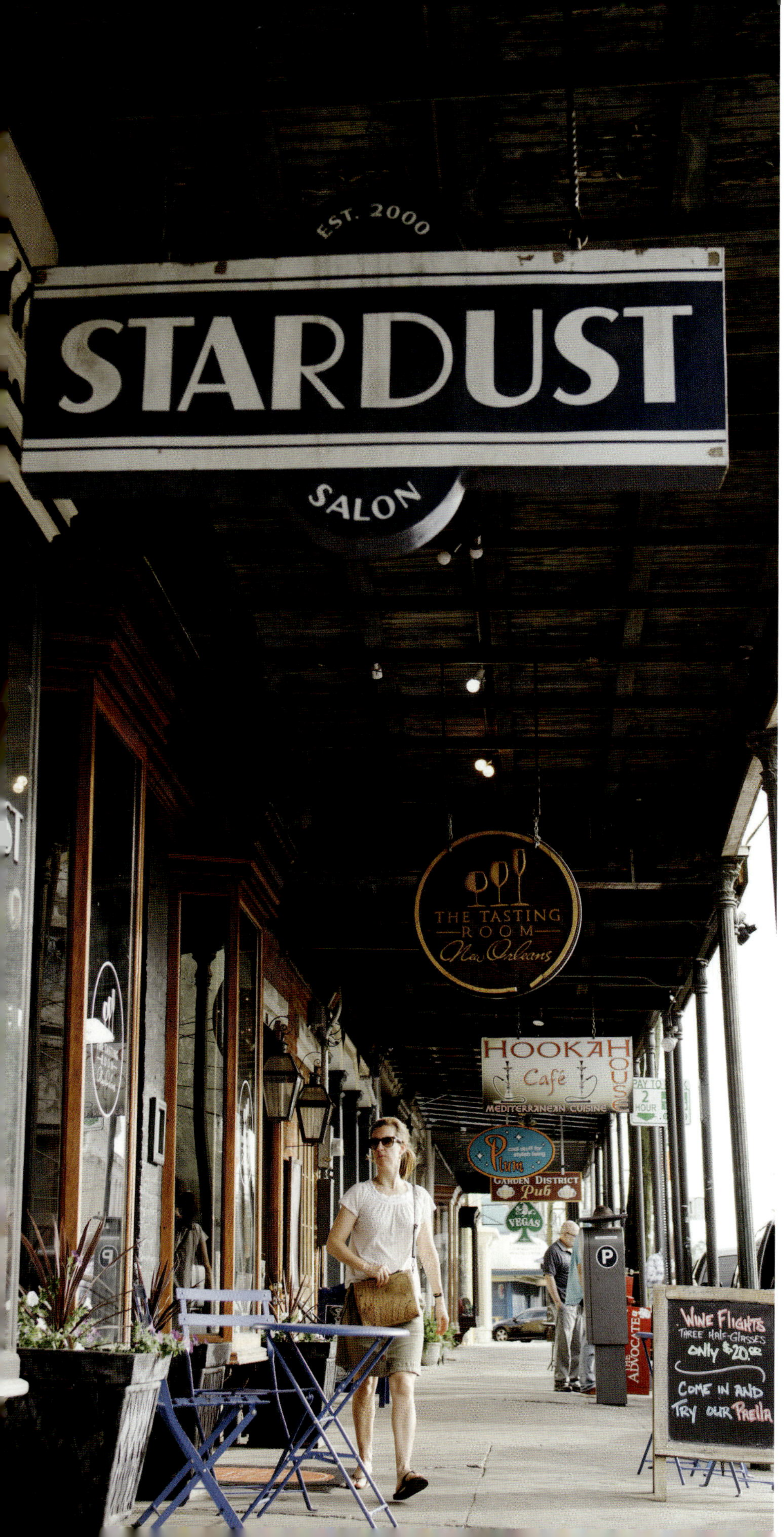

but was heavily populated with many families living upstairs in the buildings as well. One such was at Sam's Shoe Shop, a shoe repair business owned by Sicilian immigrant Salvatore Alongi. He and his wife Caterina, who did clothing alterations, lived in the back of the building that he owned. They had nine children—not unusual in New Orleans in the early twentieth century.

Alongi's granddaughter Catherine "Cath" Wilson, her parents Raymond and Mary Reidling, and Cath's brother and sister lived upstairs in a three-room apartment during the 1950s. Cath remembered that the house smelled wonderfully of food, and on Sundays her grandmother had an open house with never-ending meatballs and spaghetti. Everybody was welcome, and all the cousins would come over.

In the neighborhood she recalls a "wonderful" bakery with items like wine cakes and fresh Italian bread. She remembers Caronna's Bar as a "famous watering hole." Woolworth's, at 2014 Magazine, would open all its doors and windows and run huge ceiling fans during the summer. A remembered childhood

Pedestrian friendly 1900 block of Magazine Street.

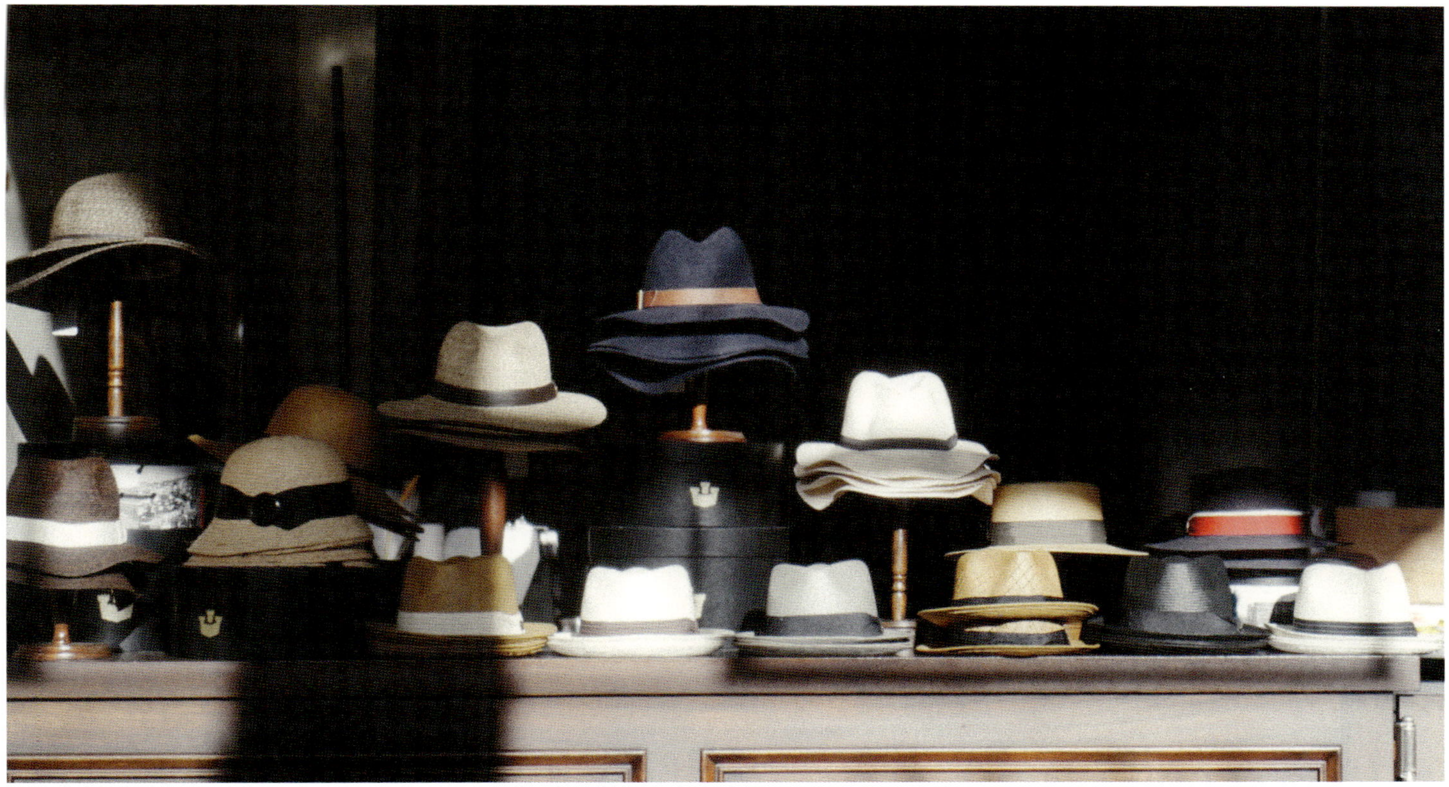

New Orleans is a hat town.

noise was the "whoomph, whoomph" of those fans. At the Happy Hour Theater, Mr. Kern was the floor walker. He made sure people kept quiet and would not allow food or drink in the auditorium. Whatever refreshments you bought had to be consumed in the lobby. Everywhere on Magazine there was a "huge amount of foot traffic," not only shoppers and workers, but also people going to and from bus stops, as so few people had cars and the population depended on public transit.

"It was a wonderful, glorious place to grow up—rich with history, culture, food. Everybody's grandparents had foreign accents or spoke a different language." During her childhood the area was safe, and Cath recalled roaming around looking at the beautiful old New Orleans architecture, which she loves. She remembers the ceiling

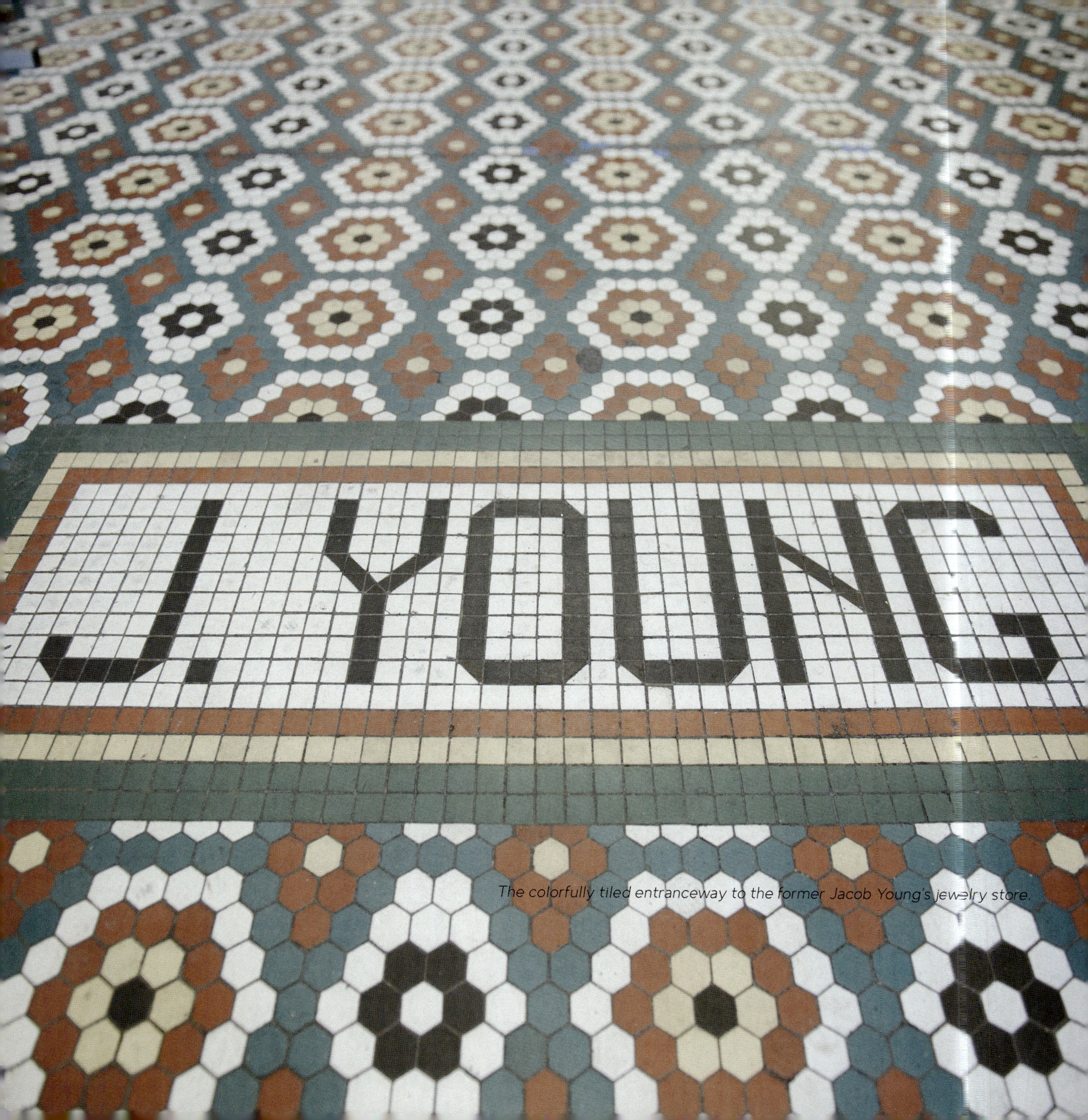

The colorfully tiled entranceway to the former Jacob Young's jewelry store.

frescoes at St. Alphonsus Church. She is an artist and credits this architecture for her inspiration to this day.

Starting in the early 1960s the old neighborhood began to change. Not only were houses falling into disrepair, but there were street gangs beginning to form. It was no longer safe, and people started locking their houses. Although Mrs. Cath's grandparents remained in the neighborhood until their passing in the '70s, her own family moved to the suburbs. Now long gone from her childhood home on Magazine, Cath is part of a gallery. Its location is, of course, on Magazine Street downtown.

By the 1990s this section of Magazine had declined badly. People said if you went there you risked getting shot. There were many vacant storefronts. The high crime rate in the nearby St. Thomas housing project, a development which dated to the late 1930s and early 1950s (and was integrated in the mid-1960s), did not help the image of Magazine at all. With the replacement of St. Thomas by a mixed-income residential development, a rapid resurgence of lower Magazine and its shopping district began to take place.

One of the pioneers in this resurgence is Dublin-born Aidan Gill, owner of Aidan Gill for Men. This elegant barber shop at 2026, just a few doors down from what used to be Caronna's Bar. Mr. Gill has also been a pioneer in the resurgence of the old-time barber shop, which had been in decline for decades, since the rise of the unisex hair salon. From barbering days in Dublin and London, he moved to New Orleans and opened a shop at Hampson and Adams Streets in Carrollton in 1990. He then moved to Magazine in 1999 at a time when there were about a dozen junk or antique shops and seven bars nearby. He bought his current location in 2010, as he foresaw the street's changing fortunes, especially with the closing of the St. Thomas housing project.

In reviving the barber business his shop not only contains the highest quality shaving creams, lotions, and colognes, but also a veritable museum of historic shaving items and decor. There is a large mirror case from the venerable Eola Hotel in Natchez. The red-and-blue barber pole from Luke's Tonsorial Parlor, which was at 4332 Magazine next to Ms. Mae's The Club, is also on display. Luke's site had long been a barber shop—in the '40s it was barber

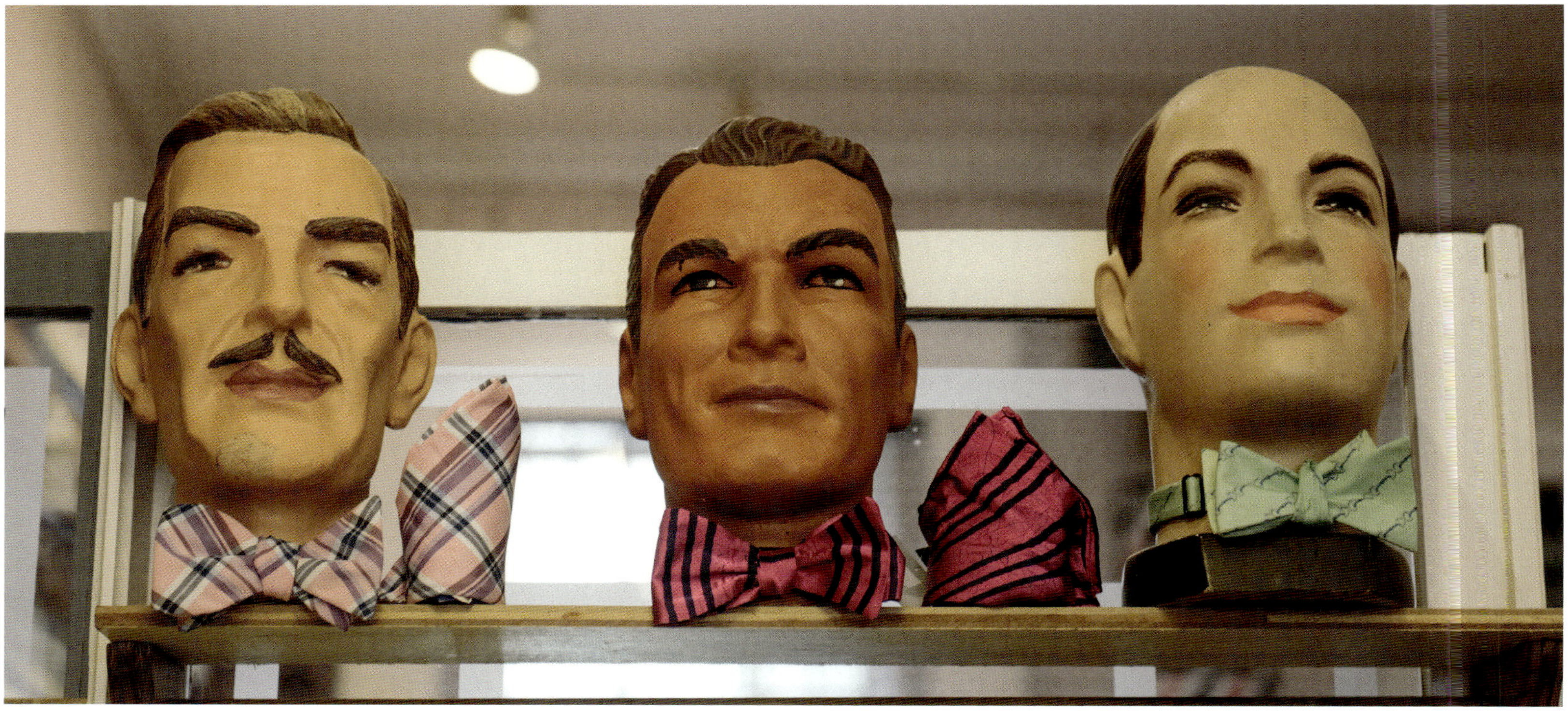

Aidan Gill, purveyor of fine bow ties and pocket squares.

Salvatore Danna's—although it is now the Hey! Cafe.

The building in which Mr. Gill is located has served men for about a century. From a flower shop in the early twentieth century, it became the Varsity Shop, a fashionable men's clothing store, in 1918. In 1932, hurt by the Great Depression, the business was reorganized by the owners as Behrman and Company. To update the look of the shop, the arts and crafts cabinets were covered with thick, white paint. Although since removed, the paint applied in the early 1930s was still there eighty years later. Like many other shopkeepers on Magazine, the family lived behind and over the store. Behrman's lasted well into the late twentieth century. Mr. Gill has the Behrman's sign that used to hang under the gallery above the front door.

Across Jackson Avenue the Magazine commercial district begins to come to an end. On the corner at 2201-09 is a beautiful row of buildings dating from the 1850s. Across Magazine from this, at 2208, was once the popular second-hand furniture shop of Bernard Regenbogen. The 1978 *Underground Shopping Guide*, by Ann H. Earhart and Diana D. Earhart, called Regenbogen's "A cluttered little place for the real digger; junque and more junque."

Paul L. Arceneaux remembers from the late 1960s that his mother, Bonnie Arceneaux, had dealings with "a used furniture store called Regenbogen who would sell and buy things from the street." Mr. Arceneaux remembers the owner as "a very good businessman," and that this trait ran in the family. He recalls that Regenbogen had a little daughter who offered to sell him a nickel for a quarter, and Mr. Arceneaux said that he took her up on the offer: "Where could you buy a smile like that for twenty cents?"

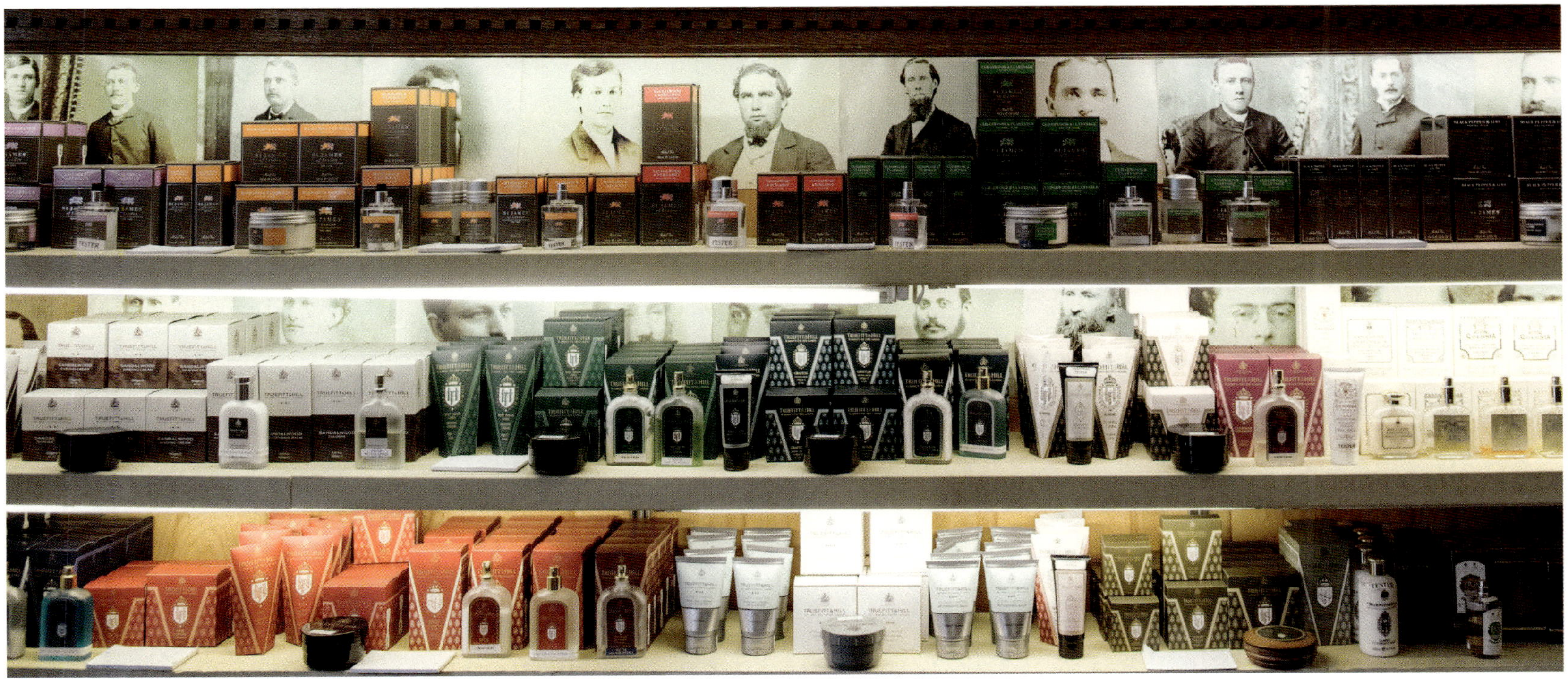

Gentlemen's toiletries at Aidan Gill.

Regenbogen's building is no longer standing. It was burned in a spectacular fire around the mid-1990s and for a number of years it was the site of a small neighborhood garden. A large, two-story building has since taken its place. On the Jackson Avenue side of this building is the shop of French-born folk artist Simon, whose brightly painted, star-studded signs can be seen gracing doorways and shop windows throughout Magazine Street—indeed, all over town.

It was also nearby on Jackson that Vera Smith died in the street in the tumultuous days following Hurricane Katrina. Her lifeless body remained exposed for several days before her neighbors built a makeshift grave to cover her on the sidewalk until her body could be removed. At the site of the temporary grave there is a brightly painted shrine that Simon built in her memory.

While Magazine has been noted for its antique shops beginning around the 1970s, earlier on it was sought out for its thriving secondhand trade, with stores like Regenbogen's, Ben Matthews, Hooter's, Young's, and many more. Many families from all parts of town helped furnish their houses from Magazine Street. Charlotte Hoggatt moved into a new house in Metairie in 1964 and said that soon afterward she bought a dining table from Ben Matthews off Magazine on Melpomene, because she "wanted something affordable."

One dealer that lasted into the twenty-first century was E.J. Hooter's, at the 1936 corner of Magazine and St. Andrew. The store was described by the 1978 shopping guide as having "lots of used furniture and occasional antiques mixed in with refrigerators and stoves . . . check here often as the stock moves rapidly." Hooter's mid-nineteenth-century building is now thoroughly spruced up as the Donald T. Erwin building.

Into the late 1970s between Hooter's and Regenbogen's were secondhand stores like Mack's, now Bella Umbrella, at 2036. Of Mack's, the shopping guide states, "If you are out for a bargain in used appliances they are here." The Council Thrift Shop at 2104 was run by the Council of Jewish Women and "Regular visits are necessary . . . as the turnover is great." Today it is the site of the Renaissance Shop. City Furniture at 2116, now Franco's Athletic Club, was "truly a used furniture store with an occasional find hidden away."

While many people found their dining tables in these shops, antique dealers with a discerning eye sometimes found things of much greater value for their own more elegant shops. By the 1970s, fancier antique emporia were replacing the old secondhand dealers. At the same time some antique dealers were shunning the French Quarter, as rents were much lower on Magazine Street. One such example was Arthur Anders, who around 1975 moved his fine furniture, china, and silver from Chartres Street to 3116 Magazine near Harmony.

The shopping district, which ends just above Jackson Avenue, is arguably one of the most significant historic retail districts in the United States. Many of its buildings date to the early 1850s and retain a nineteenth-century character. For many years regarded as little better than run down and virtually abandoned by the 1990s, it has revived significantly and is now one of the most important, historically significant sections of Magazine Street.

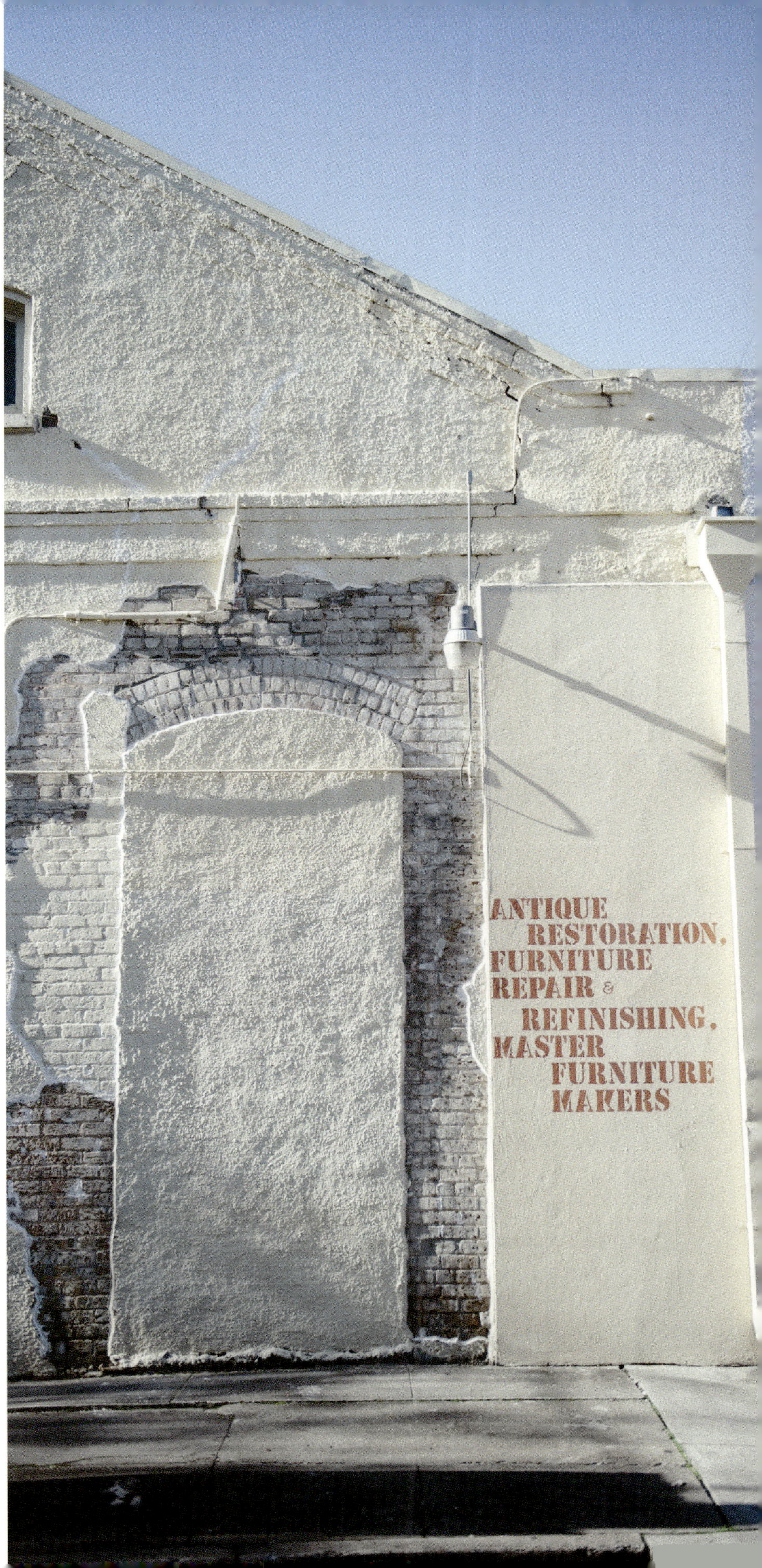

Now famous for its trendy boutiques, Magazine Street is still home to many antique shops.

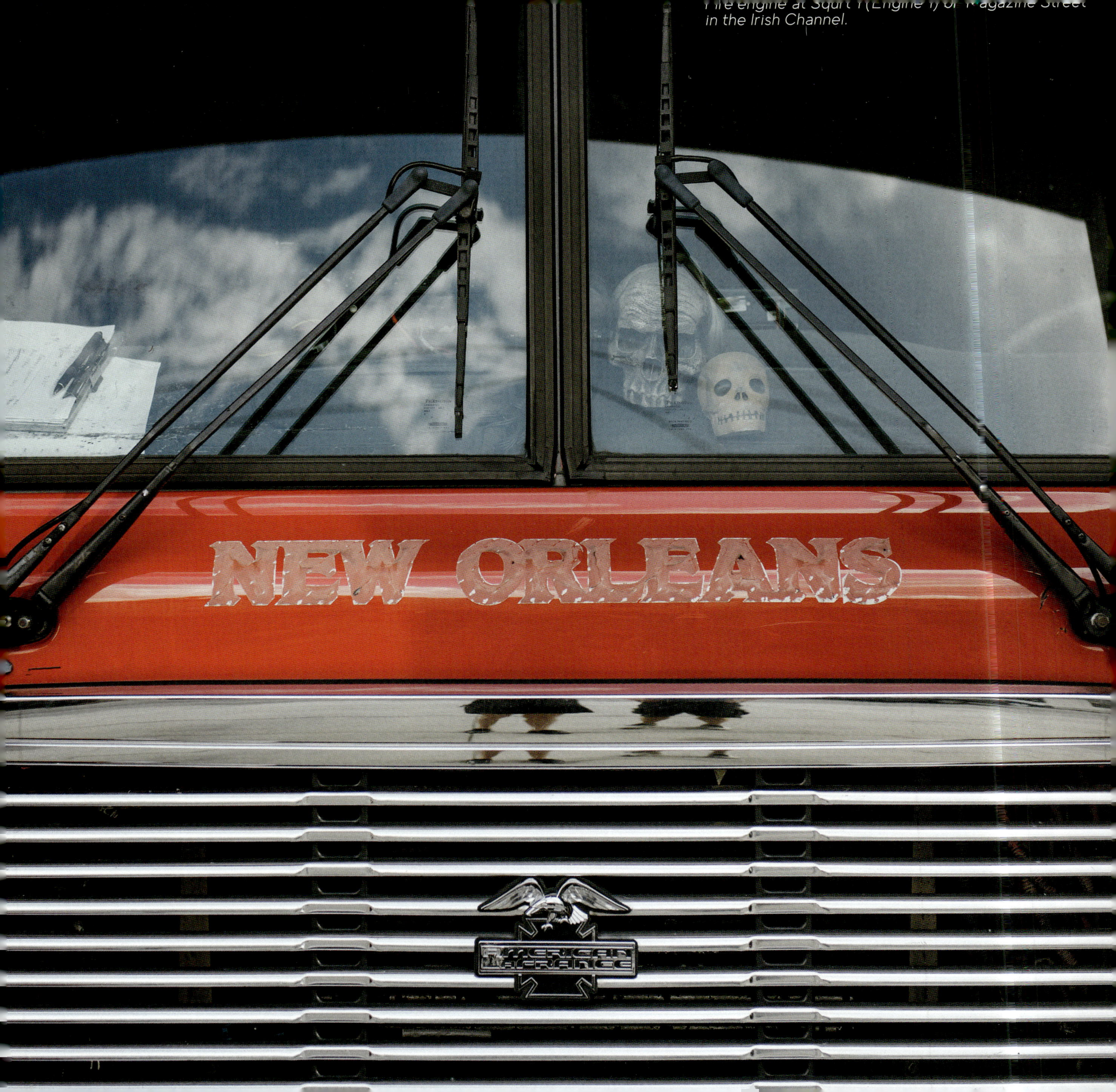

Fire engine at Squirt 1 (Engine 1) on Magazine Street in the Irish Channel.

Chapter Five

Jackson Avenue to Louisiana Avenue

Traveling up from Jackson Avenue, Magazine Street once again takes on a tree-lined residential appeal and includes only a few businesses before commerce starts again at Washington Avenue. This area was originally part of the City of Lafayette, which was incorporated in 1833. At the time it was a separate city in Jefferson Parish and was the seat of that parish.

The City of Lafayette was made up of several plantations subdivided into faubourgs. Faubourg Nuns, which had been owned by the Ursuline Sisters, was subdivided in 1810 and ended at Soraparu Street. Next up was John Poultney's plantation, which extended to First and once subdivided in 1824 was called Faubourg Lafayette. The adjacent plantation belonged to Jacques Livaudais and was sold by his wife Marie Marigny to a group of investors in 1832. It was large, extending between First and Harmony, and in 1832 the new investors hired Jefferson Parish surveyor Benjamin Buisson to subdivide it. In 1836 the heirs of Valery Delassize had Buisson subdivide their plantation, which extended to Toledano. It was

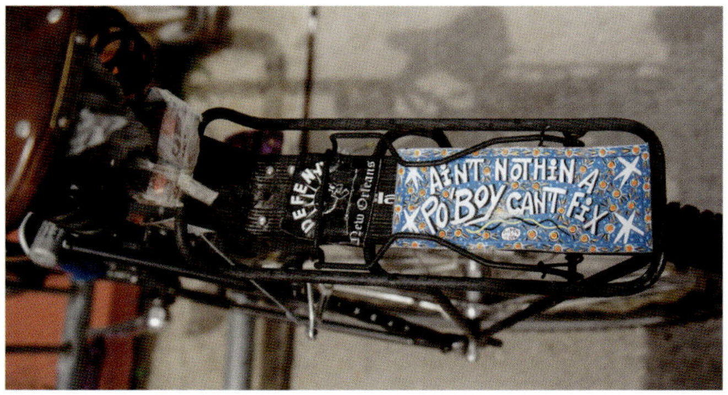

A serving of New Orleans wisdom.

initially separate from the City of Lafayette but annexed in 1844. These subdivisions continued to connect into the street plans initiated by Lafon, and the arrangement near Louisiana Avenue continued Magazine's gentle curve mimicking the Mississippi River.

During the second quarter of the nineteenth century, New Orleans was growing rapidly with its urban population approaching 150,000 in the early 1850s. As the population continued to spread progressively upriver, Lafayette became the area's main center of growth. Actually growing faster than New Orleans proper, Lafayette emerged from a village in the 1830s to a city of about 25,000 in the early 1850s. Lafayette was annexed by New Orleans in 1852, and the Jefferson Parish seat was moved to Carrollton, which was still a separate city within that parish.

While Washington Avenue had originally been designated as the main street of Lafayette, it was ultimately Magazine that took on that role. The area between Washington and Louisiana Avenue grew into Magazine Street's second important business district and another typical nineteenth-century commercial strip.

Helping New Orleans grow were large numbers of immigrants pouring in, especially Germans and Irish in the 1840s and '50s. Although scattered all over town, immigrants concentrated in the area between Magazine and the river, which was ultimately dubbed the Irish Channel, even as many Germans settled there as well. Since the aristocratic Garden District emerged to the north between Magazine and St. Charles, Magazine came to be regarded as the dividing line between the rich and the working class. The river side was "the other side of the tracks," so to speak.

Today the Irish Channel Historic District is identified as the neighborhoods between Magazine and the river and Jackson and Louisiana Avenues, while the Garden District is between Magazine and St. Charles and Jackson and Louisiana. These districts are small in area and serve modern historic district designations. In the nineteenth century the neighborhoods covered much wider areas. Historically, the Irish Channel referred to the area between and including Magazine and the river from about Lafayette Street to the end of the upriver urban area. The term

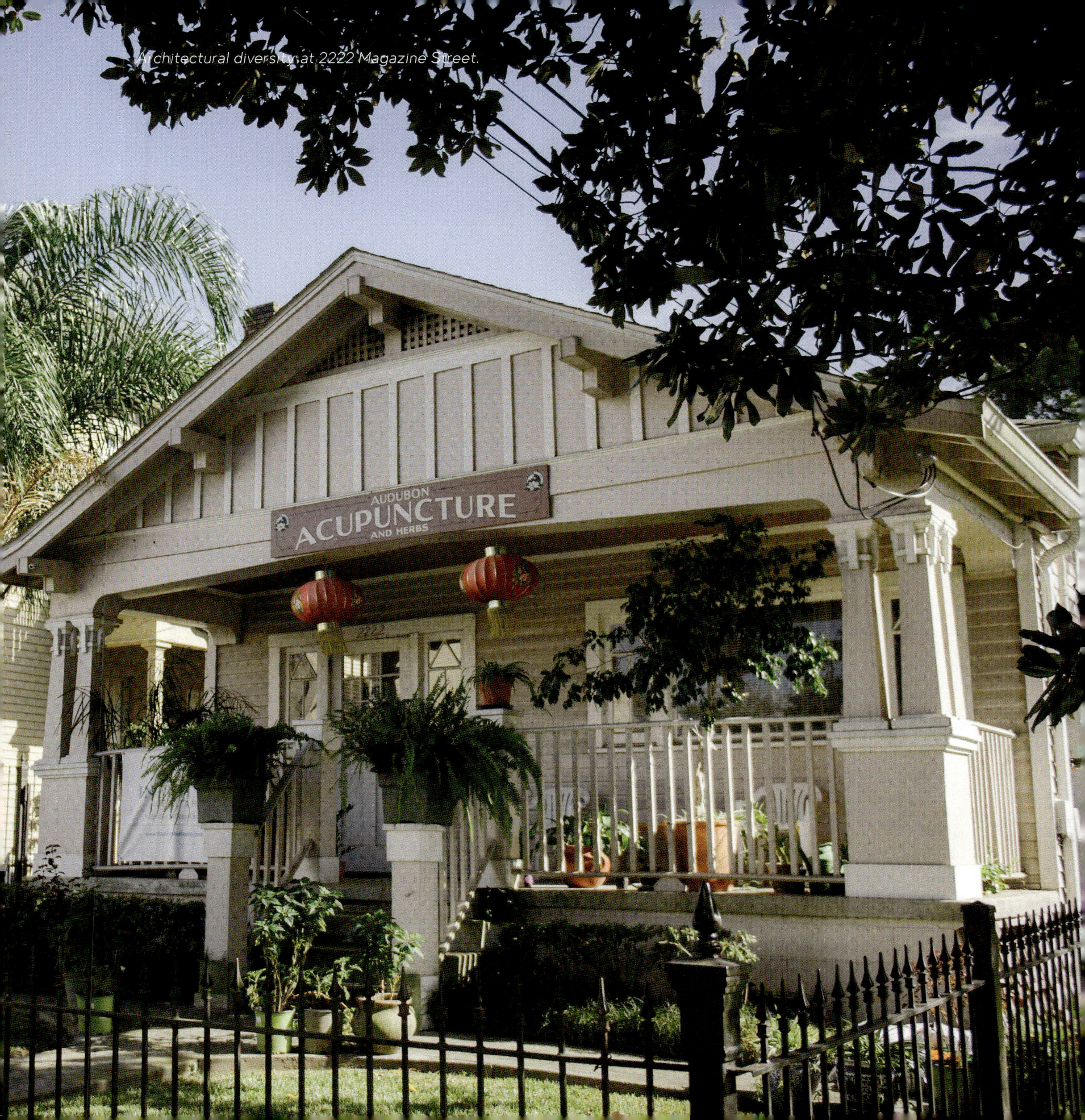

Architectural diversity at 2222 Magazine Street.

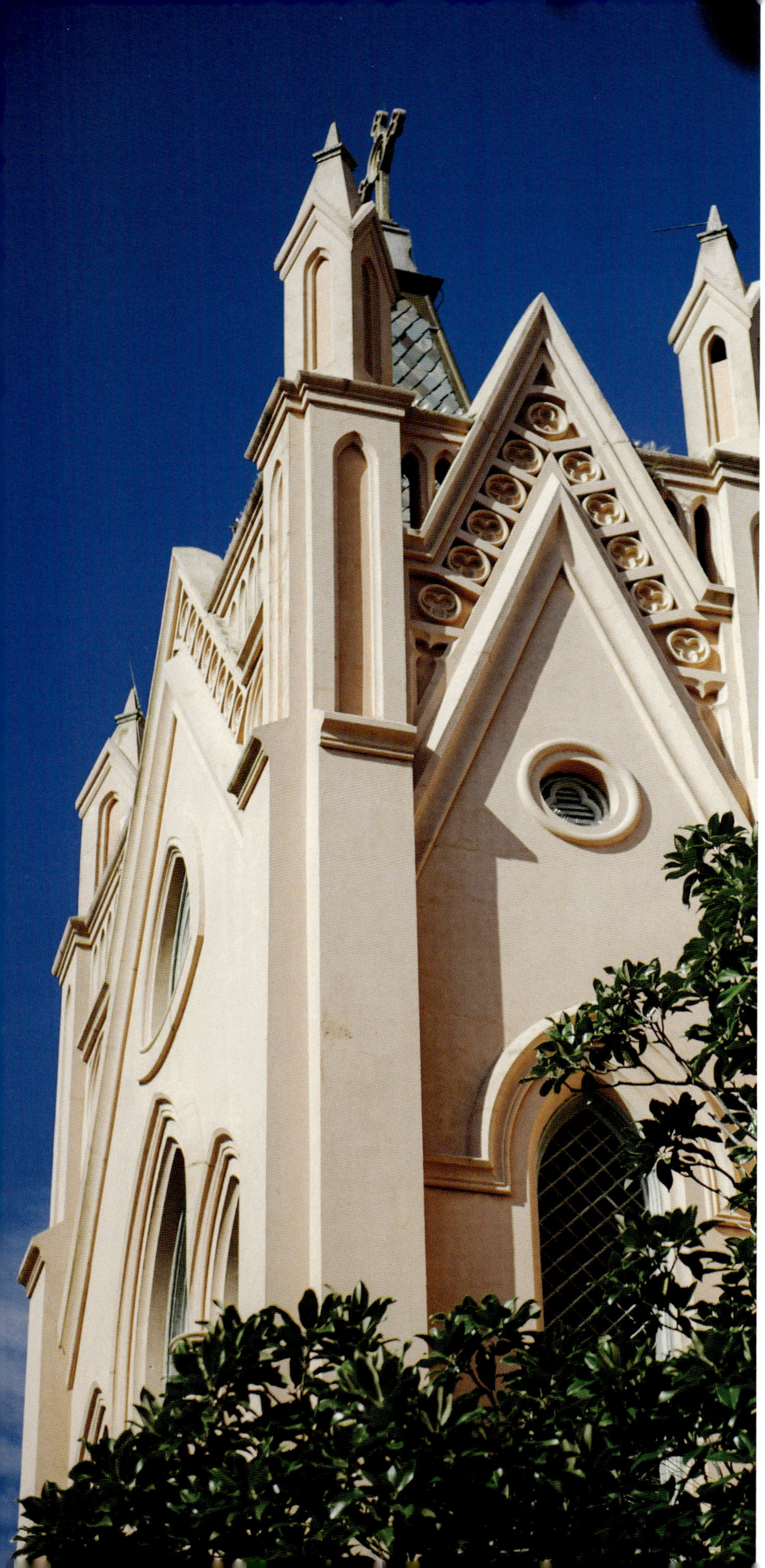

Garden District, which was in popular use by the 1850s, referred to any of the tree-lined streets in the Uptown area. Even then, Magazine was roughly the dividing line.

The upriver growth of the city in the mid-nineteenth century and its large immigrant population is exemplified by what came to be called Ecclesiastical Square. While not along Magazine, it is one block off on Constance between Jackson and St. Andrew, and the many Catholics living along this area of Magazine Street would have found their parish church in this square. Ecclesiastical Square has its roots in the Redemptorist order, which in Louisiana dates to the early 1840s. This order espoused combining religion and education, thus the Redemptorists erected not only churches, but also schools, libraries, meeting halls, and orphanages. Ultimately, three churches were built near each other in Ecclesiastical Square to serve the various language groups of immigrants. The Italianate-style St. Alphonsus was completed in 1857 on Constance Street for English-speaking Irish Catholics. St. Mary's Assumption, the first German Catholic church in Louisiana, is a beautiful example of German Baroque architecture. Located

Trinity Episcopal Church.

across Constance on Josephine, it was dedicated in 1860 for German Catholics. These were followed by Notre Dame de Bon Secour on Jackson for the French. The congregations were consolidated in 1920, and the smaller Notre Dame was ultimately demolished. St. Mary's still has an active congregation and contains the shrine to the Blessed Father Francis Xavier Seelos (1819-1867), who died of yellow fever while serving other fever sufferers. He now moves through the process of canonization to become a Catholic saint. St. Alphonsus has been closed as a church since 1979 and now serves as a community center.

For the area's Protestant population, Trinity Episcopal Church remains an important congregation. It dates to 1847 and the first service in the church on Jackson at Coliseum—two blocks off Magazine—took place in the basement in 1853. Still standing, Trinity was remodeled in the 1890s. Its first rector was Leonidas Polk, the Confederate general, who lived on Magazine Street between Third and Fourth Streets.

Several other Protestant churches in this area were located on Magazine Street itself, but they are now long gone. The Lafayette Presbyterian Church stood on the river side between Jackson and Philip. The site is now a vacant lot. The First Baptist Church stood at the corner of Second on the downtown river side and was replaced in the 1880s by a pair of handsome extant houses. First Baptist relocated to 2813-29 Magazine, where it remained for several decades, and now its site is a recently built strip mall in an 1870s style. Farther up Magazine on the Uptown lake side of Louisiana was the Louisiana Avenue Methodist Church, now site of a CVS drugstore parking lot.

Magazine between Jackson and Washington was anything but a working-class street in its early days, as many of the large surviving houses here testify with their Garden District appearance. These nineteenth-century dwellings are in a variety of styles ranging from Greek Revival (not unlike some found on the other side of Felicity), mid-century brick houses with cast iron, and ornate Victorian examples from later in the century. There are even a few twentieth-century bungalows. By the 1940s the street had declined, and many houses were converted into tenements.

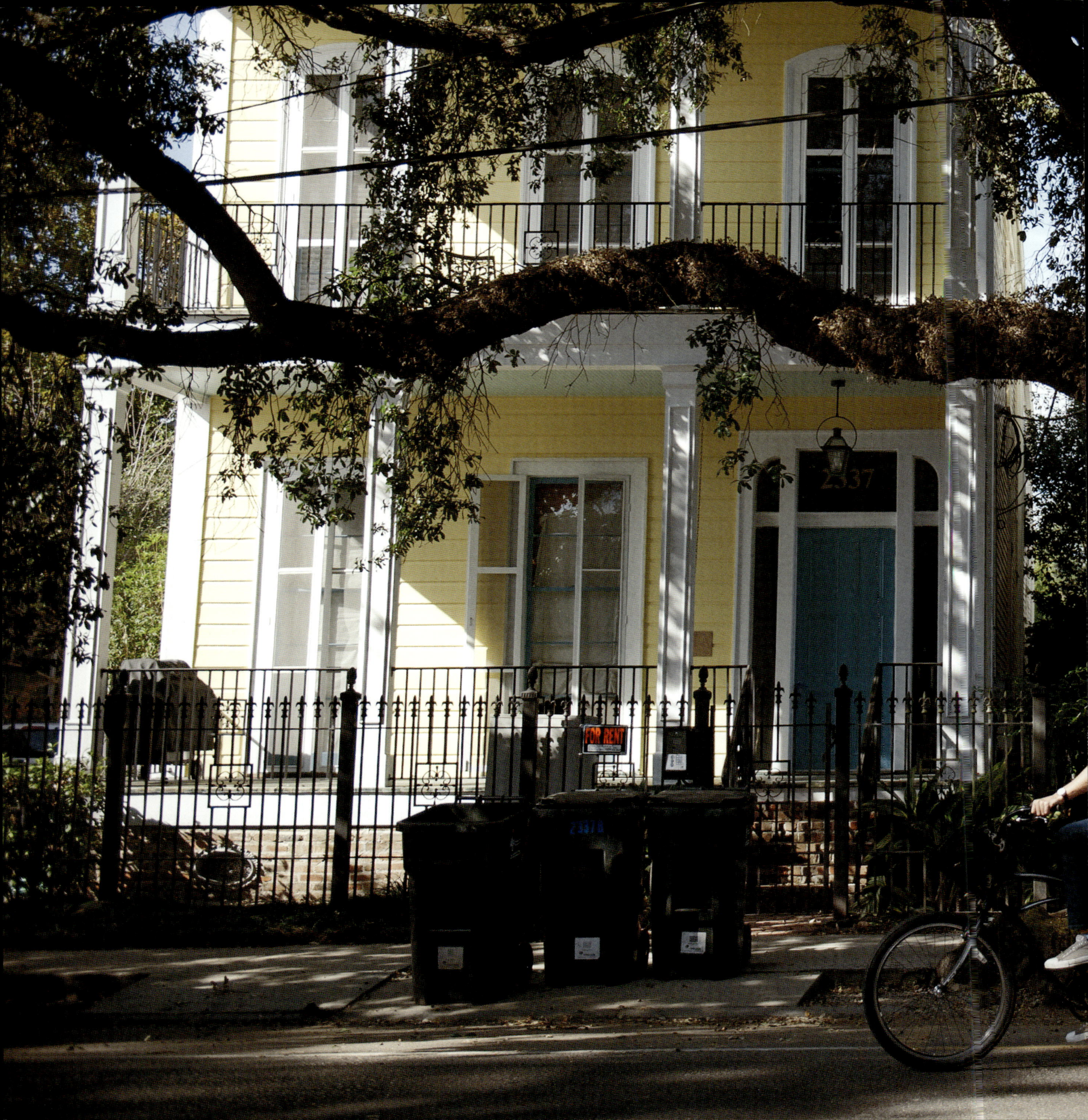
2337
FOR RENT

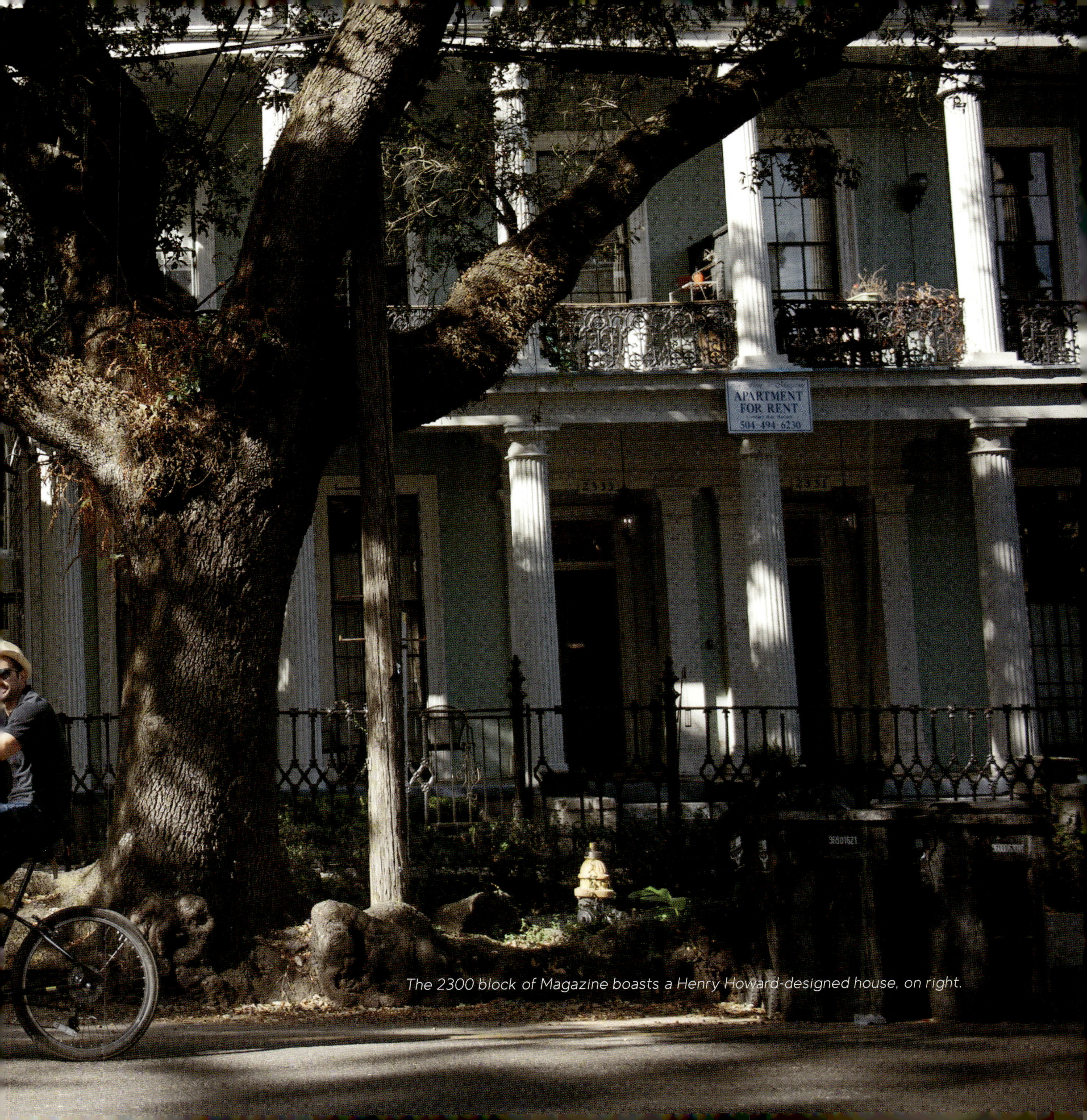

The 2300 block of Magazine boasts a Henry Howard-designed house, on right.

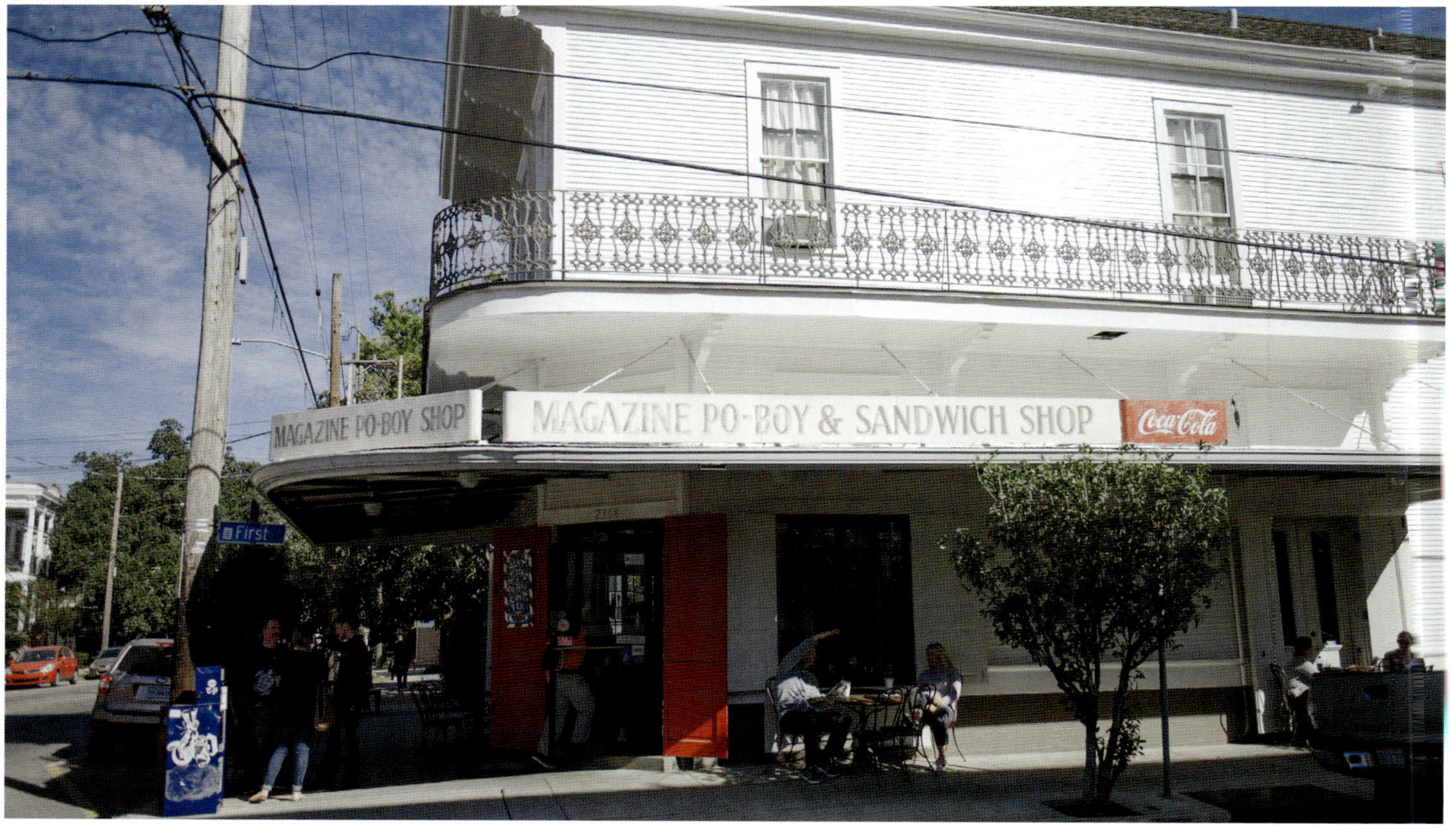

Magazine Po-Boy & Sandwich Shop (2368 Magazine).

The 2300 block between Philip and First contains several notable houses such as 2319—hidden behind a row of big trees—with its ironwork galleries. It may have been designed in 1853-54 by noted architect James Gallier, Jr. In the same block is a Greek Revival double house designed in 1859 by another famous architect of the time, Henry Howard.

At the corner of First Street are two commercial buildings. In the 1940s the one at 2369 was an H&G Hill's grocery store. Hill's was a major chain of small, pre-super market grocers that could be found across New Orleans, and there were several branches along Magazine. In some cases the groceries were just a few blocks apart. Hill's was among several chains—like A&P and Piggly Wiggly—competing with the "mom and pop" stores and public markets

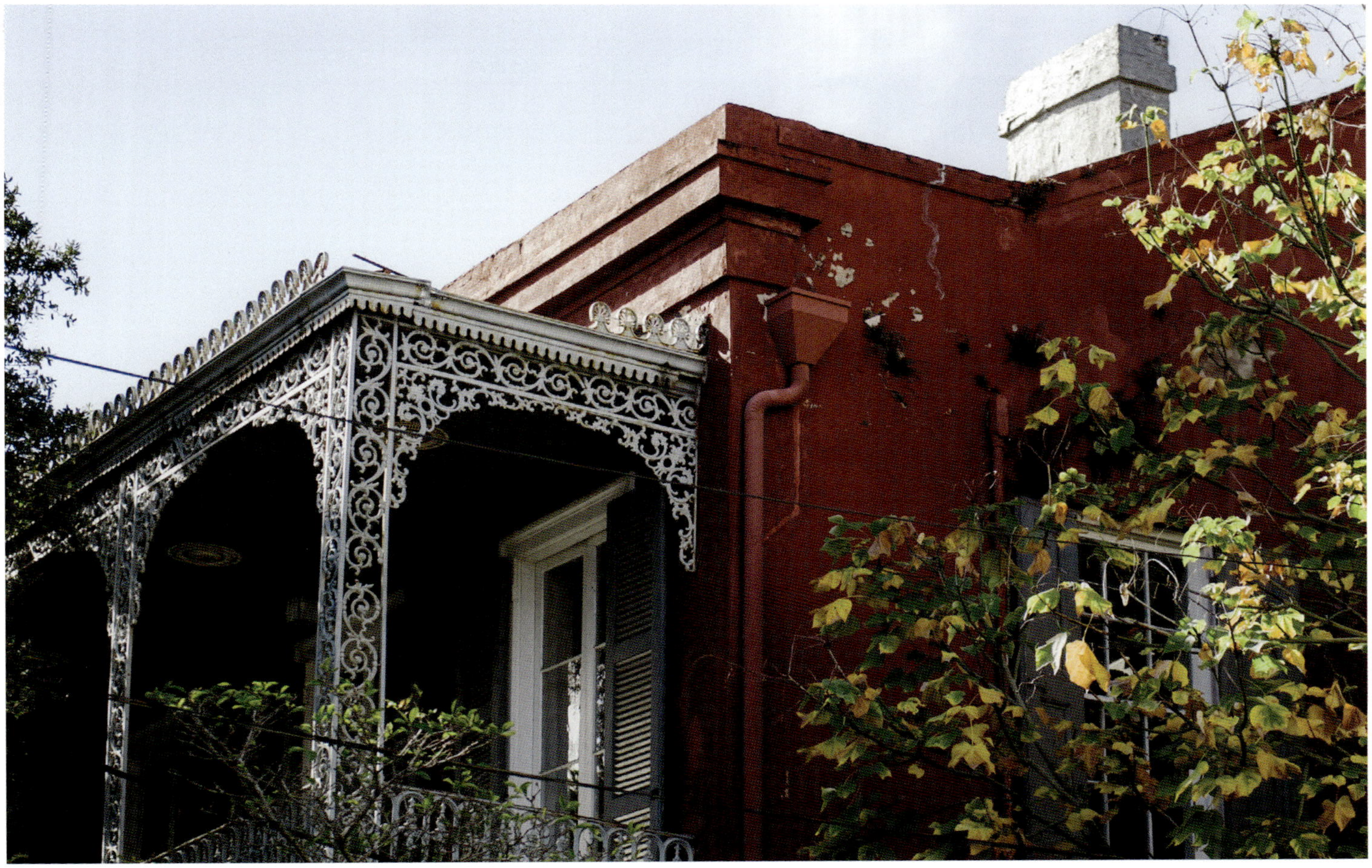

An 1850s mansion at 2319 Magazine Street.

in New Orleans, both of which were ultimately forced out of business. In the 1940s, the building across Magazine from Hill's was also a neighborhood grocer, L&G Super Store. The Hill's location is now occupied by a store, while L&G has for many years been the Magazine Po-Boy and Sandwich Shop.

The next block up continues in a strictly residential mode. On the river side at 2426 and 2428, on the corner of Second, are two handsome 1880s houses that stand on the site of the former First Baptist Church. In the early

A beautiful example of 1860s residential architecture at 2501 Magazine.

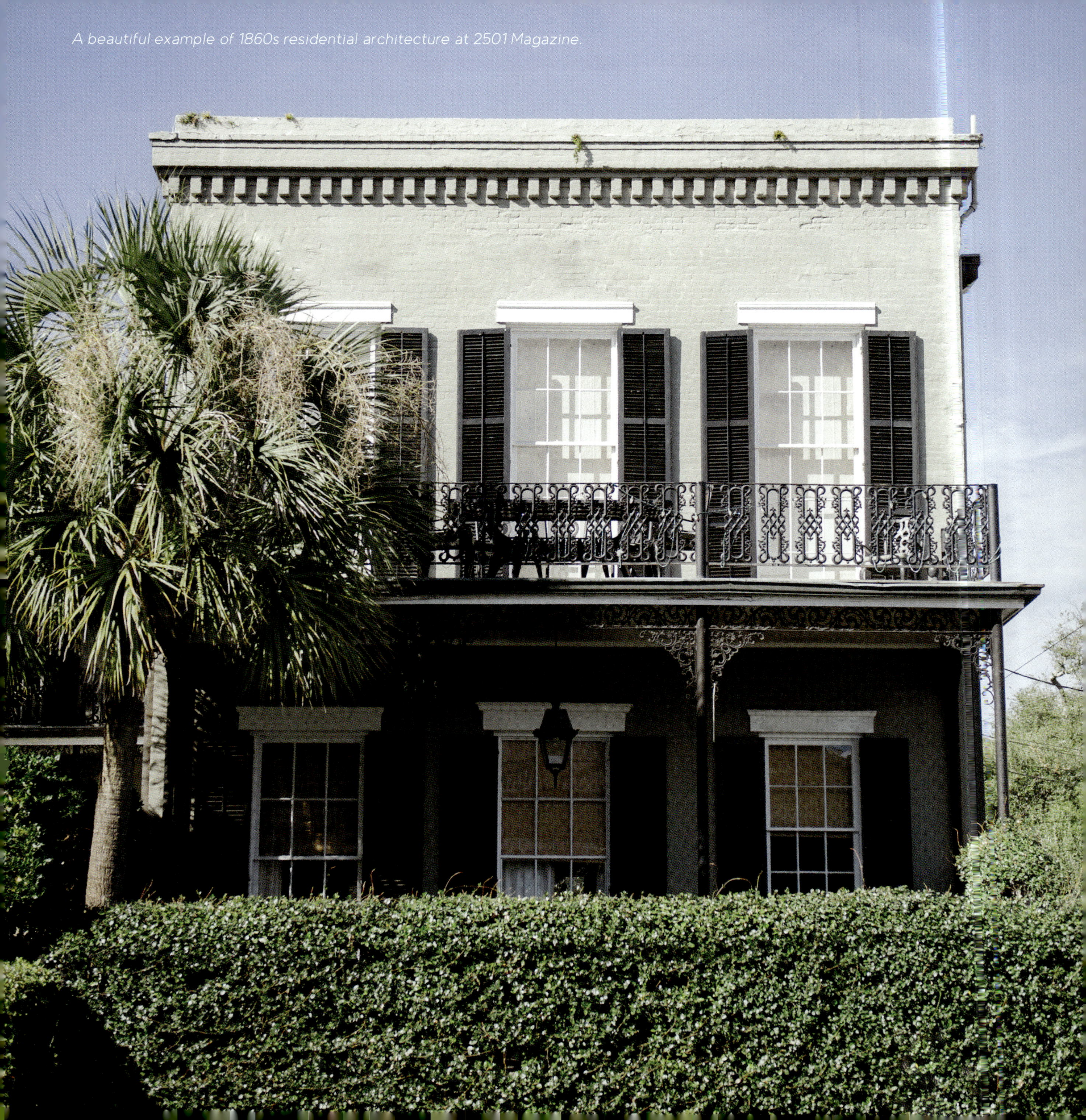

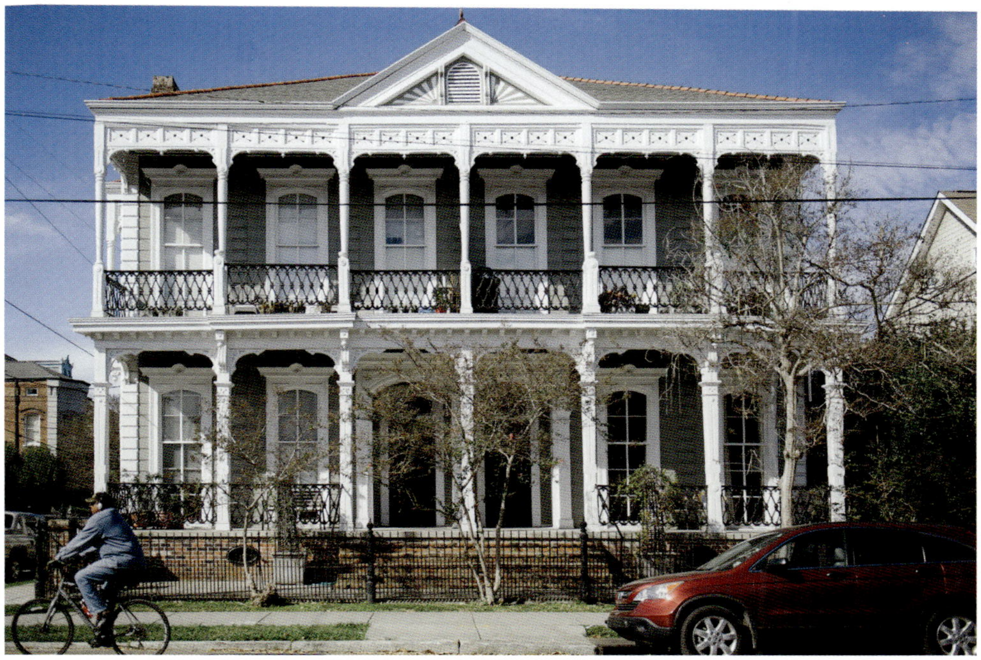

An 1880s Eastlake-style double.

1880s across Magazine from these homes was a large house on a property that covered a quarter of the square block. This was typical of the early arrangement of the Garden District, where each property covered a quarter of the block. The house is no longer standing, having been replaced by several buildings, including a large late-nineteenth-century double house on the corner of Second.

At 2501, on the corner of Third, is a circa 1860 brick house with a large side garden not unlike the Terrell House. Until at least the early 1880s a similar brick house stood directly across Magazine at 2502, but by the 1890s it had been replaced with a large Queen Anne-style house. After Hurricane Katrina in 2005 it was left vacant, but since then it has been gorgeously restored. It is now called the Ghost Manor because of its high tech and animatronic Halloween display, although it is also tastefully decorated for Christmas.

The next two blocks continue with an array of Greek Revival, Queen Anne, and bungalow houses among other styles. There is only one commercial intrusion, which is at the corner of Third. This is a substantial mid-nineteenth-century brick building ringed with a cast-iron gallery and typical of New Orleans commercial buildings of its day. During the nineteenth century it housed a furniture store and by the 1940s it was the Old Famous Bar. Now it is Tracey's Bar with its fluttering Irish flags. A large shamrock is painted with the tricolors of the Irish flag in the middle of Third Street next to the bar. Parasol's Bar

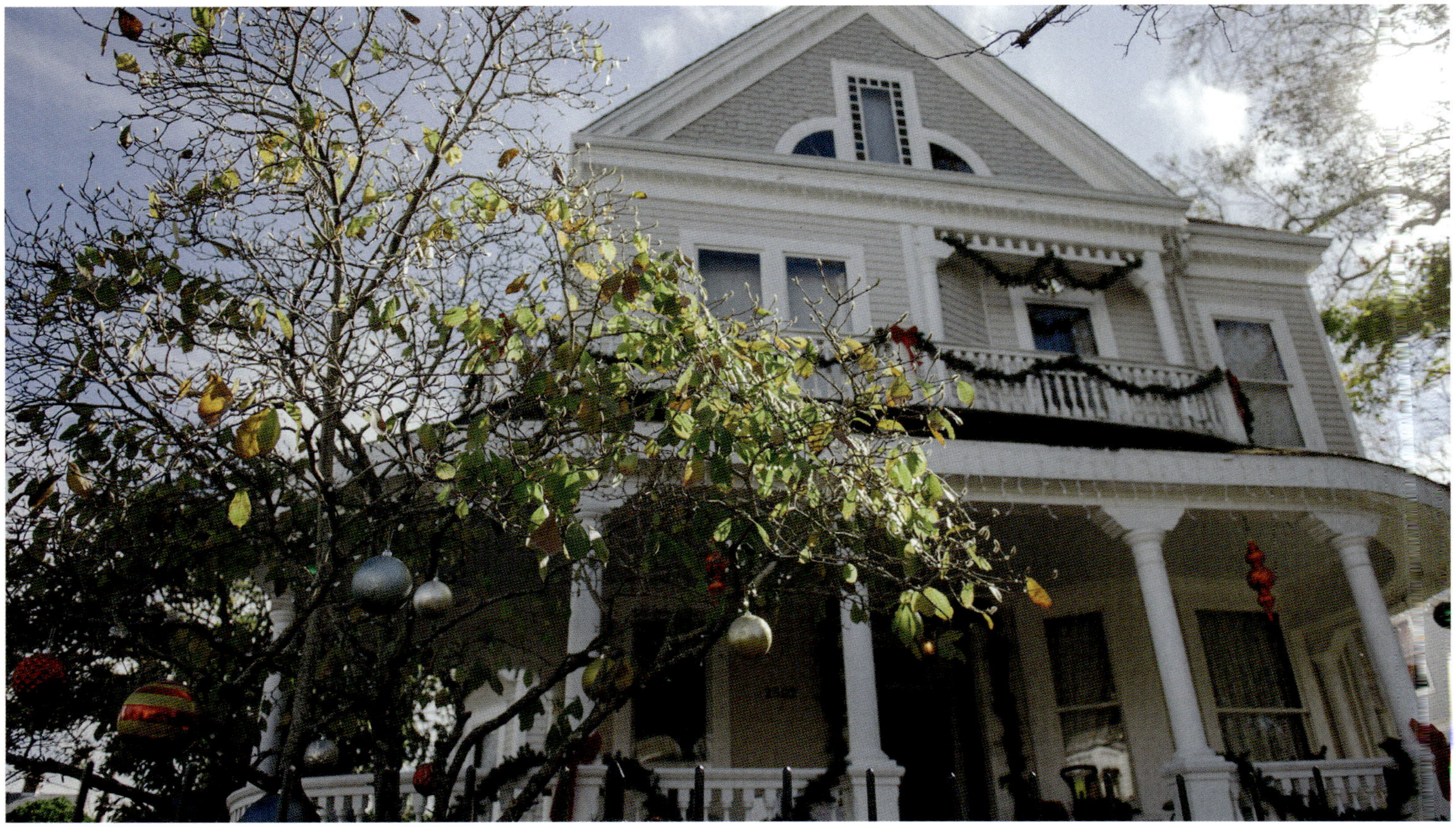

Ghost Manor (decorated for Christmas in this photo), so called for its tradition of eerie Halloween displays.

and Restaurant is a block away at Third and Constance. While Parasol's dates to 1952, there has been a saloon on the site since at least the 1890s. The proximity of these two Irish bars makes ground zero for the annual Irish Channel celebration on March 17, St. Patrick's Day. On that day what seems like a multitude of green-clad revelers fill the one block of Third Street between the two bars.

The holiday is highlighted by the Irish Channel Parade the Saturday before the big day. The parade started as a neighborhood event in 1947 and has grown ever since. In 2017 the parade began way Uptown at Jefferson Avenue and marched strictly along Magazine to Jackson, to the enjoyment of crowds of people mostly dressed in various shades of green. For many people, Irish and not, the parade is an extension of Mardi Gras, which concludes several weeks before St. Patrick's Day.

At Washington Avenue the character of Magazine takes a dramatic shift again, as it abruptly goes from tree-lined residential to blocks of shops. The Discount Zone service station at 2727 Magazine was once the site of the Washington Theater, which was in operation by 1914. It was not in business long, since it burned down in 1937. Diagonally across Magazine and Washington at 2800 stands an 1880s townhouse that almost always has had businesses of various kinds on its ground floor. In the late 1920s it was E.S. Bernadas pharmacy—at the same time Bernadas had a pharmacy on 900 Jefferson at Magazine—but by the late 1940s it had become Henry Toll's Bakery and Confectionary. In the 1970s and '80s it was an auto supply shop. Today it is the trendy, elegant Coquette restaurant—a long way from auto supplies.

The only other examples of late-nineteenth-century houses that remain on the block are at 2842-44 and 2852-58. These are all typical of the small, working-class homes that could be found throughout Magazine. Today, like many old houses on Magazine, they are businesses. Directly across Magazine from these houses is a veteran business, Usner Brothers sheet metal works, which has

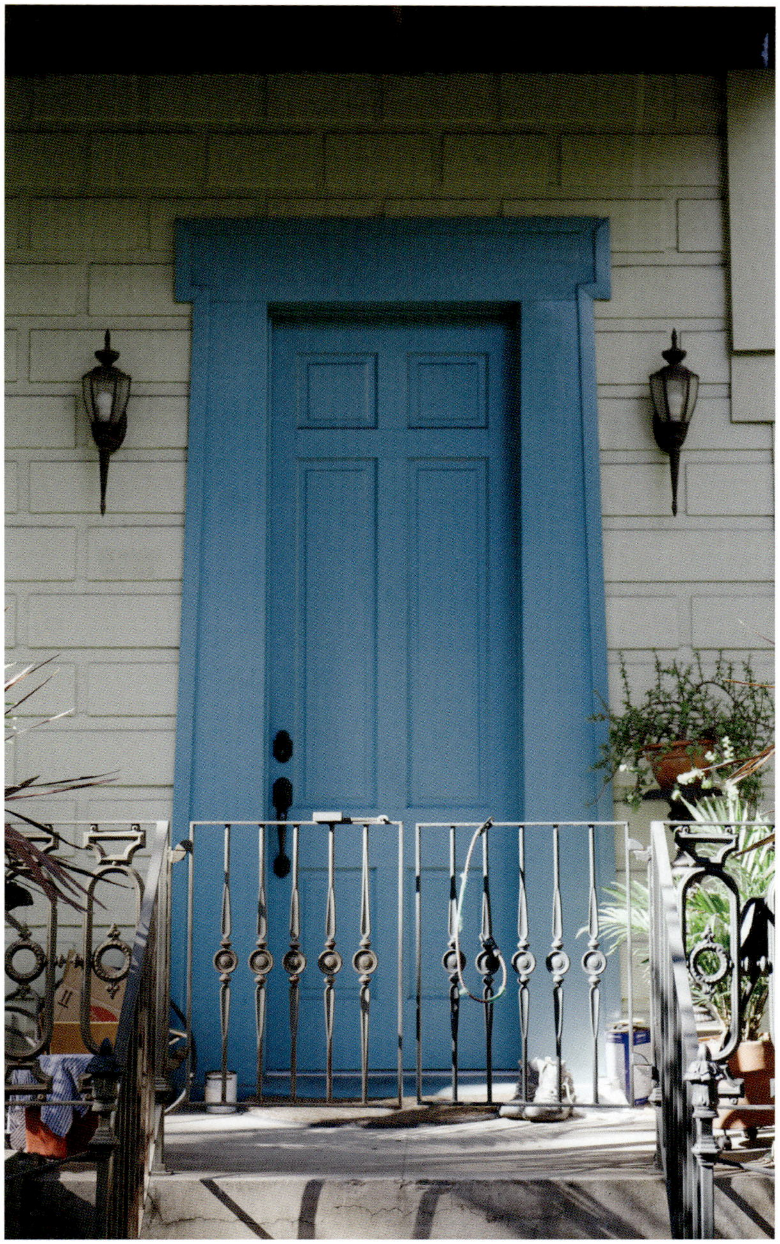

Doorway of the Garden District mansion of world-renowned artists Jeff Gladhart and Rachel Burch Williams.

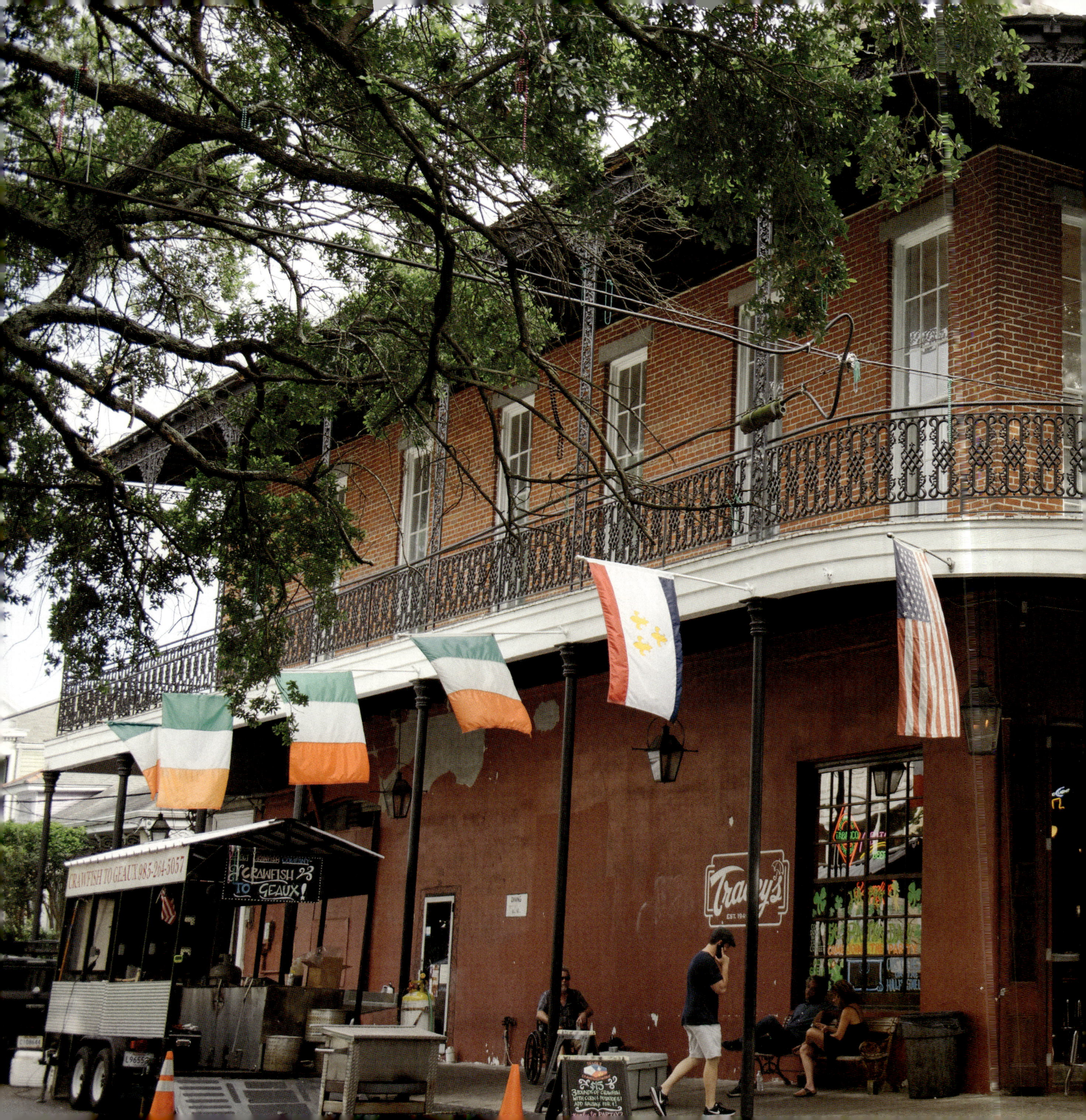
CRAWFISH TO GEAUX 985-264-5057
CRAWFISH TO GEAUX!
Tracey's

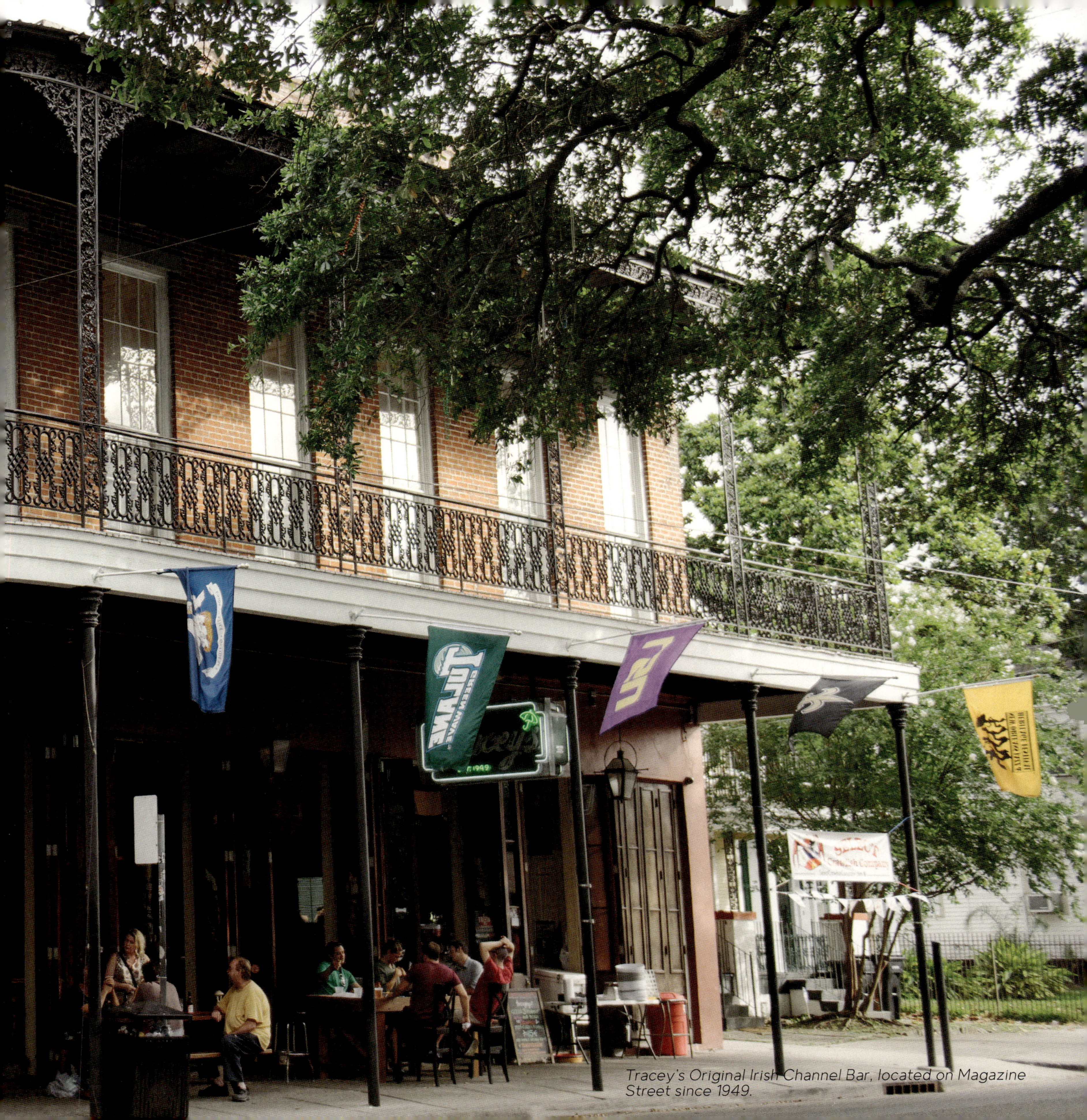

Tracey's Original Irish Channel Bar, located on Magazine Street since 1949.

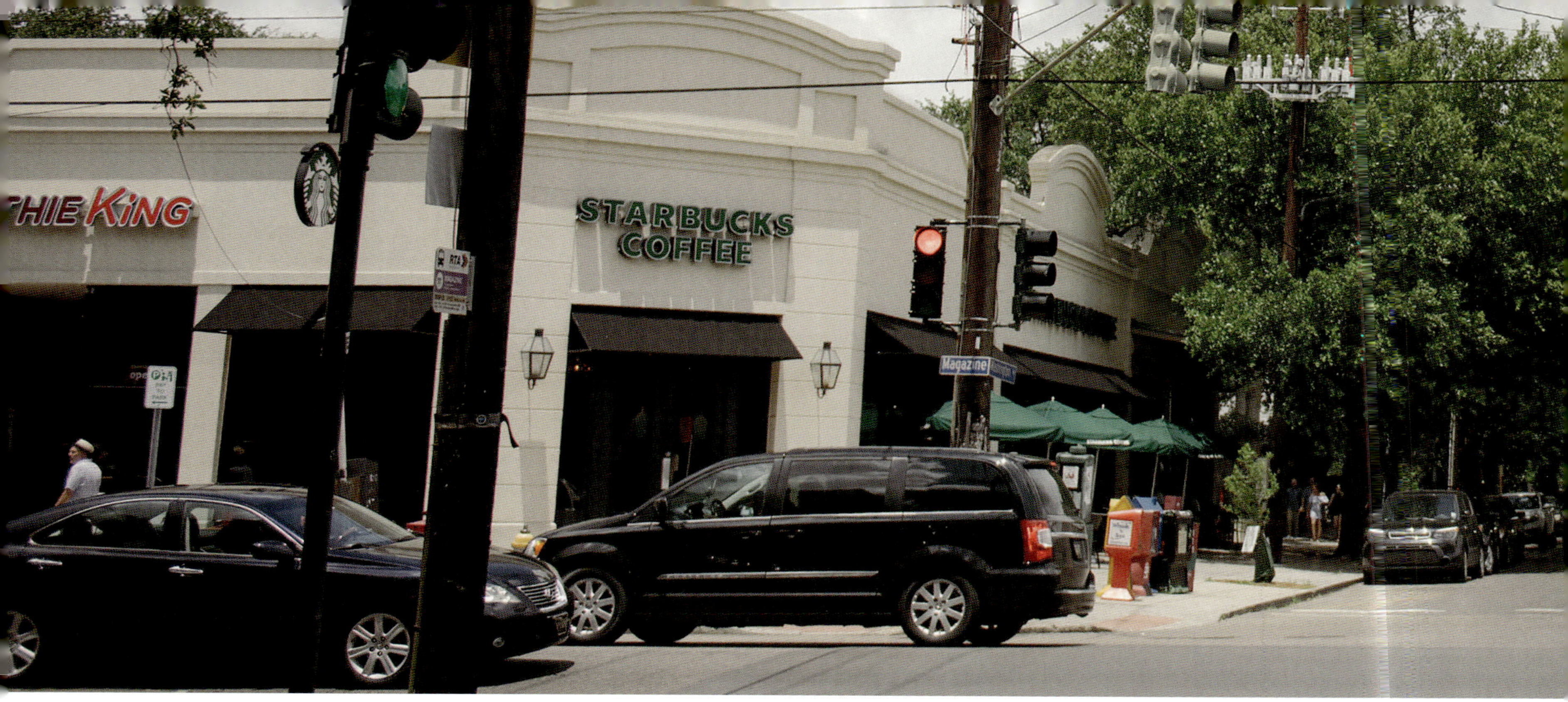

Washington Avenue looking toward the lake from Magazine Street, in the 1850s (bottom photo) and today (top photo) (Courtesy The Historic New Orleans Collection, 1982.32.4.)

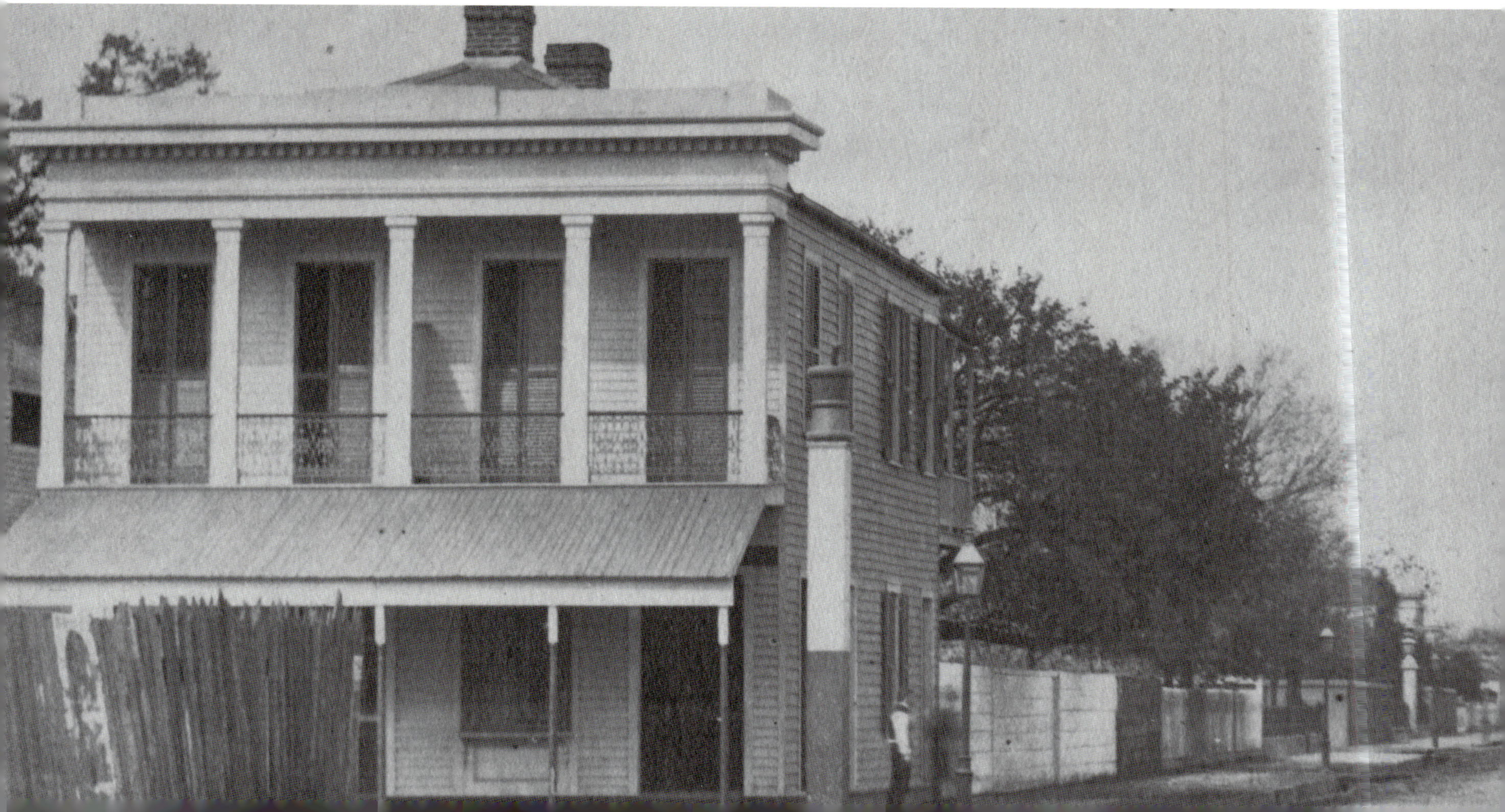

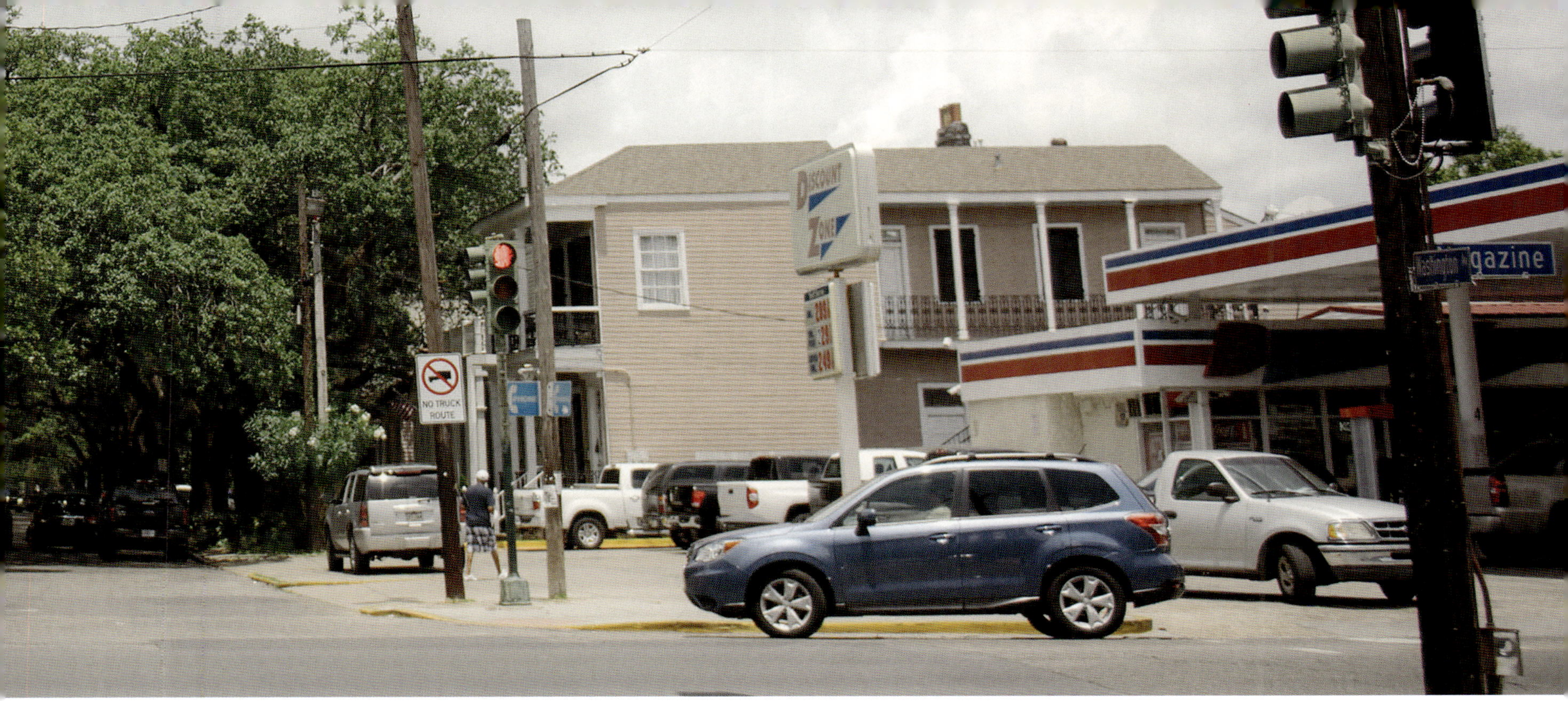
NO TRUCK ROUTE
Discount Zone
Magazine

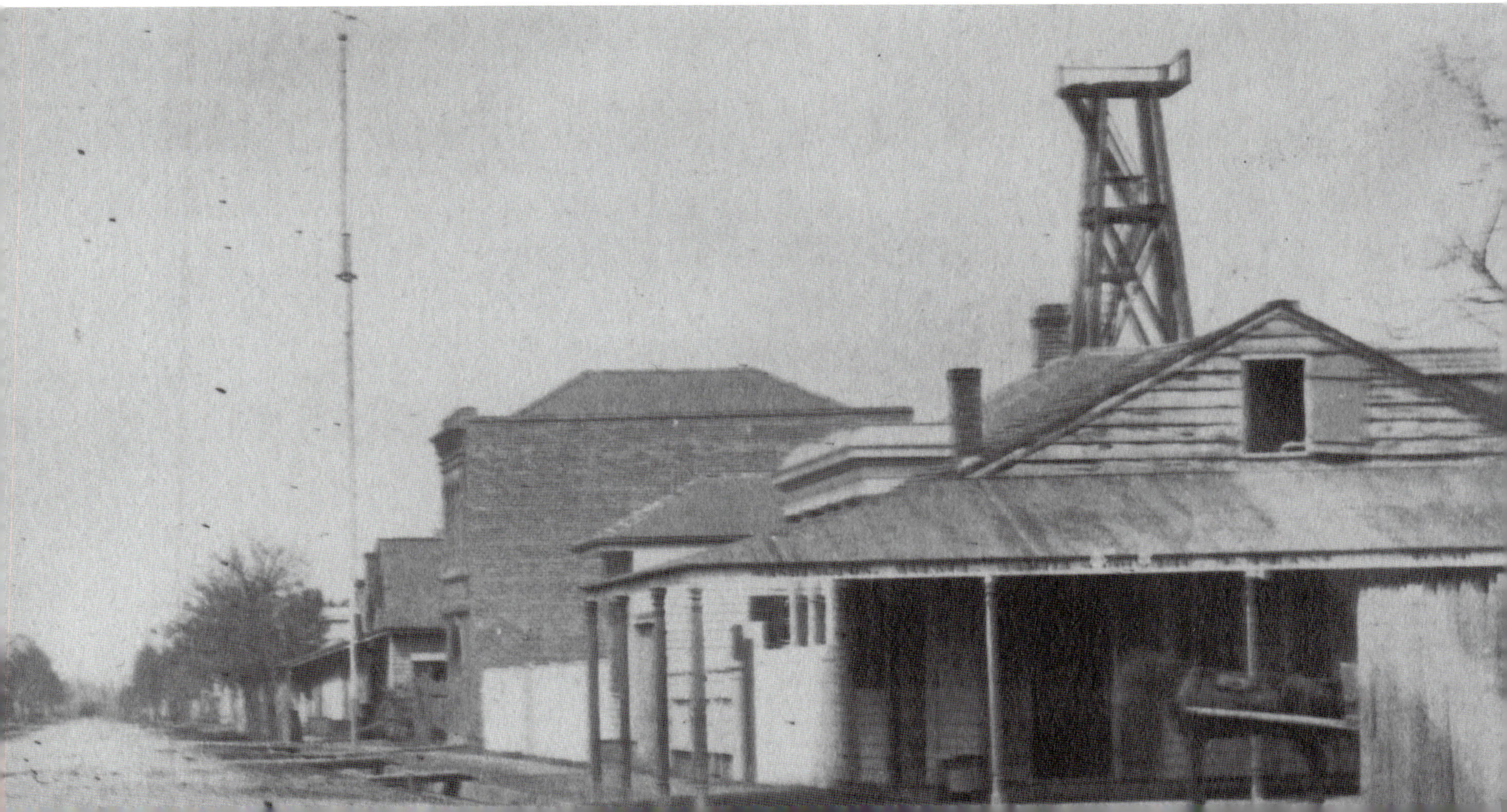

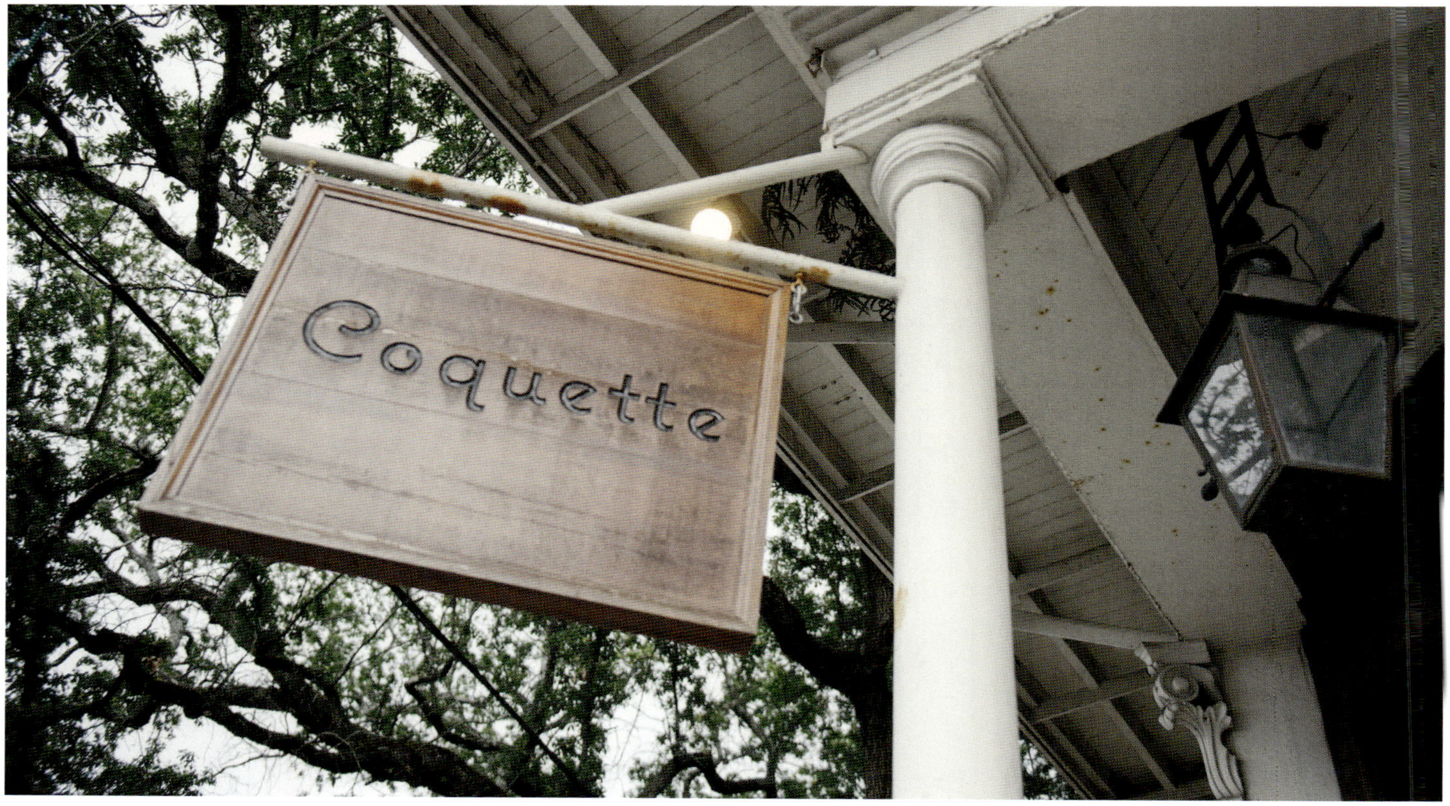

Coquette restaurant, 2800 Magazine Street.

been at 2845 since 1947. Its predecessor on the site was Gulf Galvanizing Metal Works. In Magazine's older days, before the arrival of trendy boutiques, this sort of business was much more common.

Another business representing Magazine's past would have been F.A. Martiny and Son at 2820. Now defunct, but still in existence in 1978, it was described by the *Underground Shopping Guide* as the "answer to the small town feed store. They sell feed and supplies for rabbits, birds, dogs etc." Its site is now the parking lot of Sake Cafe, a Japanese restaurant.

The next block up, between Sixth and Seventh, was once lined with rows of attached frame business buildings with a few houses scattered in between. Typical of early buildings here are the two businesses, Belladonna and GNC, facing

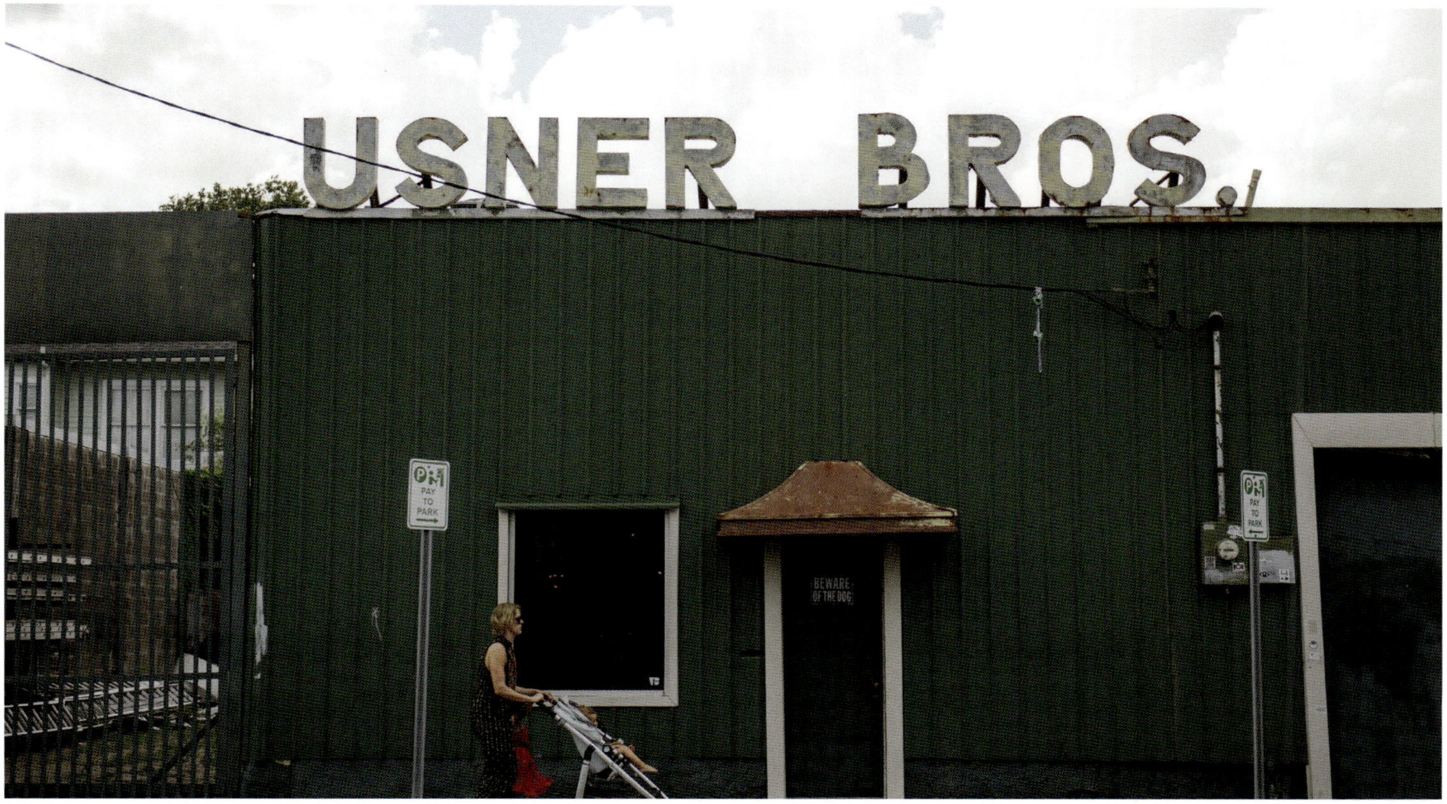

Usner Brothers, a sheet metal contractor since the 1940s (2845 Magazine Street).

each other at the corner of Sixth Street.

Buildings such as these, from the late nineteenth and early twentieth centuries, are very different in appearance from the brick rows of business blocks from the mid-nineteenth century between Jackson and Felicity and show how architectural tastes changed. With some exceptions, such as the restaurants near the corner of Ninth, they lack the ornamental ironwork galleries of earlier business blocks below Jackson. This look continues to Louisiana Avenue, and while it does not necessarily evoke a New Orleans style as in the older commercial area, with the old-fashioned display windows and doorways it offers a glimpse into an earlier age of shopping.

It was around this intersection of Magazine and Sixth that sisters Ann Trice and Kate Robinson recall the shop of Joe

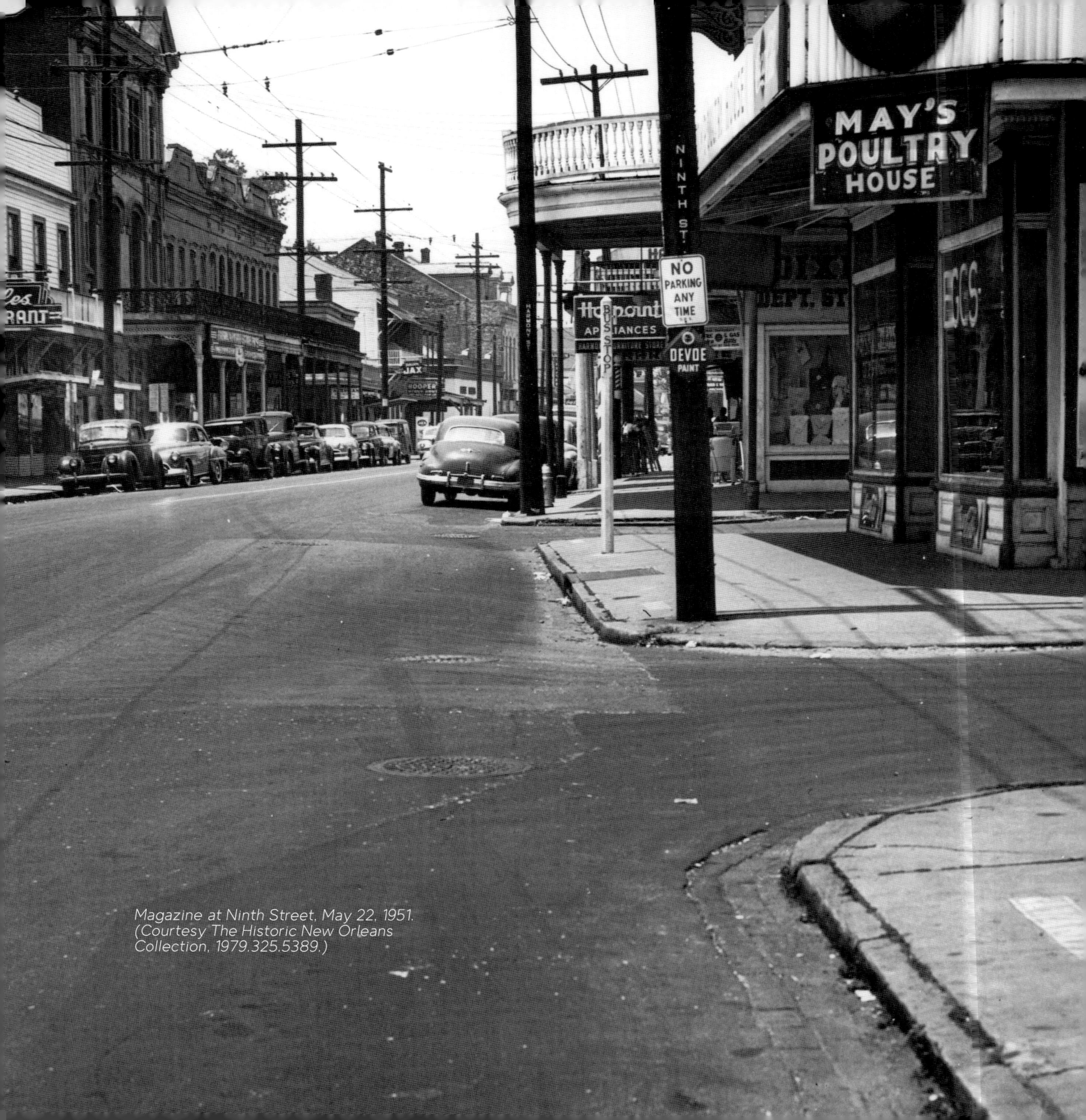

Magazine at Ninth Street, May 22, 1951.
(Courtesy The Historic New Orleans Collection, 1979.325.5389.)

Chapotel in the late 1950s. Chapotel had a furniture restoration shop, and he was a "superb furniture craftsman." His wife also had a small, separate antique store nearby. Chapotel was also a crack shot, having been a World War II sniper. The little girls would often go with their father to Chapotel's shop, and they remembered him as a "real character." He smoked a lot and cursed a lot. Mrs. Robinson said that he taught her every curse word she knows. Their father did not shoot, and Chapotel wanted him to learn how. To encourage this he would take them into the yard behind the shop where Chapotel grew cotton. He would pull out his loaded pistol and shoot the bolls off the cotton plants.

Halfway down this same block, two mid-twentieth-century buildings face each other. On one side is a modern fire station; across the street at 2917 is a former Salvation Army social center and homeless shelter which was in operation in the 1930s. Until the 1990s it served the homeless, but since then this simple building has been converted into an array of shops. An earlier building on this site was the House of Bultman, a prestigious funeral home that eventually moved to St.

Now Gulf Coast Bank & Trust Company, this building has served as a bank for more than a century.

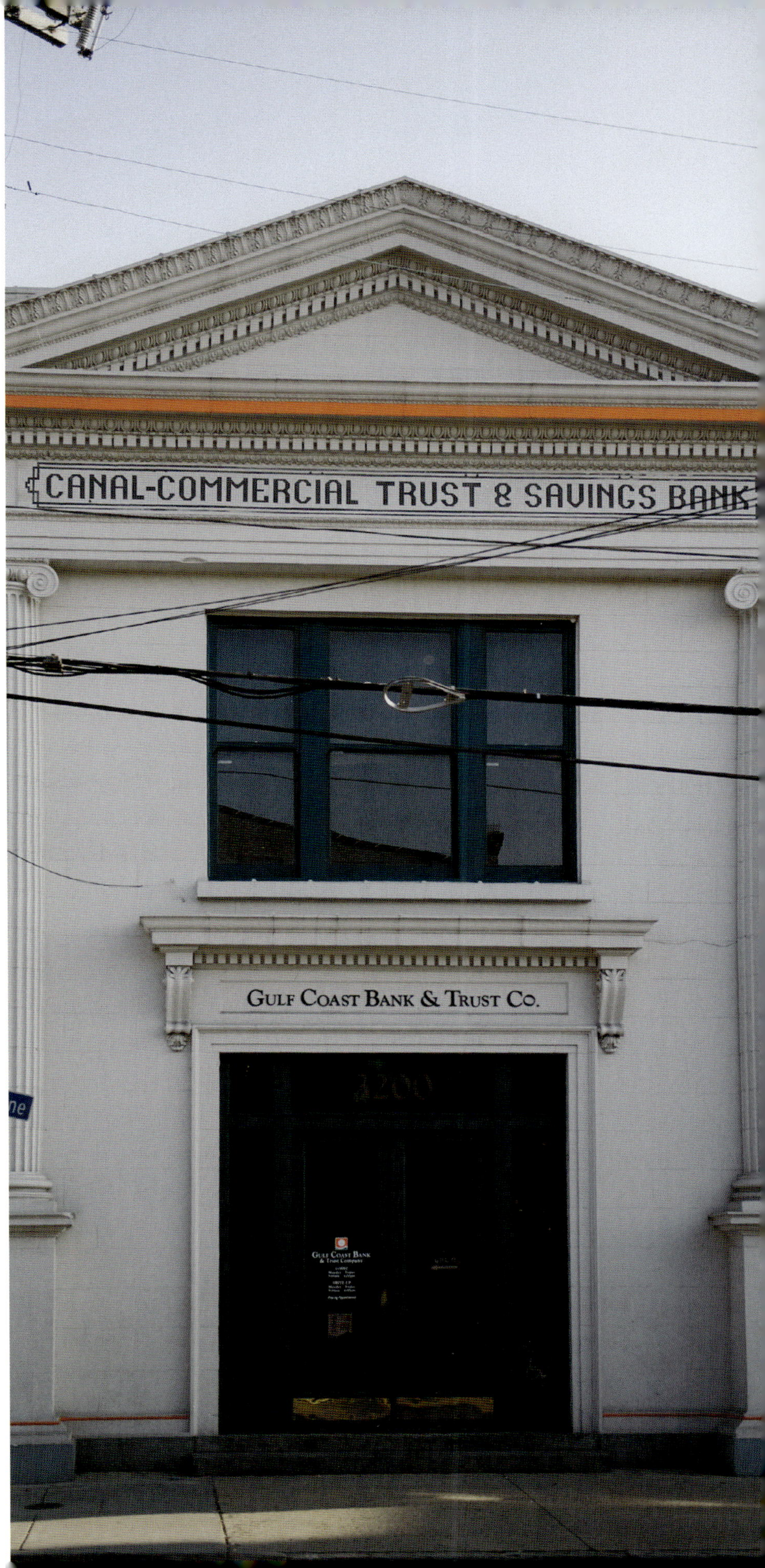

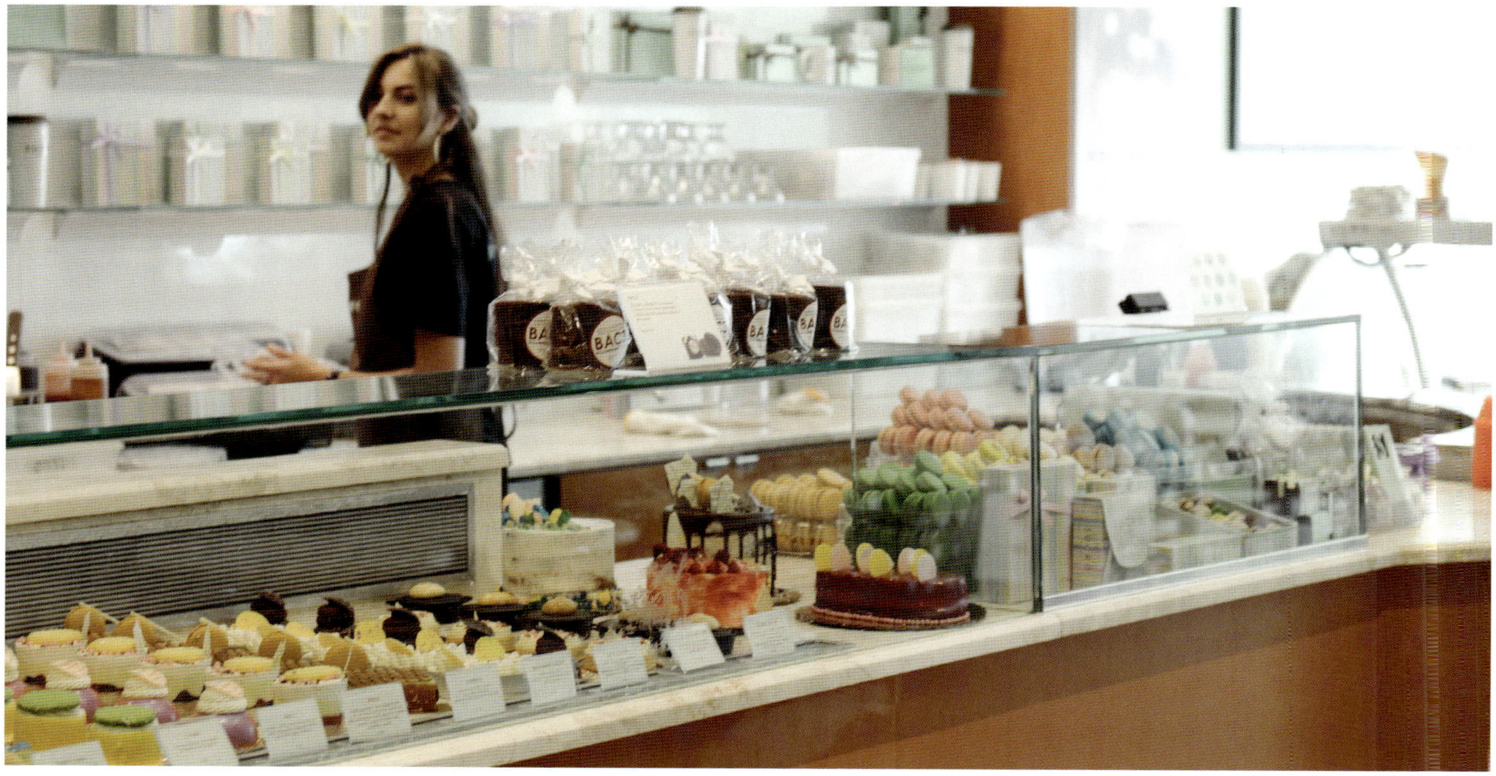

Interior of popular confectioner Sucre (3025 Magazine Street).

Charles at Louisiana but is now out of business.

Facing each other across Magazine at the corner of Seventh are simple mid-twentieth-century buildings that once housed automobile-related businesses, again attesting to the changed retail character of Magazine. A service station now houses West Elm, a decor and furniture dealer at 2929. Across Magazine, an old auto parts store houses NOLA Couture, a Crescent City themed boutique at 2928, and Pippen Lane, a high end children's shop at 2930, started in 1997 by Anna Beth Goodman, the wife of actor John Goodman. Kitty-corner from Pippen Lane is Joey K's, a popular neighborhood restaurant at 3001; this location has housed a restaurant since 1848. A few doors down at 3025 Magazine, is a popular dessert spot called Sucre.

On the river side of Magazine in the 3000 block between Seventh and Eighth are the Orphanage Apartments, whose building fills most of that side of the street. This massive Romanesque Revival-style structure was built as the St. John's Protestant Orphans' Home in the late 1880s and remained an orphanage until 1972.

The other side of the street is lined with an array of shops and restaurants and the oldest business name on Magazine is here. H. Rault Locksmiths was founded as a gunsmith's shop in 1845 by French immigrant Joseph Rault. Originally located in the French Quarter, Rault moved his business to Magazine in the 1850s. Here his son Henri learned to be a locksmith and later renamed the business H. Rault. While the business has had several locations on Magazine, including 3013

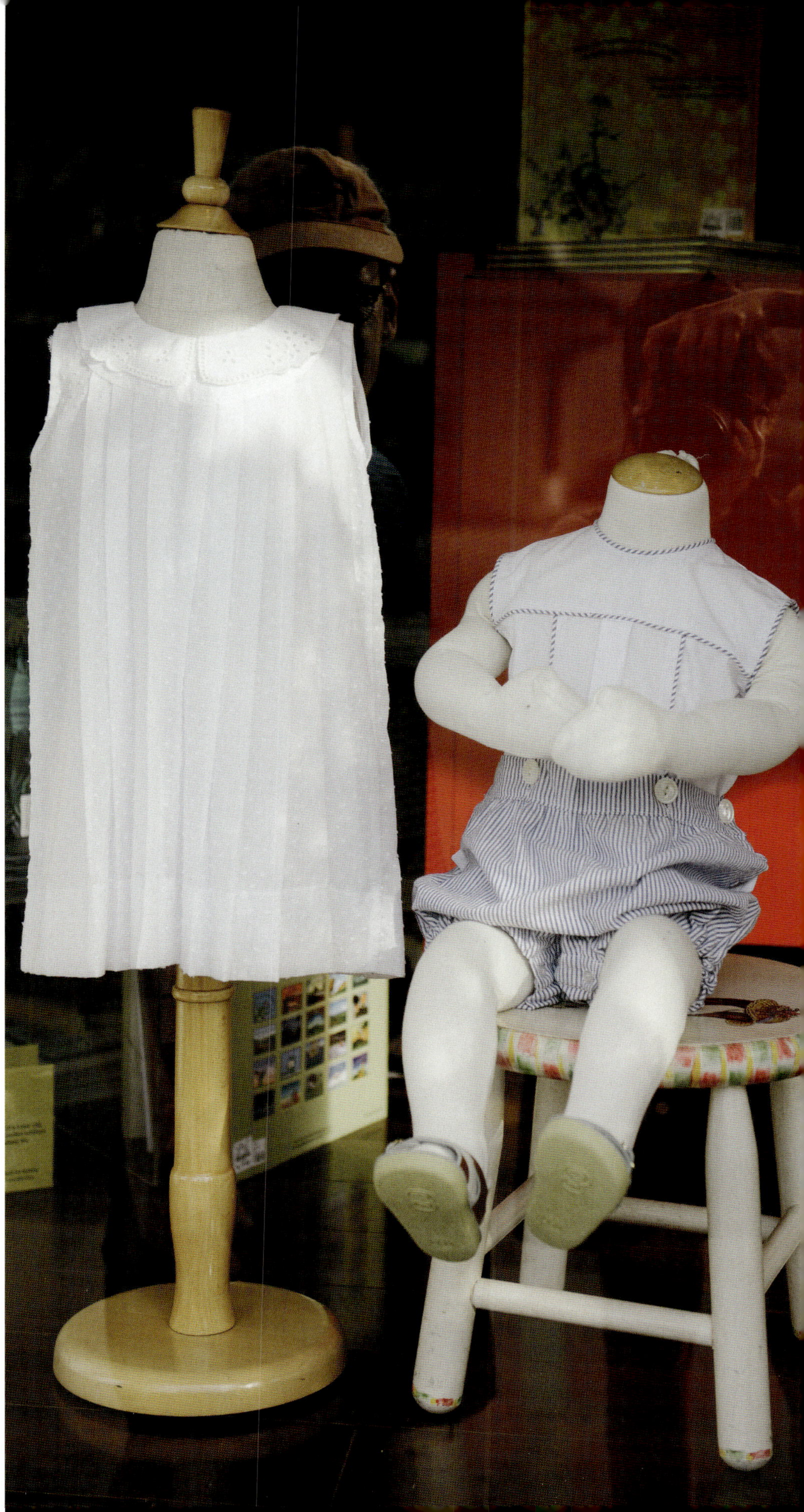

Window display at Pippen Lane (2207 Magazine Street).

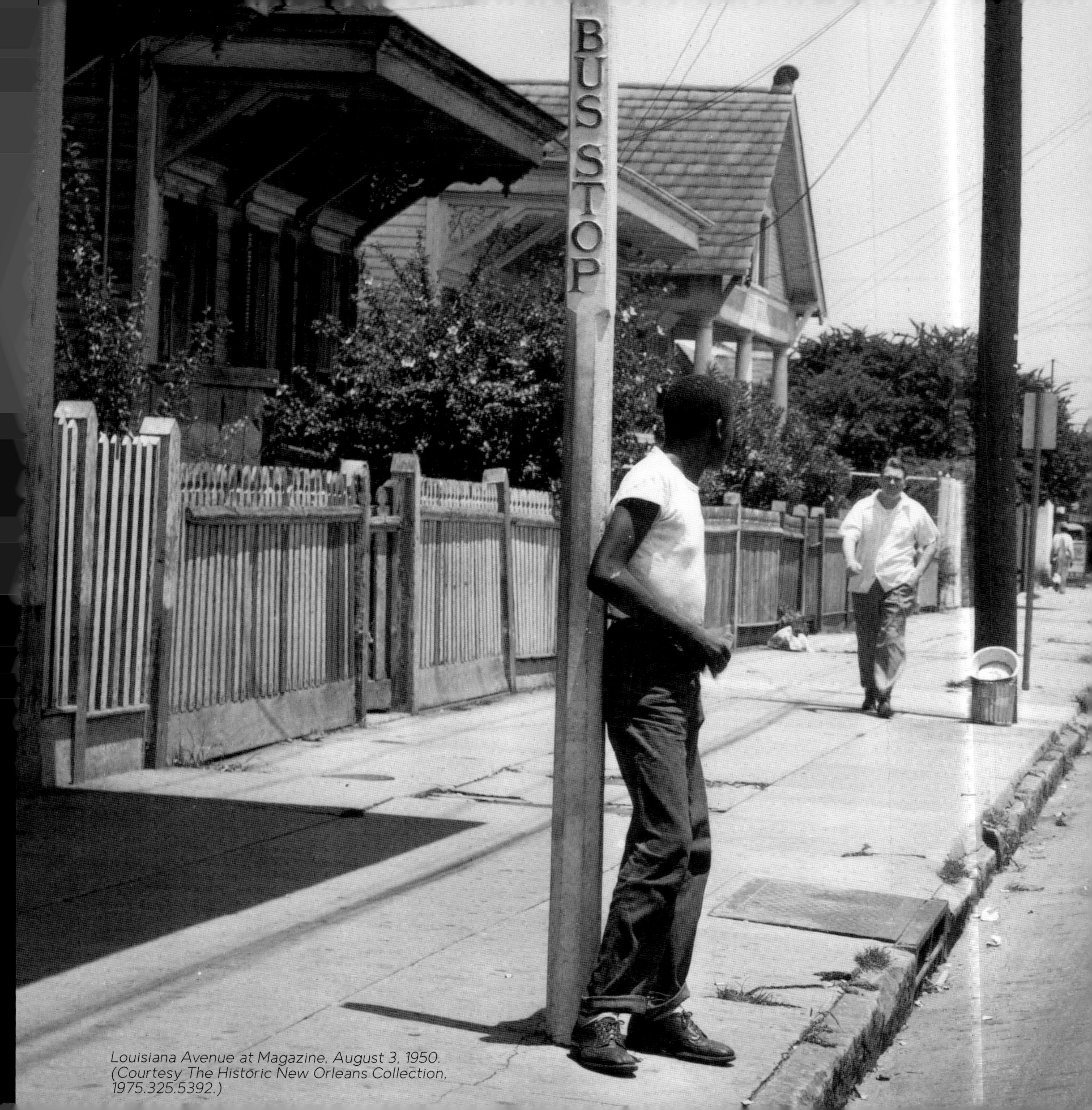

Louisiana Avenue at Magazine, August 3, 1950.
(Courtesy The Historic New Orleans Collection, 1975.325.5392.)

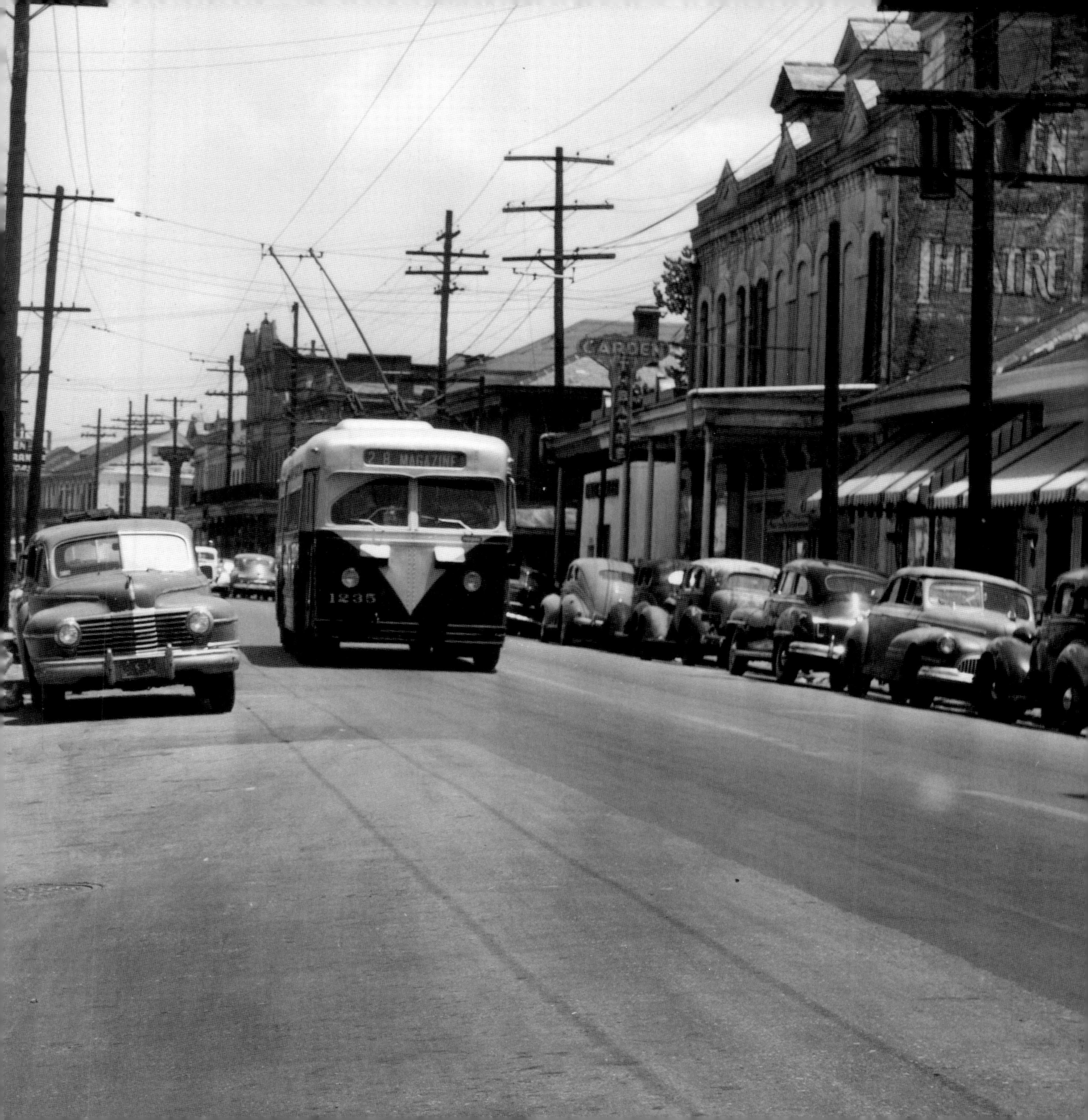
28 MAGAZINE
1235
GARDEN
THEATRE

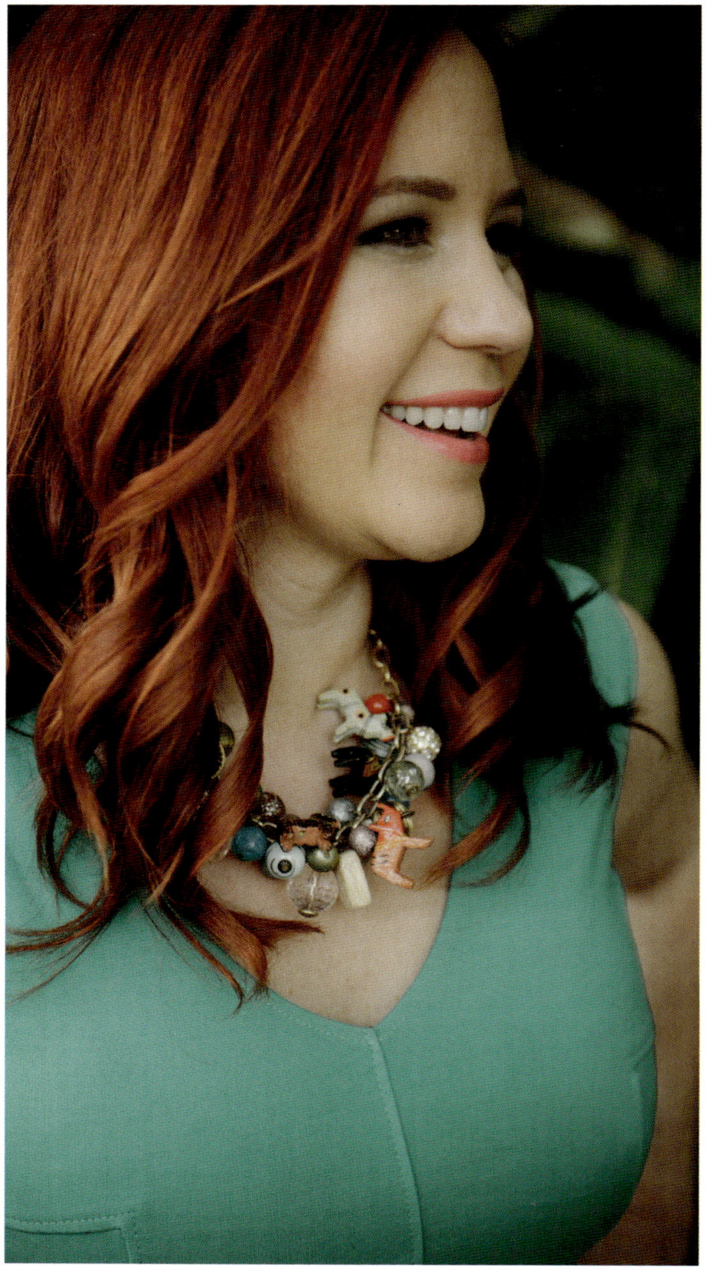

Lauren Haydel, aka "Fleurty Girl."

which is now Cella's Boutique women's store, in 1926 it moved to the current location at 3027.

At 3017 Magazine, Antique Mall is an arcade containing an array of mini shops, but in the '40s the building housed an A&P supermarket. At that time other stores on this block reflected the functional nature of most Magazine business. In the block along with H. Rault and A&P there were also a laundry, a beauty shop, a pharmacy, and a liquor store. Today the businesses tend toward trendy and upscale, ranging from ladies' shops and a silver store to a candy shop and a couple of restaurants.

Fleurty Girl is at 3117. Owned by Lauren Haydel—married to Ryan Haydel of the popular Haydel's Bakery in Jefferson Parish—Fleurty Girl originated in the owner's former home on Oak Street in 2009. It "took off way bigger" than she expected, and that same year she was able to move to Magazine Street and ultimately close the Oak location. She saw it as a good omen that the New Orleans Saints beat the Indianapolis Colts in Super Bowl XLIV on February 7, 2010, by a score of 31 to 17. The final score matches Fleurty Girl's address, and the

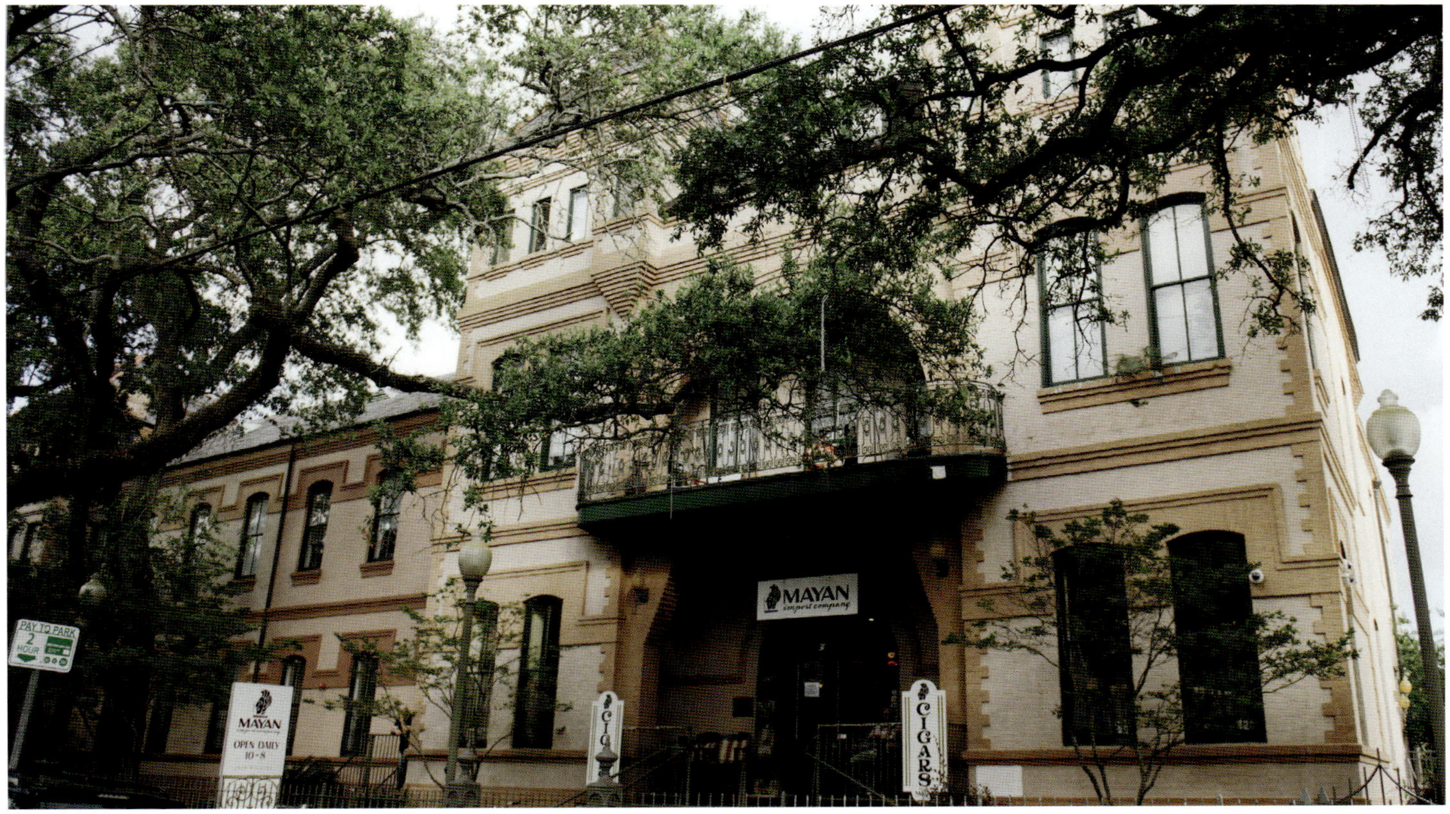

The Orphanage Apartments, formerly St. John's Protestant Orphans Home.

numbers have been good luck ever since.

Initially Fleurty Girl sold women's tee shirts with locally inspired designs, but the store has expanded to include clothing accessories, home decor items, and a wide array of locally inspired gifts. The store motto is "Curated Southern Goods," because from the start it specialized in locally made merchandise and "unexpected things." Haydel wants customers to feel that coming into the store is "an experience." Even though Fleurty Girl has expanded to five stores, the experience for customers on Magazine is indeed different. Both tourists and locals sometimes stroll in with a drink in hand from a nearby restaurant or bar, something "you can't do everywhere," Haydel quips.

Although the space on Magazine is "challenging," she says, because of the

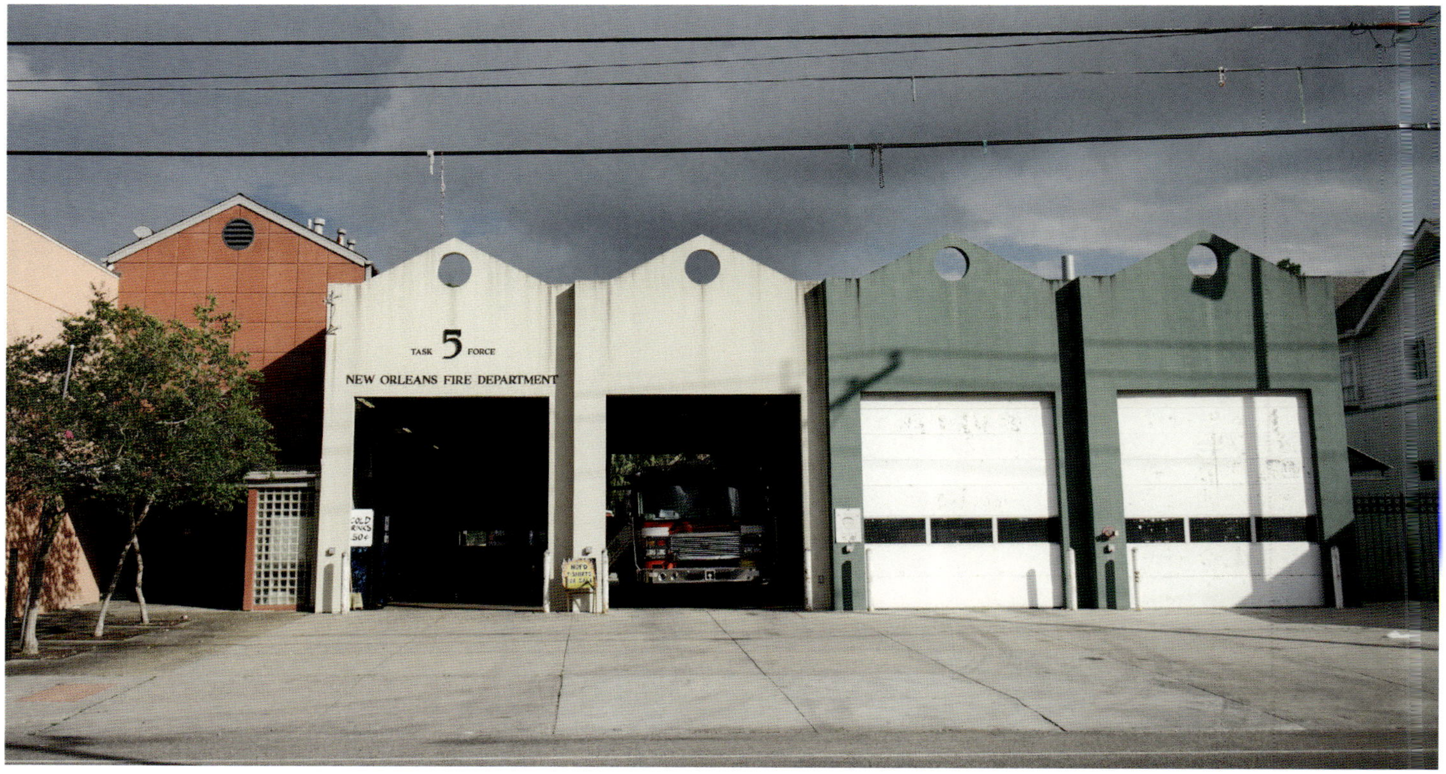

New Orleans Fire Department Squrt 1 (Engine 1), at 2920 Magazine.

limitations of the old buildings, "character is built into Magazine Street." Mrs. Haydel reflects that Magazine is "so special and so unique . . . We're lucky to have it."

Between Ninth and Harmony at 3138 is the former Ninth Street Market, a commercial anchor and the source of the business development along this stretch of Magazine Street. The market was established in the 1850s to serve this fast-growing neighborhood, and as with all New Orleans public markets, it was an open-air structure with rows of stalls and an overhang protecting the sidewalk from sun and rain. It was rebuilt along with other markets in the early 1930s. Like the Magazine Market, it survived only into the mid-twentieth century before being sold for redevelopment.

Where Breaux Mart now stands at 3233,

between Pleasant and Toledano, was once the depot for the New Orleans City Railroad. Across Pleasant Street, where Walgreens is located, was the stable for the mules that pulled the streetcars—the only streetcar locomotion until the 1890s. City Railroad entered service in 1861, the same year the depot opened, and was electrified in 1895. The barn remained in use as a streetcar barn until 1903 when it was redeveloped as the main repair shop for all city streetcar lines. It was closed in 1915, demolished many years later, and replaced by the supermarket, then an A&P, in 1969.

The City Railroad at first traveled up Camp from Canal to the depot, then used Magazine for the return trip. In 1883 the line was expanded to include Laurel Street to Audubon Park, returning on Magazine. Beginning in 1898 new electric streetcars traveled toward Canal on Camp and returned Uptown on Magazine. Other streetcar lines included Magazine Street in their routes as well. The Jefferson City Railroad, established in 1864, followed Magazine from Toledano to Joseph through what was then the separate suburb of Jefferson City. This rail company merged with the Crescent City Railroad in the 1880s and inaugurated service from Canal along Chestnut and Camp, switching over to Magazine until the end of the line at Audubon Park. By 1920 one streetcar line was established along Magazine, and its route was the same as today's Regional Transit Authority Magazine Street bus line. There was a double row of tracks along Magazine until their removal in 1948 for new trolleybuses.

Three large buildings across the street from Walgreens, between 3218 and 3244, all date from before 1880. These handsome brick buildings are among the finest and most substantial early commercial buildings along this part of Magazine Street. They appear more solid than the mostly frame buildings elsewhere along this stretch. In 1948 they housed a series of businesses including general merchandise, cleaners, and a drugstore; they now house a trio of restaurants.

Libby Bonner recalls an antique shop in this block in the mid-1980s where she saw hidden away in the back a large and nearly complete set of Johnson Brothers English dinnerware. When she enquired about it, the proprietor responded, "That ugly stuff—you

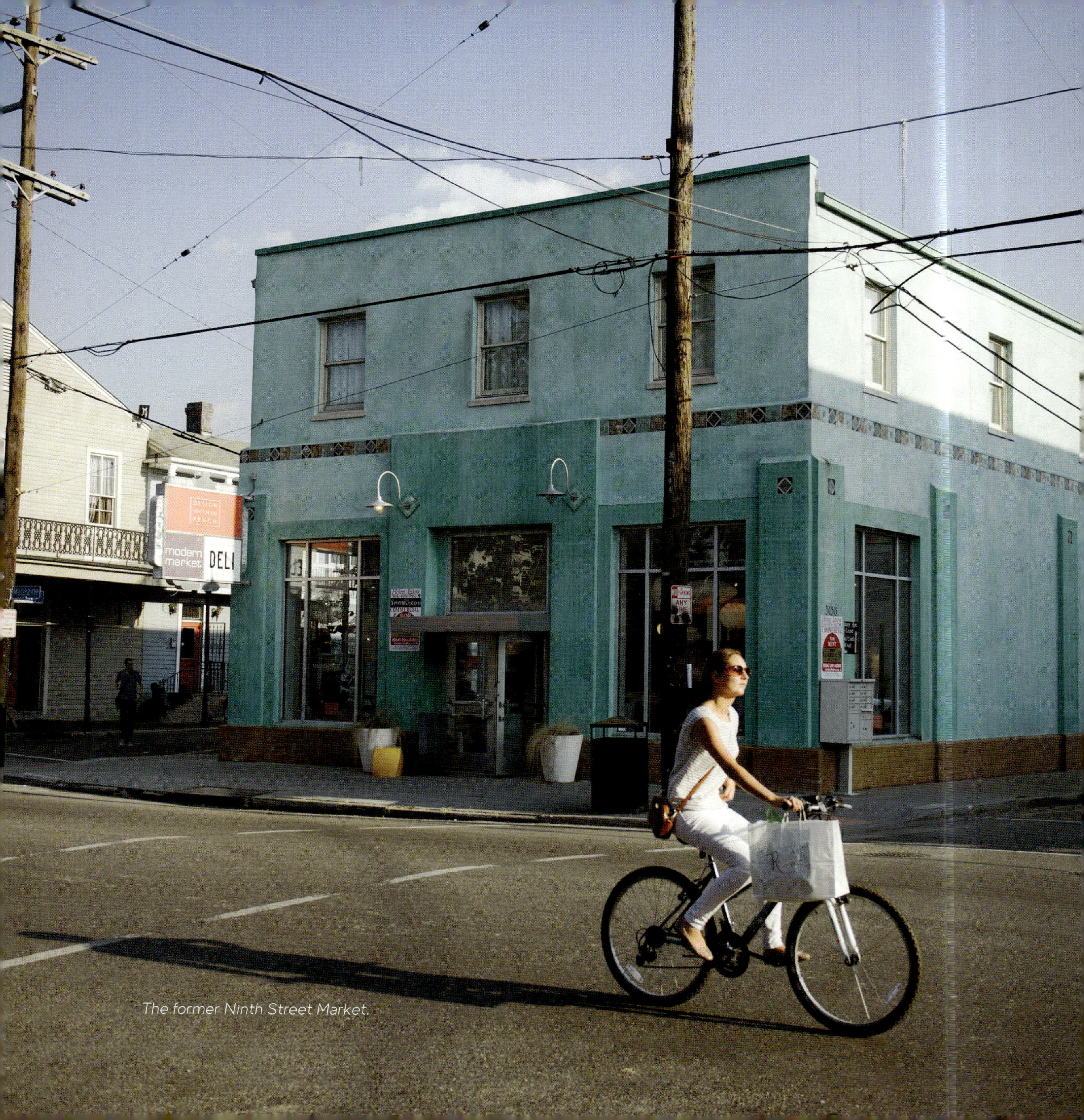

The former Ninth Street Market.

can have it for twenty dollars." Mrs. Bonner said that she "skipped out" with her buy, and she still uses it in her Northshore home.

The next block up a millworks and auto repair shop convey the feel of Magazine in the mid-twentieth century, while several shotgun houses, now shops with new storefronts, are typical of the street in its more residential days. Across the street, the building on the corner at 3300, now Smashburger, looks fairly modern, but its roots date to the 1890s. The large building next door was built in 1894, and while now all retail, 3312 Magazine once contained the Garden Theater. In 1914 the Garden opened as the United States Theater but changed its name in 1917. It shifted to Spanish-language pictures in 1959, finally closing in 1965 to be converted to retail use. Several people remembered when Edward Fuhr's Bakery was at 3336 in the 1940s and '50s, recalling that "the best doughnuts were sold" there. Dat Dog hot dog restaurant is at this address now.

John Van Vranken was the owner of a barroom and liquor store at the corner of Louisiana. The bar is gone and is now the parking lot for a condominium building facing Louisiana where Stan Levy Antiques was located in the 1970s and '80s. In a 1948 interview, Van Vranken estimated that the bar had been around for almost 100 years. Although Van Vranken's age was not provided, he said that, "when I was a kid all the business was on Tchoupitoulas Street . . . But a new interest was born in Magazine when the Magazine Market was back. It drew both people and business back to Magazine."

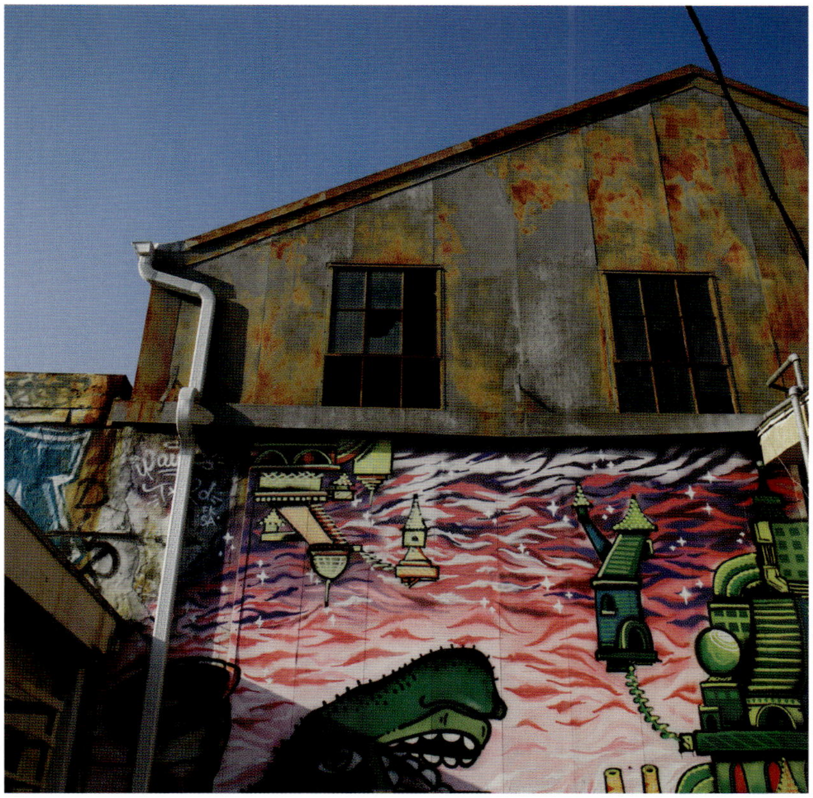

Magazine is not all high fashion.

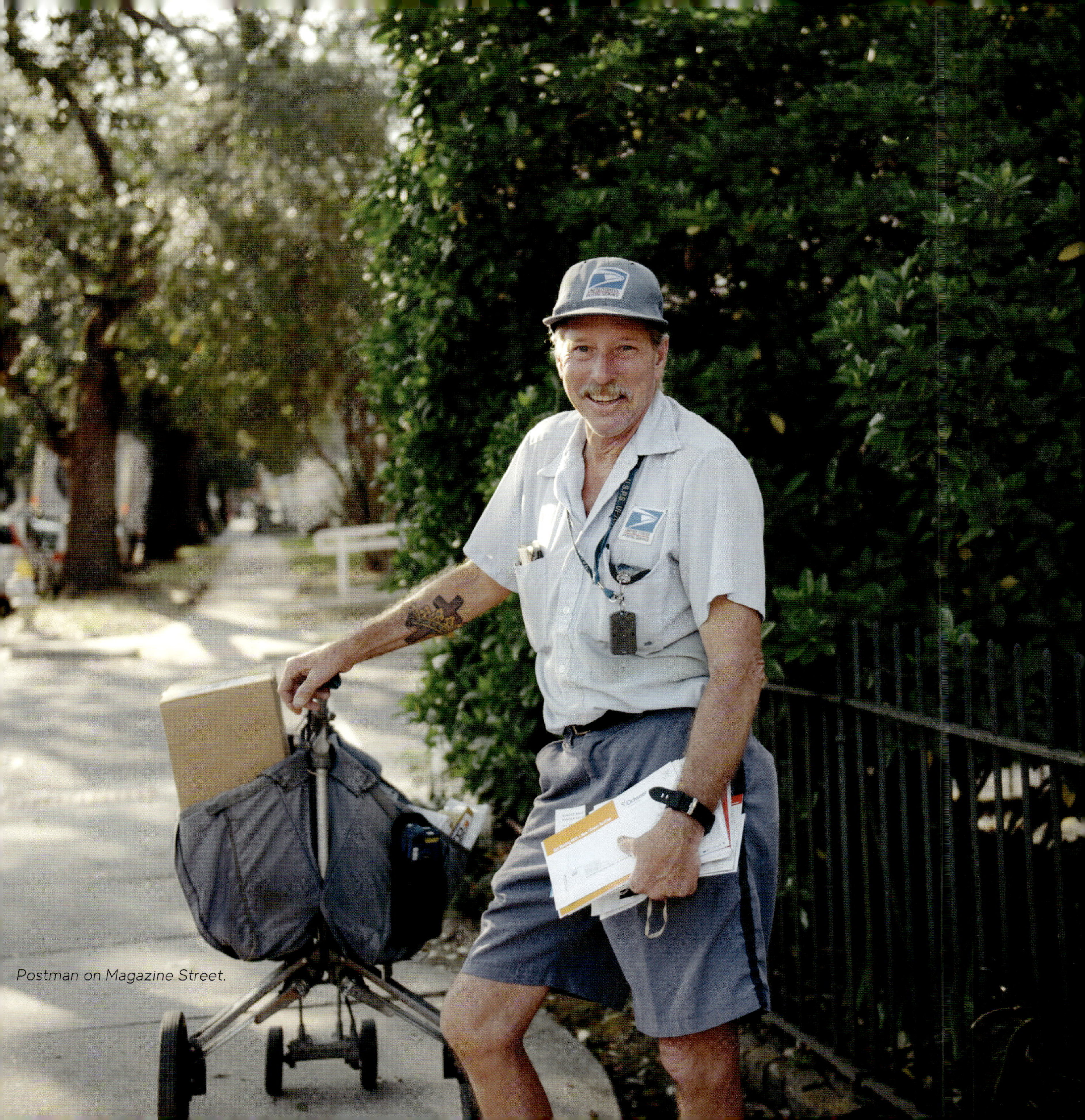

Postman on Magazine Street.

Chapter Six

Louisiana Avenue to Napoleon Avenue

Beyond Louisiana Avenue, Magazine Street takes on a decidedly residential appearance, recalling when this section was mostly homes prior to the 1970s. Now it is heavily retail with many businesses located in what used to be dwellings. As with earlier Uptown neighborhoods, this section was also created from a series of plantations, and Magazine Street continued to grow as the most important commercial link in the Uptown grid.

Immediately above the former City of Lafayette was a plantation acquired by Joseph Wiltz in 1800. He had Jean Hyacinthe LaClotte subdivide his tract in 1807 and called it Faubourg Plaisance, or "pleasure" in English. Bounded by Toledano and Delachaise, its main street was called Grande Cours Wiltz, later renamed Louisiana Avenue. Above here the land extending to

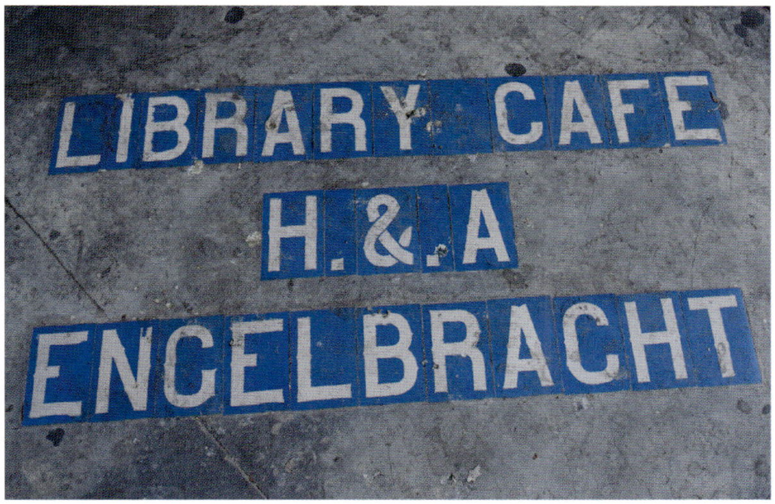

Sidewalk tiles in front of Ms. Mae's The Club identify the former business at that location.

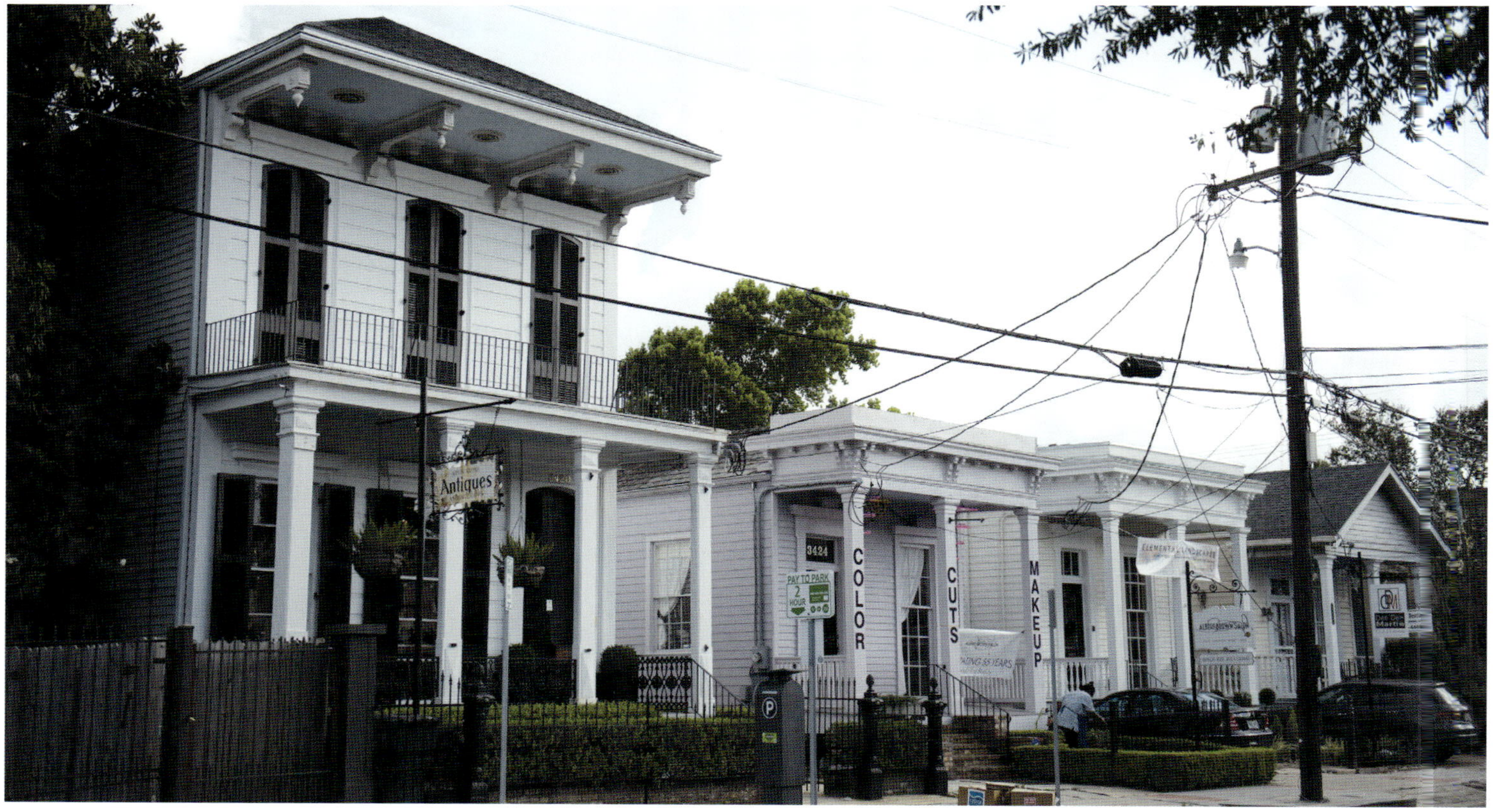

Homes dating from the 1860s and '70s have been turned into shops in the 3400 block of Magazine.

Amelia belonged to the heirs of Philippe Delachaise, who had his plantation subdivided in 1855 as Faubourg Delachaise. Faubourg St. Joseph reached General Taylor Street and was subdivided by Benjamin Buisson in 1849 at the request of the widow of Louis Avart.

Louis Bouligny owned a large plantation extending from General Taylor to Upperline Street. He sold half of it to Samuel Kohn and Laurent Millaudon in 1831 and three years later the properties were subdivided by Charles Zimpel, who was one of the builders of the New Orleans and Carrollton Rail Road Company, chartered in 1835. This subdivision was prompted by the growth that the railroad was expected to generate. The plantation was divided in two by Napoleon Avenue and the separate sides of the faubourg were called East and

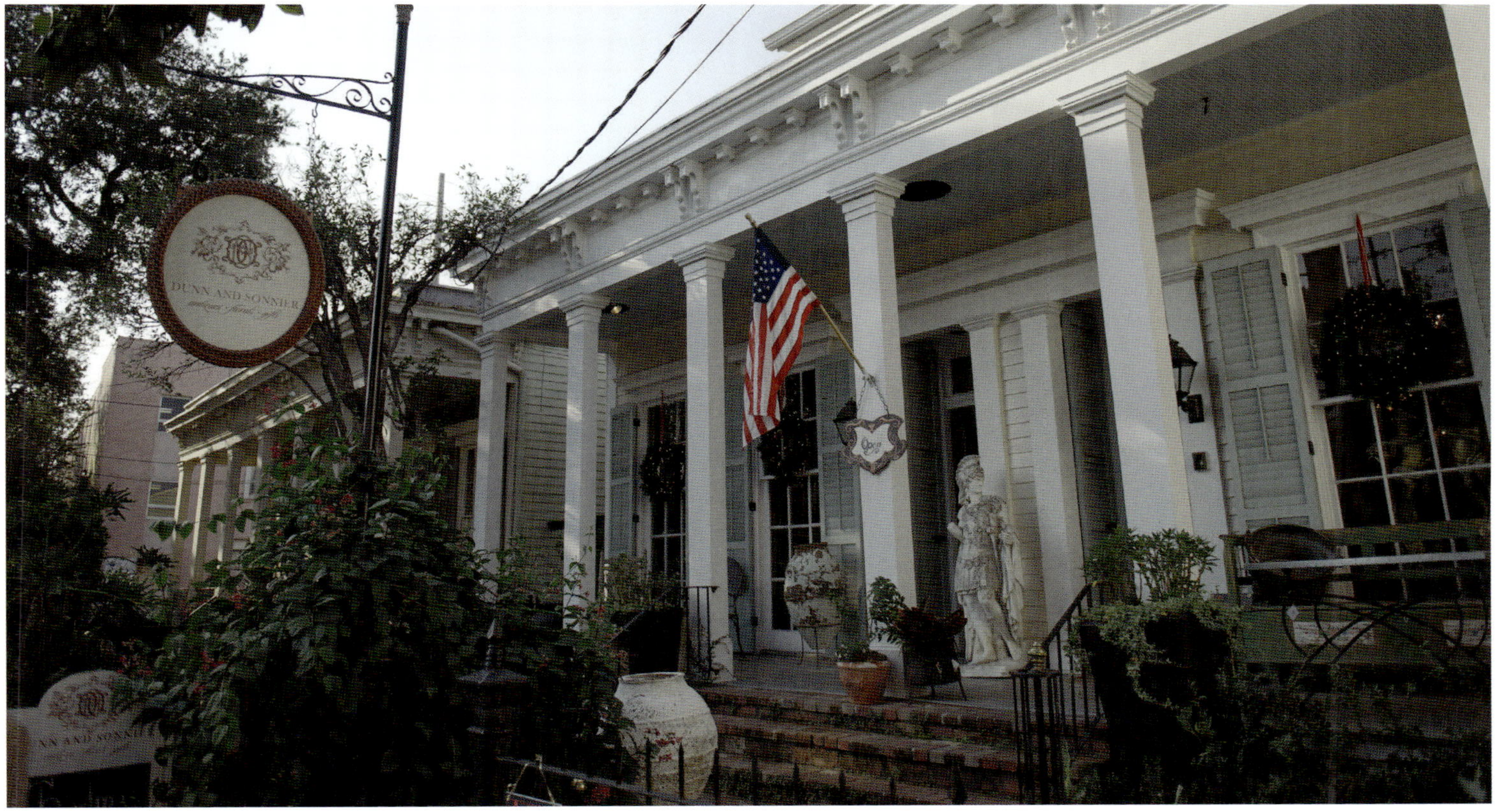

Dunn and Sonnier antiques and interiors, 3433-3439 Magazine Street.

West Bouligny. The original plan included Laurence Square—sometimes shown as Lawrence Square—at the intersection of Magazine and Napoleon and was named for Laurent Millaudon.

Extending from Upperline Street to Valmont was the property of Francois Robert Avart, who had it subdivided in 1841 by H. Maulhauser as Faubourg Avart. Adjoining this and up to Joseph Street was a property owned by several investors, including the City Bank of New Orleans and Samuel Ricker, Jr. It was subdivided by Buisson in 1849 and named Rickerville. The main street of Rickerville was Peters, renamed Jefferson Avenue in the 1920s. Old blue-on-white tile street markers can still be found throughout older sections of New Orleans, and in the case of Jefferson Avenue, they still spell out the street's original name.

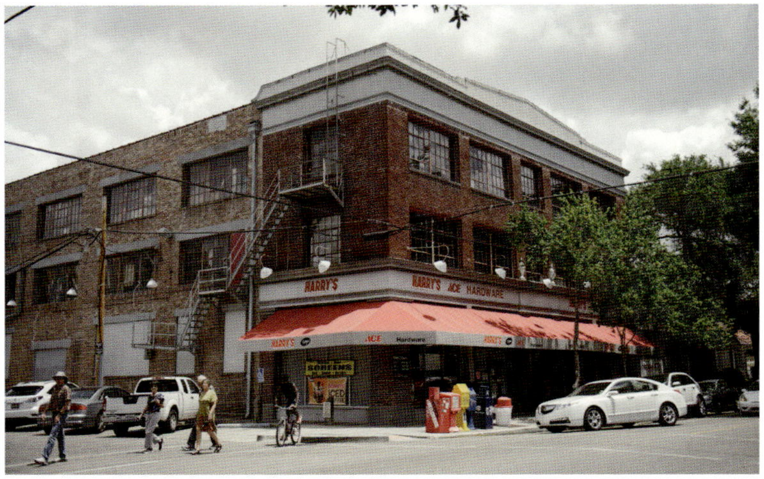

Harry's Ace Hardware, formerly a car dealership, then a bakery.

In 1846 the area between the upper limit of the City of Lafayette at Toledano to what became Audubon Park was incorporated as the town of Free Port. In 1850, Free Port lost its status and was reincorporated as Jefferson City, which extended from Toledano to Joseph Street. Midway between the Mississippi River and the St. Charles railroad, Magazine quite naturally became the main street of Jefferson City.

In a highly controversial move unpopular with its residents, Jefferson City was annexed into New Orleans in 1870. This occurred during the violently charged political and racial climate of post-Civil War Reconstruction (1865-1877), when the Louisiana state legislature, based in New Orleans during Reconstruction, forced the annexation. Previously the town had had its own mayor, council, courts, market, and schools, but with annexation it lost control of these.

From the 1850s until the end of the century, Jefferson City was the fastest-growing section of New Orleans. From a few scattered households in 1850, it grew to a population of 5,107 in 1860. Ten years later it exceeded 25,000. In the 1870s it was still a big, spread-out neighborhood marked by large stands of trees, but by the end of the nineteenth century it had become a well-developed part of the city.

Prior to the 1870s, Louisiana Avenue marked the end of the heavily built city. Above this, Magazine was similar to a country road, marked mostly by scattered cottages and double houses. They would become much more prevalent by the 1880s. Houses were interspersed with some businesses; during this pre-automobile age they were not only welcome additions to serve the neighborhood's needs but also gathering places within walking distance of home.

The *Daily States* of July 8, 1948,

interviewed Waverly Greathouse, who was aged eighty-two and lived at 3421 Magazine—now site of the House of Flowers and Gifts—in a house that had been built in 1883. He recalled that in the 1870s his family had lived much farther up Magazine in a house that was then the only one on the block. He remembered Magazine above Louisiana as being all mud until 1882, when wooden planks were laid crosswise on top of the mud, and horse-drawn trolleys ran down the middle of the street. He added that the gutters remained mud. His section above Louisiana, he said, began to build up commercially about 1878, but "At that time the Magazine Market was the only business in the area." Lamplighters, he recalled, turned off the gas lamps if a full moon came out. Then about 1913, he said, the gas lamps were replaced by electric streetlights.

Several early residential buildings can be found in the blocks of Magazine above Louisiana, attesting to the growth in the area during the 1860s and '70s. The house at 3420, across the street from where Waverly Greathouse lived, has the appearance of the 1870s, while next door, at 3424 and 3426, small, matching shotgun houses with classical columns and Italianate ornamentation date from the late 1860s. These buildings are now all shops. Across Magazine at 3433-35 and 3437-39, on the corner of Delachaise, are two elegant, nearly identical Greek and Italianate structures dating from about 1869. In the late 1970s these were respectively Blackamoor Shop and Didier, Inc., upscale antique galleries at a time when fine antiques were beginning to appear in increasing numbers along Magazine. Now it is Dunn and Sonnier, antiques, flowers, and gifts.

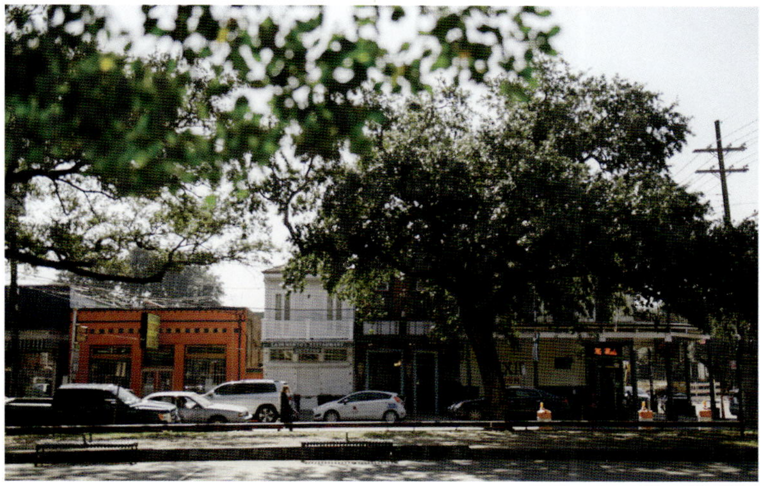

Laurence Square.

In the next block after Delachaise on the river side at 3444-50 are three nearly

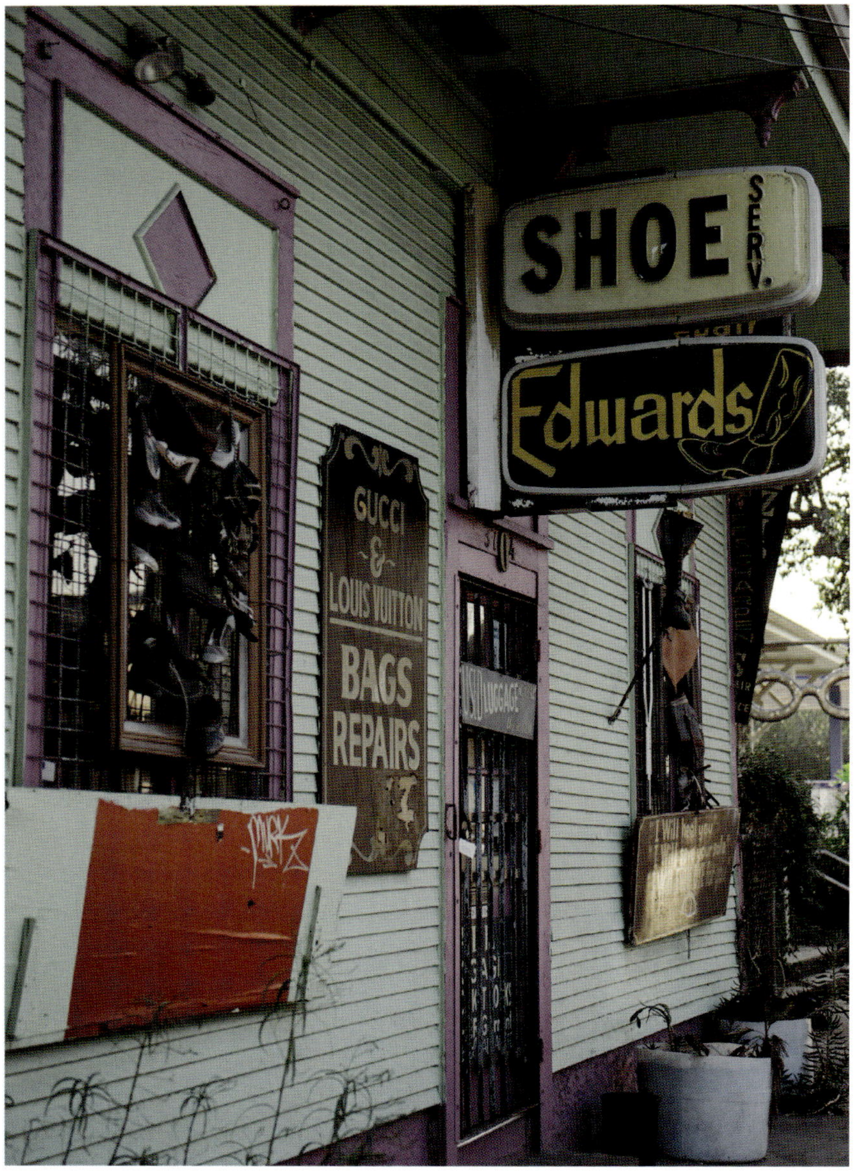

One of three shoe repair shops remaining on Magazine Street (3704 Magazine). At one time there were dozens.

matching houses, two of which are now shops, dating from 1892. Across Magazine is a massive brick building that now houses HomeLife in the Gardens, a retirement facility. Until the construction of this building in the mid-twentieth century, one of the grandest houses on Magazine stood here. Built in 1860, it was a raised wooden structure with a mansard roof. It later became the convent of the Catholic Missionary Servants of the Most Holy Eucharist, who had the new structure built.

The next block up after Aline continues to maintain the residential character of a middle-class nineteenth-century neighborhood although it is now mostly shops. The Italianate building at 3504-06 dates from the early 1870s, while its larger next-door neighbor at 3508 is from the late 1880s. Farther up the block, the house at 3516-20 is from about 1870, while the two identical double houses at the corner of Foucher date from 1893.

Across Magazine at 3535, on the corner of Foucher, there was once a row of similar double houses until they were removed sometime around 1920 to make way for the large building of the Menger-Fisher Motor Co. showrooms. By the late 1930s

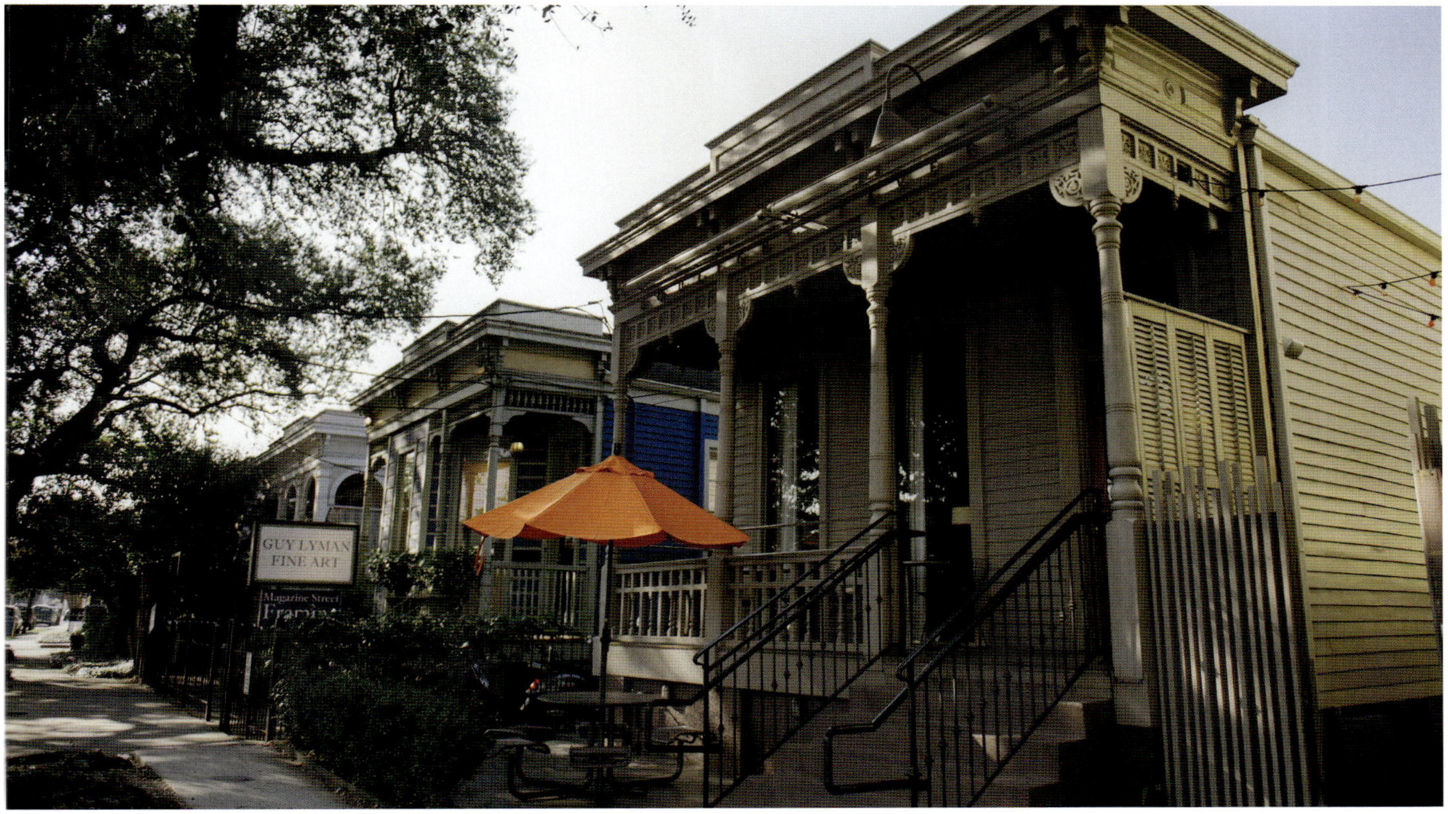

Modern businesses are housed in former Victorian residences in the 3600 block.

this building was a bakery called Mother's Home Made Pies, but since about 1970 it has been Harry's Ace Hardware. Harry Offner started the business at 326 South Rampart Street in 1910 before moving to Magazine. The street once had numerous hardware stores, but Harry's is now one of only two that remains; the other is Clement's at the corner of State Street. In 1978 the *Underground Shopping Guide* called Harry's "Magazine's largest Hardware store" with "everything from concrete and nails to . . . pitchers to serve bloody Marys."

Mary Shelly has lived nearby on Magazine since 1970.

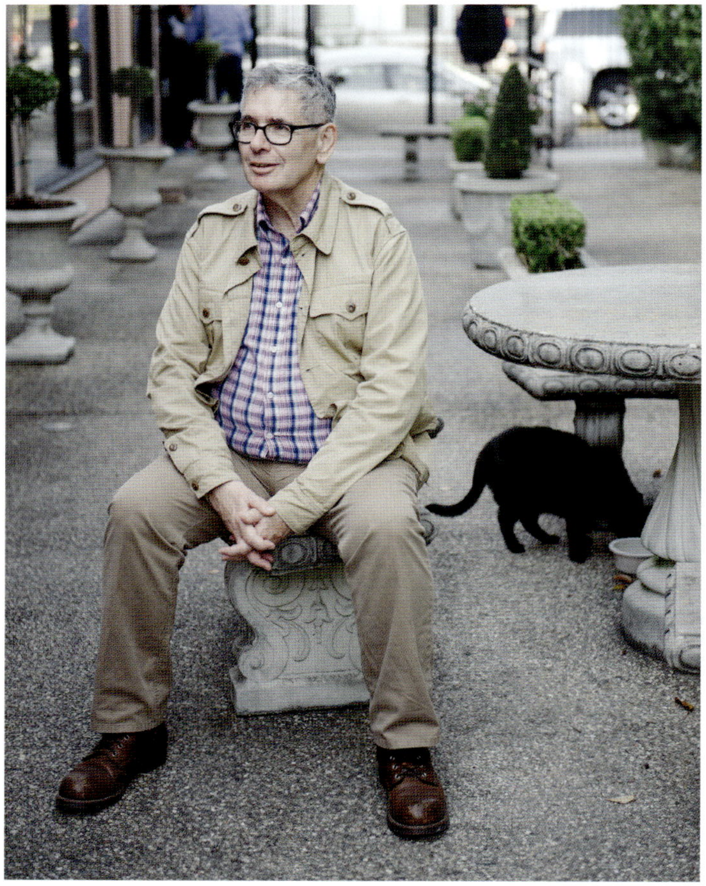

The author and a new friend taking a break near the shops at 3806 Magazine.

When she and her husband, Ceaser, bought their house, this area of Magazine was entirely residential except for Harry's. Today it is mostly commercial with houses converted to businesses. Mrs. Shelly's maternal grandfather was noted jazz player Louis D. James, Sr., who lived in Carrollton where she grew up. She and her husband lived Uptown and as they were looking for a house chose this area of Magazine. Mrs. Shelly did not want to buy a shotgun, which is the style of this house, but she fell in love with the kitchen—so they bought it anyway. As the family grew, they raised four children. Bedrooms and a bath were added across the driveway of the house, a common expansion all over New Orleans. This was an all-white neighborhood when the young couple bought their home, and the Shellys were the first African American family to move along this part of Magazine. She said that it did not seem to make a difference, since everyone got along. Some nearby neighbors were elderly, having been there for many years. Mrs. Shelly helped care for some of them, and they grew to become very close friends.

For the next two blocks Magazine continues with a residential feel and boasts several large houses. Diagonally across Foucher from Harry's, at 3606, a circa 1881 house serves as the studios of radio station WRBH 88.3 FM, Radio for the Blind and Print Handicapped. While the station's roots go back to 1975, it has been located on Magazine since 1994. In 1932 it became the first 24-hour reading radio station in the United States. The buildings next to WRBH are typical of the 1870s, while farther up at 3641-53 is a series of four small houses also from the 1870s, some of which are now in commercial use. Across Magazine from WRBH, at 3607, is another large residence which dates from 1883. This elegant structure is now Cavan Restaurant & Bar.

When these middle-class houses were being built, this section of Magazine up to about Marengo was strictly residential, as well as quietly countrified. Now there are rows and rows of fine, upscale shops. A number of single and double cottages remain standing. A few are residences, but most house retailers. In the early twentieth century the businesses that emerged here, especially approaching Napoleon, were mostly grocers, bakers, pharmacies, laundries, cobblers, barbers, hairdressers, hardware stores, plumbers, and bars with an occasional family clothing store or jeweler for extra discretionary spending. The names of all the quality stores here now are quite simply too numerous to mention, but a selection indicates how the character of the street has changed.

Since 1999, the Magazine branch of New Orleans-born jewelry designer Mignon Faget has been at 3801. In the late 1940s the building was the Peniston Bar and Restaurant, and by the late '70s it was the Brass Gallery.

One of the newest shops on Magazine is Pilot and Powell at 3901. This is "a luxury retail space . . . in the heart of vibrant Magazine Street" co-owned by Katherine Bullock Joyner and Coeli Hilferty. Mrs. Joyner said that Magazine was chosen as the location for their store because it is now the "epicenter for commerce in New

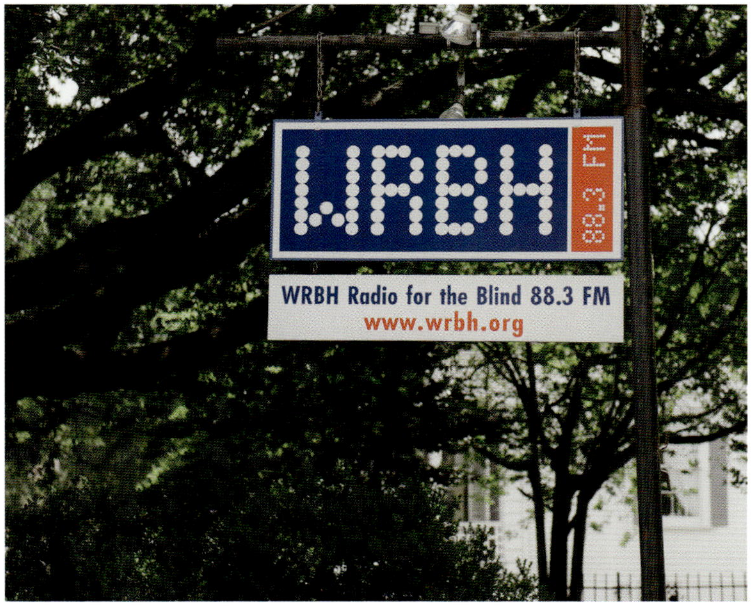

WRBH Radio for the Blind and Print Handicapped, at 3606 Magazine Street.

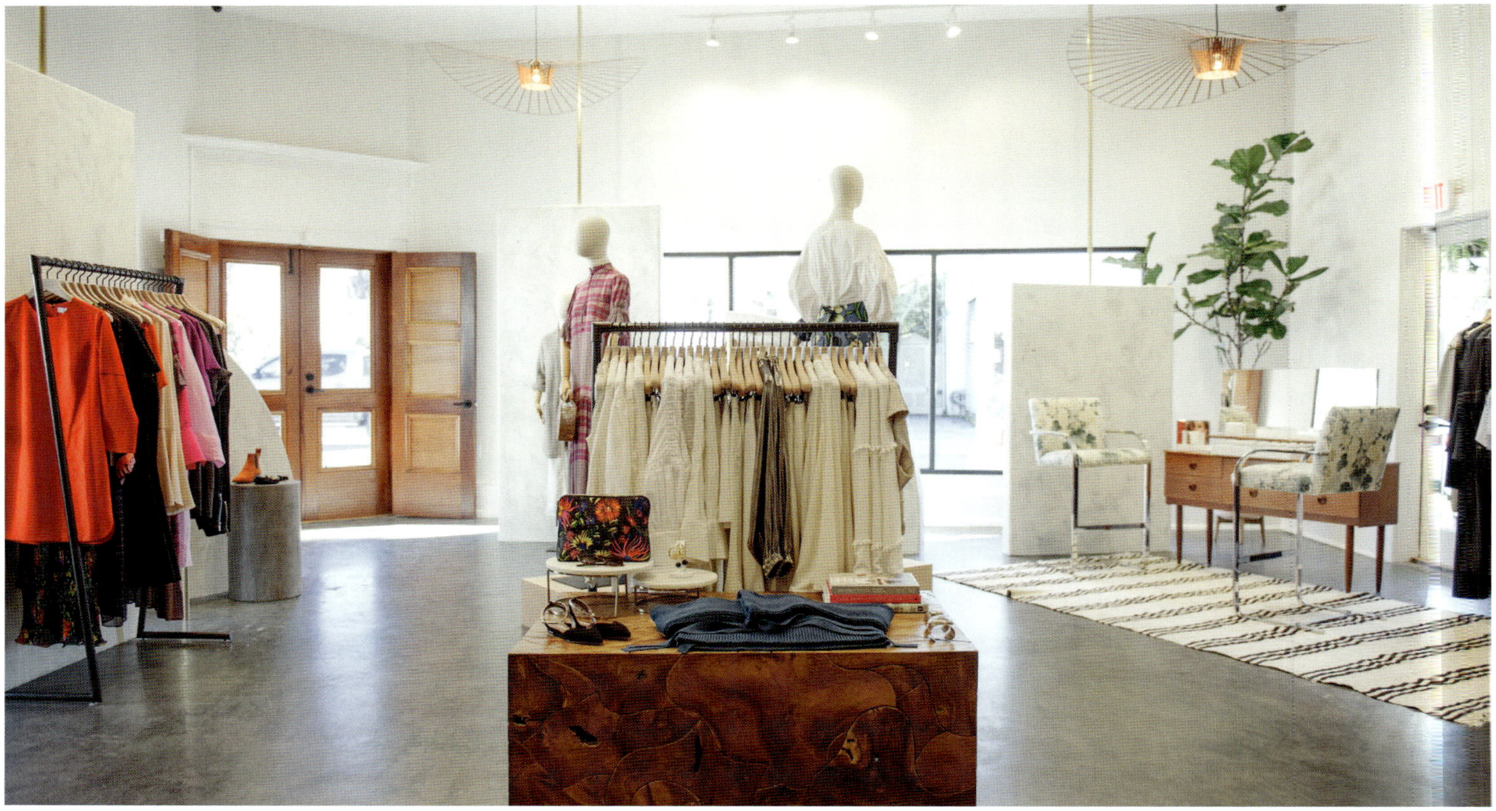

Pilot and Powell, at 3901 Magazine Street.

Orleans." It is a draw, because the stores here are mostly locally owned and are attractive to locals and tourists alike. In the 1940s this building was shared by the Best Ice Cream Shop and Jack Cefalu's Shoe Repair.

Billy Reid, a Louisiana native from Amite, is a designer of luxury men's and women's clothing and has several stores nationwide. One of his shops is at 3927 Magazine in a building that was Frank Manale's grocery store in the 1940s then in the '70s, Knight's Antiques.

Still farther up Magazine is another elegant women's

shop, Weinstein's, at 4011. Dating to 1971 in the French Quarter and for a while in The Shops at Canal Place, Weinstein's relocated "to the hustle and bustle of Magazine Street." Its building, formerly housing a dog groomer, is relatively new and stands on the 1940s site of C&D self-serve food store. Co-owner Bonnie Wilson hypes Magazine as "pretty cool" and "where it's at."

Another recent shop is at 3811, and it is also one of the most unusual. The French Library is owned by Katrina Greer, wife of former New Orleans Saints player Jabari Greer, and has found a successful niche selling children's French-language books and gifts. Her bookstore has become a destination, because there is nothing else like it in the region. It is also a lifestyle shop including a café and children's play space, with child-sized furniture and French reading and art sessions.

According to Mrs. Greer the shop fits the neighborhood and its nearby French-themed businesses such as Aux Belles Choses, specializing in French décor, at 3912; La Riviere Confiserie, with its French savories and sweets, at 3719; Lilette, a French restaurant, at 3637;

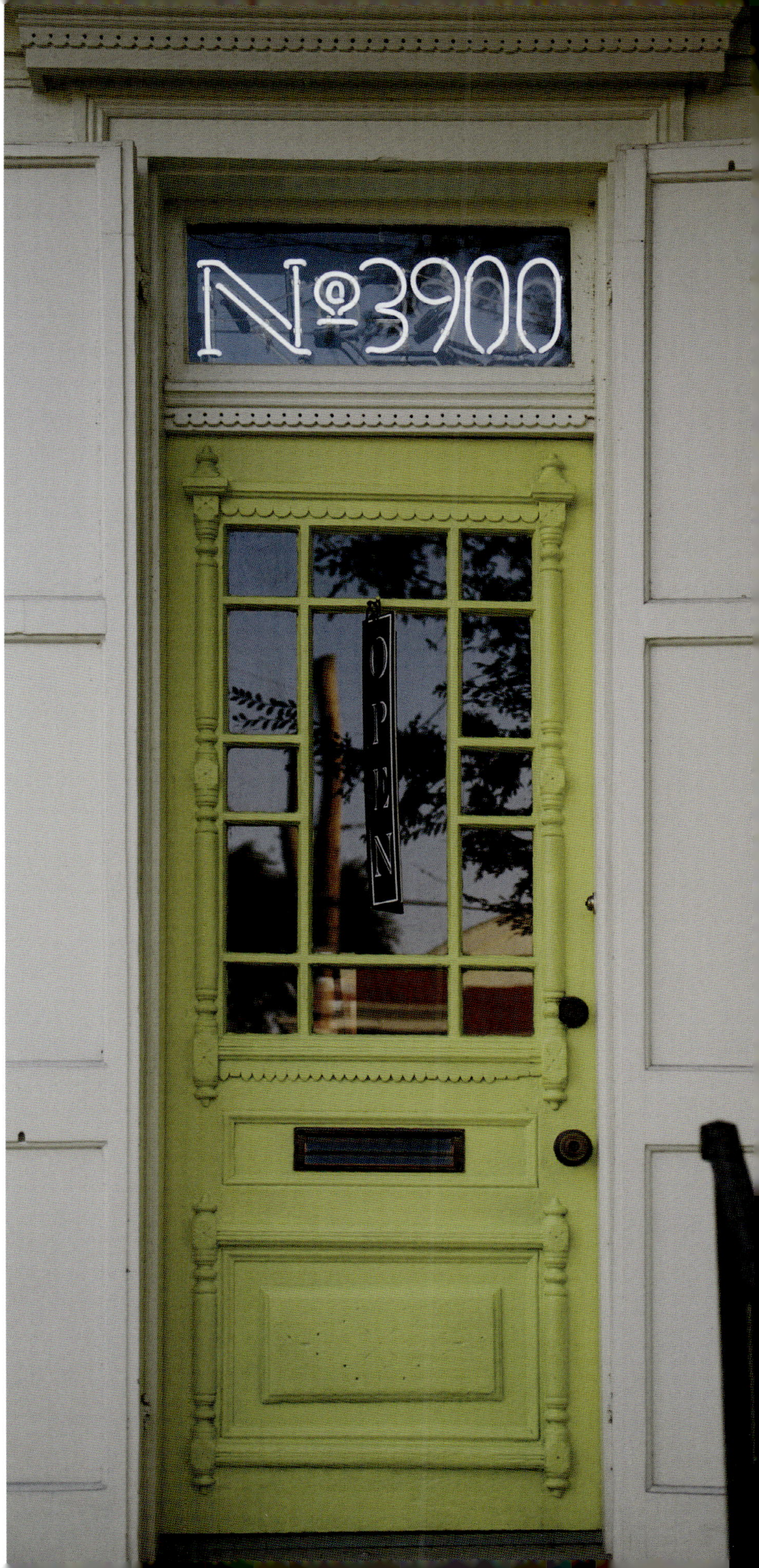

The original residential doorway is still in use at Box Paper Scissor.

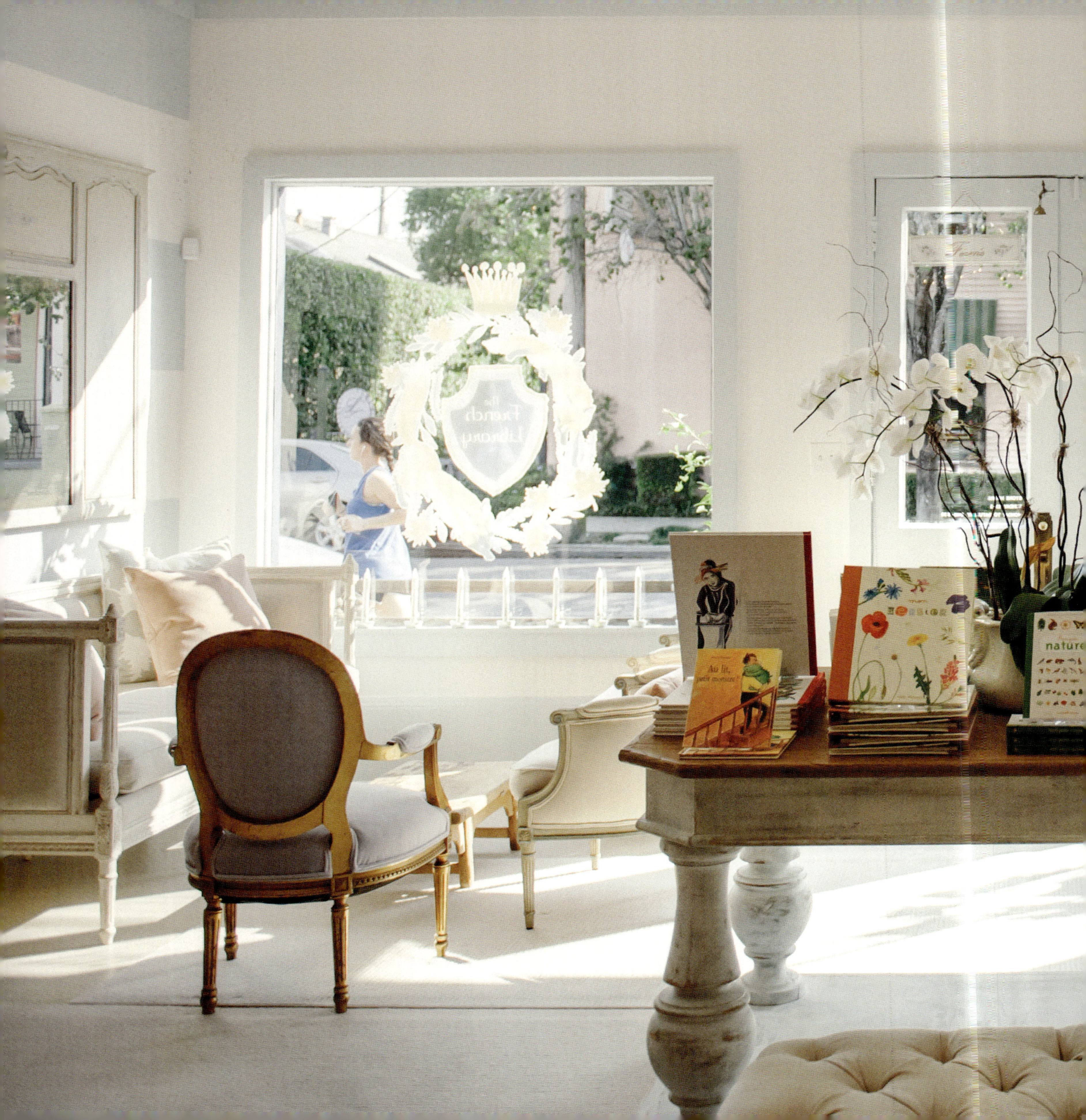
nature

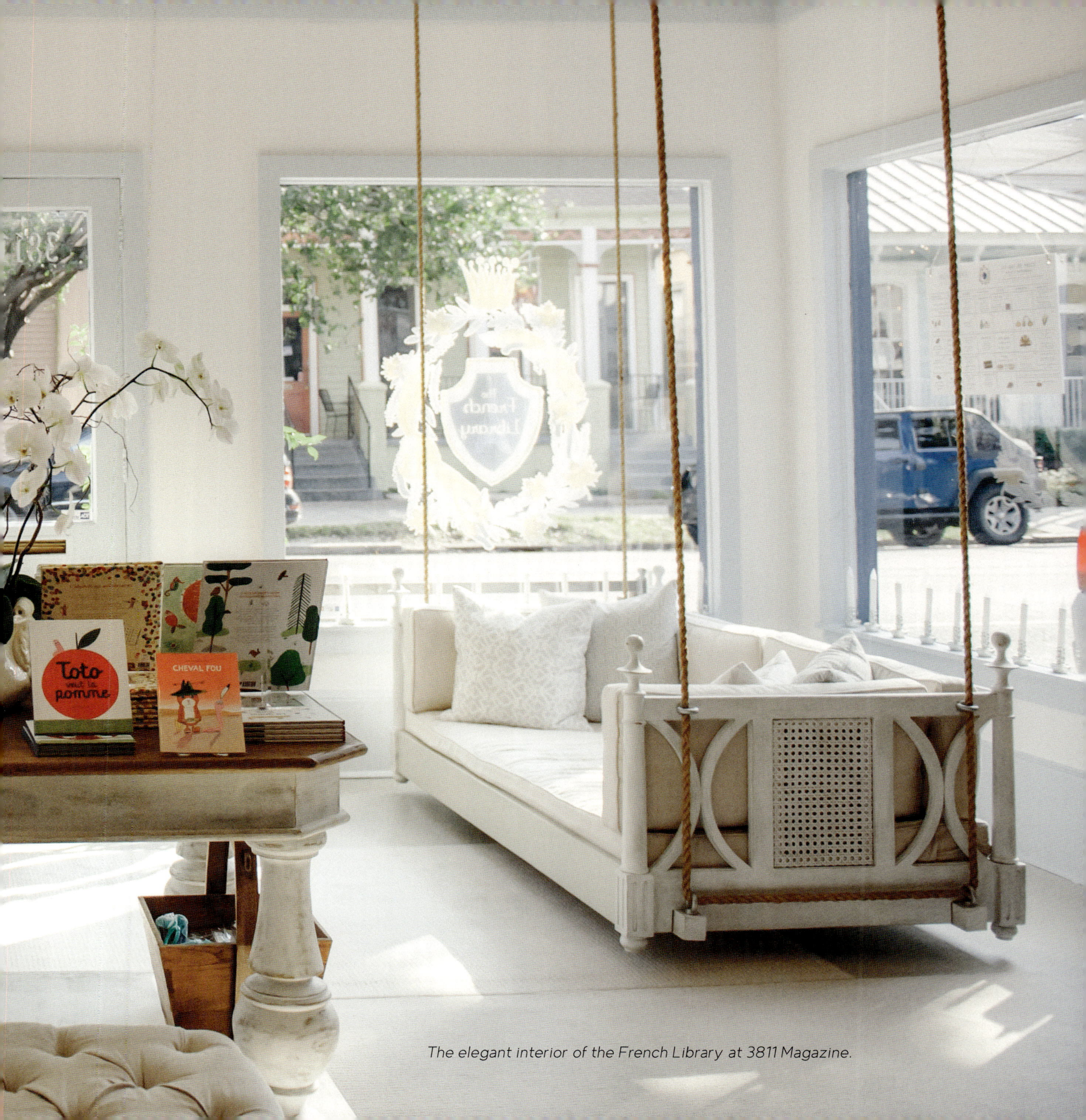

The elegant interior of the French Library at 3811 Magazine.

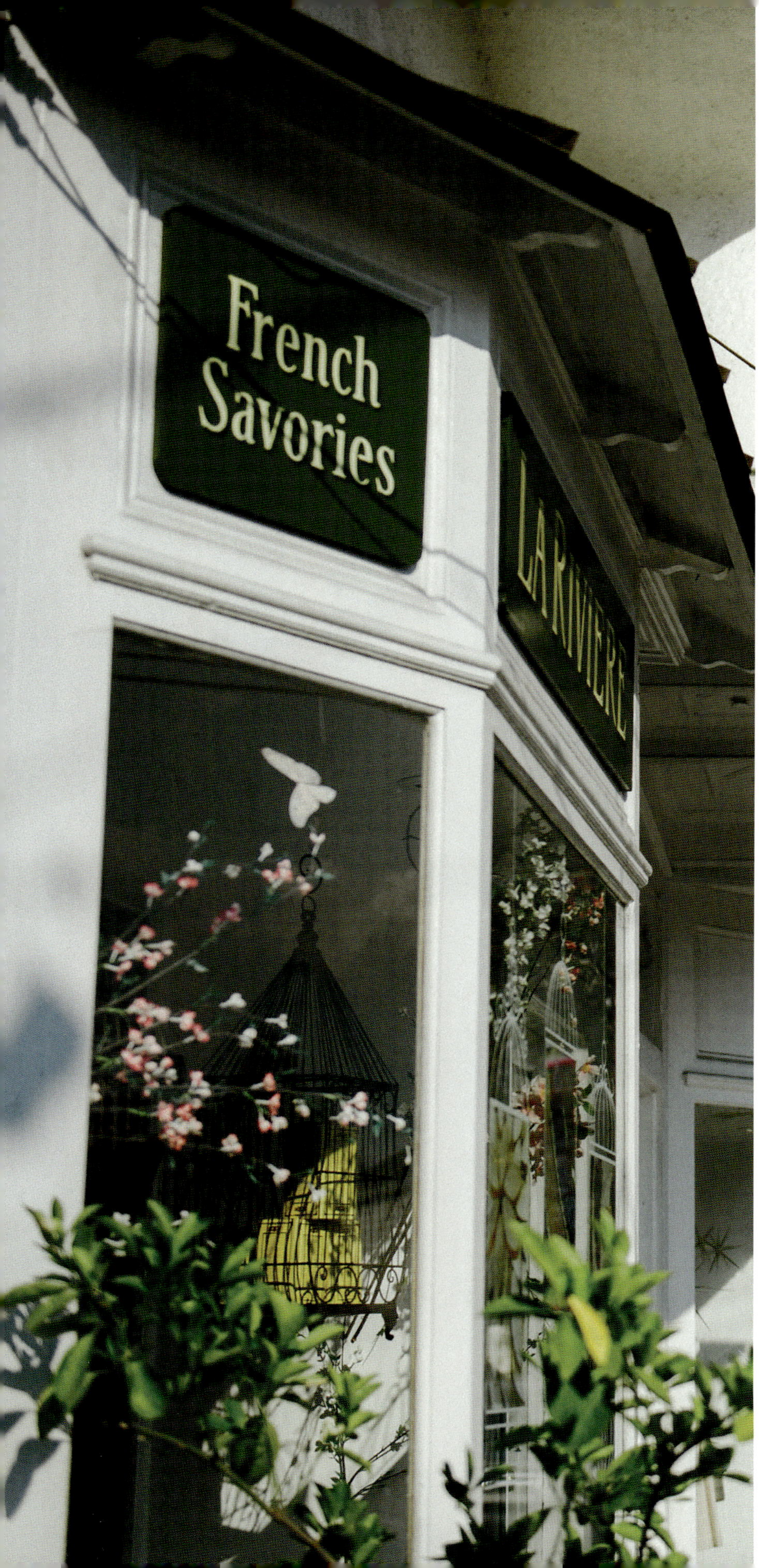

and Verduré Olive Oil Co. at 3636. There are several French-immersion schools Uptown, including Ecole Bilingue de la Nouvelle-Orléans on General Pershing near Magazine. The school's annual Fete Français, honoring the city's French heritage and connections, has been held since 2000.

With stores frequently opening and closing on Magazine at a breakneck pace, Mrs. Greer feels that "if you can make it on Magazine Street, you can make it anywhere." She regards Magazine shopkeepers as family, helping each other and supporting everybody's businesses. Previously the store had housed a decorator shop, but in the late 1940s the business was more typical of Magazine at the time. A plumber, E. Hagardorn & Son, was located there.

At 4100 a parking lot sits in front of the former Home, Hook and Ladder fire station. This was a private enterprise (one of many), that predated the New Orleans Fire Department. The old firehouse faces Marengo Street and still has its 1884 facade. Although the Magazine side of the building was rebuilt for a restaurant, it now hosts Fine & Associates law firm.

Several French stores such as La Rivière Confiserie make their home on Magazine Street.

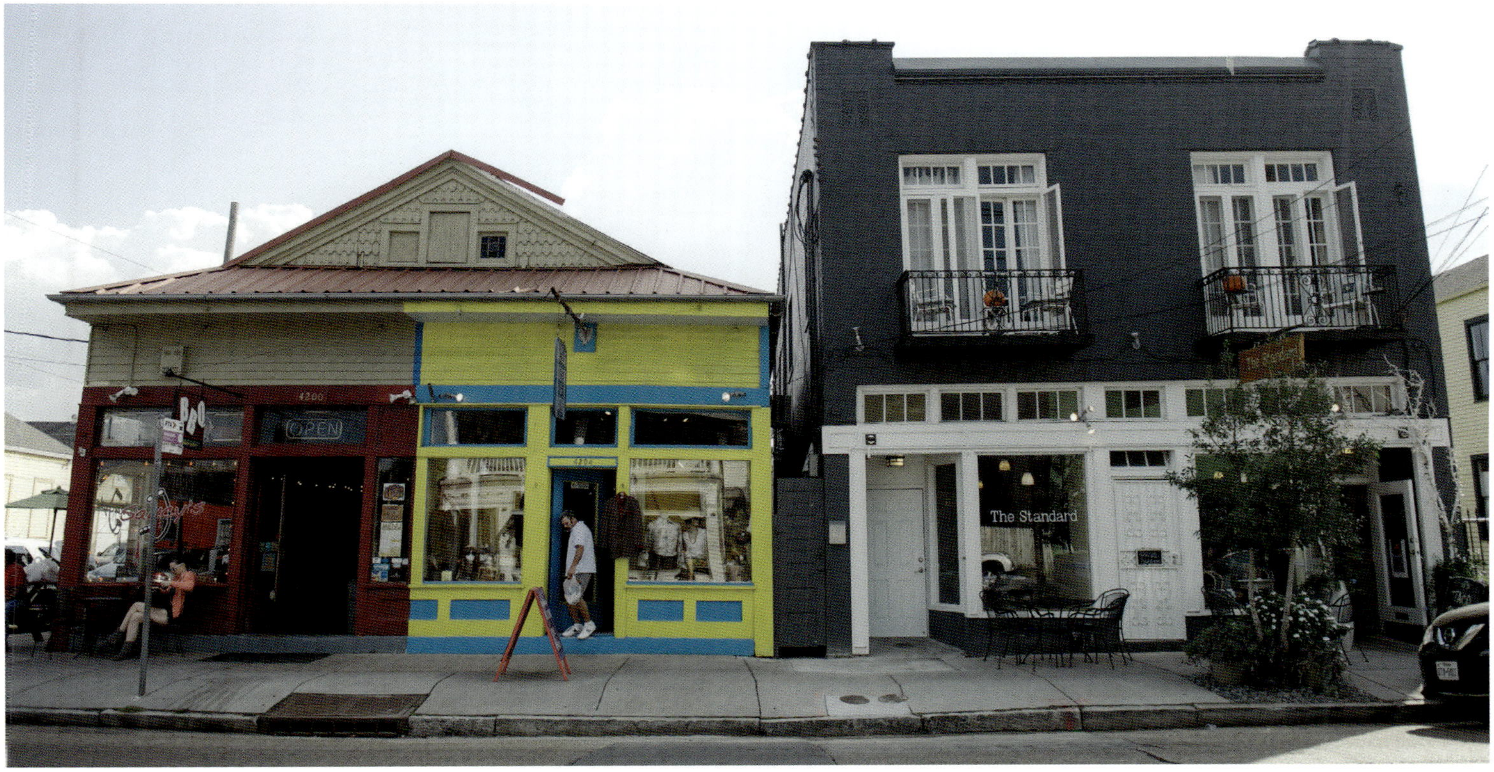

Colorful shop fronts on the 4200 block.

A number of decorators and furniture dealers can be found throughout this section of Magazine now, and they are a link to the past, when several furniture stores operated here. In the 1940s, Brown's Appliance and Furniture Co. was at 4112. A new building on the site is the home of Villa Vici, an elegant furniture and design store. Brown's competition included the longtime Itzkovitch Furniture Co. across Magazine at 4119, which dated from about 1923. The name Itzkovitch was set into concrete over the front door, and although the lettering has since been filled in, the name is still discernible, if obscured by the sign for the

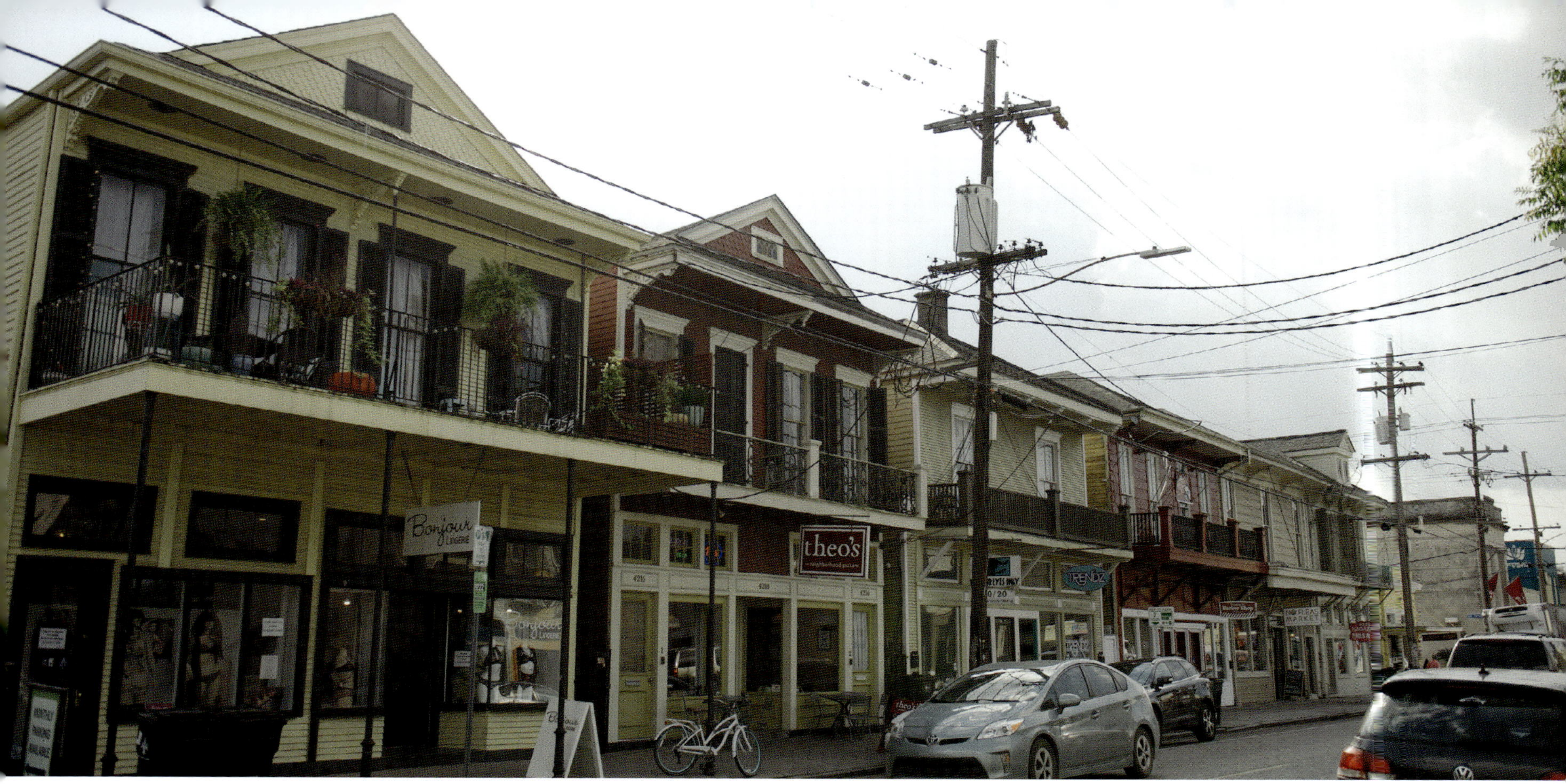

These buildings on the 4200 block replaced those structures destroyed in the 1908 fire.

Buffalo Exchange clothing store. The Neal Auction Company at 4038 and the corner of Marengo is housed in the building that was once Kottermann's Furniture Co., in business by 1916. The rather nondescript building at 4018, next to Neal's parking lot, was called the Ragin Cajun in the 1970s. An antique store, its sign read, "We buy junk and sell antiques." Diagonally across Magazine from Kottermann's, in the '40s was Weinstein's Department Store, which in 1978 housed Wiley's appliance and furniture repair. Today it is Lanier & Associates, an engineering firm. In the same block, at 4139, was Handleman's, a branch of the Dryades Street department store. It is now Sherwin-Williams paint store.

In 1948 Max Miller, one of the owners of Miller's Jewelry Store at 4214 Magazine, in business since 1921, remembered the great fire of 1908 that burned down two square blocks of Magazine. Miller's Jewelry building is now Bonjour Lingerie Shop. Miller recalled that the fire started in a shoemaker's shop when the proprietor accidentally kicked over a lamp. The fire quickly grew out of control and burned down rows of mostly one-story frame

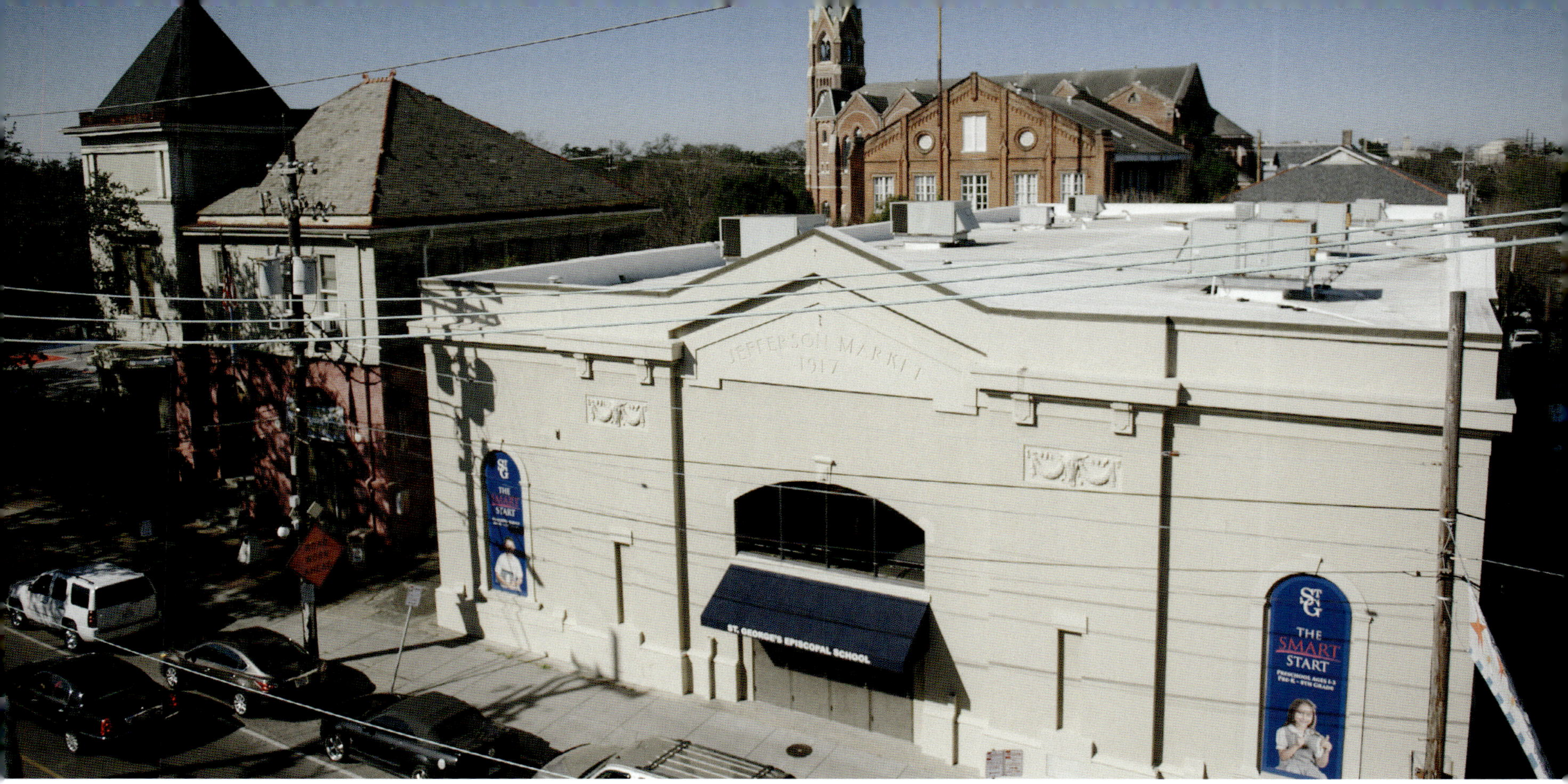

Jefferson Market, the Second District Police Station, and St. Stephen's Church.

stores—some dating from the 1870s and '80s—along both sides of Magazine in the 4200 block between Milan and General Pershing.

The fire also badly damaged the Pioneer Engine Company #1 fire station, established in 1853 at 4213 Magazine. It was rebuilt and is now home to the Israeli restaurant Shaya. Born in Israel and brought up in Philadelphia, Alon Shaya moved to New Orleans in 2003. In 2014, he opened Pizza Dominica at 4933 Magazine and a year later opened Shaya. In 2016, Shaya received the James Beard Award for best new restaurant in the country, and in 2017, Shaya's chef Zach Engel received the award for the nation's best new rising chef.

Of Magazine Street, Mr. Shaya says, "I feel I can be a consumer and a local. . . . It's where I want to hang out." He chose the street for his restaurants because he sees it as the place where the majority of locals do their dining and shopping. To Mr. Shaya, Magazine Street is like "a small town." His barber is across the street from the restaurant, he can go to Harry's Hardware, and he and his wife can walk the dog in Audubon Park.

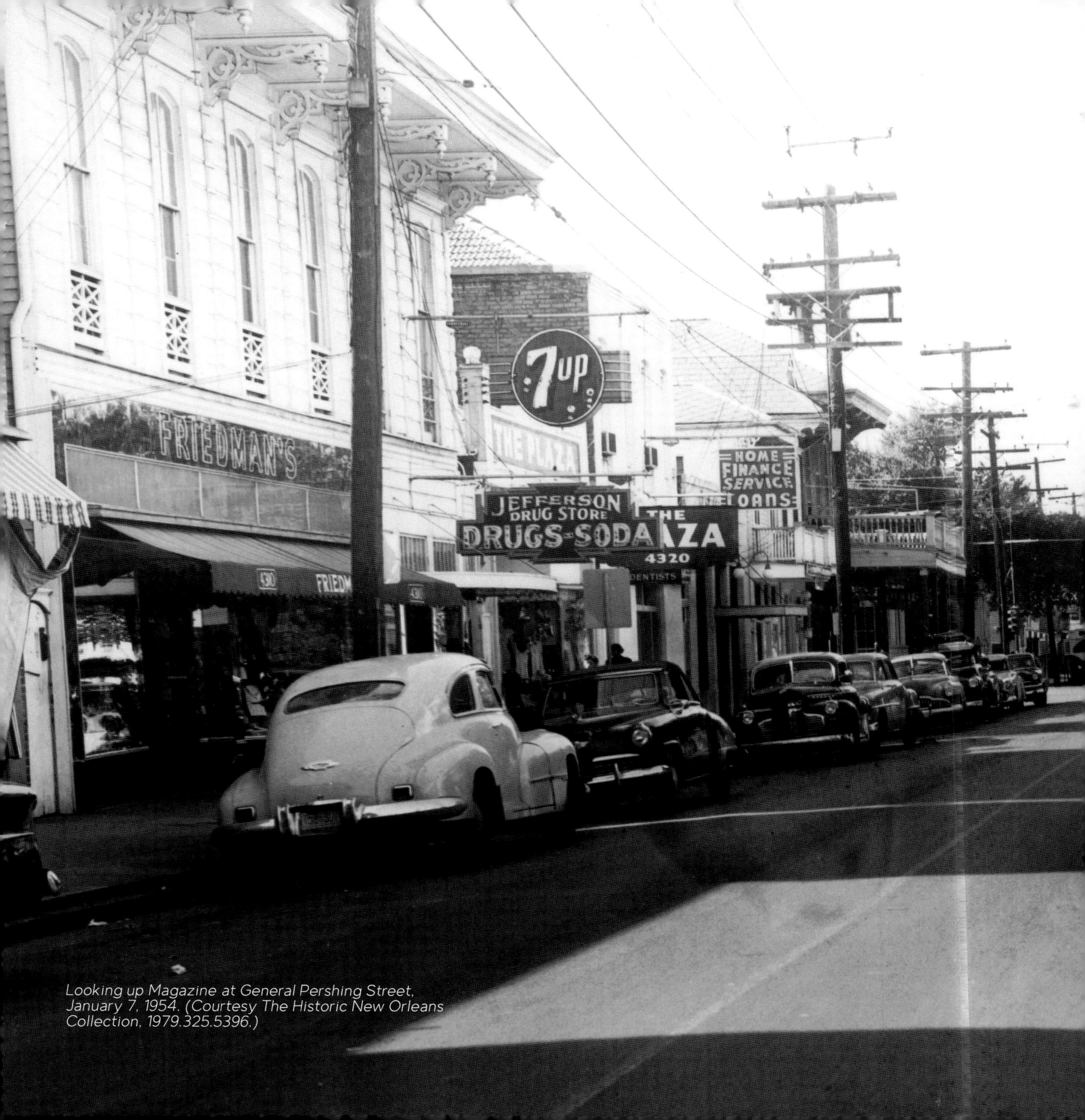

Looking up Magazine at General Pershing Street, January 7, 1954. (Courtesy The Historic New Orleans Collection, 1979.325.5396.)

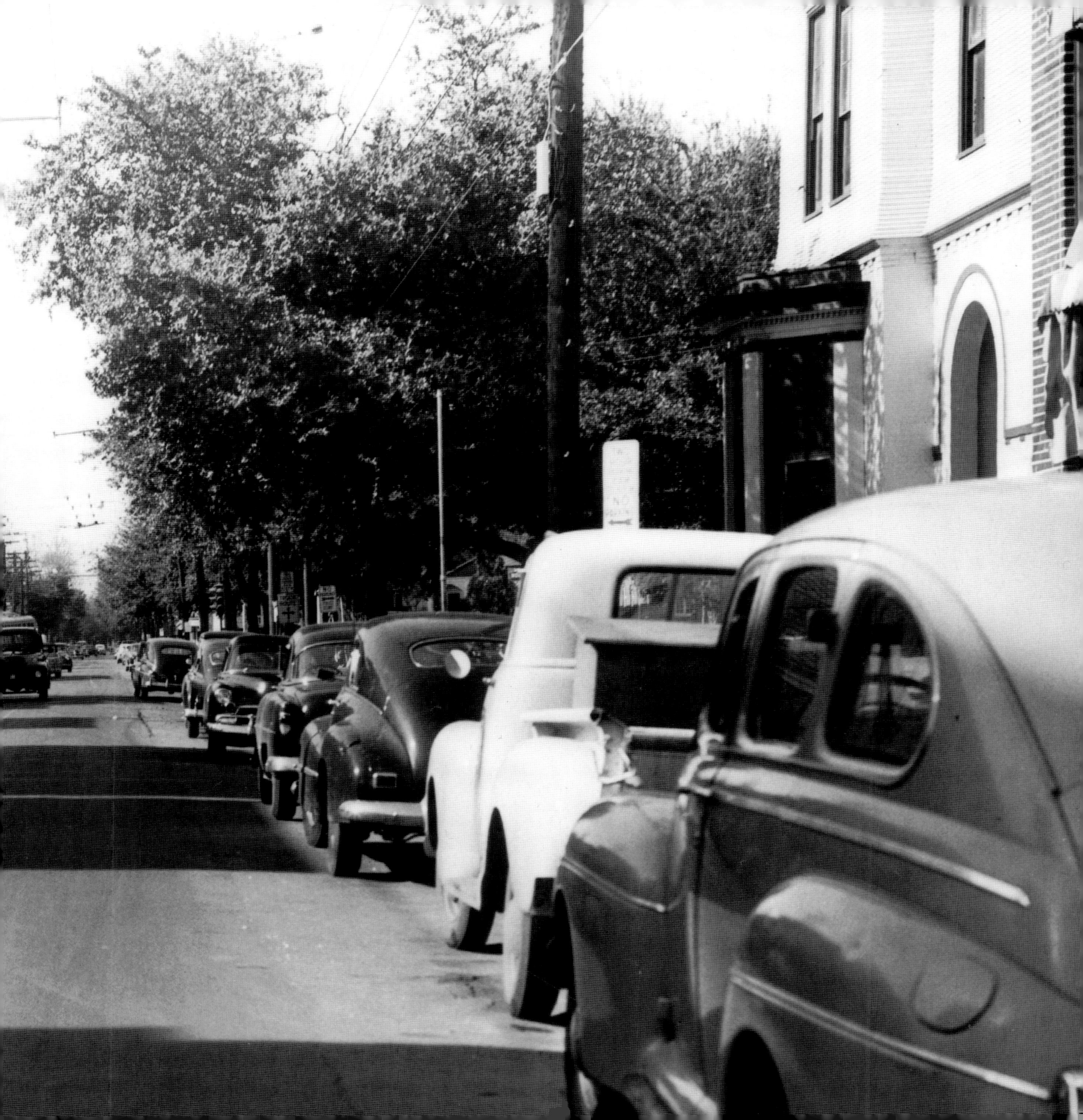

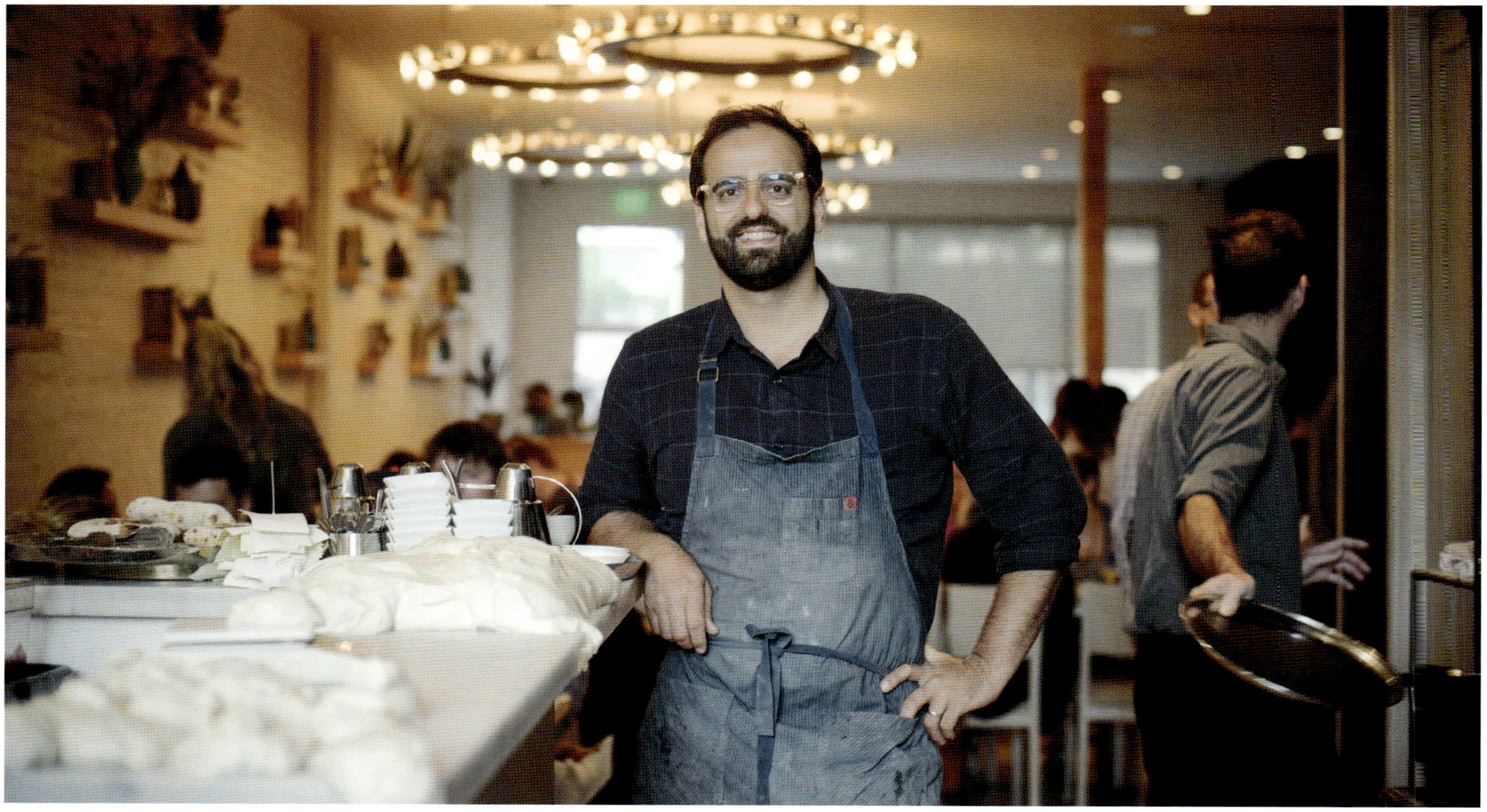

Alon Shaya in his signature restaurant at 4213 Magazine Street.

While tourists do visit Shaya, he feels that the majority of his customers are local. He likes to think of it as a "neighborhood joint," because in the dining room he sees many familiar faces: "ladies who lunch, businessmen, and people who walk there with their children from the neighborhood." He is pleased with Shaya's events space, where people celebrate wedding rehearsal dinners, baby showers, birthday parties, and other events that are part of people's lives. Shaya's is "a dream come true," he says, since it is not just a restaurant to sell food, but a gathering place. In spite of the restaurant's awards, Mr. Shaya thinks that "Magazine does more for the restaurant than the restaurant does for Magazine."

Around the corner on General Pershing—its name changed from Berlin Street in a rash of anti-German patriotism during World War I—the 1908 fire consumed St. Henry's Catholic Church and school. The school, now Ecole Bilingue de la Nouvelle-Orléans, was quickly rebuilt, although the church was not completed until 1926. Despite public outcry from parishioners, the church was closed for services in 2008. It reopened for daily mass in 2012.

Another victim of the fire was Frank W. Mackie grocery at 4238 Magazine. It was rebuilt into a full-service store that specialized in fancy foods and delivery. Soon after Mackie's death in 1942 the store was sold to Frank Von der Haar. He operated it as a purveyor of fine foods and meats, and it became a mainstay of Uptown dining and entertaining until it closed in 1982. Customers recall that it was more like an office full of desks where orders were taken, rather than a regular grocery store. The building was later used as a florist, but today it is La Petit Grocery restaurant, a name commemorating the site's grocery store days.

Diagonally across Magazine from Mackie's was the Jefferson Market. This public market opened in the 1860s serving Jefferson City, and like other markets, it served as a catalyst for the growth of the surrounding business district. The market house was rebuilt in 1917 and remained a public market into the 1950s, when it became a Winn-Dixie Supermarket. It closed in 1986, replaced by a large Winn-Dixie on Tchoupitoulas. The Jefferson Market is now the gym of St. George's Episcopal School, which is located around the corner on Napoleon Avenue, facing Laurence Square. The school is in a former McDonogh public elementary school that was built for African American students in 1875.

Next door to the Jefferson Market is the Second District Police Station. Built in 1899, this grand building contains a wooden staircase that would befit any St. Charles Avenue mansion, as well as an intricate cast-iron staircase. The station is to be replaced by a new, state-of-the-art facility in another part of the police district, while the old building is slated to become part of St. George's school. Near

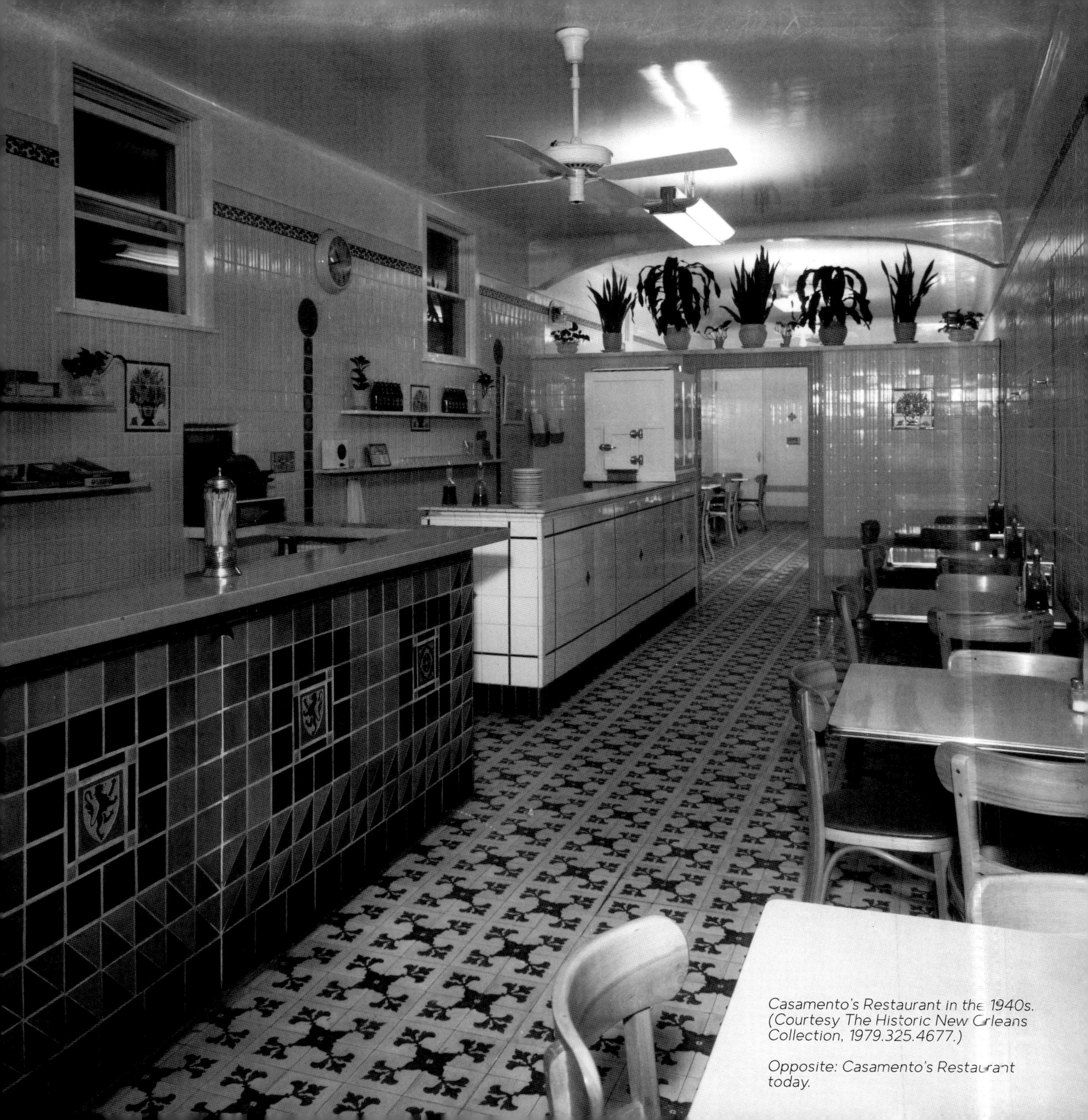

Casamento's Restaurant in the 1940s. (Courtesy The Historic New Orleans Collection, 1979.325.4677.)

Opposite: Casamento's Restaurant today.

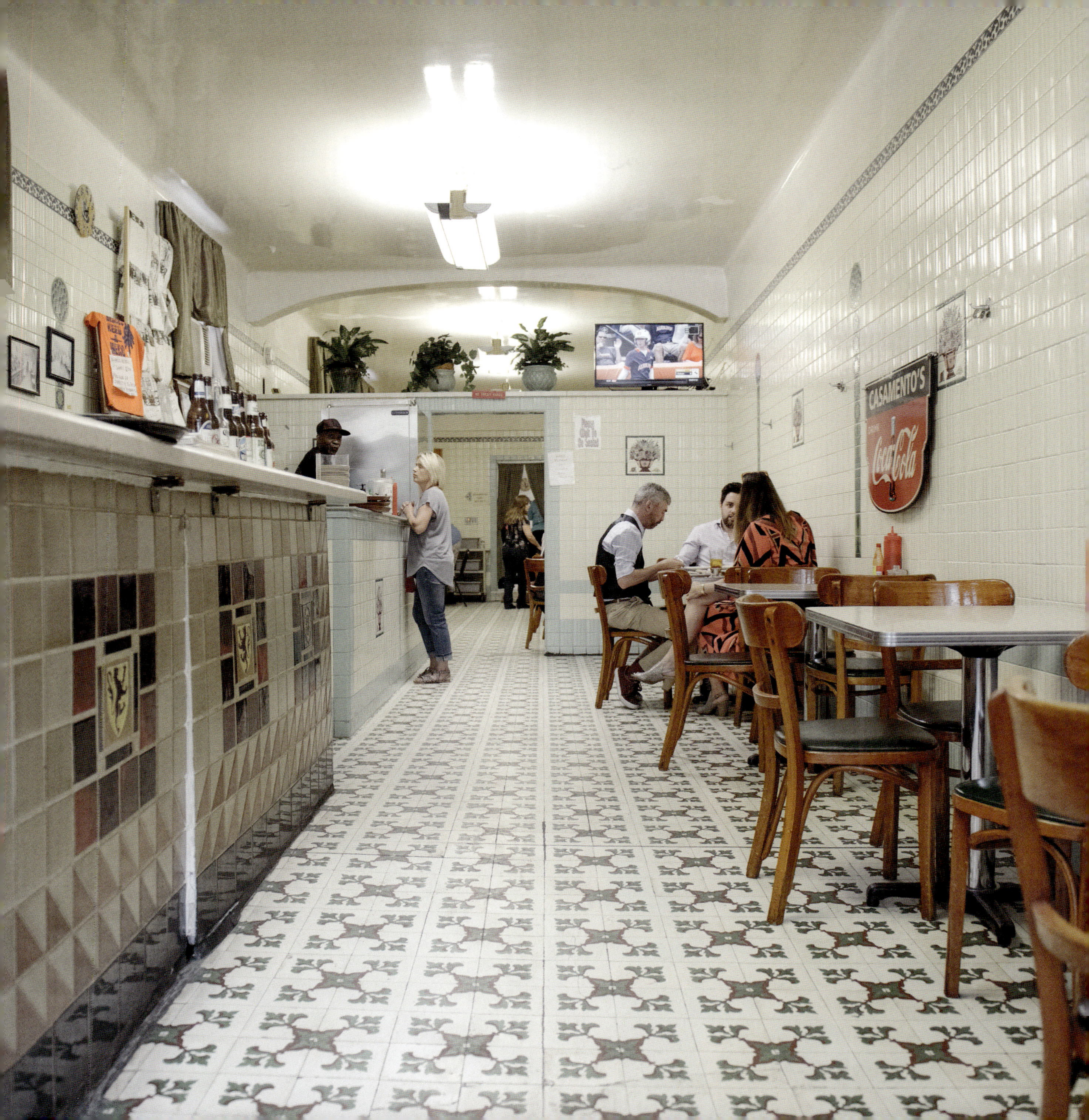
CASAMENTO'S
Coca-Cola

the police station in Laurence Square is a children's branch of the New Orleans Public Library. It was constructed about 1905 from a donation given by Andrew Carnegie to build libraries in New Orleans.

A block away on Napoleon is towering St. Stephen's Catholic Church, built between 1868 and 1887. The spire, which was not added until the early twentieth century, rises over two hundred feet. This is the second-largest Catholic church in the city and is now Good Shepherd Parish, combining the congregations of St. Henry's and Our Lady of Good Council on Louisiana Avenue at Chestnut, still standing two blocks off Magazine.

At the 4300 corner and General Pershing is a circa 1920 branch of the Hibernia National Bank. It is now the design center for Mignon Faget, one of the nation's leading jewelry designers. Mignon Faget began as a clothing designer and maker on Dublin Street in the Riverbend section in 1969. In 1976 she ceased clothing manufacture and focused on jewelry, the designs of which are based on flora and fauna of her native state. In 1997 she acquired the closed bank building for use as her corporate headquarters. While the bank interior was extensively renovated for the new use the massive and impressive bank vault has been left intact.

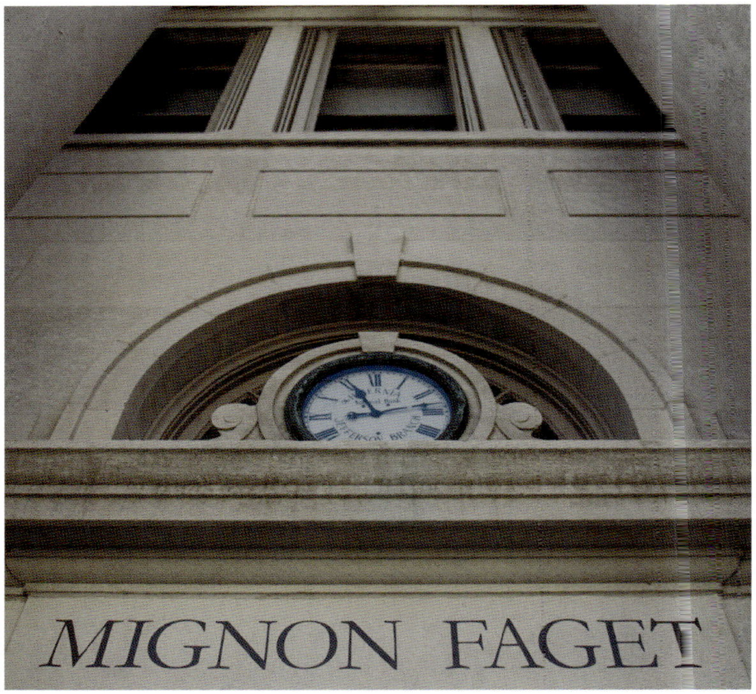

Mignon Faget corporate headquarters, formerly a Hibernia National Bank, at 4300 Magazine.

Magazine across from the police station and market was a busy shopping block anchored by Friedman's Department Store at 4310, which specialized in school uniforms and Halloween costumes. Another anchor was F. W. Woolworth's five and dime, which in the 1940s was at 4308—now Nirvana Indian Cuisine—but in the '50s it moved to a bigger store at 4318. It is now Peaches Records, where Woolworth's unused soda fountain is still preserved. From the early twentieth century Winsberg's was a popular shoe store at 4304-06, where it remained in business until the 1980s. NOLA Boards, a purveyor of cutting boards, and The Parlor on Magazine hair salon are now in this building. Farther up Magazine at 4330 is Casamento's Restaurant, called by the 1978 *Underground Shopping Guide* "an institution in this neighborhood," and it still is. Established in 1919 by Italian immigrant Joseph Casamento, the restaurant is noted for its seafood as well as for its heavily tiled interior. The founder considered tile easy to clean.

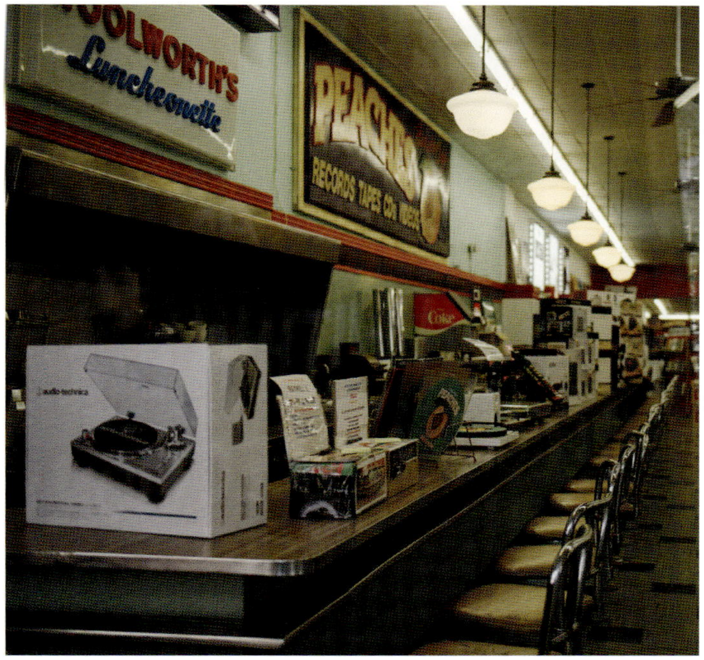

Peaches Records uses the former F. W. Woolworth's lunch counter to display merchandise.

The early 1880s building at 4336 and the corner of Napoleon has long been a bar. It was a bar in the early twentieth century, and by the 1920s it was Henry F. Engelbracht's liquors. As this was during Prohibition, it was identified as either a grocery store or a restaurant. For many years it was called just The Club before merging with Ms Mae's, another popular hangout formerly at the corner of Magazine and Joseph. It now operates as Ms. Mae's The Club.

While Magazine remains commercial across Napoleon and Laurence Square in West Bouligny, the street takes on a more residential appearance again and frequently passes under a canopy of well-established trees as it moves toward Audubon Park and the Mississippi River.

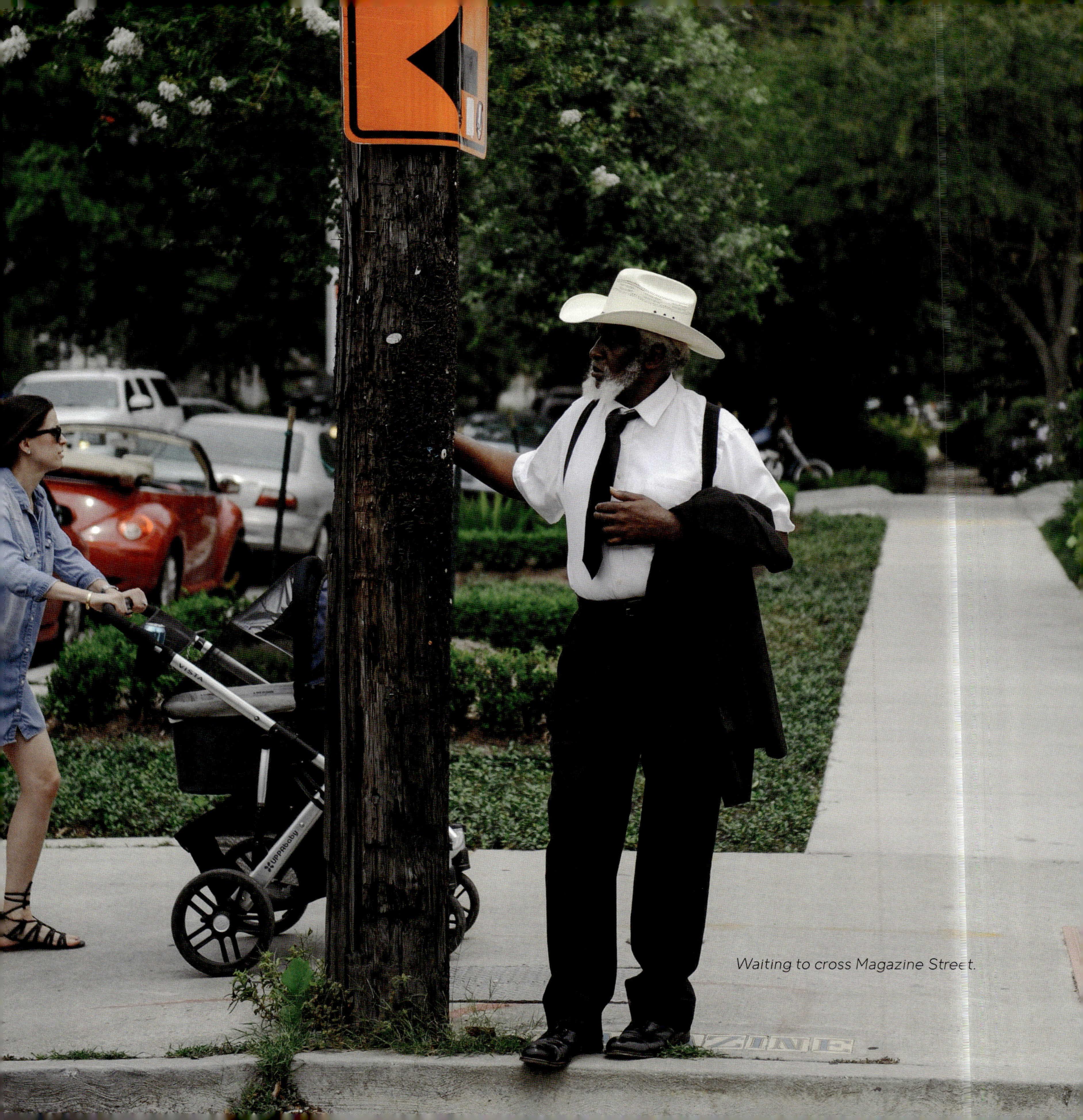

Waiting to cross Magazine Street.

Chapter Seven

Napoleon Avenue to Nashville Avenue

Crossing Napoleon and continuing Uptown, the nineteenth century begins to disappear and slowly merge into the twentieth century, with the oldest houses dating from the late 1880s and '90s. In the early 1870s, Laurence Square blended into the surrounding grazing lands, but by the early 1880s Magazine was filling with commercial buildings up to Cadiz. Closer to Audubon Park, buildings along Magazine were few and far between with at most one or two per block. It was eighty-two-year-old Waverley Greathouse who recalled that as a boy his family's house was in this area of Magazine. In the 1870s it was the only one on the block.

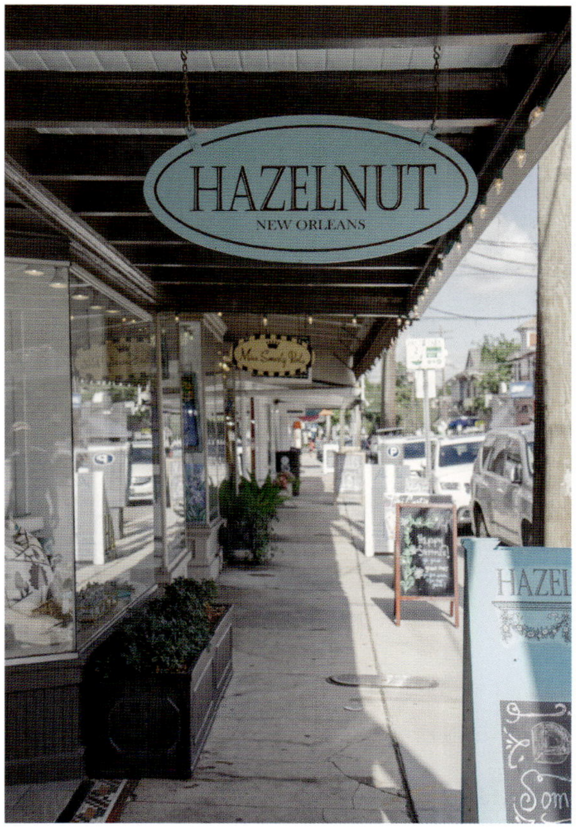

Hazelnut and neighboring shops along the 5500 block of Magazine.

There were a few large houses—now long gone—on very large properties that testify to the countrified nature of Magazine

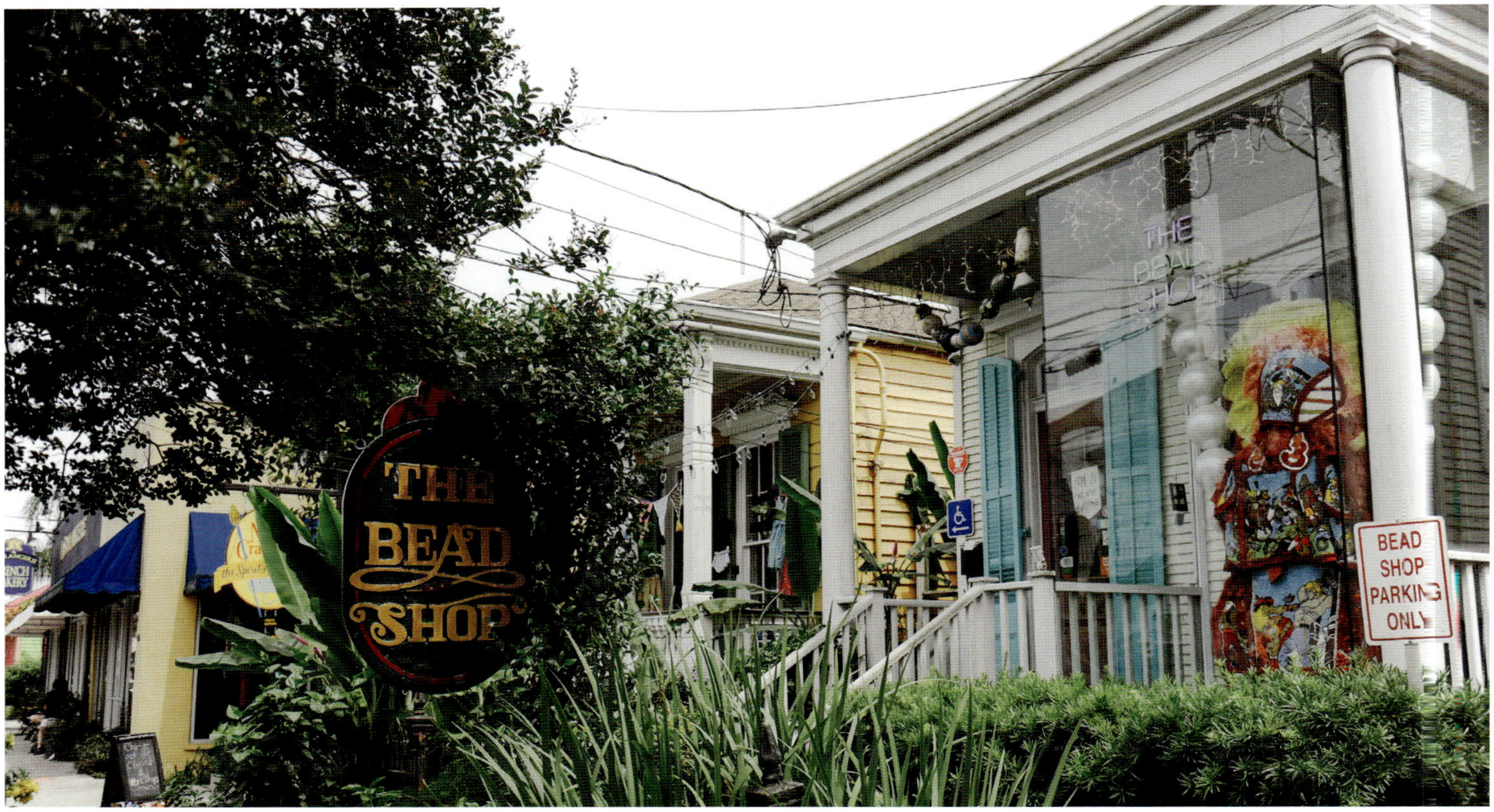

The Bead Shop, a former residence turned retail, at 4612 Magazine Street.

then. On the river side of the street between Upperline and Soniat, today's 4900 and 5000 blocks, there were only two houses per block on properties covering entire squares. On the lake side of the 5300 block between Valmont and Leontine stood a massive house in the center of another property that covered a whole square. Now more modest homes sit in its place.

Above Peters—now Jefferson—even though blocks were already subdivided, buildings of any kind were even more greatly scattered. By the late 1880s and '90s this was changing quickly as this part of the former Jefferson City was in the path of the steady upriver growth of New Orleans. Early in the new twentieth century, Magazine was fairly well built all the way up to Audubon Park.

As early as the 1870s, there was a fire station at 4521 Magazine. It was later

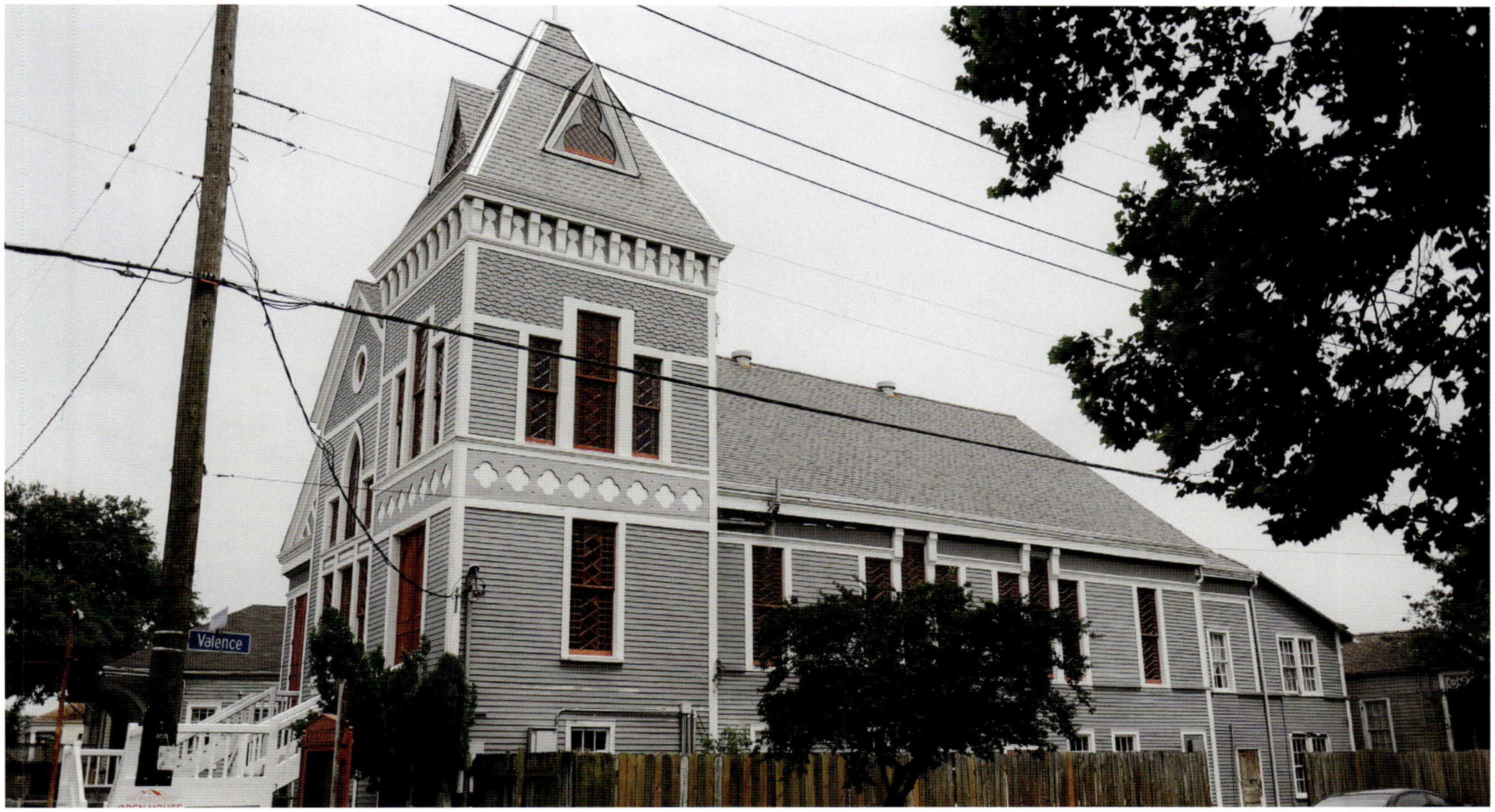

Valence Street Baptist Church.

rebuilt and is adaptively reused for Temple Gym. A block away on the river side of the street at 4610 and 4612, just beyond Cadiz, are two simple shotgun-style cottages dating from 1896. These were typical of the many small, working-class residences in the area, and today these house Uptown Needle & CraftWorks and the Bead Shop. Across the street from these two cottages is a large commercial building of the same vintage that is now an urgent care center.

Farther up the block at the corner of Valence is the Valence Street Baptist Church. This congregation has roots dating back to 1845, and the church was built in 1885 to accommodate the growing neighborhood population. It was designed by Thomas Sully, who designed some of the finest houses on St. Charles as well as several of the earliest high-rise buildings

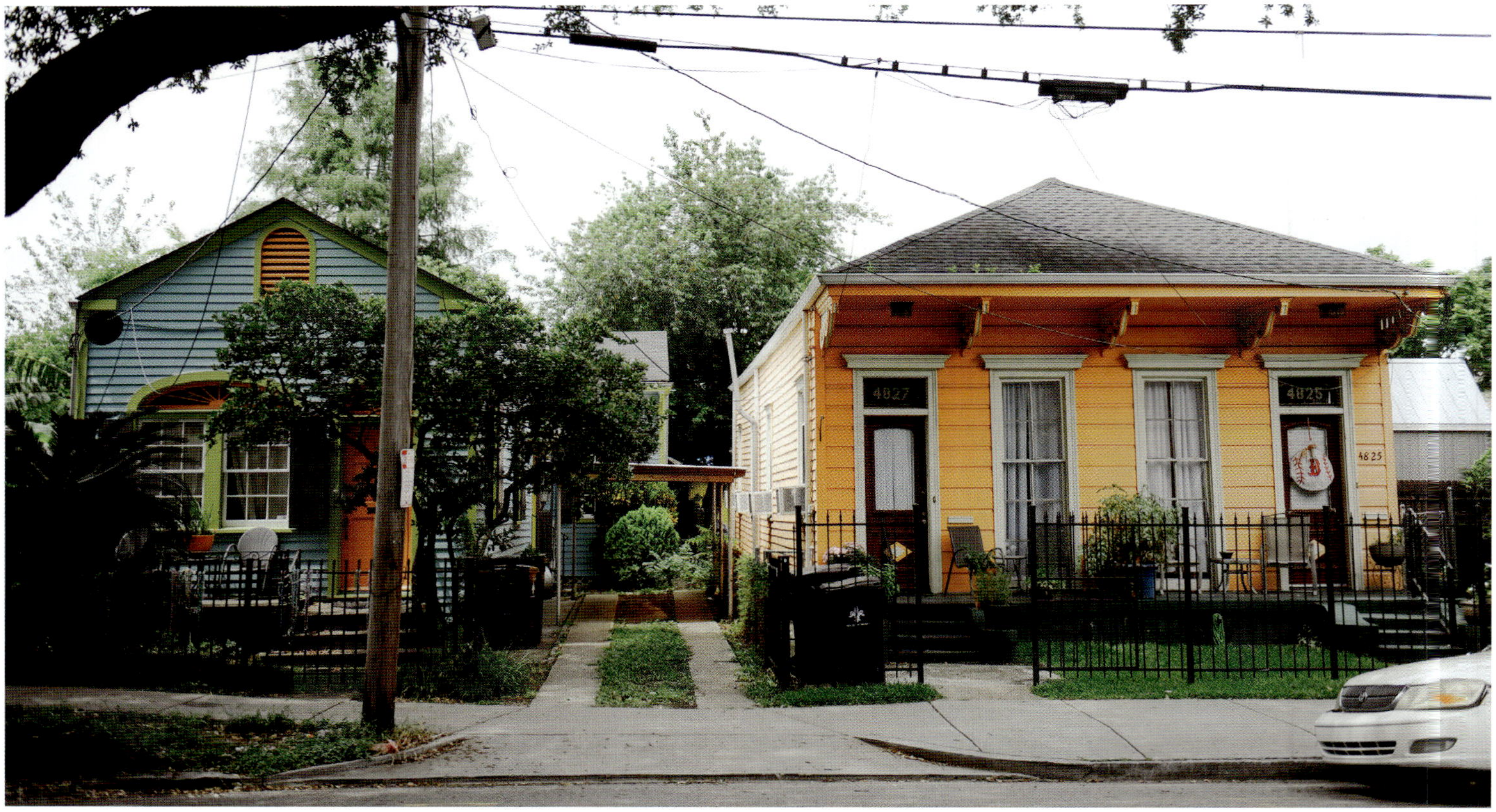

Colorfully painted residences.

downtown. Initially the church faced Valence Street—thus its name—but it was eventually reconfigured to face Magazine and raised to provide more school space. It was badly damaged in Hurricane Katrina but has been restored to its pre-storm appearance.

Between Valence and Bordeaux at 4719 to 4729, there are three 1890s houses typical of this period. Today these buildings are used for a mixture of residential and commercial purposes. Edward Jones, the national investment firm, maintains an office at 4719 in half of a double house. This is an unusual location for a financial business like Edward Jones, which generally prefers a professional building or storefront. Even the signage had to be redesigned, because this is not a typical neighborhood financial office with a shop window for display of the company

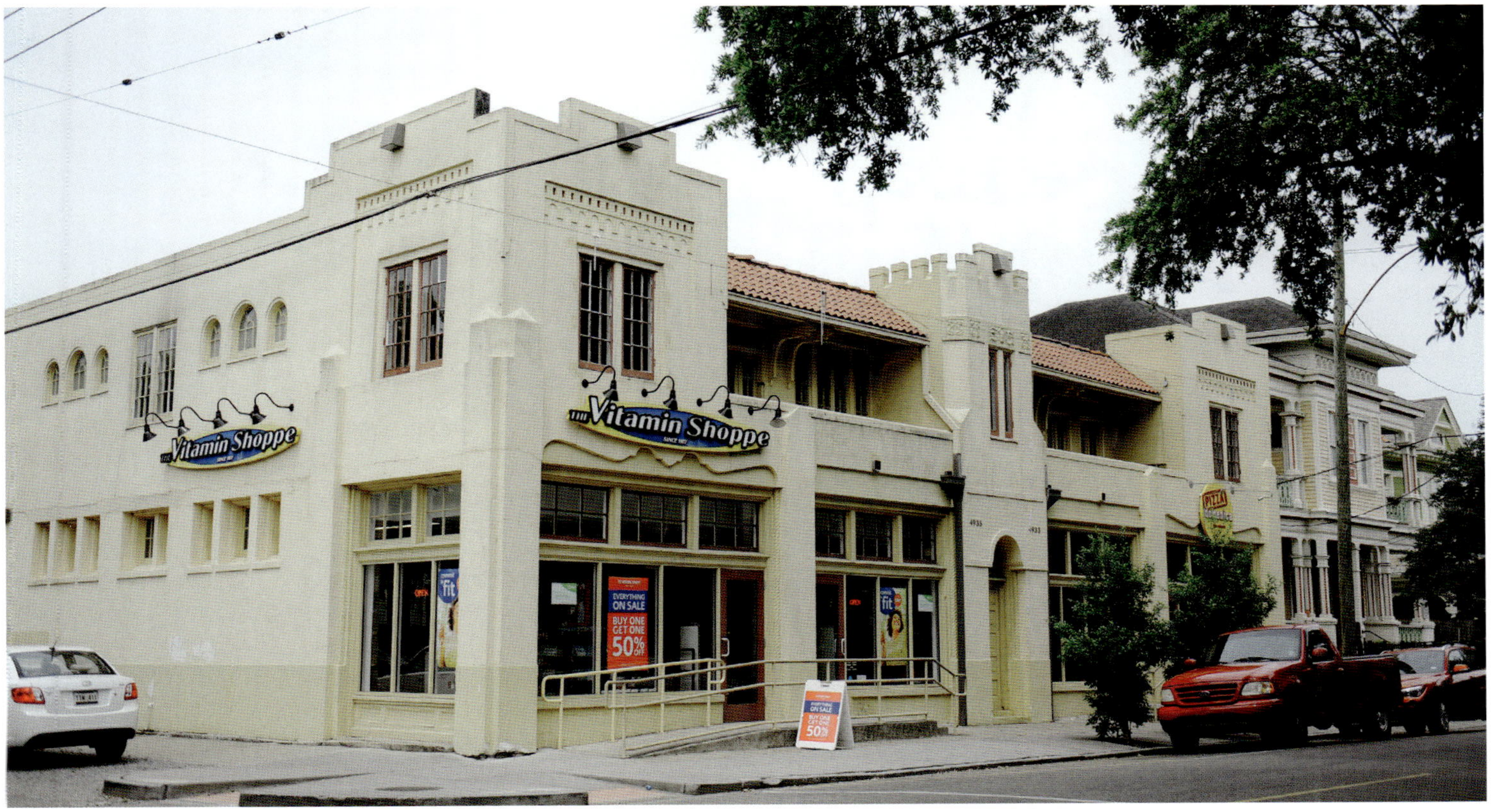

A mixed-use commercial and residential building from the 1920s.

sign. It is also rare to have a residential tenant on the other side of the wall. Debbie Hughes, the financial advisor here since 2012, said that there was a situation where a tenant smoked marijuana during business hours and the smell of weed came through the walls.

Ms. Hughes, who used to work at a Metairie Edward Jones office, commented that in Metairie "you never get what they get on Magazine." The first week in their Uptown location she told her assistant to paraphrase a line from *The Wizard of Oz:* "I'm not in Kansas anymore." This branch, according

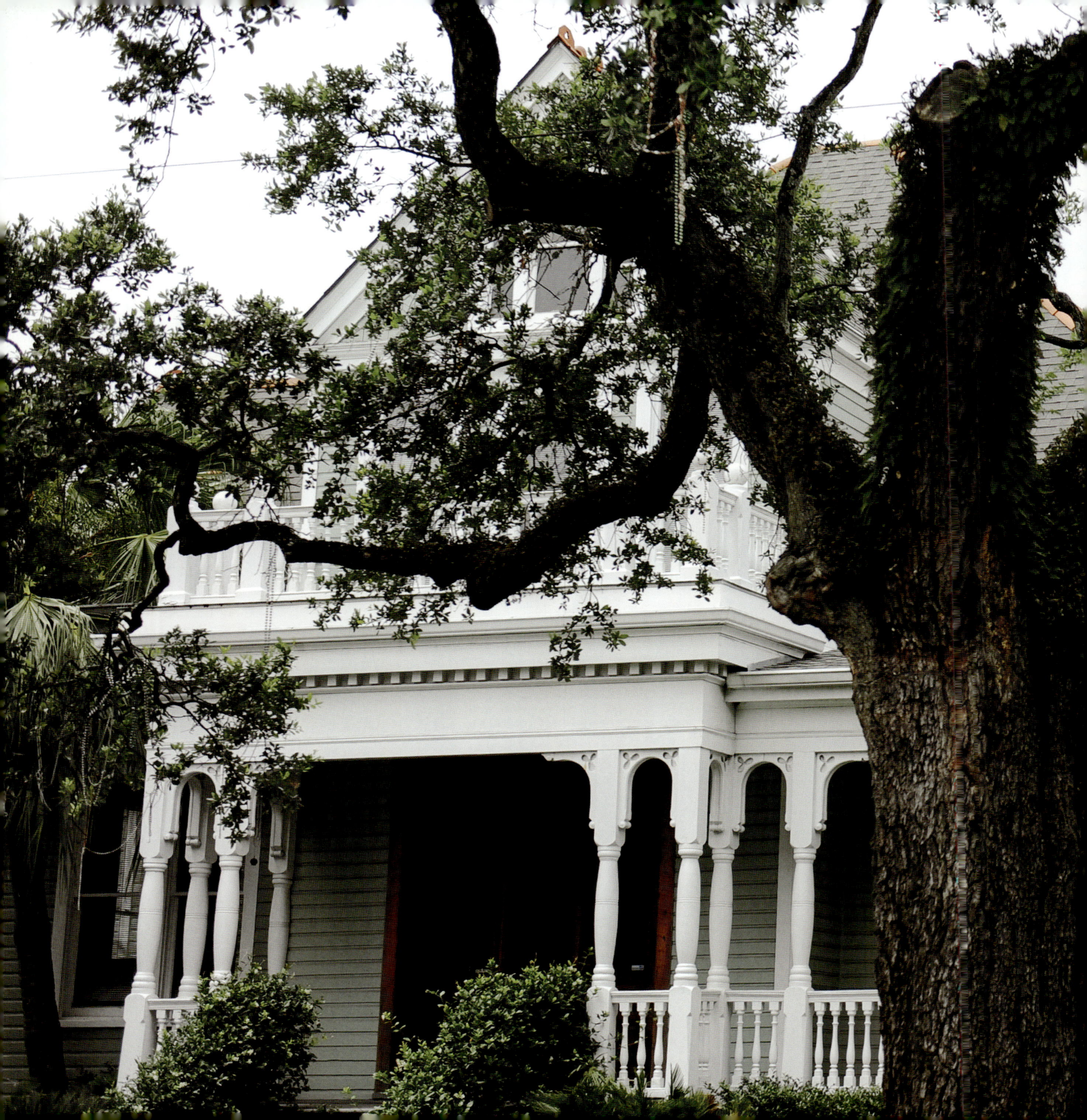

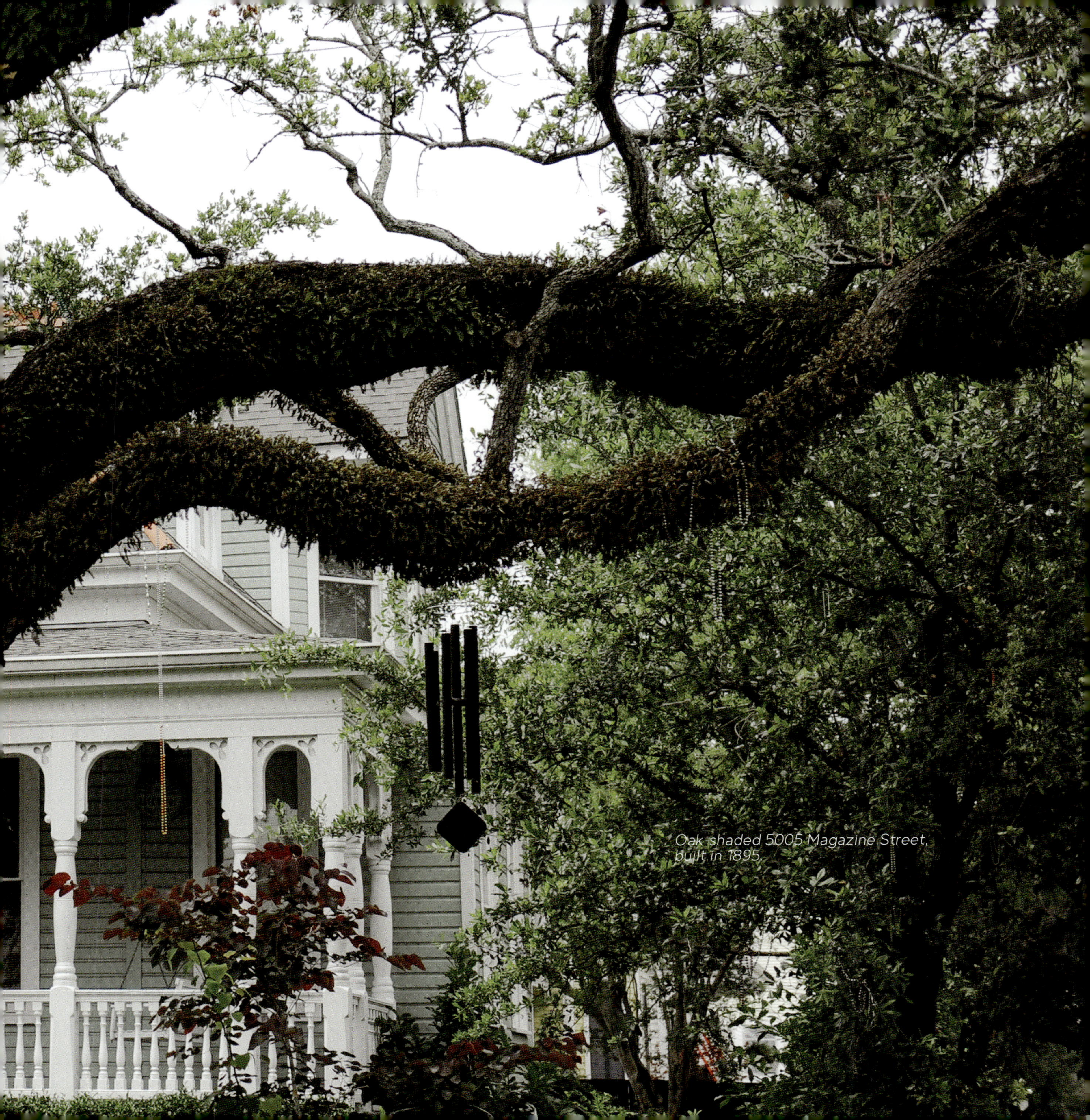

Oak-shaded 5005 Magazine Street, built in 1895.

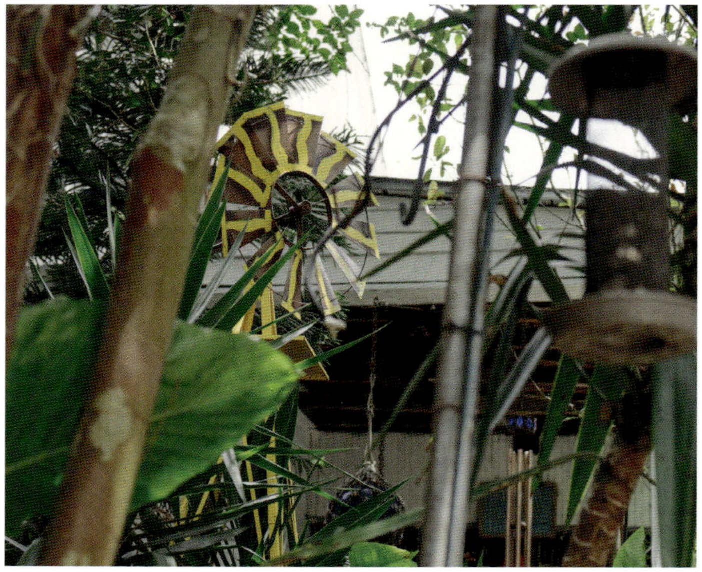

Lee Harvey Oswald's former residence.

to Ms. Hughes, has a very diverse investor base from many different backgrounds and cultures. This is something that, she feels, fits well with Magazine's eclectic mix of population. Edward Jones investors and advisors from out of town often make a point of visiting here just to say hello and see how different a branch based in an old house is from elsewhere.

Ms. Hughes loves Magazine because it still has a mom-and-pop atmosphere, and no matter where you go, "you get to know the people behind the counter, and you are welcome to go in and visit." She summed up Magazine by saying that "within a few blocks where else can you talk about your finances, get a good meal, buy vintage clothes or designer clothes, and then get a tattoo [in reference to the numerous tattoo parlors along Magazine]."

A bit farther up at the corner of Upperline are two commercial buildings. The one at 4866 houses Charlotte Williamson Salon in a building dating from 1891, while across Magazine at 4861 in a building of more recent vintage is Long Life Massage. In the 1940s these buildings respectively housed Wolf's Pharmacy and Bienvenu's Crab Depot wholesale seafood. This is a typical juxtaposition of corner commercial establishments of their periods. By the late 1970s they were both antique shops—Limited Editions and Les Bijoux, Ltd.—an indication that the character of Magazine retailing had changed in the intervening thirty years.

Across Upperline on the river side was once the site of a huge property covering the whole square. Subdivision of the property began in the late 1880s, about the time during which 4904 was built. In the 1970s and '80s it was Sixpence, an antique store, but is now Cognitive Behavioral Therapy Center. Across Magazine at 4901-03

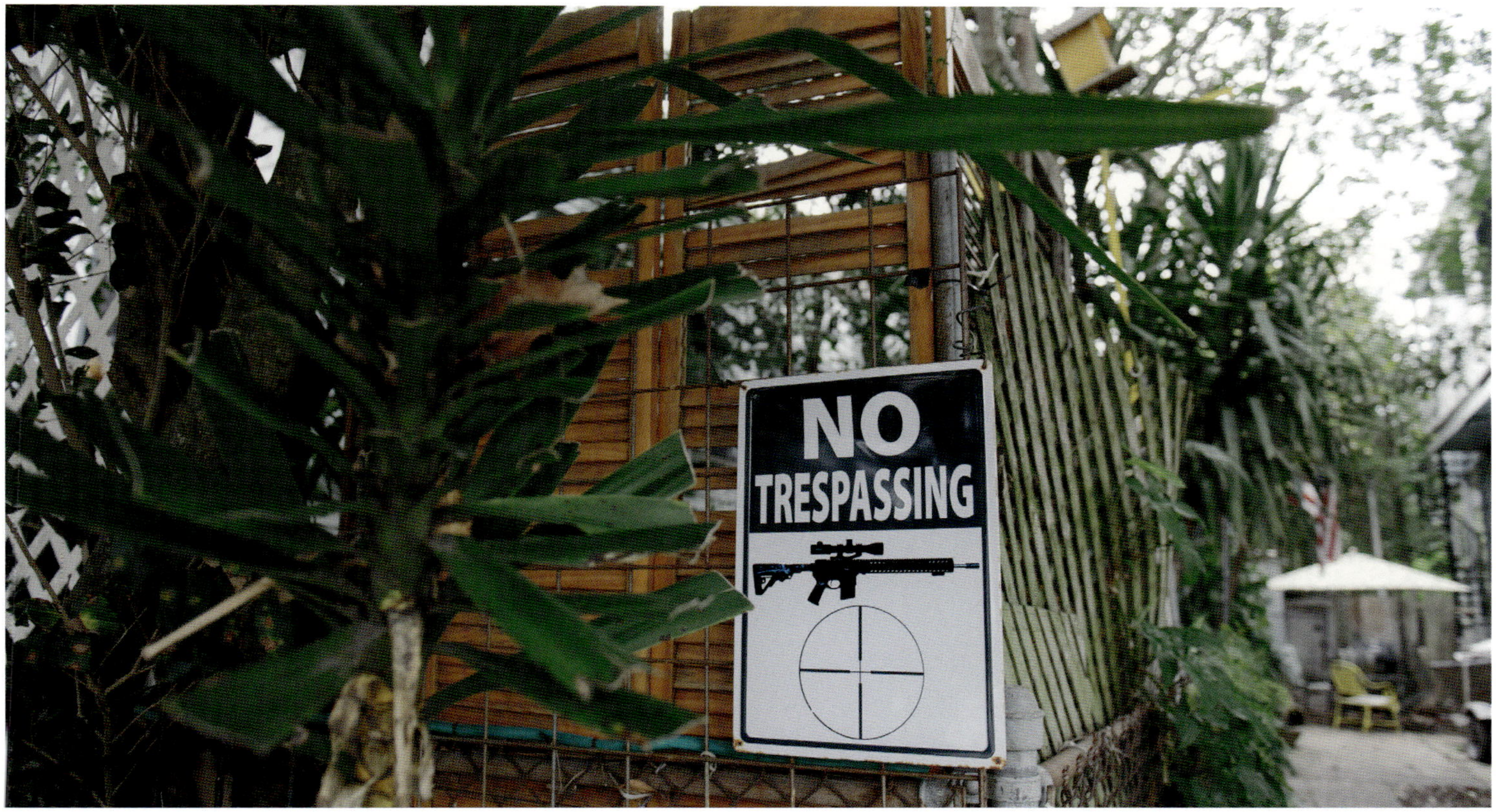

Signs discourage the curious from exploring Lee Harvey Oswald's former residence.

there is a large double house from the mid-1890s, while farther up the block at 4919-21 is yet another large double house, in this case dating from the late 1880s.

Between these two double houses are several additional circa 1900 buildings, but there is also a slice of American history from sixty-three years later. On one side of the double at 4905 Magazine lives ninety-four-year-old Harold Cavillier, a retired navy man and veteran of World War II who rides his three-wheeled bicycle every day. He has lived in the house for more than twenty years, but it is the rear apartment adjacent to Mr. Cavillier's double that has gained some notoriety. It was the rented home of Lee Harvey Oswald and his wife Marina between May 9, 1963, and September 23, 1963, before they relocated to Dallas, Texas, where Oswald

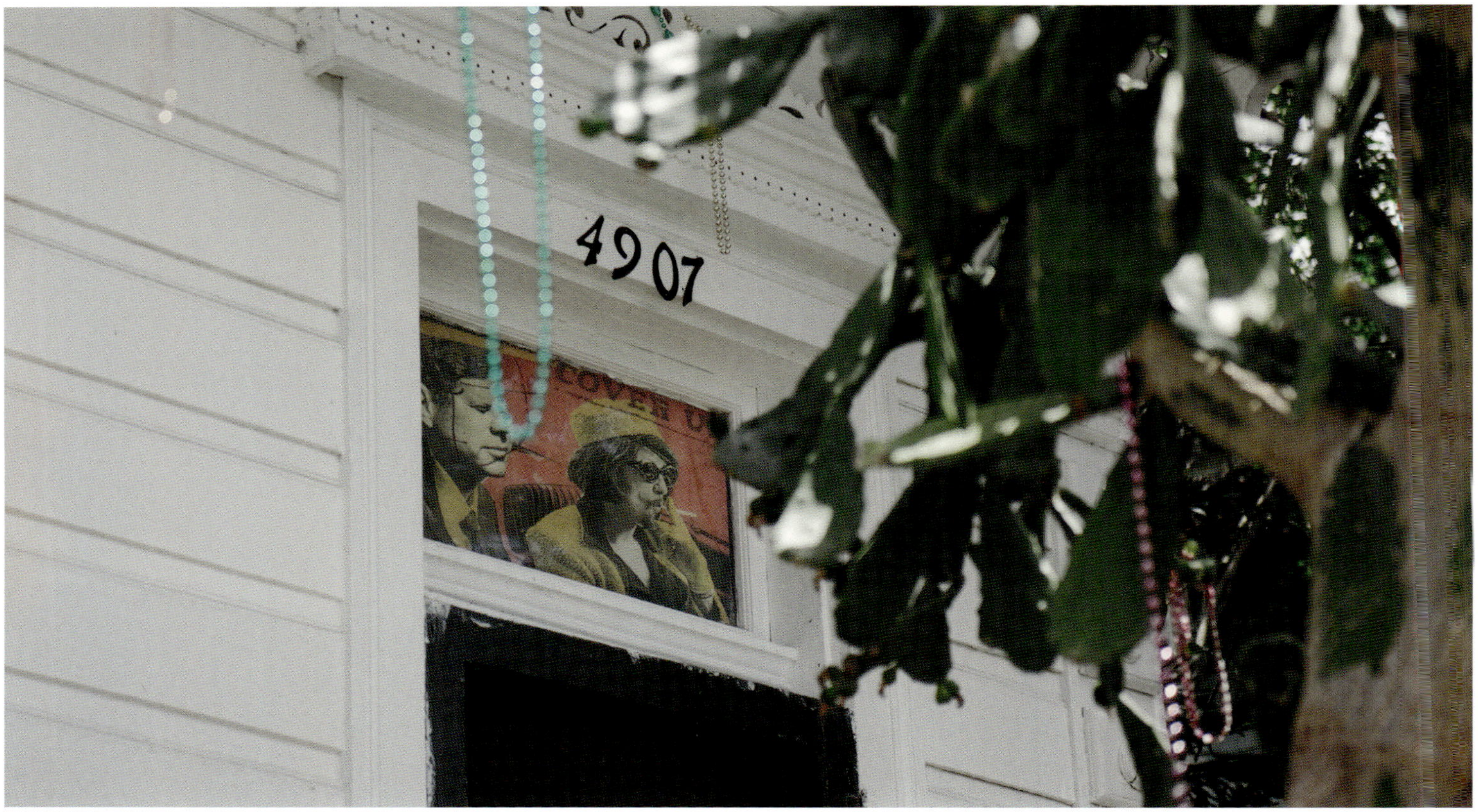

The transom of the home in front of Oswald's former apartment depicts the moment before JFK is assassinated.

was accused of assassinating President John F. Kennedy on November 22 of that same year. Mr. Harold says, "Lots of people have come by over the years to see the Oswald house, but we don't let them back there."

The next block up across Robert, except for a service station in the middle of the block, is predominately residential with buildings dating from the late nineteenth and early twentieth centuries. One of the finest houses on Magazine is the rambling country house at 5005, built in 1895 for Walker and Lulu King Saxon. Mrs. Saxon was a painter and one of her paintings, called "Uptown Street," is in the collection of the Ogden Museum of Southern Art. It is a handsome work executed in 1890 and believed to depict Magazine Street. There are no streetcar tracks in the view, although by 1890 tracks already went as far up as Audubon Park. Still, it offers a charming glimpse into the tree-lined, rural atmosphere of Magazine—and Uptown in general—in 1890 when there were dirt streets, numerous trees, and few houses. By the late 1940s the Saxon house had become the Louise Davis School; today it is the Torre Design Consortium.

The mid-twentieth-century building of St. Katharine Drexel Preparatory School, a Roman Catholic girls' school, fills the river side of the 5100 block of Magazine. This block is one of the most important sites in the history of African American education in Louisiana. Southern University was formed in 1879 and in the 1880s moved into a large and impressive building in the center of the square. Southern remained here until 1914 when it was moved near Baton Rouge, where it remains today.

Born to a wealthy Pennsylvania family, St. Katharine Drexel (1858-1955) was founder of the Sisters of the Blessed Sacrament, an order devoted to furthering the education of Native Americans and African Americans. In 1915 she established Xavier High School on the former Southern University site. This evolved into Xavier University, which moved to its current campus on Palmetto Street

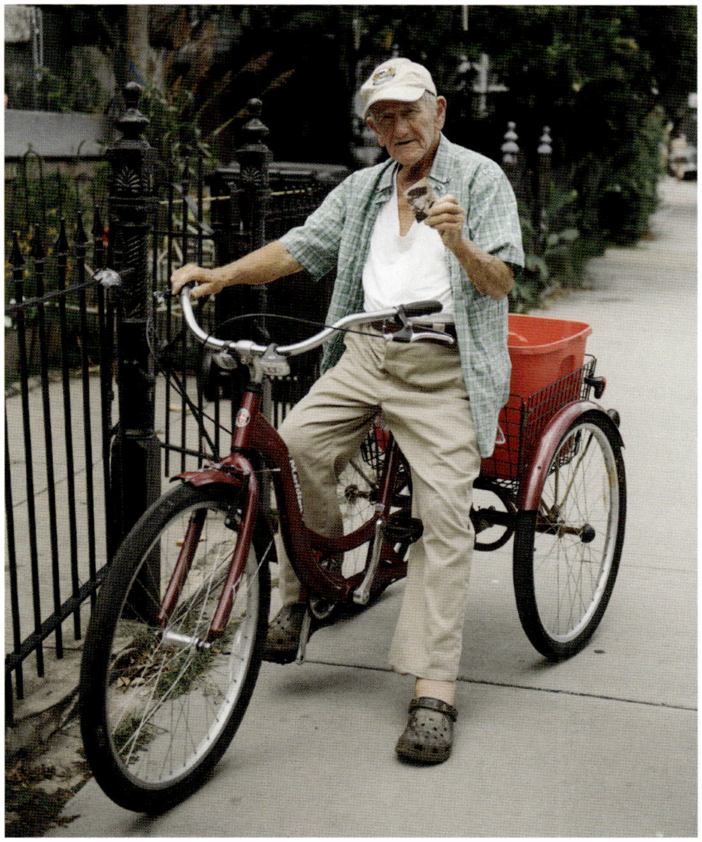

Harold Cavalier, resident of 4905 Magazine, holds a World War II-era photo of himself.

in 1929. The Magazine site then became Xavier University Preparatory School, a Catholic girls' school. In the 1950s the old university building was replaced by the present structure. When Xavier Prep ceased operations in 2013, the property was purchased by members of the alumni who reopened it and renamed it in honor of St. Katharine Drexel.

Across Magazine at 5101 and the corner of Soniat is another old neighborhood institution of a very different sort and with a very long history. Henry's Uptown Bar dates from 1900 and remains in the hands of the original family. Henry's motto is "Serving Beer Before You Were Born." Founded by Irish immigrants James and Margaret Tully Lee, it was at first called James Lee's Saloon. Later owned by their son-in-law Edward Crone, it was called Crone's Bar. The next generation's son-in-law was Henry Gogreve, and since Hurricane Katrina the business has been officially called Henry's, though it is now owned by Henry's son, Steve Gogreve.

Henry's is the oldest family-run business on Magazine as well as the oldest business operating out of its original building. But the property's history as a bar pre-dates Henry's. Before Henry's opened in 1900, 5101 Magazine was already the site of a saloon. The footprint of the building appears to fit exactly with part of an older structure shown on an early 1880s map which might help date parts of the building back to the 1870s or before. Like many buildings in New Orleans, it is constructed of barge board. Barges came downriver and were sold at the port along with their

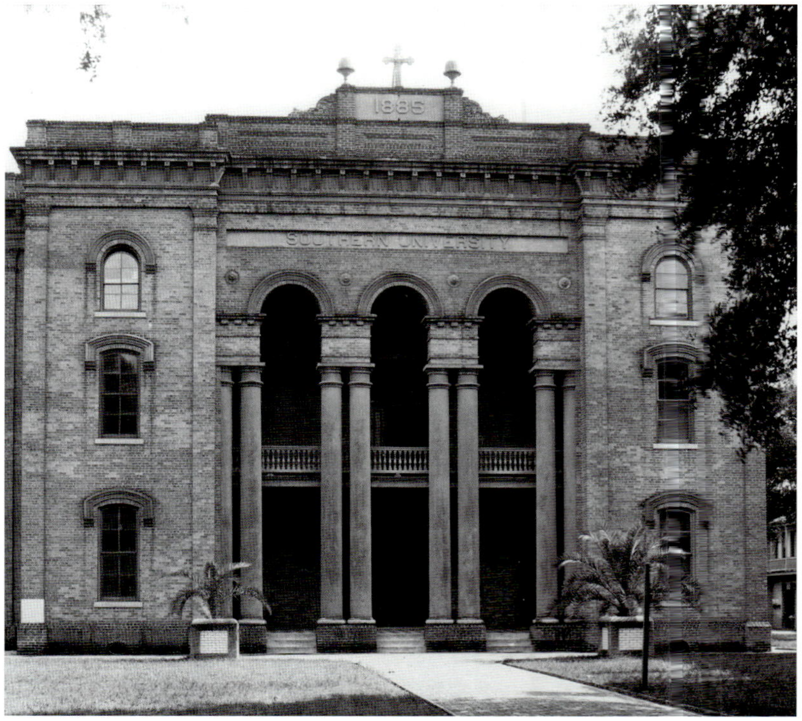

Southern University, later Xavier University, then Xavier Prep, circa 1930. (Courtesy The Historic New Orleans Collection, 1979.325.1950.)

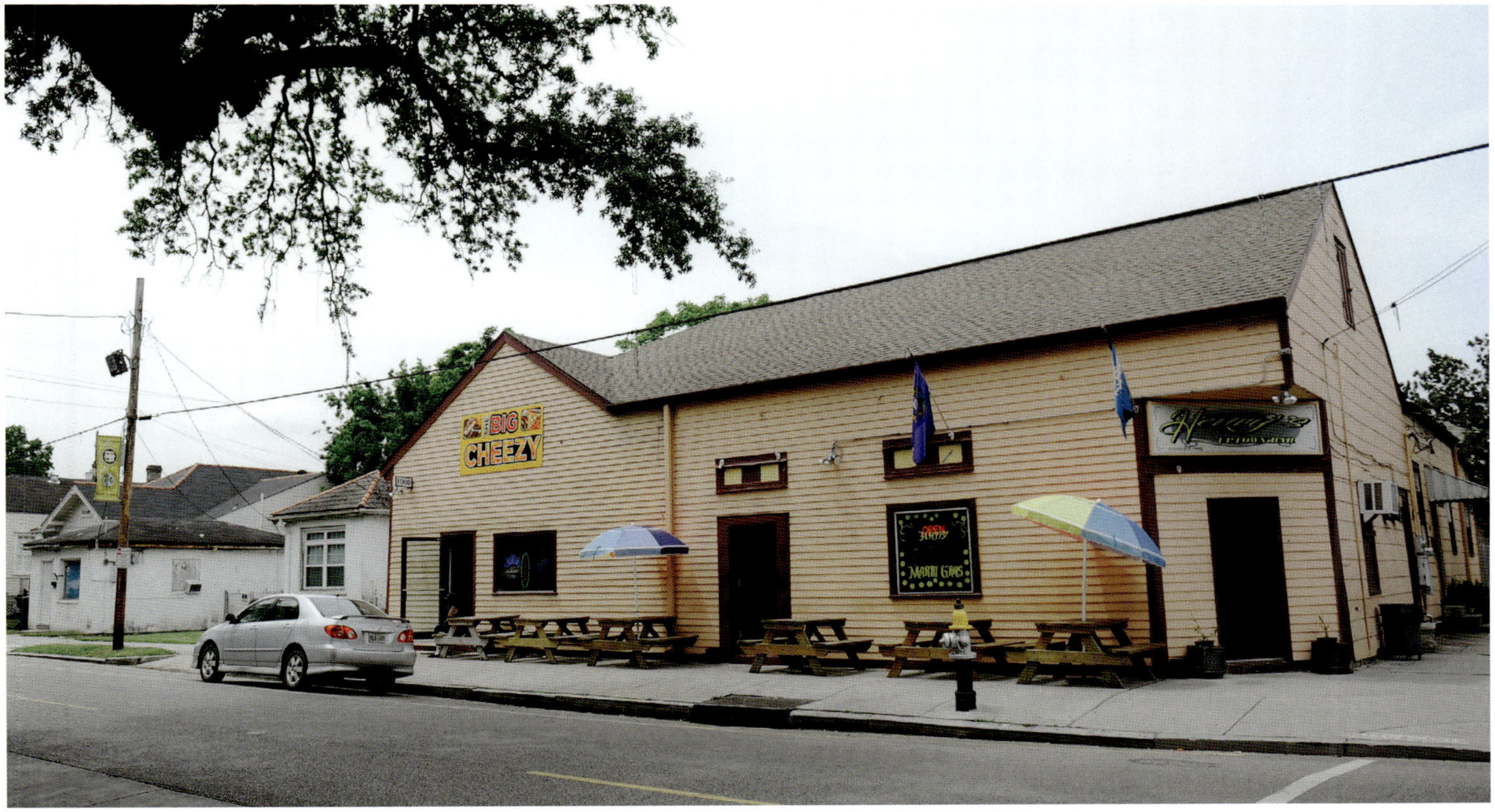

Henry's Uptown Bar, owned by the same family since 1900.

cargoes, after which the barge was cut up for its lumber. The bar was a speakeasy during Prohibition, and in the early 1930s, it was the first place on Magazine to serve draft beer with frosted glasses and mugs.

Henry's—called Crone's at the time—was also visited by Lee Harvey Oswald when he lived a few blocks away in 1963. Oswald was not a big drinker, according to Steve Gogreve, but he frequented Henry's Meat Market, adjoining the bar and also owned by Mr. Gogreve. Oswald would go in and check food prices, and his wife would return later to make the purchase. After Oswald was arrested and filmed handing out pro-Castro leaflets on Camp Street, he later went to the bar to see himself on television, to the disgust of the owner. Soon Oswald stopped showing up and he was not heard of at the bar until the assassination. Henry

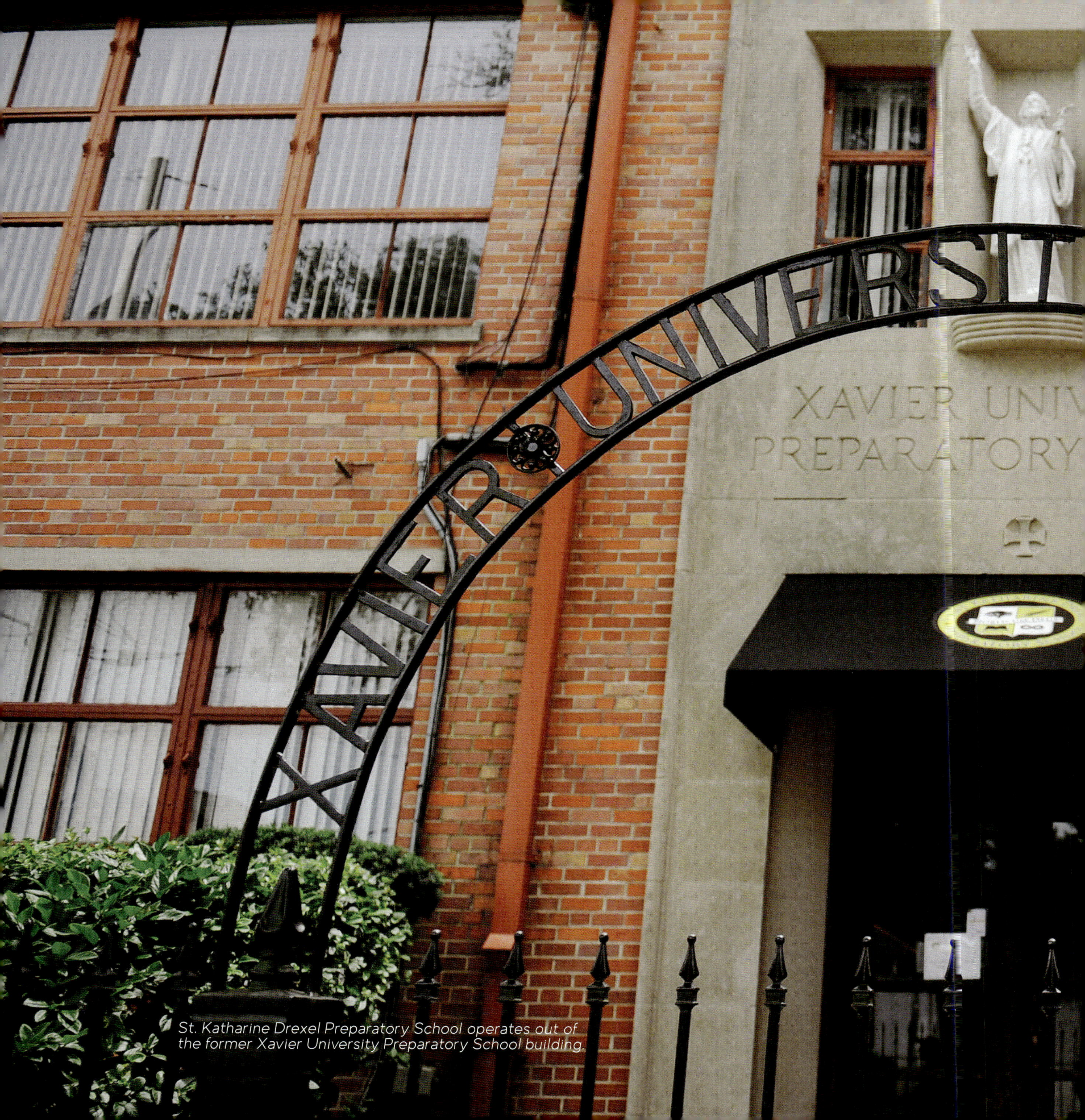

St. Katharine Drexel Preparatory School operates out of the former Xavier University Preparatory School building.

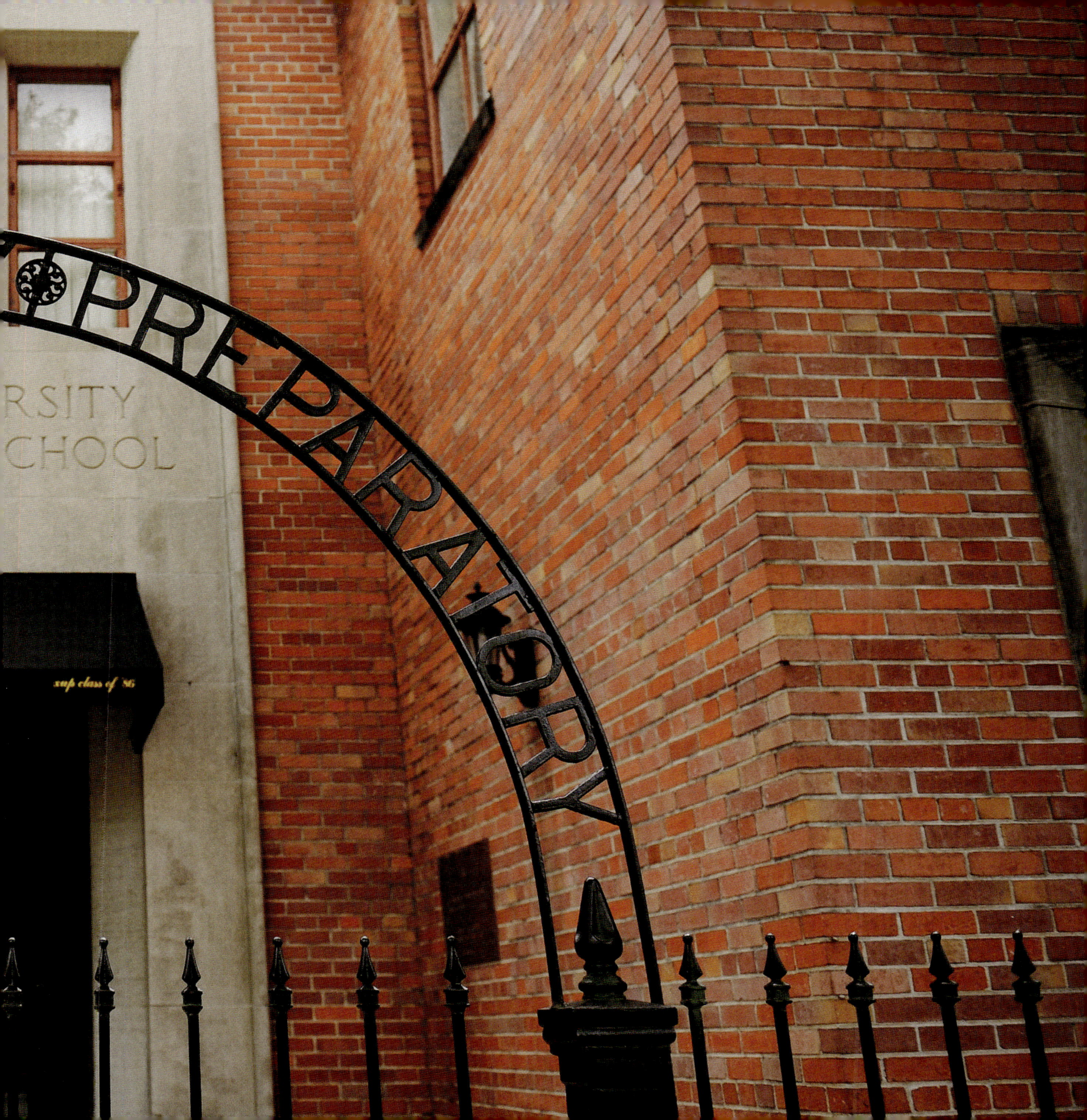
PREPARATORY
RSITY
CHOOL

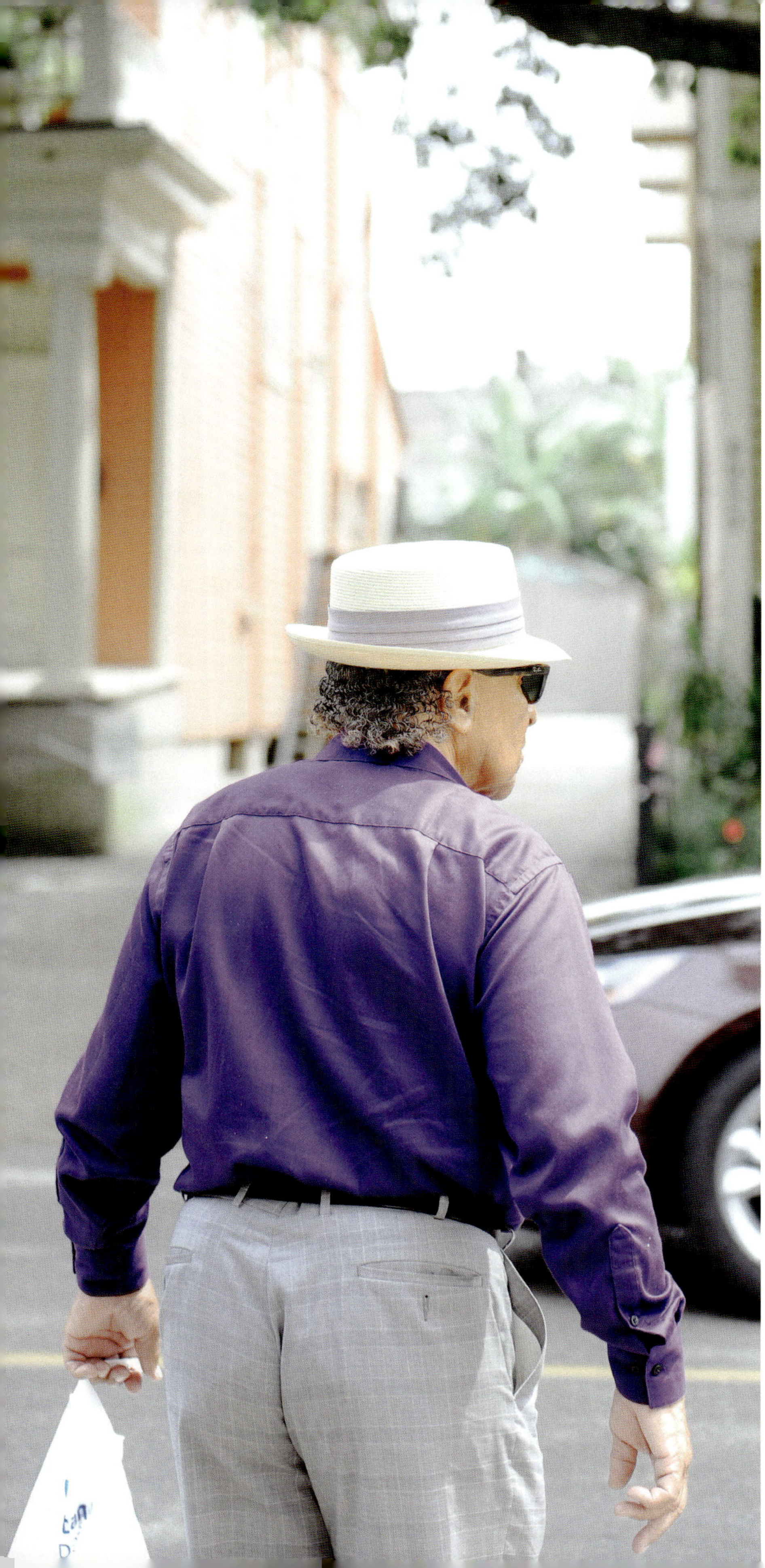

Gogreve was interviewed by national television networks the day after the Kennedy assassination and later by the Warren Commission, which investigated the president's death.

Le Bon Temps Roulé, a bar at 4801 Magazine, also claims that Oswald was a patron. A plaque affixed to the bar testifies to the claim. This longtime bar has gone through a number of name changes. In 1963 it was Gerald's Jackpot Bar, while fifteen years earlier in 1948 it was T&T Beer Parlor.

The next few blocks present a jumble of late-nineteenth- and twentieth-century residential and business buildings. One earlier example is a fine mid-1890s double house at 5221-23, while along the lake side of the 5300 block is a series of early neighborhood dwellings with gingerbread ornamentation dating from the early 1890s. These are on the former site of a large country mansion whose property comprised the entire block. By the late 1890s this country neighborhood was becoming more and more town-like, and after the streetcars were electrified in the 1890s it grew even faster since a trip downtown took less time.

One of the finest houses of this period

A sharply dressed gentleman crosses upper Magazine Street.

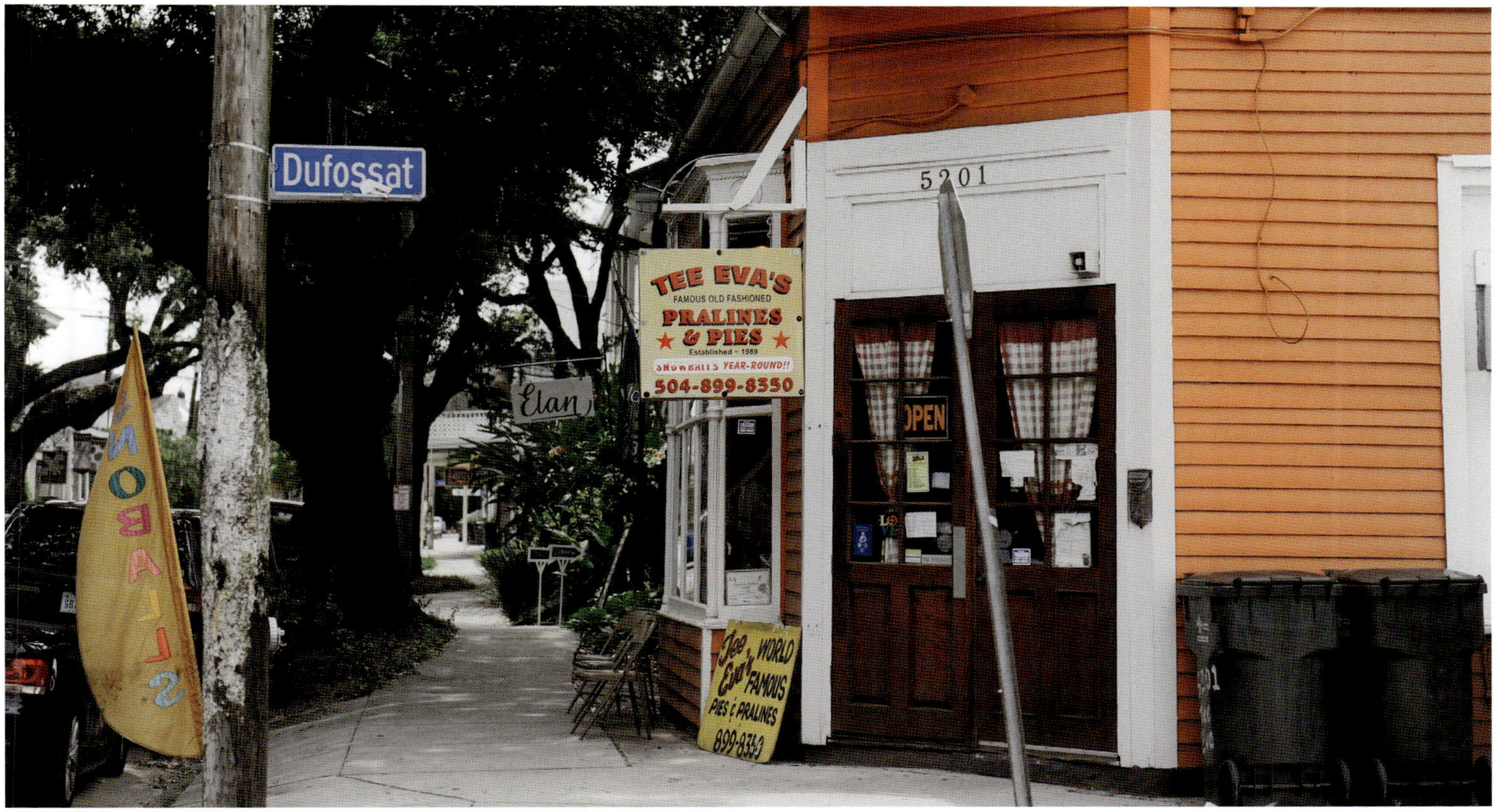

Tee Eva's Pralines & Pies.

is located at 5256 on the corner of Valmont. It is a large 1883 mansion that now houses the New Orleans Academy of Fine Arts. The school was founded in 1978 by Auseklis Ozols and fostered through the interest of Mrs. Dorothy Coleman. It is open to all comers and has a large enrollment. Its original school was at another Magazine location at 3218 in an 1870s commercial building that now houses Amici Ristorante & Bar. The house at 5256 was renovated into a small shopping center called Valmont Square in the 1970s, and the school took over in 1980.

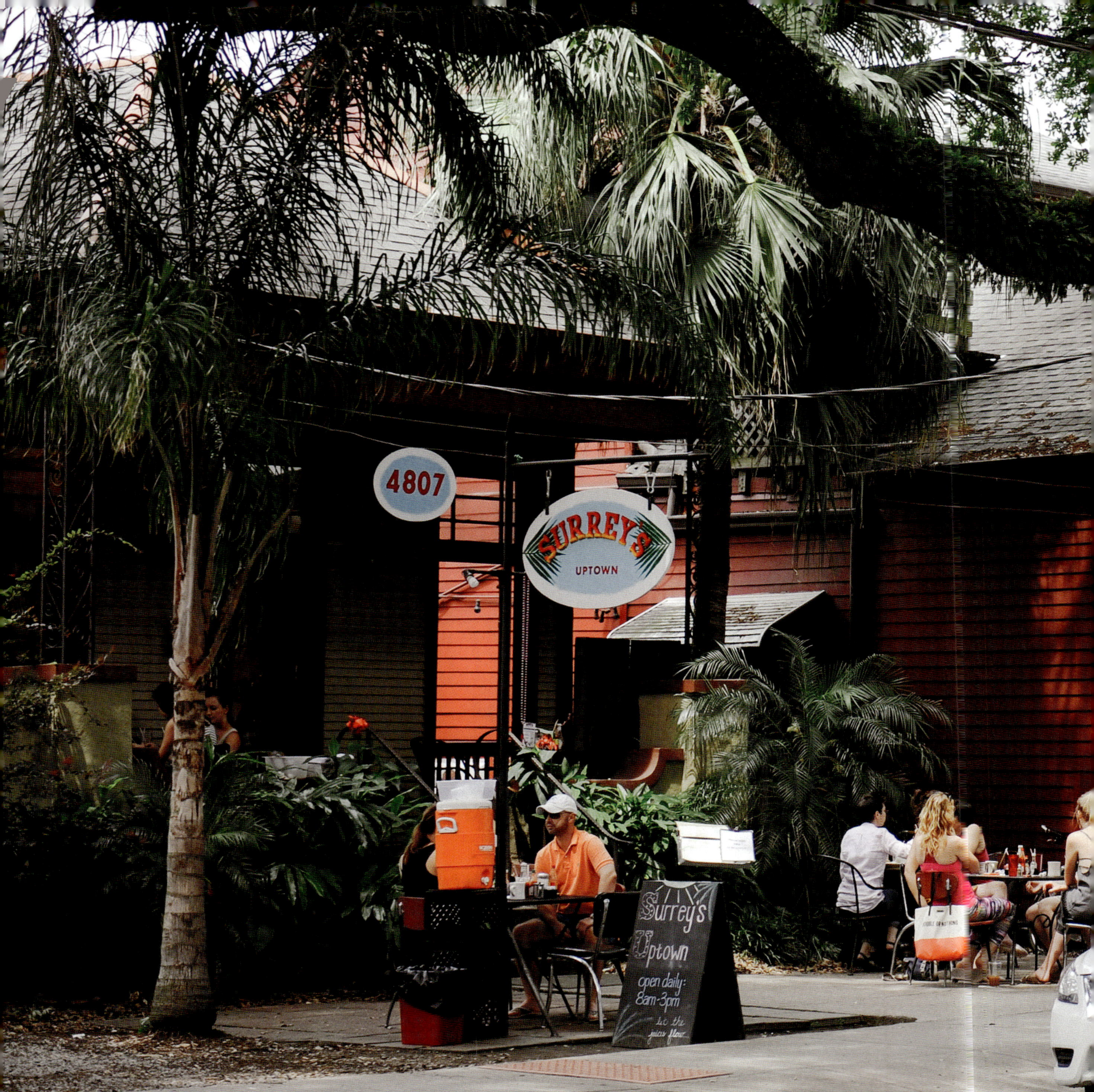

Surrey's Café & Juice Bar and Le Bon Temps Roulé (4800 block).

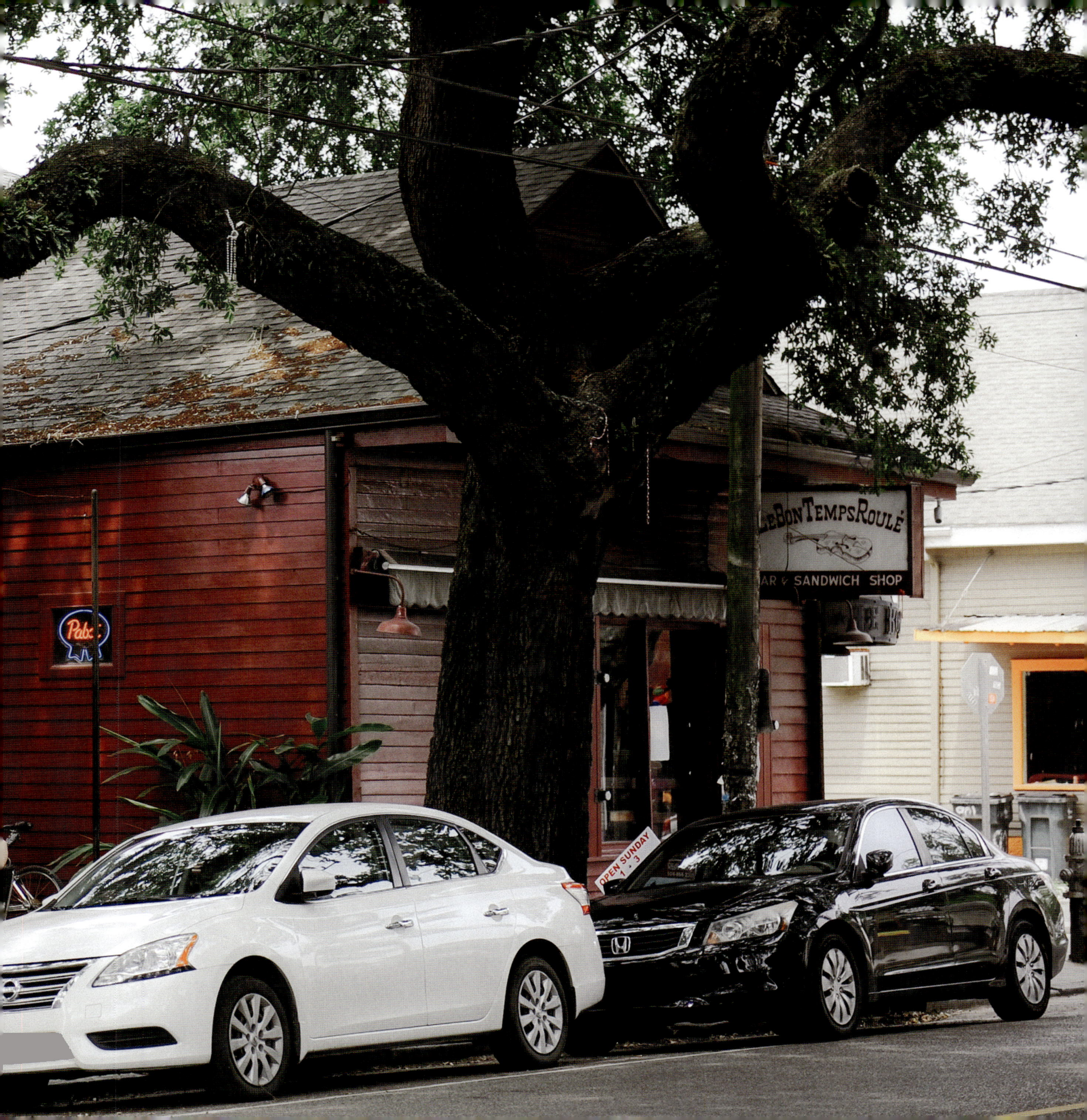
LeBonTempsRoulé
AR & SANDWICH SHOP
OPEN SUNDAY
1 - 3

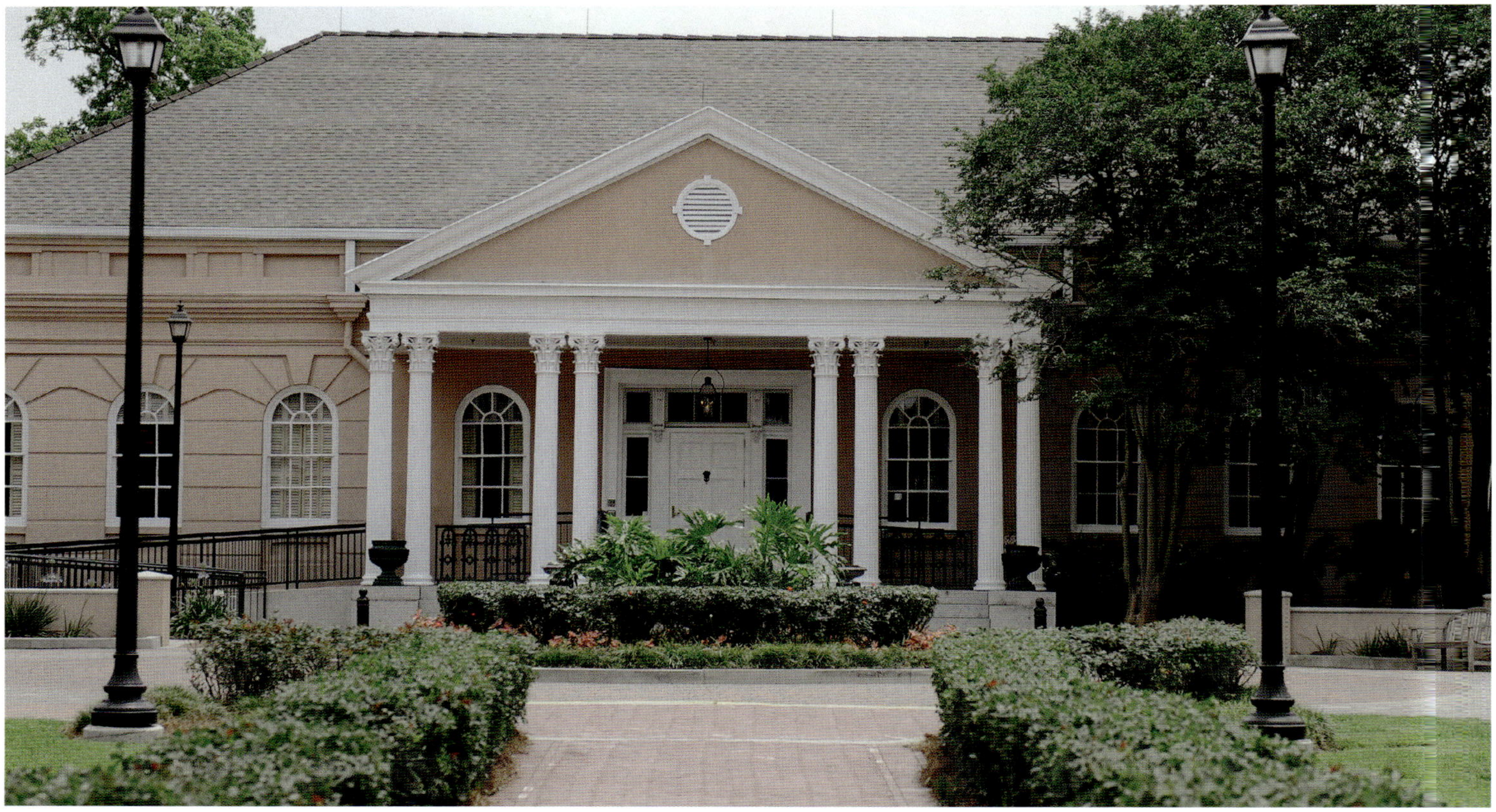

Poydras Home.

The Poydras Home fills the huge square on the river side of Magazine in the 5300 block between Leontine and Jefferson. Founded by philanthropist Julien Poydras (1740-1824) in 1817 as an orphanage on Julia Street, it moved to this location in 1857. Then the home was in rustic countryside and shaded by large oak trees. It was originally three stories, but the top two floors were removed in 1959 when it became a home for elderly ladies. Now open to both sexes, the complex has expanded dramatically.

Crossing Jefferson Avenue another important Magazine Street shopping district emerges, heralded by a tall Queen Anne-style landmark dating from 1899-1900, built as a pharmacy and operated under various names and owners for the first eighty-eight years of its life. Unti

1923 it was Walsdorf's, and through the '20s it was E.S. Bernardas, who also maintained a pharmacy at 2800 Magazine at Washington. By 1930 it had become Baumann's pharmacy. Throughout all these years the pharmacists and their families lived upstairs. By the 1940s it was Mayeux Brothers who operated the pharmacy, and the building ended its drugstore days as Dupont's, when in 1988 the enterprise was renamed Uptown Delivery Pharmacy and relocated to 741 Nashville at Magazine into a building that in the 1940s had housed an A&P grocery store. Uptown Delivery Pharmacy remains one of the last independent pharmacies in the entire area, and as its name implies, it still delivers.

In the late 1940s, 5415 Magazine was Klein Brothers Furniture Company, but even before that it was a tailor shop. Libby Bonner, manager of British Antiques, which has been at this address since 1981, was told a story by an unidentified elderly lady who said that her father and uncle owned the tailor shop. This was most likely in the 1930s after the lady's mother had passed away. In looking after the little girl the two men built a big doll house inside the counter, which was not far from the front of the store. Here the girl "spent many happy an hour" playing in the doll house, while customers transacted their business just inches above the little girl at play.

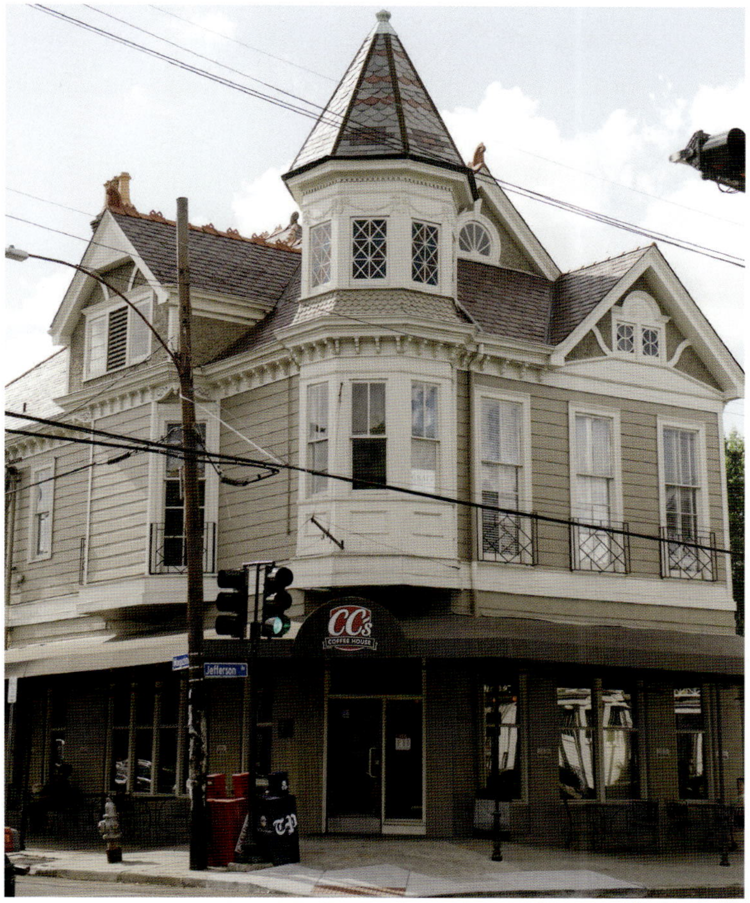

Long the site of a drugstore, the Queen Anne building on the corner of Jefferson Avenue is now a CC's Coffee House.

In the 1960s and '70s the building was Dionysian, a dark college hangout bar

New Orleans Academy of Fine Arts.

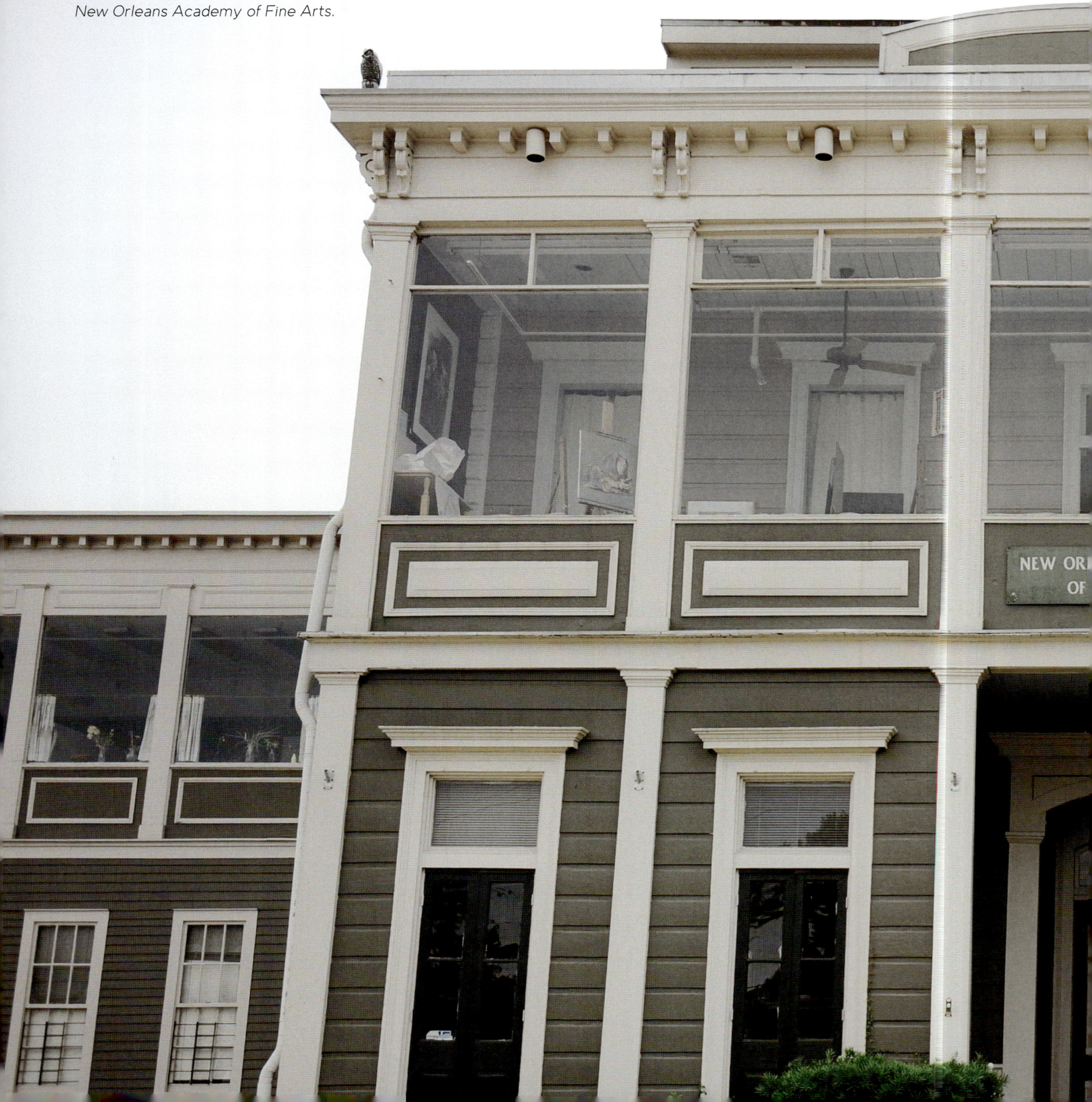

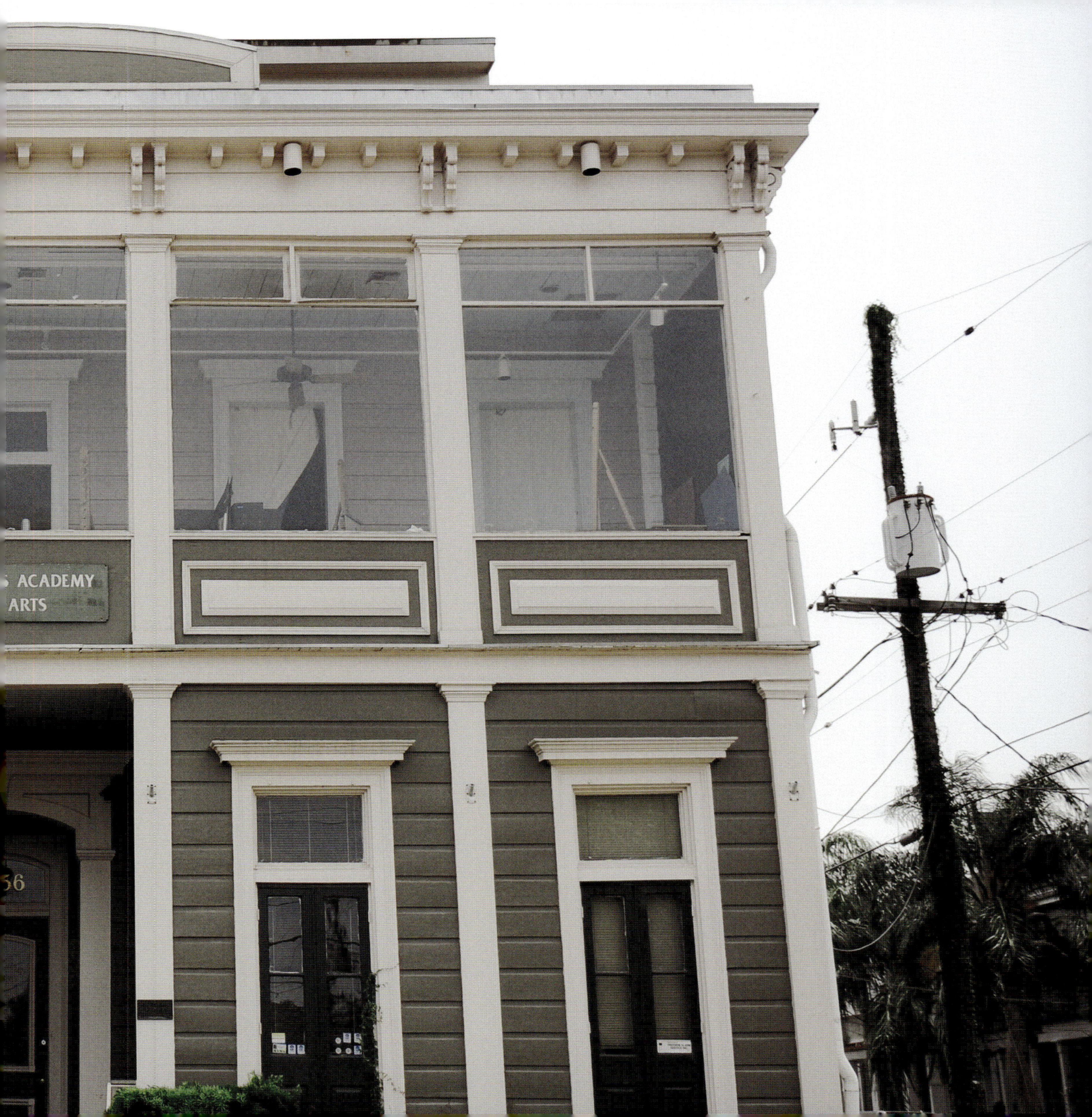
ACADEMY
ARTS

with few frills. When the building was Dionysian, according to a former bartender and Tulane student who related the story to Mrs. Bonner, David Ferrie (1918-1967) would come in every afternoon to have a drink and just sit and talk. Ferrie was implicated later in the 1960s by New Orleans District Attorney Jim Garrison as being part of a conspiracy to assassinate John F. Kennedy. The bartender recalled that his daily customer was "very, very weird."

The building was purchased by Bennett Powell for his mother, Hazel Powell, who opened British Antiques in 1981; it is now owned by Bennett Powell and his wife, Evon. It is constructed of barge board, and the bay windows were added for the antique store. The overall feel of the glittering shop is a far cry from the building's darkened Dionysian days, which this writer remembers from a visit in the late '70s.

Farther down the block, there was an H.G. Hill grocery store at 5429 in the 1940s, which by the 1970s was T&S, a good quality mom-and-pop store that, like so many others, closed in the early 1980s. Its site is now a parking lot, but in the 1880s it was the location of a beer hall and beer garden, attesting to the large German population in Uptown New Orleans.

In the 1970s and '80s the Greenery was a popular destination at 5434, where there was a wide array of plants sold in a crowded, tropical atmosphere. The owners had a big black Pyrenees dog named Toulouse who could frequently be found in a sleepy state sprawling in the doorway. At an earlier time this building was the popular Henry Reuther Bakery and is now a hairdresser, Paris Parker salon.

Despite the present commercialization of this area, in the early 1880s this was still a countrified village with the mule-drawn streetcar line ending at Joseph Street and the streetcar barn at the corner of Octavia. To this day there is a slight jog at the intersection of Magazine and Joseph to accommodate the end of that early car line. Later this helped accommodate electric cars turning into the Arabella car barn, which was built in 1893. This huge structure was designed to serve the expanding streetcar lines as electrification took place, and the old barn at Octavia was torn down.

The Arabella barn covers a full square

block—including the former storage yard behind the barn, it once covered two square blocks—between Joseph and Arabella. The barn was initially built by the Crescent City Railroad Co., but ultimately served most Uptown streetcar lines. In the late 1940s it was again refurbished to serve bus and trolleybus lines with the phasing out of streetcars. In the 1990s it closed and remained vacant until 2002 when the Arabella Station Whole Foods adapted the huge building with its soaring, cathedral-like ceiling for a market.

Although many neighbors opposed the coming of Whole Foods, the store has become an important anchor in this shopping area and is a modern counterpart to the old Ewing's public market which was established at 5500 Magazine, on the corner of Octavia, in 1907. As with the street's other public markets, this one was rebuilt in 1931 in an Art Deco style, then in the '50s it was transferred into private hands. Ewing's remained a private neighborhood grocer into the 1970s, after which it became Leisure Landing, a popular record store; then a branch of the women's shoe store Feet First, which still has a shop at 4122 Magazine Street; then MiMi, an elegant women's store.

More recently it became another fine women's store called Joseph, based in Memphis. Co-owners are Philip Jacobson and Barrie Wurzburg. Mr. Jacobson said that he had family in New Orleans and wanted to open a store here. The company once owned the shoe department of the former Gus Mayer on Canal Street, and

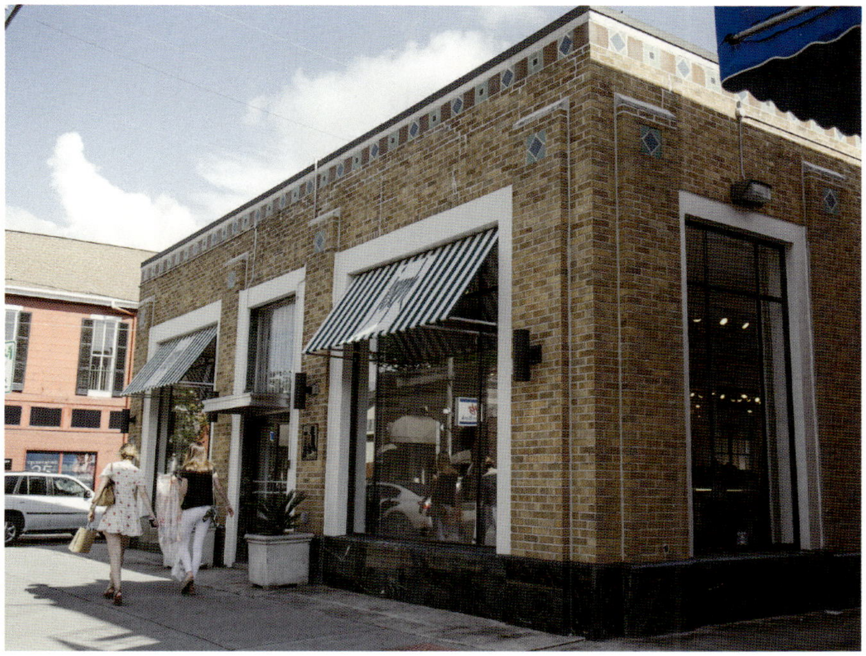

Joseph's, site of the former Ewing Public Market, at 5501 Magazine Street.

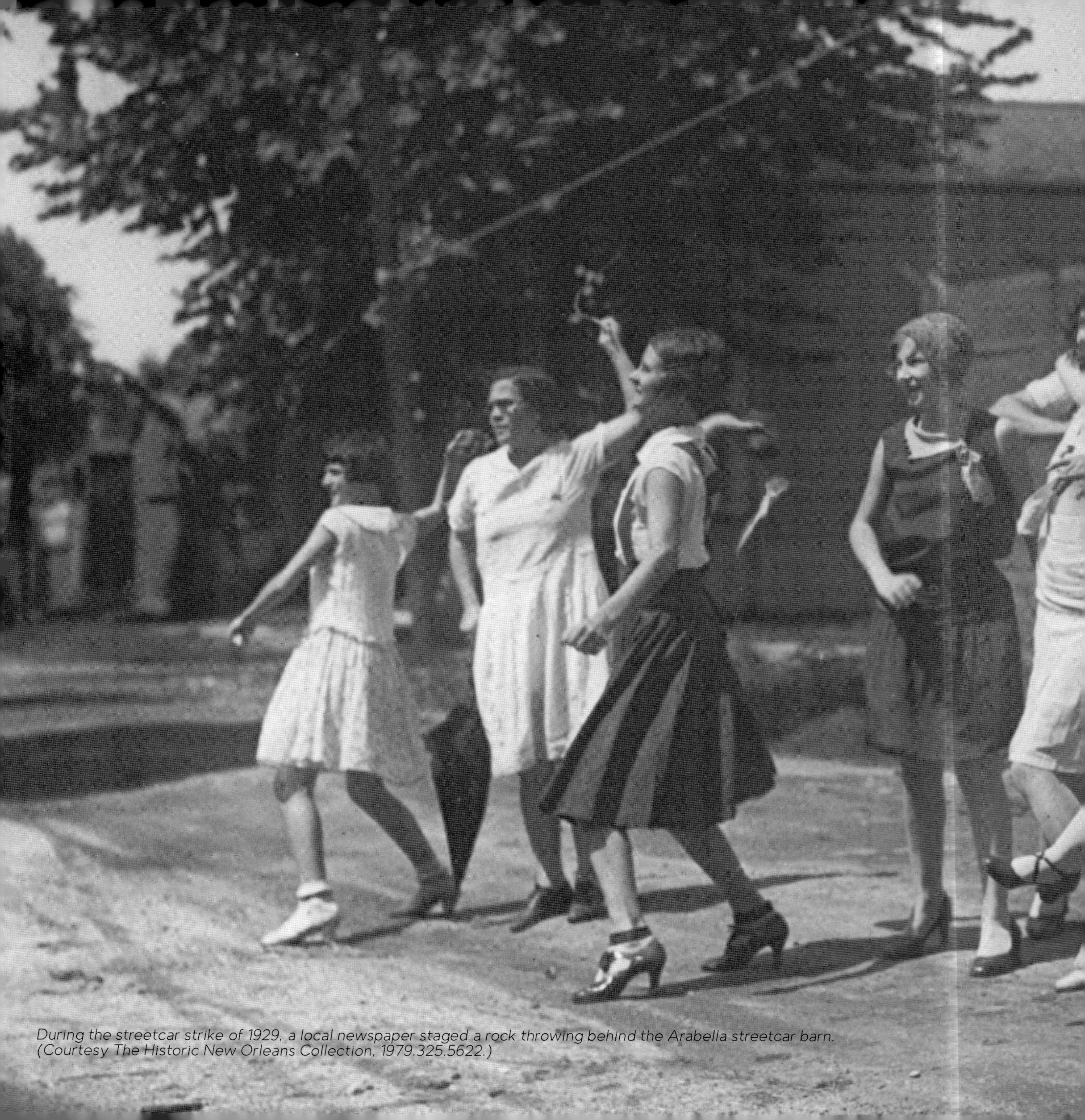

During the streetcar strike of 1929, a local newspaper staged a rock throwing behind the Arabella streetcar barn. (Courtesy The Historic New Orleans Collection, 1979.325.5622.)

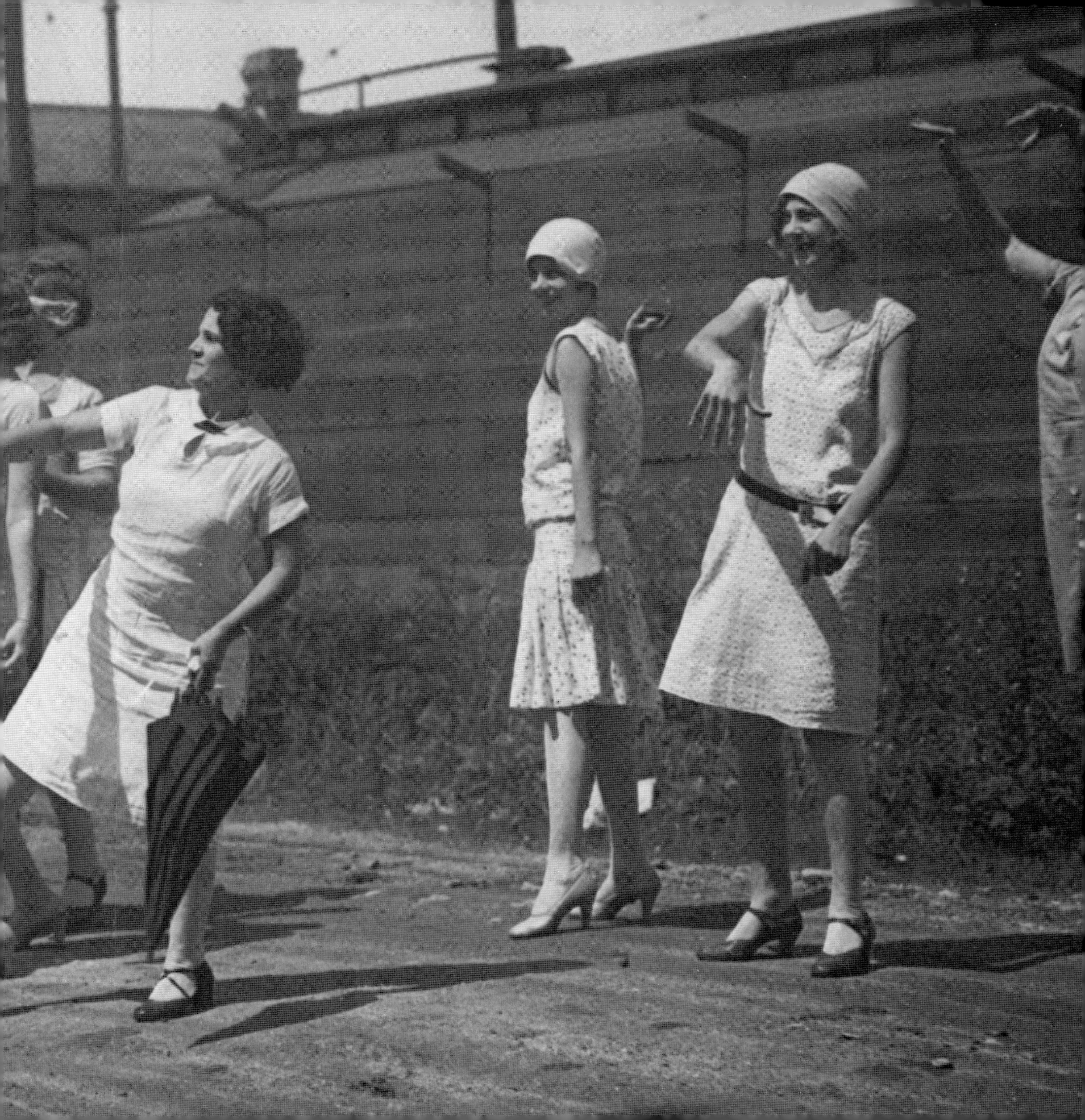

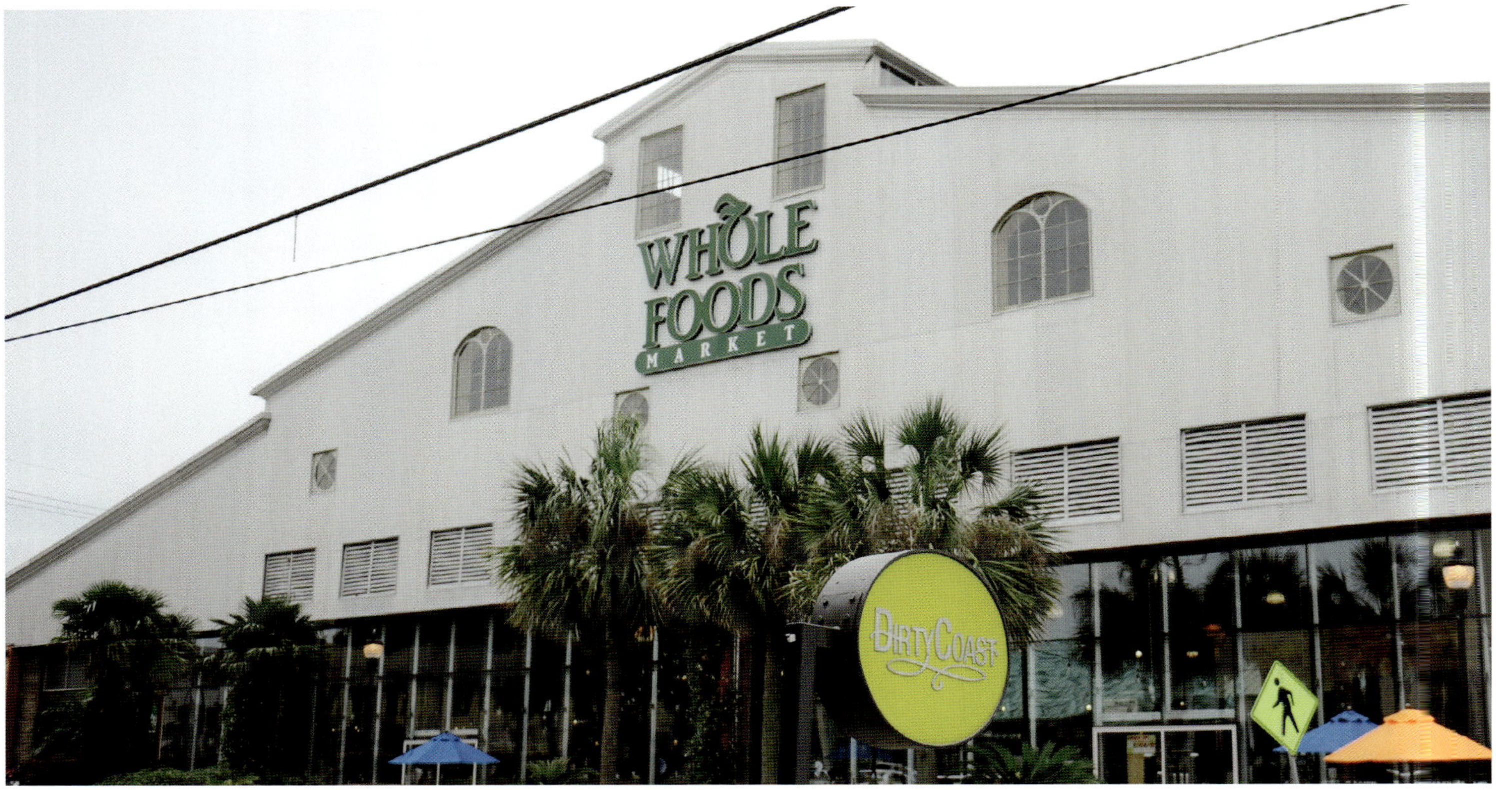

A local boutique of original, New Orleans-inspired goods, Dirty Coast shares the block with national giant Whole Foods Market.

he said that if the company was going to open a store in New Orleans, it was going to be on Magazine and in a building with history. Mr. Jacobson commented, "There is no street like Magazine anywhere."

Ewing's, just as with the other public markets, attracted an array of businesses to the vicinity, which by the late 1920s was an attractive, well-established shopping district that would extend beyond Nashville Avenue.

In the 1920s, tailor Tobias Zoller opened at 5519 Magazine before moving to 5422. Here men could rent formal wear well into the twentieth century. The store now houses B Kids children's shop, which started in Baton Rouge and is owned and run by three sisters with locations in Louisiana, Texas, and Alabama, but the Zoller name is still emblazoned in tiles in the doorway. Across the street, on the

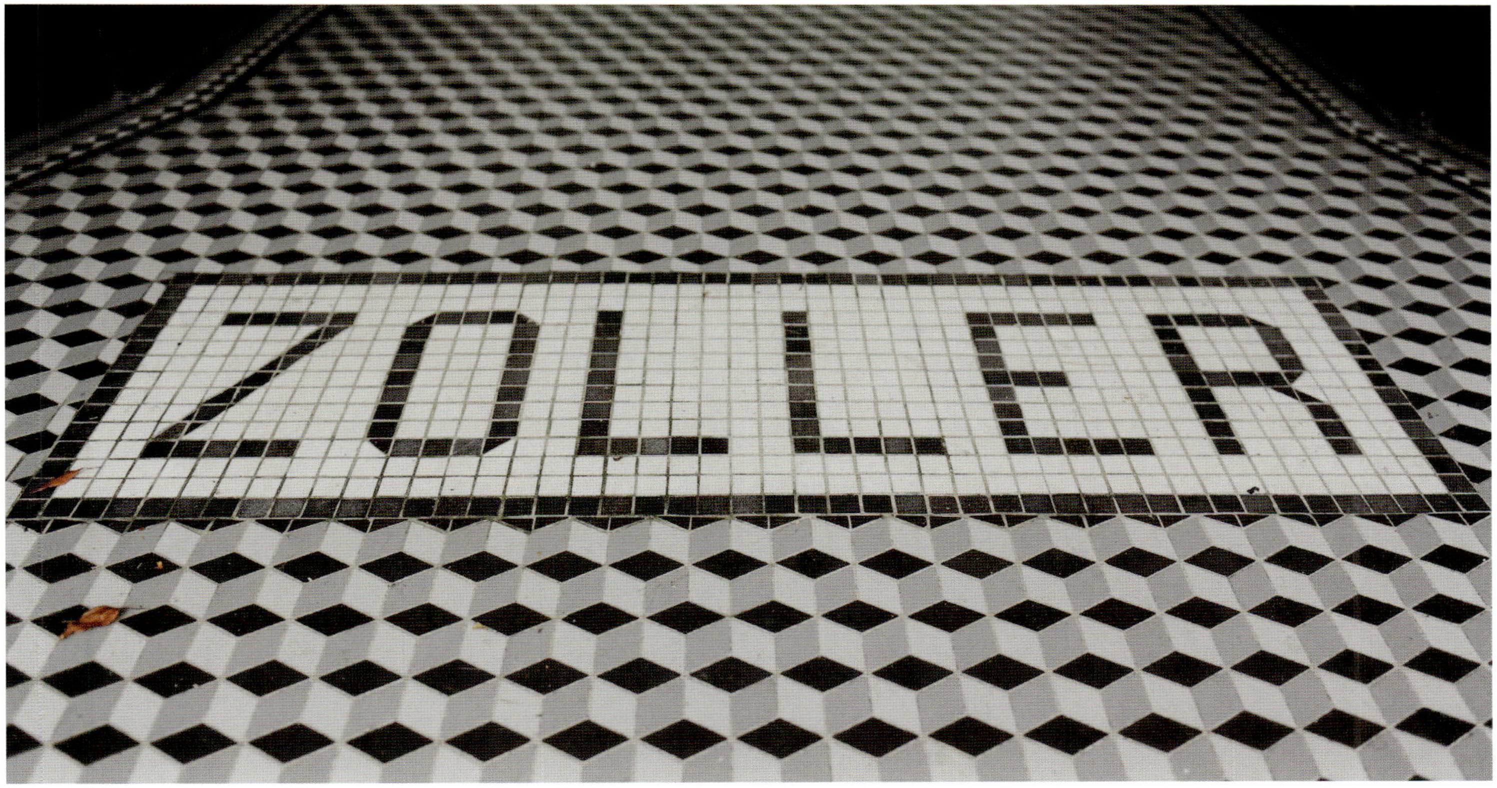

Entrance tiles to Zoller's tailoring shop.

corner of Octavia at 5501 Magazine, is Earth Savers, a full-service spa with three Greater New Orleans locations.

Ott's Pet Shop was at 5505, now Jean Therapy, and of Ott's the *Underground Shopping Guide* said, "If you have tried everywhere and can't find it, try here; I'll bet they have it." It was a leading pet shop from the 1940s until its demise more than half a century later, and many people recalled that when they were children in the 1950s they would catch and sell lizards to Mr. Ott for a nickel apiece, and he would sell them for seventy-five cents each.

For many years Friendly House Restaurant & Bar—now Slice Pizzeria—stood across Joseph from the Arabella bus barn at 5538 and was popular with bus barn employees. The *Underground Shopping Guide* called Friendly House a "Super 'Blue

Plate' restaurant" with "big portions . . . local color is plentiful." In the 1920s, it was called the Standard Restaurant.

Diagonally across Magazine from Friendly House, at 5606, was Tranchina's Restaurant, which also had "Plenty of local color and busy at lunch time." Its site is now a parking lot for a small strip mall dating from 1986. At the same Joseph intersection, at 5535 is a longtime bar location. In 1916 it was W.F. Ernst's saloon, but in the 1920s during Prohibition it was Robert J. Fee's grocery. In the 1940s it was Dud's Bar, owned by Dudley Dees, and today is remembered by some as Ms. Mae's from the 1980s and '90s, a popular college hangout prized for cheap drinks. Ms. Mae's is now merged with The Club at the corner of Napoleon, while the old bar is the much more upscale St. Joe's Bar.

Many of those recalling Magazine in the 1940s and '50s mentioned Oldenburg's at 5525 as the shoe store of choice. It had been around since before the 1920s. In the '70s the address was well known as Melange, which sold antiques, reproductions, home décor, and children's clothes. In the 1980s and '90s it was the very popular needlework shop Persian Cat. Today Bryan Batt and his partner Tom Cianfichi own Hazelnut at this location. Mr. Batt is well known nationally as an actor and author and locally his family founded and owned Pontchartrain Beach Amusement Park. Hazelnut is a home decor and furnishings shop that opened in 2003 at 5515 before moving to its current location. Mr. Batt appreciates the renaissance that has taken place on Magazine Street. Like many others, he says, "Magazine is a destination for the whole area . . . across the lake . . . all over." Mr. Batt loves "the old neighborhood feel . . . the street is tried and true." He added that he "wouldn't want to be anyplace else in New Orleans," and "it's unlike a mall. Magazine is a great avenue, stores are individually owned . . . No one from corporate tells me what to put in my window or what I can have or can't have."

People from all over come to Magazine to shop, and Mr. Batt gets many repeat customers from out of town. This was echoed by Peggy Gundlach, manager of Basics Underneath Fine Lingerie at 5513 and 5515, an earlier Persian Cat then Hazelnut location. Basics started at the beginning of this century around the corner on Octavia Street. Ms. Gundlach loves Magazine because it is surrounded by neighborhoods, and while she gets many repeat customers from nearby, she has visitors from the entire region and out of town. Many shoppers come every year for Jazz Fest and want to shop where the locals go. She said that the 5500 block is thriving, and that the coming of Whole Foods and the Walgreens Pharmacy in their beautiful new 1870s-style building on the site of an American Legion Hall across Magazine "have been a benefit to the area."

Chez Nous, at 5701, is a popular Uptown gourmet takeout and caterer. The shop opened in 1981, and Ben Tanet has owned it since 1990. He said that there was little takeout even from supermarkets then, and the only other business similar to Chez Nous was Magazine Cuisine across from A&P—now Breaux Mart—on Magazine Street. Chez Nous is in a circa 1900 house, and this is the first business ever established in the building. A garage on the property serves as Chez Nous' kitchen, but it was a cobbler shop before the catering enterprise moved in. This writer remembers an elderly lady who came out on the front porch every morning in the 1970s to pick up her *Times-Picayune.* The

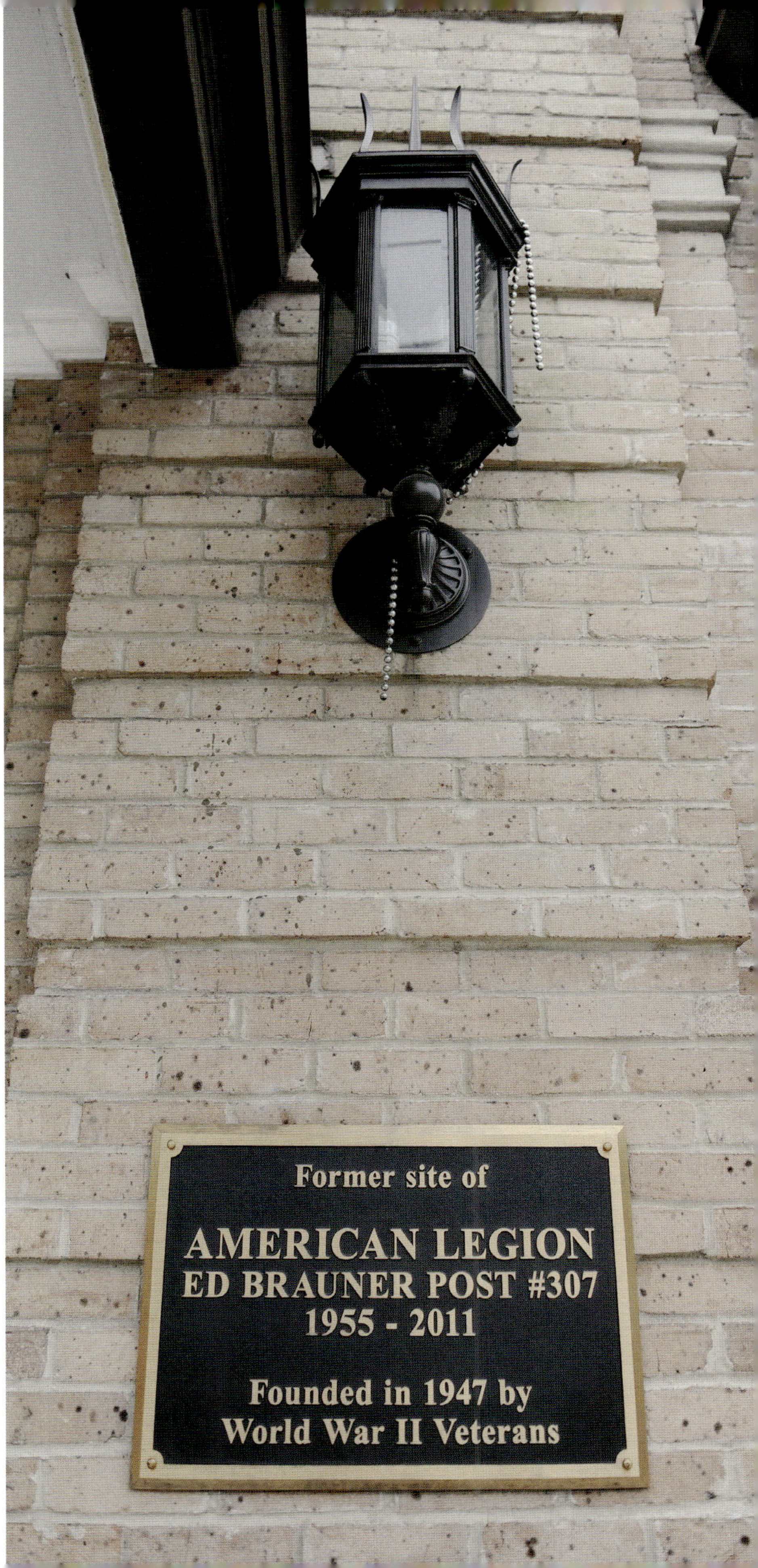

The Walgreens Pharmacy at 5518 Magazine bears a plaque commemorating the site's use as American Legion Post 307.

'70s was still a time when Magazine was far more residential than commercial. It also had an older population, with numerous families having been in their homes since the early part of the twentieth century.

When Whole Foods opened, Mr. Tanet said that business was "hard at first, but catering helps," and eventually Chez Nous was able to "feed off the anchor, so to speak." Ironically Hurricane Katrina helped Chez Nous establish itself in the face of its competition. The storm left Chez Nous with "a lot of rotten food" and a company had to come in and clean it all out, but they managed to reopen in October 2005 and prepared that year's Thanksgiving menu. Whole Foods did not reopen until February, which was good for Chez Nous' business. As to Magazine Street, Mr. Tanet, whose family lived on Exposition Boulevard next to Audubon Park, did not go to Magazine except to shop at Perlis men's store.

Not long after Chez Nous opened, the Switzerland Bakery across Magazine at 5722 closed. This bakery specialized in European pastries, cakes, and bread. When the Swiss Consulate in New Orleans closed around 1970, some of the former employees, wishing to stay in New Orleans, got together and opened the bakery.

Leading up to the busy intersection of Nashville Avenue, several turn-of-the-twentieth century houses now contain shops, while several other old houses have been thoroughly restored. The totally new building for Kenton's Food & Bourbon restaurant at 5757, on the corner of Nashville, was an Esso service station in the late 1940s and '50s.

One of the early pioneers in this section of Magazine was Joshua Mann Pailet, owner of A Gallery for Fine Photography. Upon graduating from college, he came to New Orleans in 1974 and drove along Magazine from Audubon Park to the French Quarter and settled upon renting half of a double house at 5717 Magazine, now remodeled for Kendra Scott jewelry boutique with the new address of 5757 Magazine. He chose this area of Magazine because it was near the park, the rent was cheap, and in the tradition of Magazine businesses he could live in his gallery; otherwise he could not have afforded it. His gallery was a "hole-in-the wall" and there was still a tenant on the other side of the double. He began the name of his business with an "A" so that it would be the first in the phone directory.

Mr. Pailet recalled that there were few commercial places on Magazine then, and a lot of storefronts were closed. He recalls—as does this writer—the Ewing Market and the elderly ladies who ran it. Much of the floor space had been walled off to concentrate activity in the front of the big building. Mr. Pailet was able to buy one of their chopping block tables for a good price. At the same time, the writer remembers canned foods at Ewing's that must have been on the shelves for years.

When Mr. Pailet first arrived on Magazine, he felt that the street was on its way back and that it was "kicking into gear." In the late '70s it was mainly antique shops, but the first galleries were also beginning to open. By the 1980s the Magazine Street Merchants Association had begun, and he was one of the first members.

In 1977, Mr. Pailet moved the gallery to 5432 Magazine, where PJ's Coffee is today. He recalls a nice cobbler next door at 5430, which is now site of The Elizabeth Chronicles boutique. In 1980, the gallery moved across the street to what had been Roy Slocomb's A Antiques Shop at 5423. Here the gallery remained until 1991. A second Gallery for Fine Photography was opened at 313 Royal in the French Quarter in 1989, with the one on Magazine closing in 1991, although Mr. Pailet continued to live at that address until 1998. The former Magazine gallery is now Scriptura stationery shop. Since 2002, A Gallery for Fine Photography has been on Chartres at Bienville in the Quarter, but Mr. Pailet still lives Uptown a block off Magazine.

Another store off Magazine, but very much a part of the street, is Octavia Books. At 513 Octavia, it is a block and a half off Magazine in an award-winning restored old business building. The bookshop serves the Upper Magazine population and is deeply invested in the area's independent business. For their now annual "Find Waldo Local" event, a Waldo book character figure is hidden at various local shops, mostly along Magazine Street, since the event celebrates and promotes Uptown's independent businesses.

This important shopping district, which begins at Jefferson Avenue, continues beyond Nashville Avenue, where homes are interspersed with retail venues and the street takes on a more residential character.

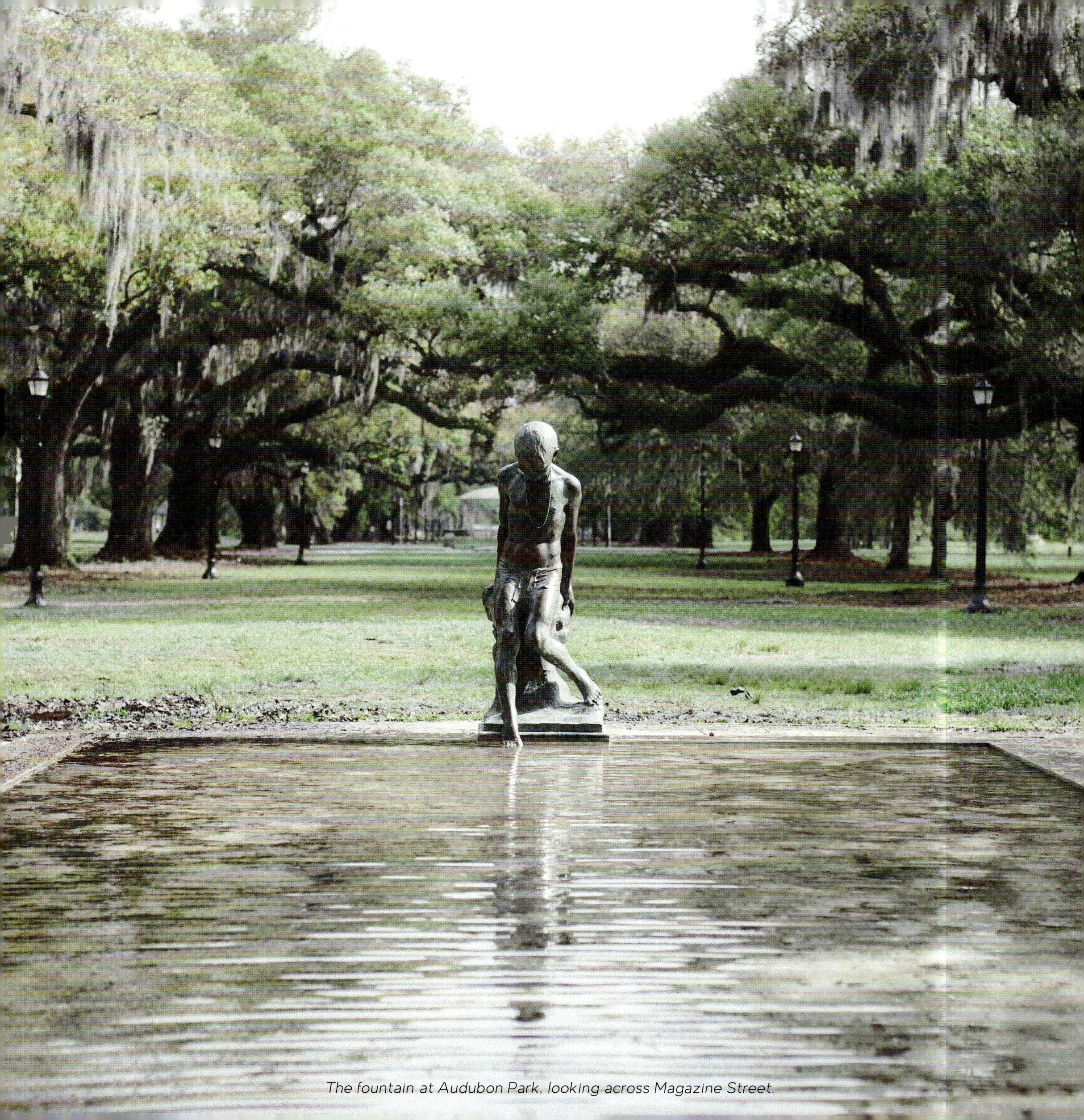

The fountain at Audubon Park, looking across Magazine Street.

Chapter Eight

Nashville Avenue to the Levee

Above Jefferson City there were four subdivisions, as well as Audubon Park, along which Magazine Street was subdivided before reaching Leake Avenue, several railroad tracks, and the Mississippi River levee.

From Joseph Street to a line between Eleonore and State was the town of Hurstville, which was named for plantation owner Cornelius Hurst and subdivided by Benjamin Buisson in 1837. Arabella Street was named for Hurst's daughter and Eleonore Street for his wife. The plantation house which was near the river has been moved to Garden Lane, now known as Bamboo Road, off Metairie Road. Hurst planned Nashville Avenue to incorporate the tracks of the New Orleans and Nashville Railroad line. The railroad was never built, but the width of Nashville attests to the plan. Had the rail line become reality,

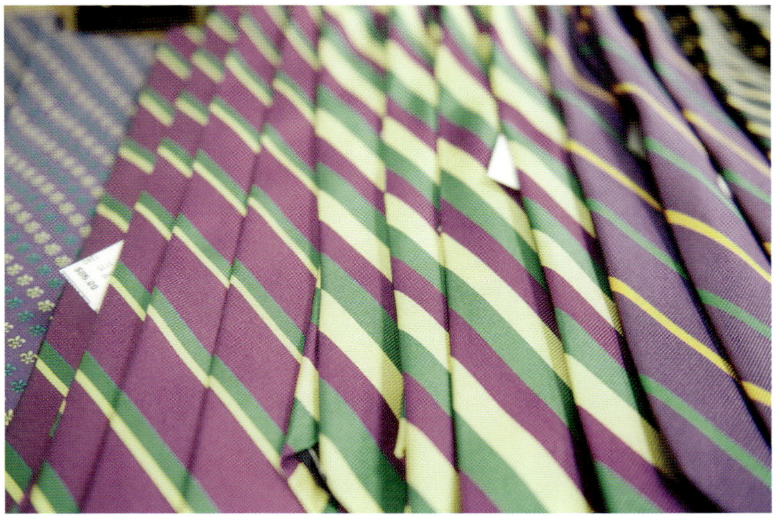

Carnival season at Perlis.

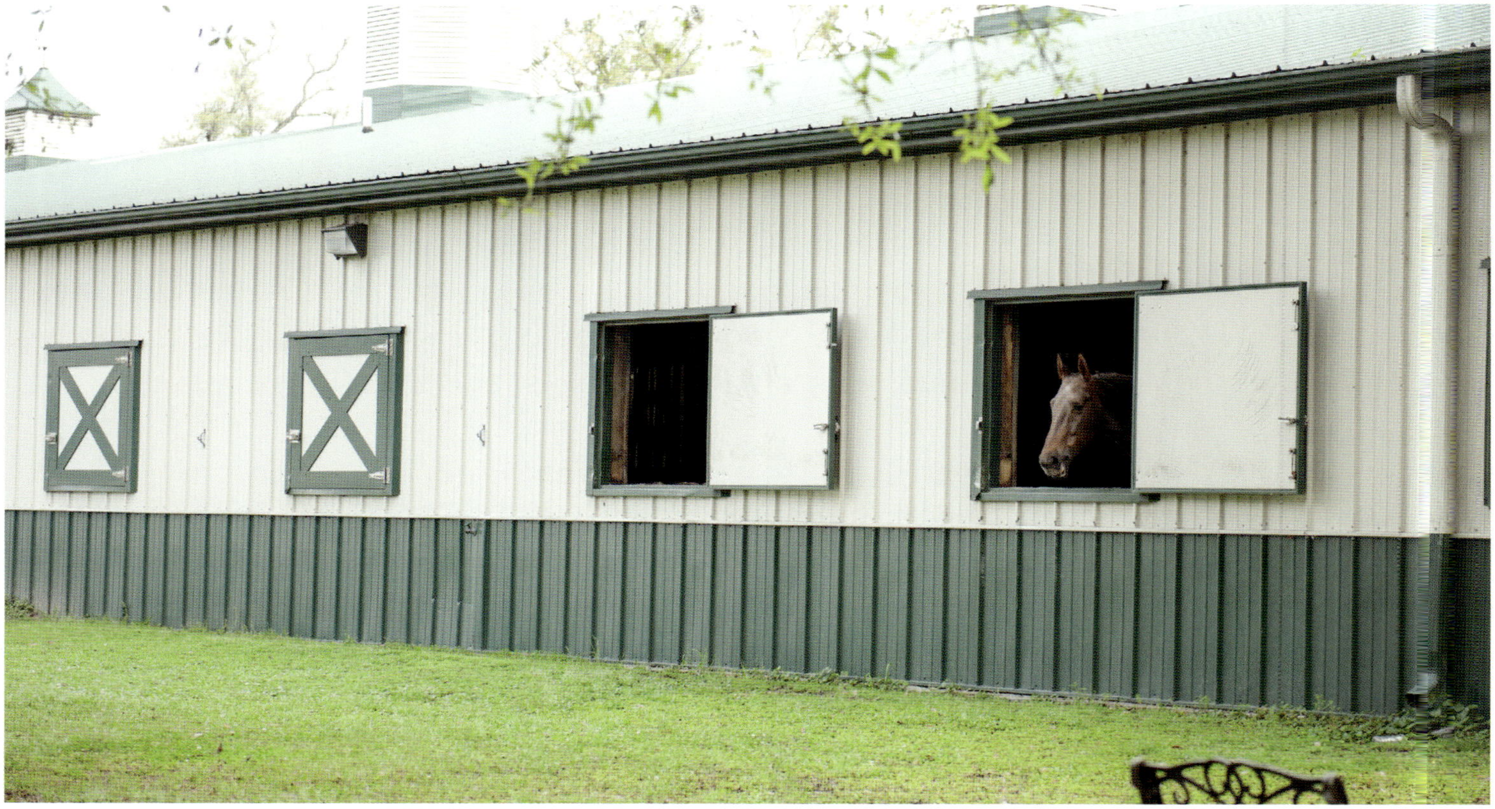

Cascade Stables, Audubon Park.

Uptown would have been a very different environment indeed.

In 1836 the next property past Hurstville belonged to John Green, who had Buisson subdivide it into the town of Bloomingdale. It was a very narrow, long lot of land that extended up to a line drawn between State and Webster, and its only street running perpendicular to the river is State. The next plantation belonged to Dominique Burthe and extended to what became Audubon Park. Burthe's land was subdivided in 1854 by a surveyor named Numegger and called Burtheville.

In the 1790s, Hurstville, Bloomingdale, and Burtheville had been the plantation of Jean Etienne Boré, and it was here that the Duc d'Orléans, future French King Louis Philippe, visited in 1798. Boré's daughter Francoise married Pierre

Foucher, who owned the neighboring plantation that is now Audubon Park. In 1825, Foucher bought the Boré tract from his wife's nephew, historian Charles Étienne Gayarré. Foucher combined the plantations but ultimately sold what had been Boré's to Hurst, Green, and Burthe. Contrary to popular belief, only a narrow strip of today's Audubon Park was ever part of Boré's holdings. It was on the Boré plantation where the first granulated sugar was successfully produced in the United States, not on the Audubon Park or Foucher tract.

While the Boré plantation was good land noted for its lush gardens and stands of trees, the Foucher property next door was unsuccessful. Antoine and Louis Foucher inherited the plantation from their parents Pierre and Francoise Foucher, and in 1834, Louis became sole owner. The plantation was unprofitable, and not caring for his role as a plantation owner, Louis abandoned the failing plantation and moved to Paris.

During the Civil War the Confederates commandeered the unused land as Camp Lewis, and then with the fall of the city in 1862, the Union took it over as Sedgwick Hospital. It was used as a staging ground

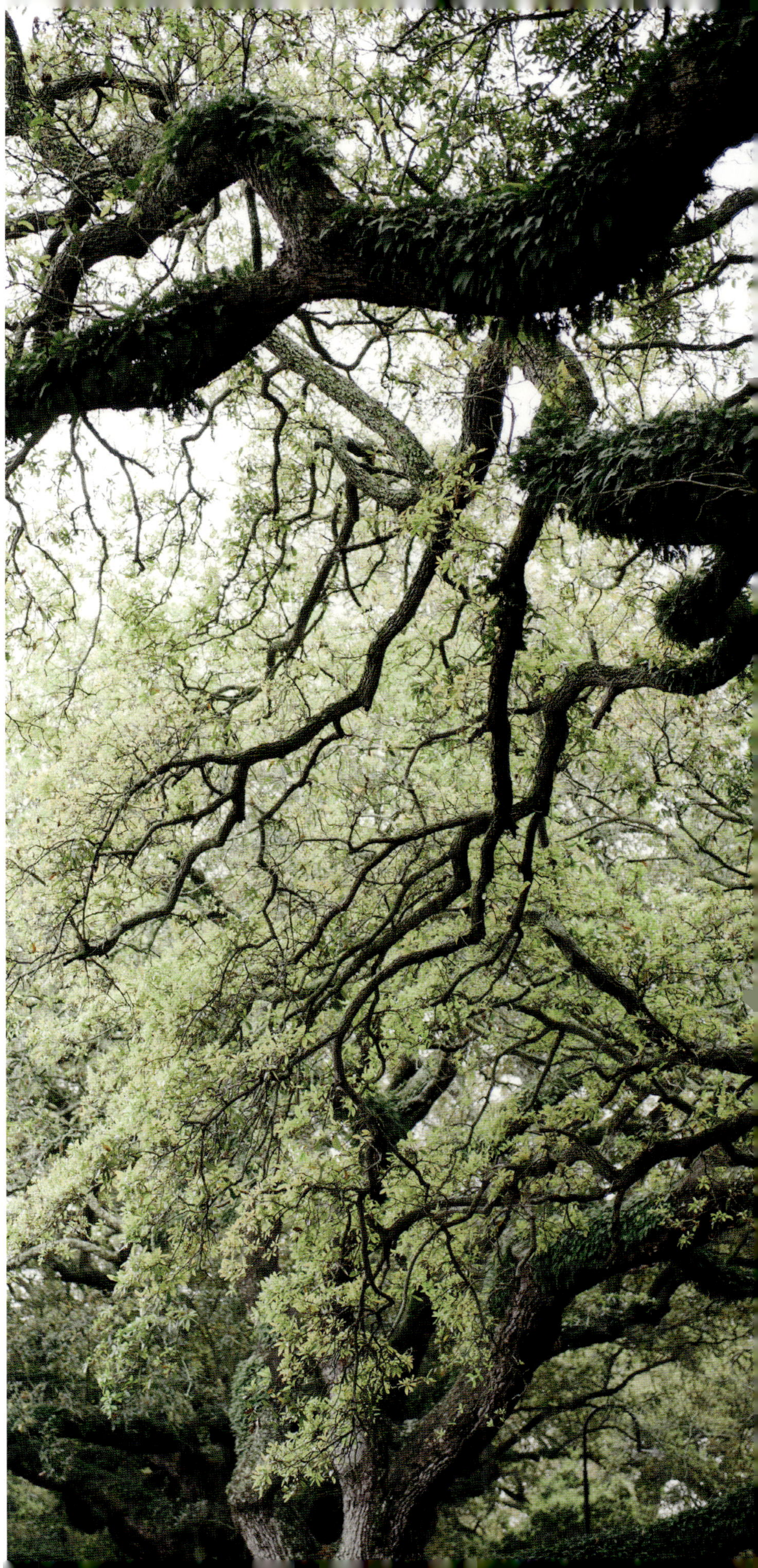

Live oaks in Audubon Park.

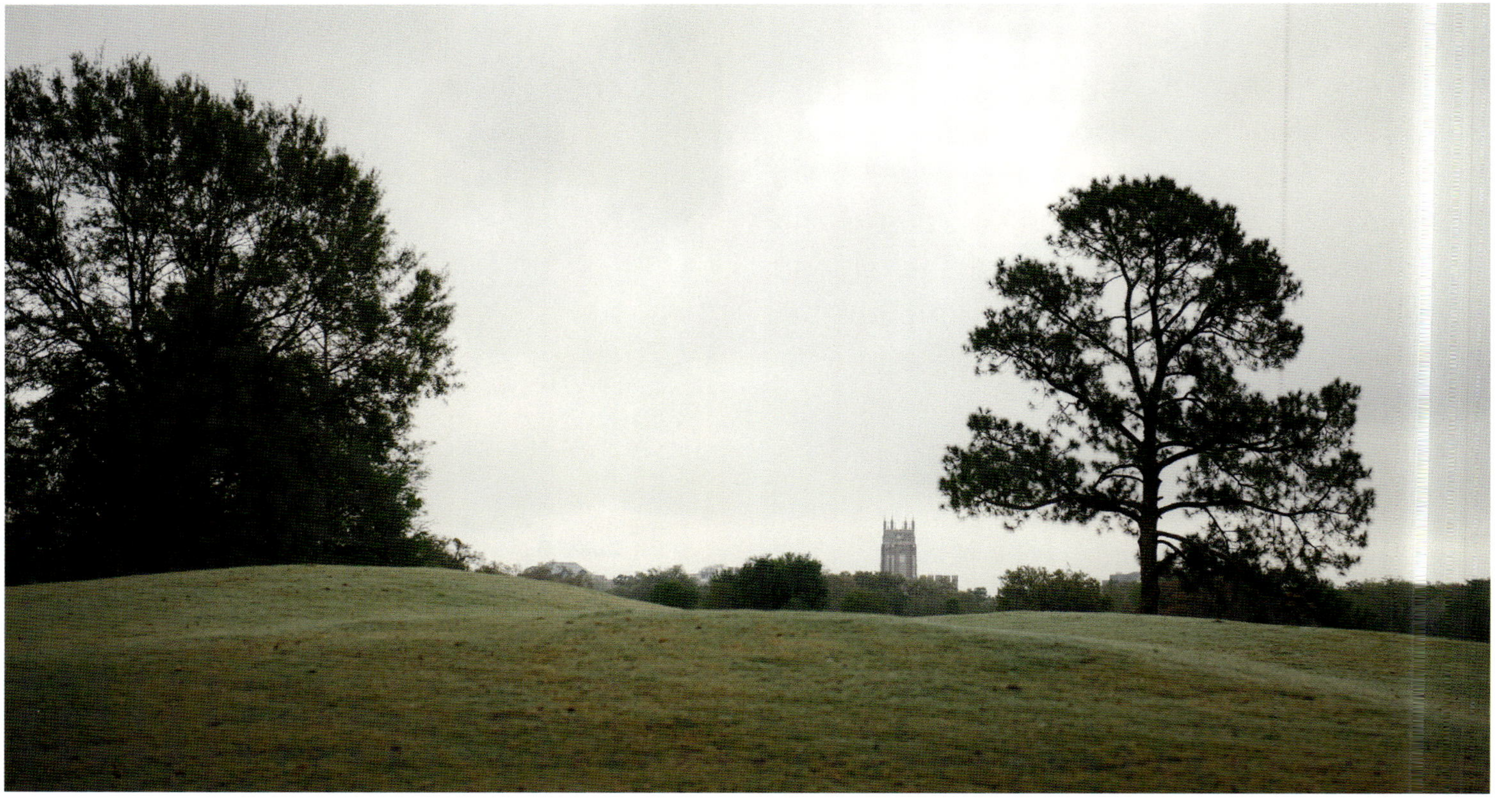

Holy Name of Jesus Catholic Church on St. Charles Avenue, viewed from Magazine Street across Audubon Park.

for the African American Buffalo Soldiers after they were organized in 1866.

Since few lots in nearby subdivisions were selling during the Civil War and Reconstruction, Foucher sold the forlorn, overgrown tract to a pair of shady speculators. Even before exchanging money, the swindlers promptly lobbied the state legislature for funds to buy the land to use as a park and site of a new state capitol building. During Reconstruction, New Orleans had temporarily replaced Baton Rouge as state capital. The speculators succeeded in selling the land to the state at a hugely inflated price, but soon after, in 1871, it was relinquished to the virtually bankrupt city for use as a park.

What would become Audubon Park was initially called Upper City Park. City Park then was called Lower City Park. The upper park remained a virtual wasteland until 1884-85, when the World's Industrial and Cotton Centennial Exposition, a world's fair, was staged there. The fair was a financial failure and to try to recoup money, its organizers made a second run the next year. The grounds contained several large wooden structures, including the main building, which housed most of the foreign exhibits and a huge music hall. So mammoth, the main building essentially covered the land comprising the entirety of the current golf course and at the time was said to be the largest free-standing wooden structure in the world. Upon the fair's closure in 1886, most of the buildings were dismantled and sold off as huge quantities of fine quality lumber. There was so much of it available, that many houses Uptown—which was beginning to grow dramatically in the 1880s—were built from world's fair leftovers.

The only things left from the fair were a piece of Alabama iron ore and the popular Horticultural Hall, which was incorporated into what became Audubon Zoo. The iron ore remains, but the six-hundred-foot-long Horticultural Hall was leveled by the hurricane of 1915.

The park was renamed in honor of artist John James Audubon in 1886, but it was in such poor state that *The Mascot*, a local scandal sheet, said that it was an insult to the man. For a number of years the land served as the state's sugar experimental station, but not until the early twentieth century was it landscaped into its present form. John Charles Olmsted of Olmsted Brothers, famous park designers, was hired to beautify the park. Incorporated among its lagoons and lawns are some ancient live oak trees as well as privately donated sculptures and fountains.

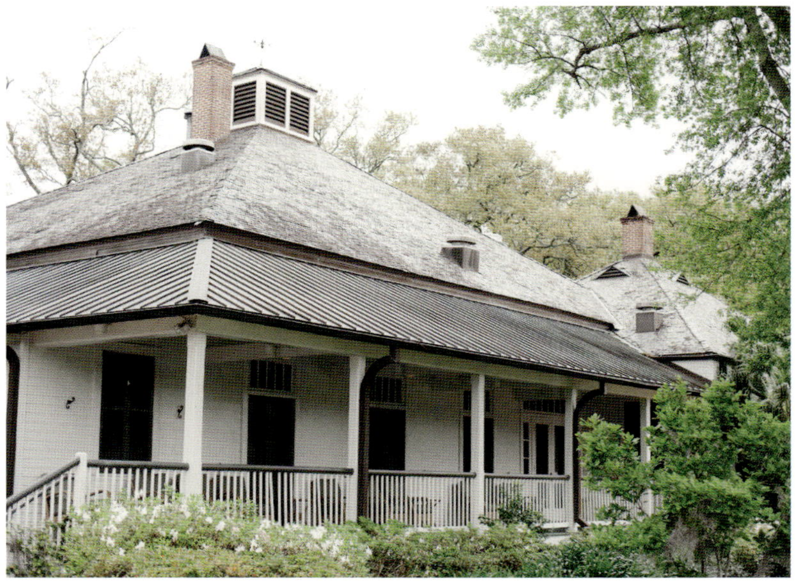

Audubon Park Clubhouse.

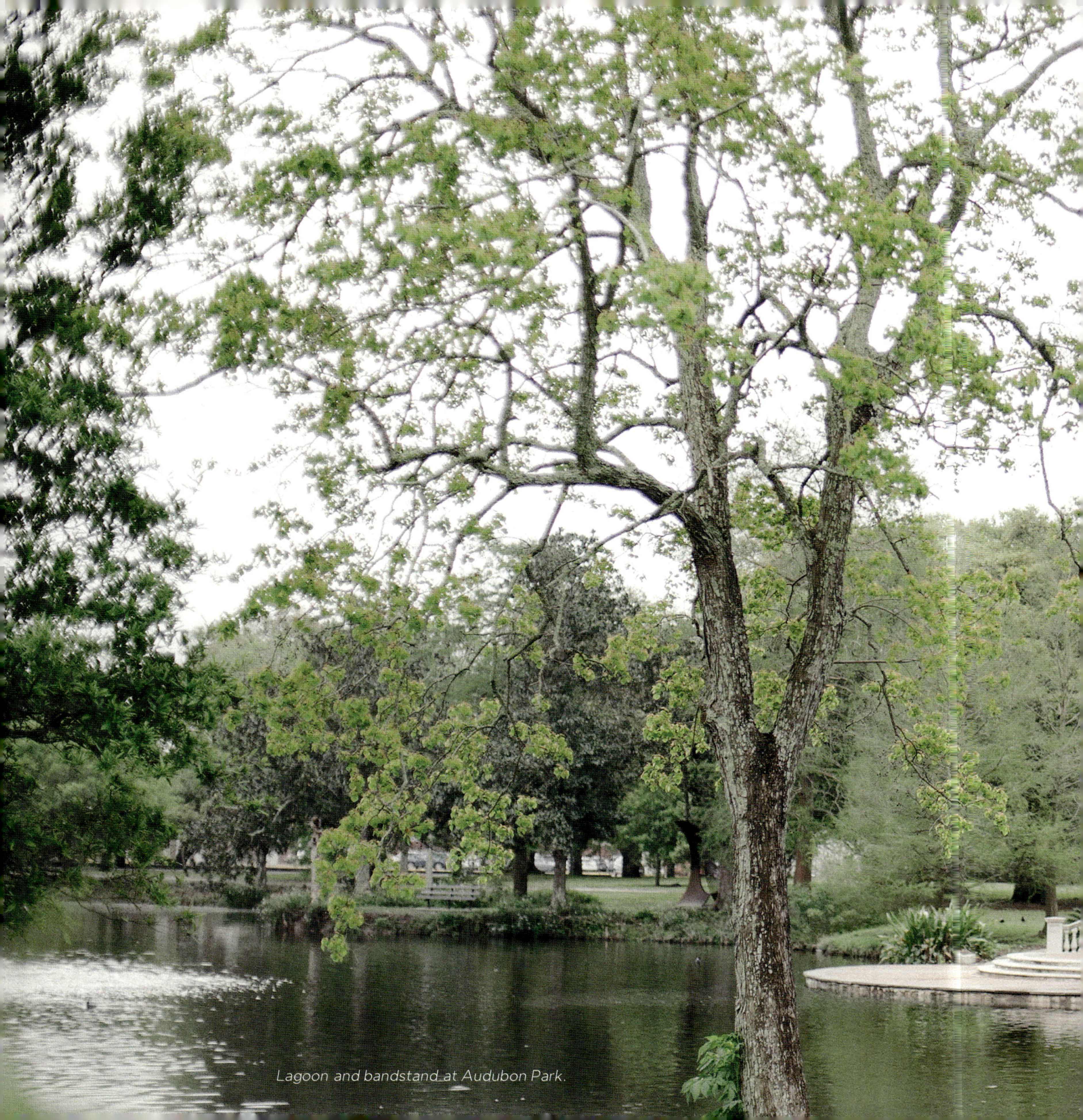

Lagoon and bandstand at Audubon Park.

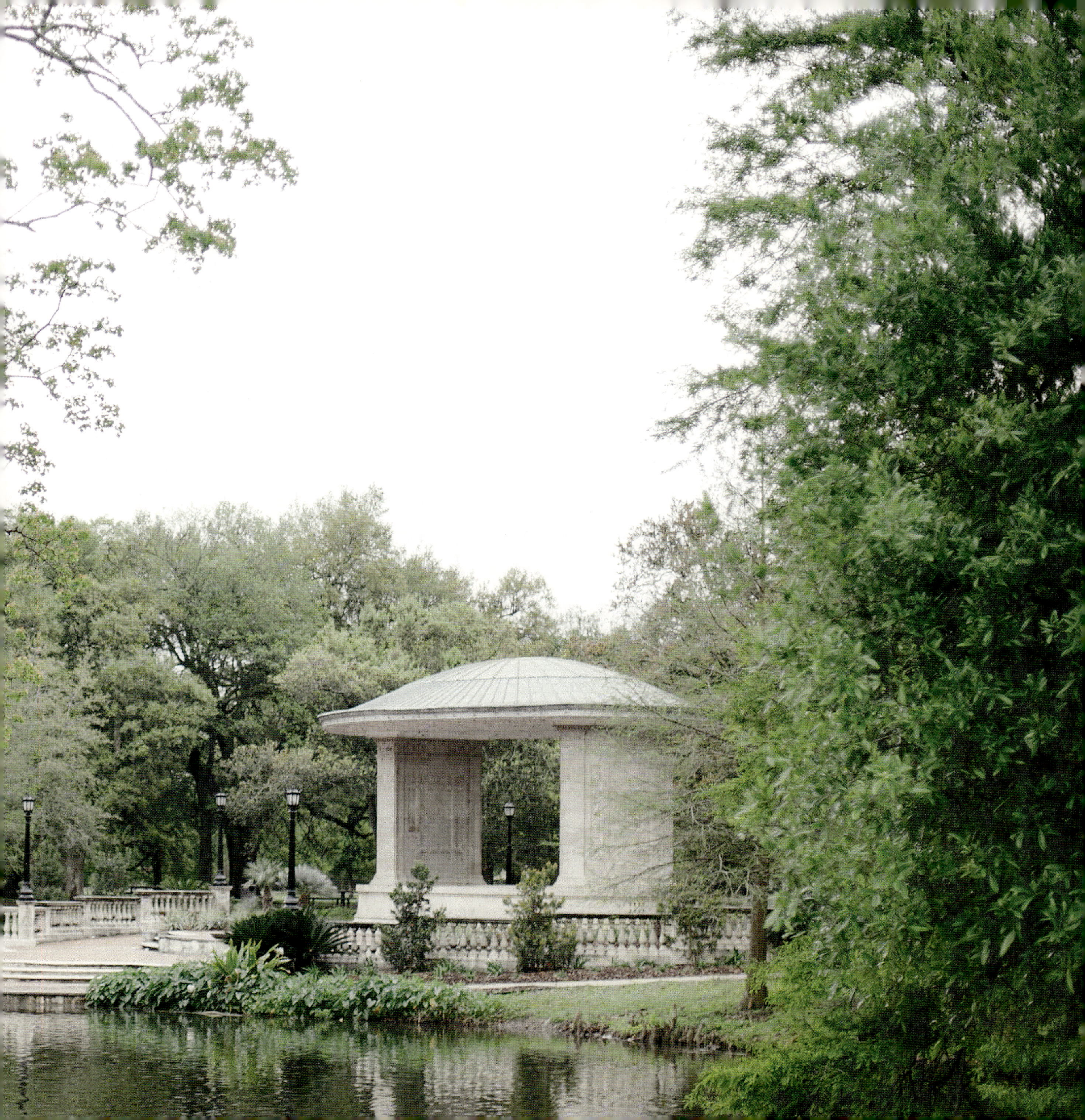

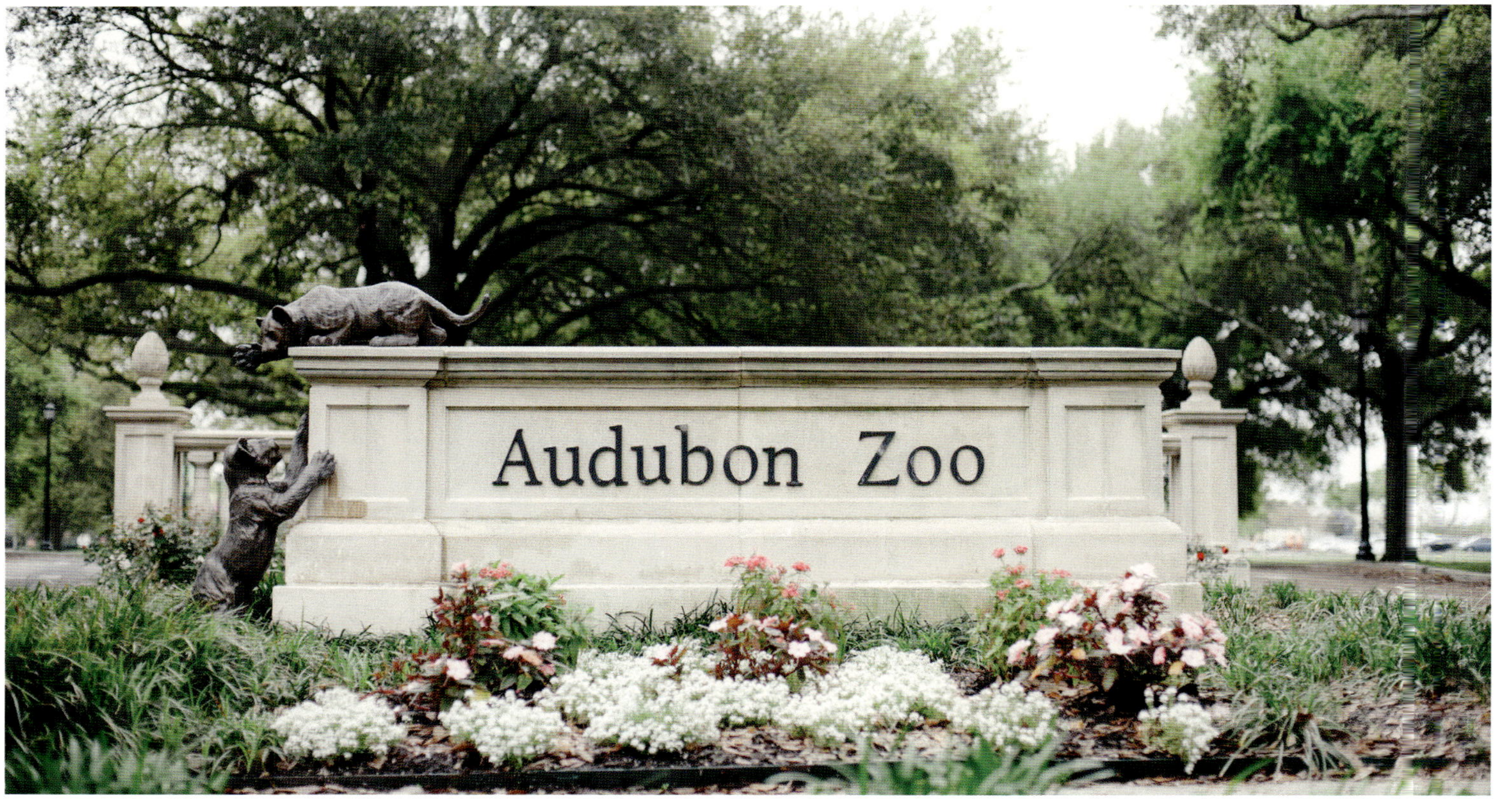

Entrance to Audubon Zoo.

A star attraction along Magazine is Audubon Zoo, whose entrance stands virtually at the end of the long street. The roots of the zoo date to 1916, and in the 1930s it received major upgrades through the auspices of the Works Progress Administration (WPA). By the early 1970s the zoo had fallen into disrepair and was threatened with closure. Current Audubon Nature Institute chief executive director Ron Forman described the state of the facility in the '70s as a "menagerie, not a zoo." With the aid of city government, business leaders, private donors, and a city election, finances became available to upgrade the zoo dramatically. In Mr. Forman's words, it was transformed from an "urban ghetto" to an "urban Eden."

Ron Forman began his tenure at the zoo in 1972 and has been CEO since 1977. It

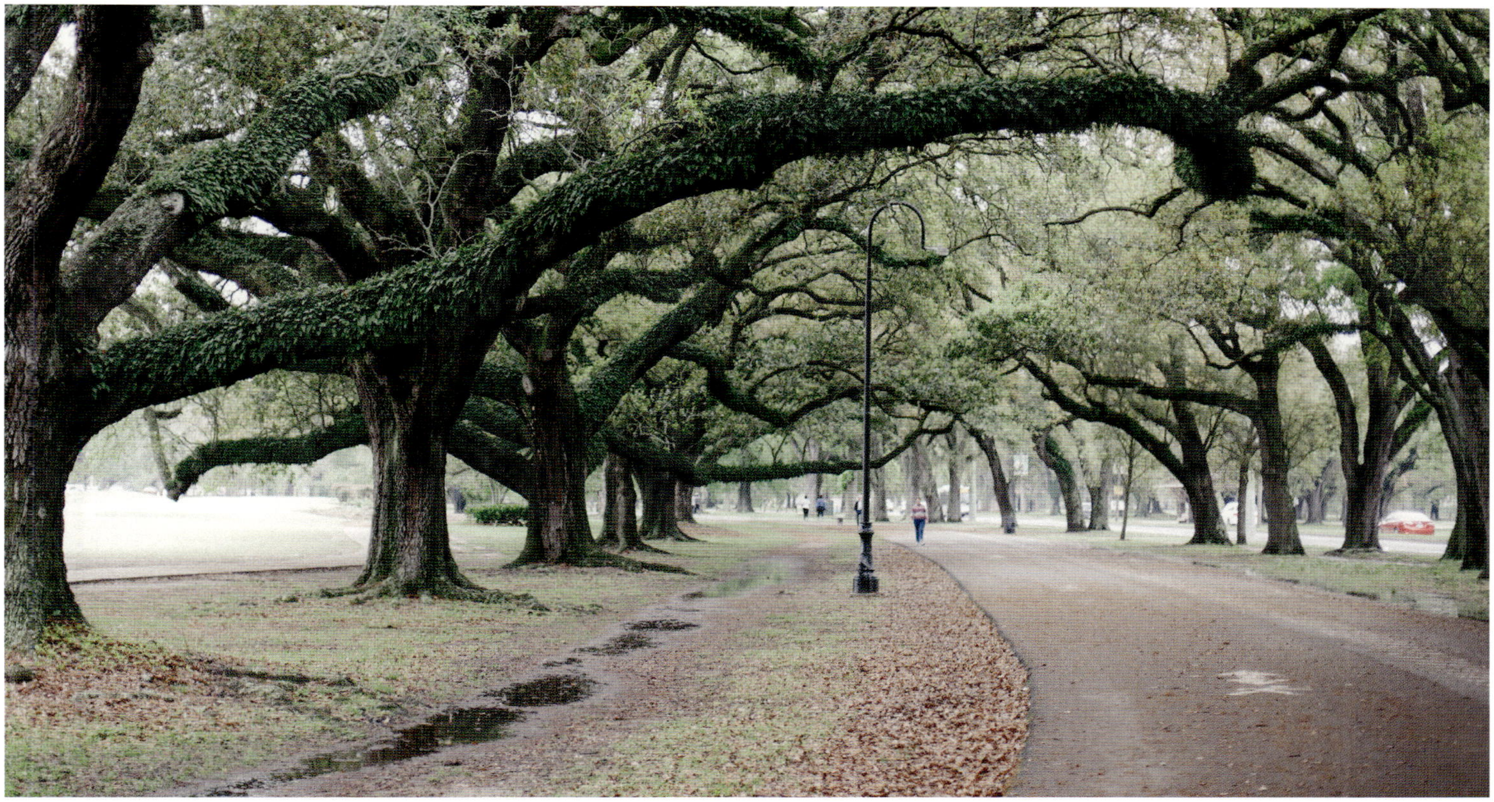

Audubon Park's jogging path parallels Magazine Street.

s under his leadership that the zoo has reached its modern prominence. In 2017, *USA Today* ranked it as the ninth best zoo in the country, while the Audubon Aquarium of the Americas, which is near the foot of Canal Street downtown, ranked fourth in its poll of best aquariums in the country. The Audubon Insectarium, located in the U.S. Custom House on Canal Street, is also part of the Audubon Nature Institute's large system of attractions. The zoo has as many as six hundred volunteers and hosts about one million visitors a year, most of whom come from greater New Orleans. The aquarium and insectarium welcome higher numbers, since they cater more to tourists, according to Mr. Forman.

In his office at the zoo Mr. Forman is in his childhood stomping grounds. He grew up off Magazine near Jefferson Avenue,

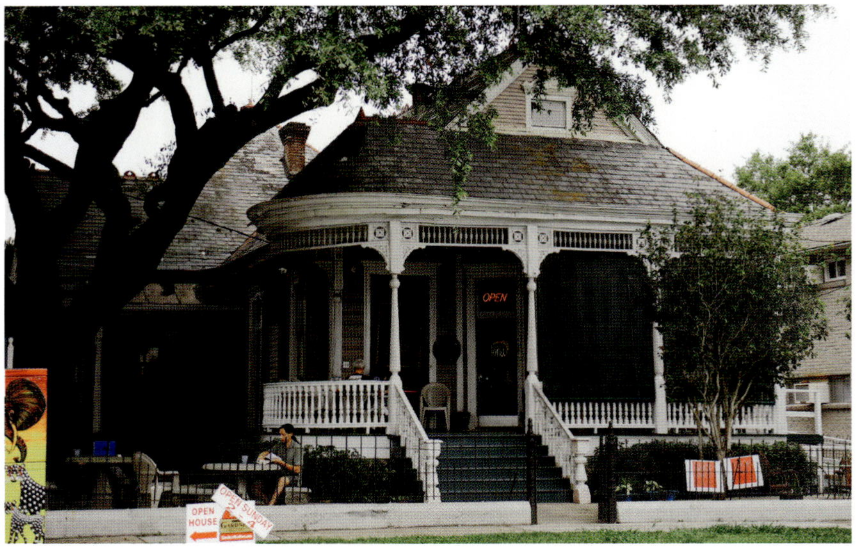

Café Luna, on the corner of Nashville, a residence-turned-business.

and much of his childhood revolved around Magazine Street. He recalls that people walked everywhere. The family doctor and family dentist were on Magazine. He remembers that when he was about seven or eight his mother sent him to one of the neighborhood stores. Mixing up his instructions, he asked the grocer for "a loaf of milk and a quart of bread." As a boy an outing would be a bike ride to Audubon Park to climb Monkey Hill. This manmade, twenty-nine-foot hill is another project of the WPA.

Mr. Forman's first job as a boy of eight was at Audubon Park. He was hired to tie up the popular swan boats—fondly remembered by many baby boomers—that plied the park's lagoon. These boats ferried a number of passengers and received their names from the profiles of swans that embellished the stern of each vessel. His compensation was free boat rides.

As zoo director, he recalled the day a man brought to the zoo a bag of hatchling white alligators. It was determined the man had poached them from a nest, which is a federal offense. Before they could proceed with the matter the guy ran off, leaving the zoo with the rare reptiles. The zoo promoted the gators as bringing prosperity and happiness, and for many years white alligators have been featured attractions at both the zoo and the aquarium, bringing happiness (if not prosperity) to many people.

Visitors to Audubon Zoo pass by a small parcel of land that, like Audubon Park, was once owned by Pierre Foucher. This parcel, which extends to the curve of the Mississippi River, was acquired by several investors in 1836 and subdivided by Buisson. It was called Greenville for one of the buyers, John Green. Here Magazine Street was initially and briefly called Foucher Street, and here Magazine met the Mississippi River.

In 1870 these towns and all of Jefferson City were annexed by New Orleans. The city now extended as far as Lowerline Street to the boundary of the City of Carrollton, incorporating territory that had been Jefferson Parish. Carrollton had been the parish seat of Jefferson Parish since Lafayette was absorbed by the city in 1852. When Carrollton was annexed by New Orleans in 1874, the parish seat was moved across the river to Gretna, where it remains today. The historical roots of the development of Uptown New Orleans and Magazine Street from the 1830s to the 1870s were not as the city of New Orleans, but rather of east Jefferson Parish.

As turn-of-the-century New Orleanians made the trek from Uptown and crossed over Nashville Avenue, they would have been traversing the heart of the former Faubourg Hurstville. Today across Nashville from Kenton's Food & Bourbon is a charming, tree-shaded, late-nineteenth-century home that now houses Café Luna and Bouffant Beauty & Barber. Although now business premises, this house gives an excellent impression of what residential upper Magazine would have looked like around 1900.

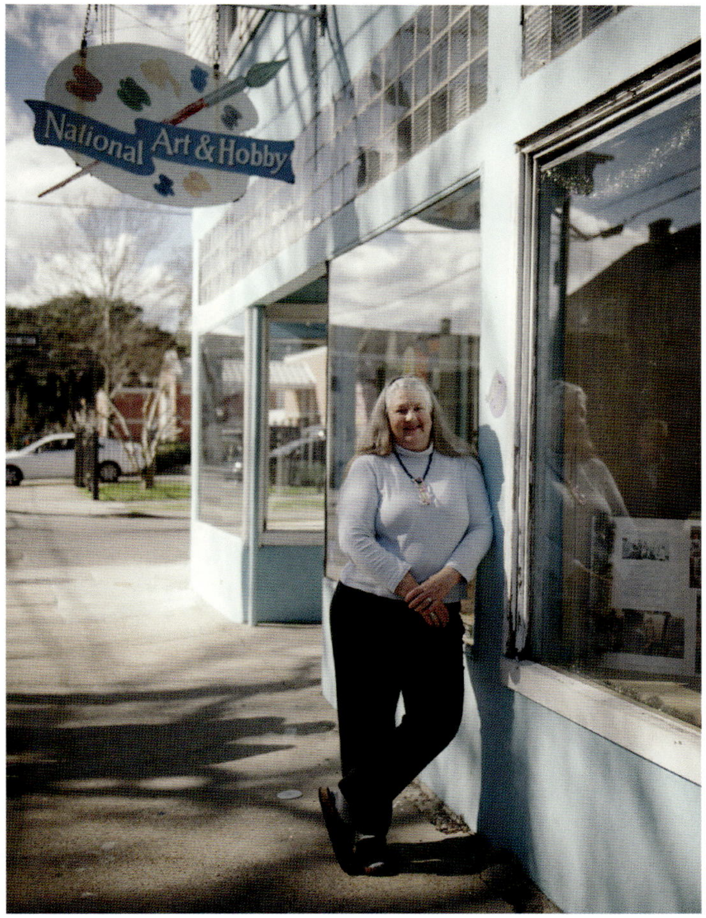

Nat Ward Bergeron, owner of National Art & Hobby.

A block up Magazine at 5835 and the corner of Eleanore was National Art & Hobby. Ben Rauch is the former owner and recalled that his mother and father, Bernard and Marguerite Rauch, opened the business in 1931, but not as an art and hobby shop. It was the Great Depression, and Bernard Rauch had lost

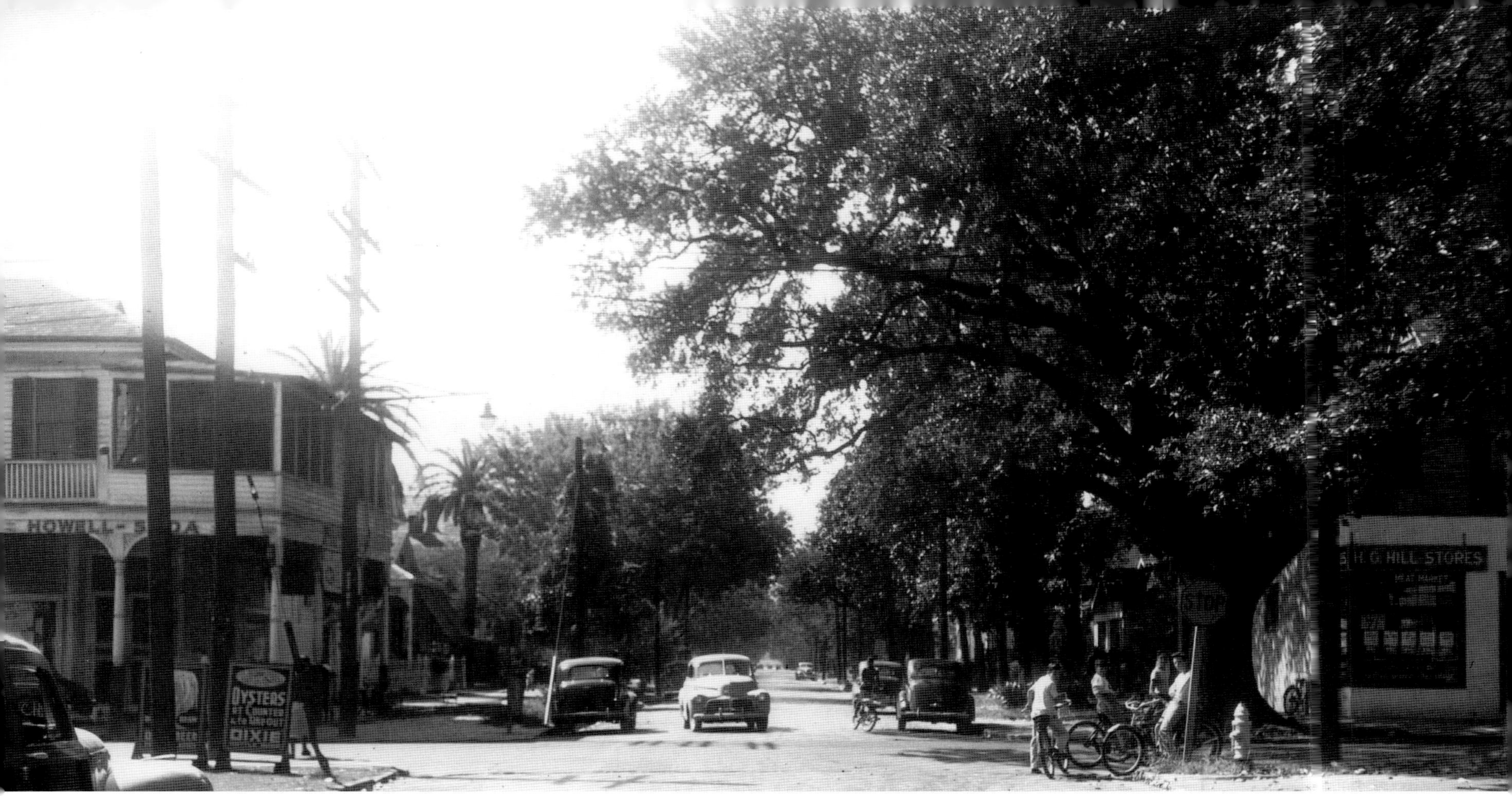

From State Street, looking across Magazine toward the river, October 1, 1947. (Courtesy The Historic New Orleans Collection, 1979.325.5622.)

his job as a meter reader for New Orleans Public Service, Inc. To pay the bills, he started a radio and appliance repair shop and installed radio antennas. Aside from the repair and installation business, he sold electric fuses. Before long the business expanded with the addition of notions like sewing threads and needles. By the late 1930s the store was stocking hardware along with crafts and sport supplies. In 1948 the business was being called the National Craft and Hobby Shop. Ultimately the store's name was changed from "craft" to "art." The store closed in 2017.

Early on, as with many retailers along Magazine, Mr. and Mrs. Rauch lived in a house next to the shop. In 1950 the whole building was raised and a new ground floor incorporated, allowing the family to live above the store. A decade later a hip roof serving as a third-floor warehouse was added. In 1995 the building and business were sold to a nephew, John Ward, and the store is now owned by Nat Ward Bergeron.

Between Eleanor and State, at 5936, a condominium building was once a movie house. It opened in 1920 as the National and in the 1930s, like so many Depression era theaters, presented other events along with movies to help fill seats. Imported art movies were popular in the 1960s and the National became a local venue for this genre. In 1965 it was renamed the Plaza, which it remained until shutting down in the mid-1970s. After serving as a porno theater, then a church, the Plaza was rebuilt in its present guise. While the facade was changed considerably, some of the 1920s architectural elements have remained intact along the roofline.

Not far down at 5924 was Herwig's Bicycle Store, which opened about 1929 and remained in business into the twenty-first century in a building that is now City Surf Fitness. Across Magazine Street at 5919 is the Covenant Nursing Home, and while its facility is late twentieth century the home dates back to 1885 as the Protestant Home for the Aged. In the same block several houses provide another glimpse of how residential upper Magazine would have once looked. While the large house at 5941 dates from the early 1890s, the bulk of the surviving dwellings date mostly after 1900.

Except for business changes, the intersection of Magazine and State has not been altered too dramatically over the last century or so. Reginelli's Pizzeria at 5961 is in the building that has long housed restaurants like Rondo's in the 1920s, Manale's in the 1930s, then Compagno Brothers Liquor and Restaurant. Across Magazine at 741 State is the former Noodle & Pie, which in the 1940s was a pharmacy like Howell's and then for many years Mozer's Pharmacy. In the 1920s and '30s the building housed the Cupid Beauty Shop. Diagonally across State is the biggest recent change to the intersection. Since the 1920s a prominent filling station called McGovern's stood here, but in 2017 it was demolished to make way for condominiums.

Across Magazine from the former filling station, at 6000-10, is a row of shops with a house sitting on top. The one-story dwelling was built on the site by the 1890s, but by the 1920s it had been raised and a ground-level brick retail building constructed along the sidewalk.

Today the business at the corner of State

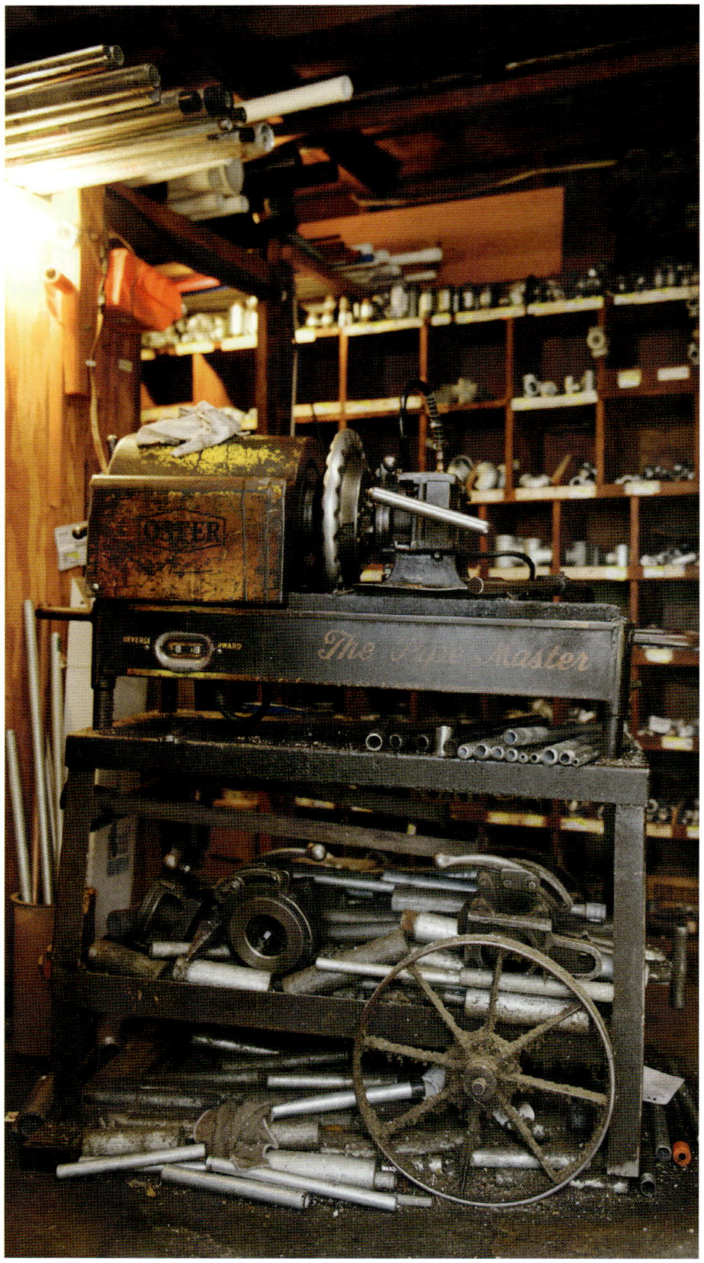

Antique pipe threader, still in use at Clement Hardware.

is Clement Hardware & Variety at 6000. The store was purchased by Leon Clement in 1980, having previously been Marquette Hardware & Variety, established by that family in 1968. Of Marquette's, the *Underground Shopping Guide* in 1978 said "If you are a professional looker; you have found paradise! Literally everything within imagination is in here . . . We loved the crowded aisles."

The hardware store hasn't changed much since. Mr. Clement calls this "a true family business," as he has four sons who have all worked here, and the current owner is one of those sons, Darren. In its current incarnation, Clement's remains a delightful jumble of every imaginable hardware item one could want. It is a personalized Magazine business evoking an earlier time. Even the billing is not computerized; it's found in a box of hand-written receipts.

Prior to becoming a hardware store, the building was the home of H.G. Hill's grocery from the 1930s and later became a Winn-Dixie market until the 1960s. This was one of the many Hill's that dotted Magazine beginning in the 1920s and '30s. At that time there was a hardware store, Silverman's Hardware and Paint, a couple of doors down at 6008. Today the Golden Shears, an old-fashioned barber shop, is at this address and has been in business for decades. In the 1940s, Joseph Alphano at 6006 was the neighborhood barber here.

Clement's is one of only two hardware stores left on Magazine; the other is Harry's Ace Hardware at 3535. When Clement's opened there were about six hardware stores left on the street. In the early 1900s, hardware stores were as prevalent as grocers and pharmacies, in some places separated only by a few blocks.

Clement's was among the first stores to reopen after Hurricane Katrina, and WWL-TV covered the event. According to Leon Clement, business quadrupled compared to pre-Katrina levels since so few hardware stores had reopened in the city at this point. He had to go to wholesalers three times a week and was forced to stock the shelves at night so that he and his employees could help customers during the day. This lasted a few months, until after the big box stores reopened and business began to return to normal.

The business at the end of the building at 6010 for many years was a laundry. In the 1940s it was called Unique Cleaners.

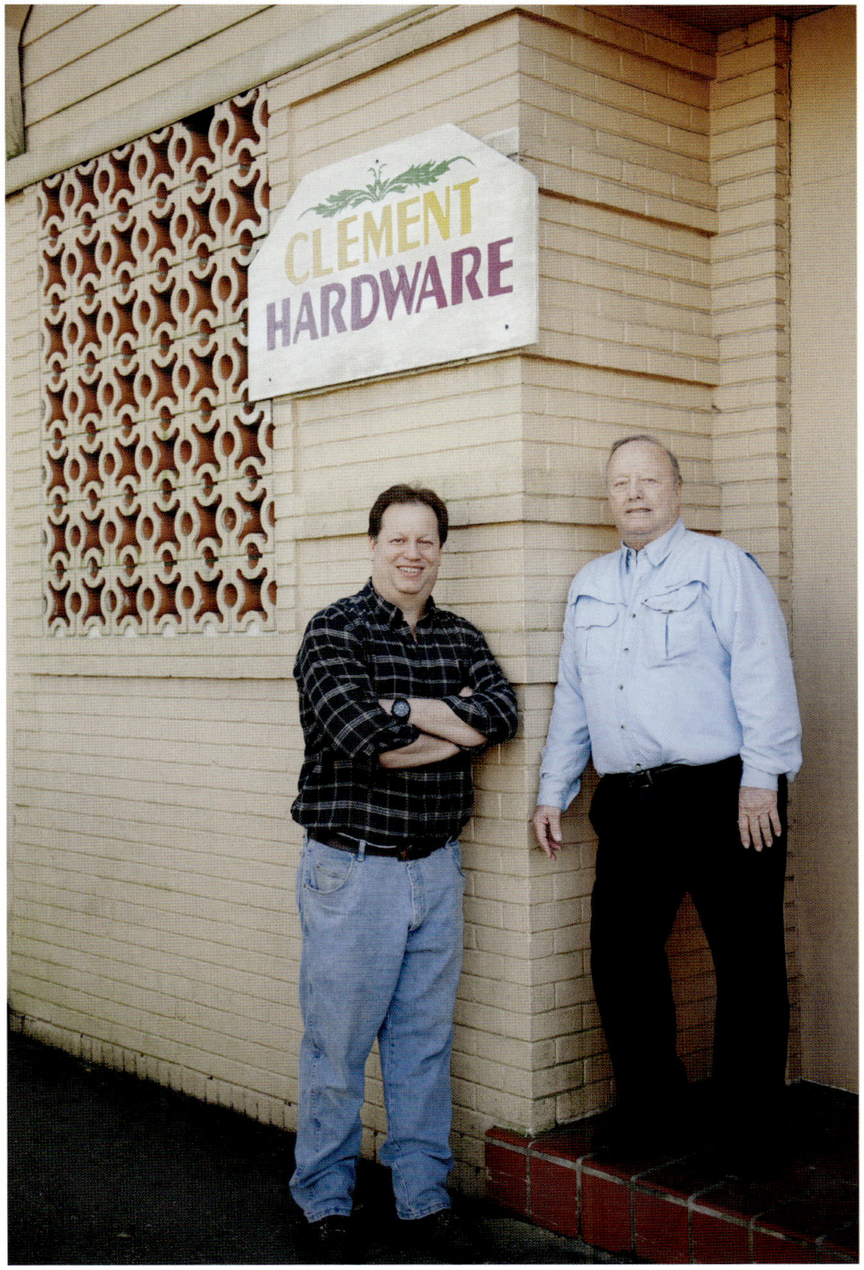

Leon and Darren Clement of Clement Hardware.

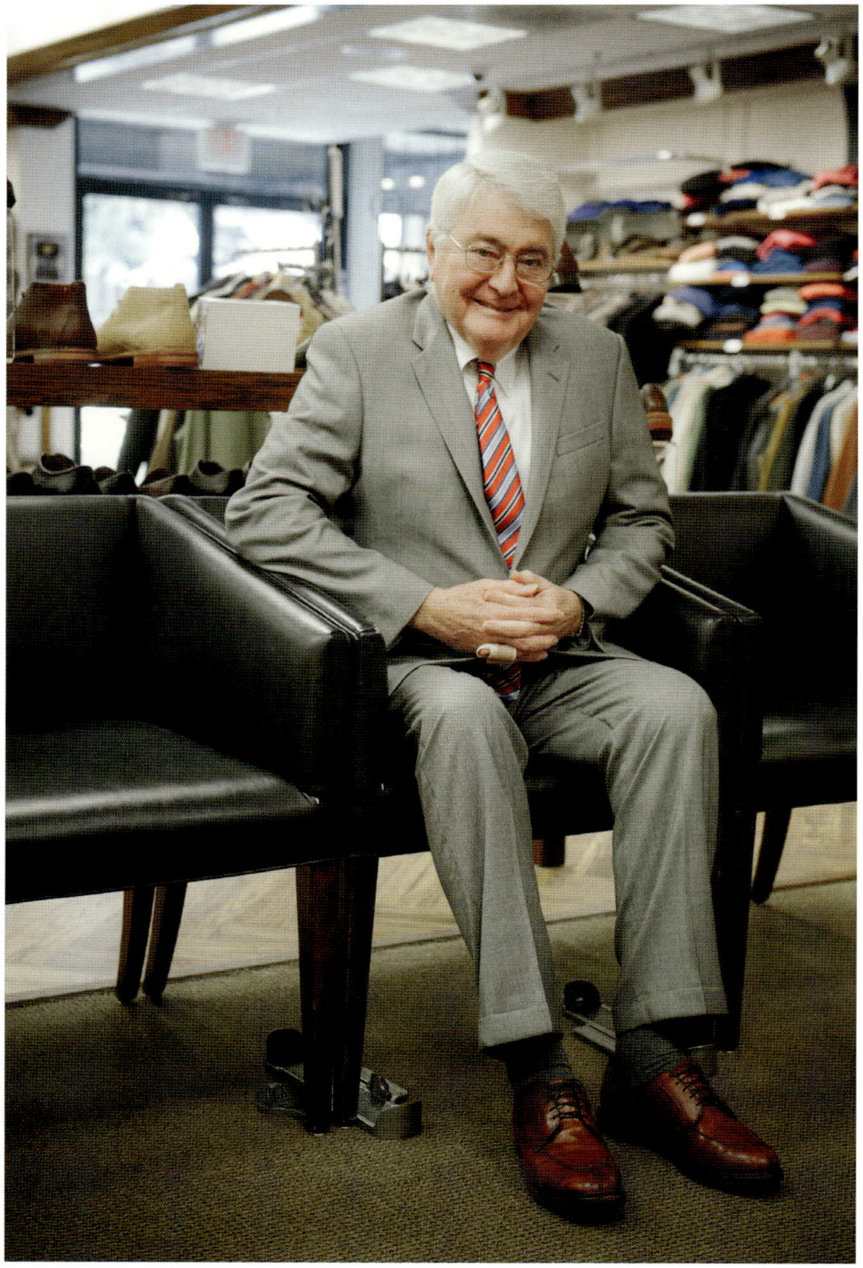

David George Perlis.

Located at the rear of the building is a large and intact fireproof cinderblock room that was the clothes dryer of its day. This business gave way about 1959 to the more elegant Nina Sloss Antiques. As one of the first antique shops on Magazine, and with its eye-appealing inventory of real antiques rather than second-hand goods, it was an early symbol of the new Magazine retail scene that was beginning to emerge. With the 1970s other antique dealers began to find their way to the street.

At the end of this block is another old-time family business, in this case an elegant men's store where several generations of local men have acquired linen and seersucker suits for summer and formal wear for Carnival. According to owner David George Perlis, the store dates to 1939, when his father, Rogers I. Perlis, opened a small men's shop with two hundred fifty dollars' worth of merchandise in front of a house near the center of the block where the Circle K parking lot is now. Business was good. Only six months later, Rogers Perlis was able to move to the corner of Webster into what had been Joseph Bentz's grocery store, which had been around since the 1910s. The address was 6070 Magazine, and this is the same address Perlis uses today. In typical Magazine Street fashion of the day, Mr. and Mrs. Perlis lived behind the store.

With the acquisition of several surrounding properties beginning in the early '70s, Perlis has been able to expand. In 1981 a new, larger building was built a bit down the block. During construction the store never closed, and when the new space was ready the old store was torn down and a parking lot put in its place. In 1999 a new addition was added to the building, and expansion has taken Perlis branches to Mandeville, Baton Rouge, and a small shop in the Jax Brewery. According to Mr. Perlis, today more business is done the day before Christmas than in a whole year in the late 1940s.

Business directories—and memories—attest that until about the 1970s there were small grocery stores up and down Magazine Street. These were mostly mom-and-pop stores, although chains like Hill's and A&P were making inroads. Some people have memories of a more casual time when some storekeepers sold bread and baked goods from a box outside their store. Customers were allowed to take what they needed and pay for it later.

An old-time family store was at 6101 Magazine and the corner of Webster. About 1920 the grocery was opened by an immigrant couple from Sicily and called Frank Cicero's Groceries. The religious life of this family long revolved around St. Francis of Assisi Catholic Church on State Street, which was just a few blocks from the grocery store. In 1920 the grocery owner's daughter Anna Cicero Drago graduated from the church school, which no longer operates but now is the site of Lycée Français de la Nouvelle-Orléans, a French-immersion public charter school. Frances Drago Hymel lived with her grandparents at the grocery on Webster and recalls as a child hearing church bells ringing to announce the end of World War II.

In 1948 the grocery had become a Best Ice Cream shop and today is Fresh Bar, a salad bar. Also in '48 an A&P branch operated across Magazine at 6100. Now that building is Monkey Hill Bar, although during the 1970s, '80s, and '90s it was the popular and notorious college hangout Audubon Tavern II.

Another member of the grocer's family was Jack Cefalu. Born in Sicily in 1892, he came to the United States at age

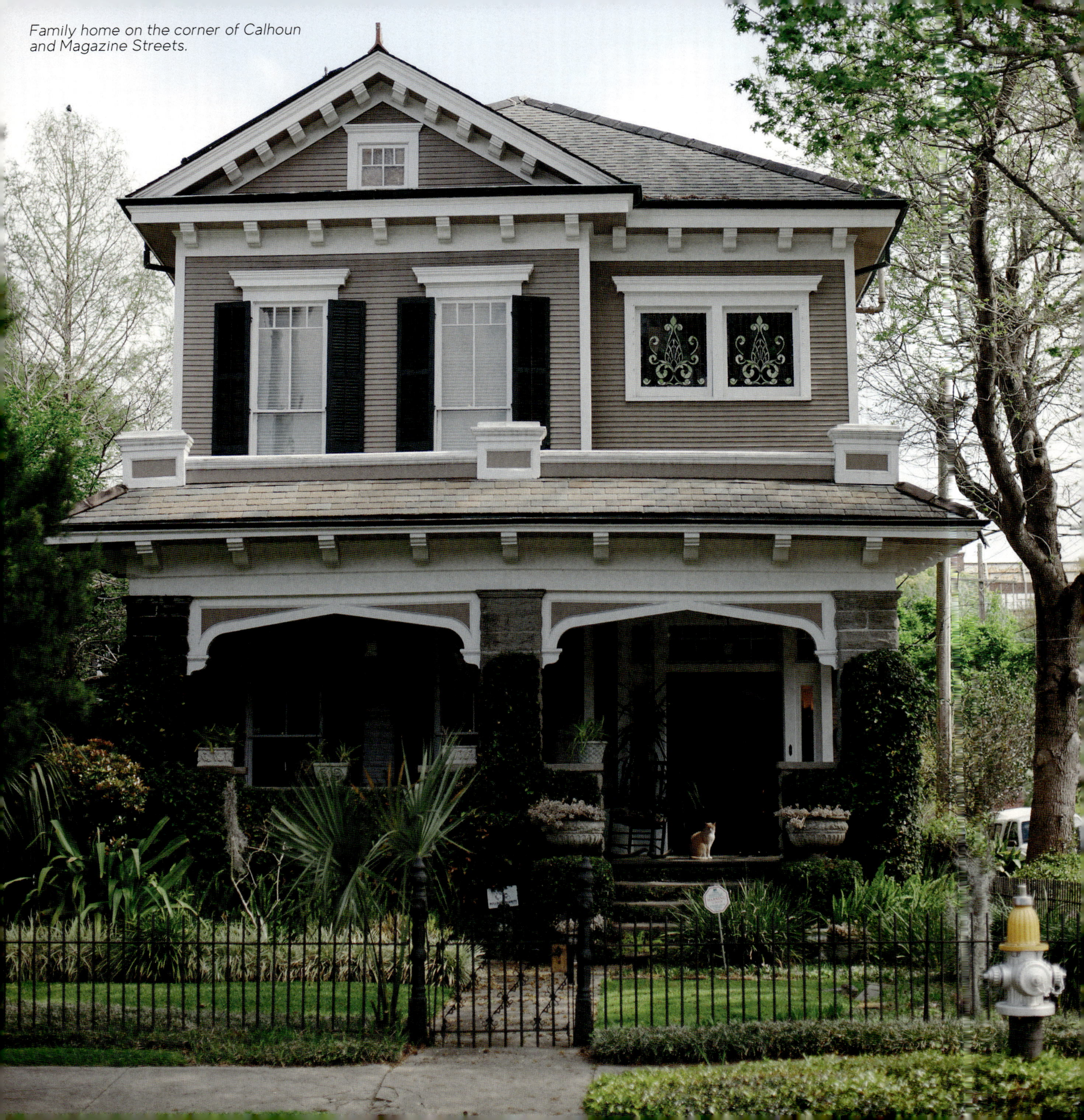

Family home on the corner of Calhoun and Magazine Streets.

twenty-one. He was a cobbler at 3903 Magazine, the same building that Pilot and Powell now occupies. Family members remembered that every day he left home in a suit but changed into his work clothes at work.

The family reminisced that as youngsters they were not allowed to go beyond Napoleon Avenue, except to the library or Woolworth's, but after a certain age they could venture all the way to Canal Street, as long as they were dressed up. They also recalled that in the 1940s and '50s everybody in the neighborhood got along. While white families lived on Magazine, there were African American families on side streets; however, there was no real division, and kids of both races played together.

In the 1930s and '40s, at the intersection of Henry Clay, where the Henry Clay Apartments now stand, was Charles Van Hoven Florist and Nursery. Diagonally across Magazine from here is the stately brick monastery of the Franciscan order of Poor Clares nuns. This contemplative order arrived in New Orleans in 1885 and built a monastery facing Magazine on this site. The current building, which faces

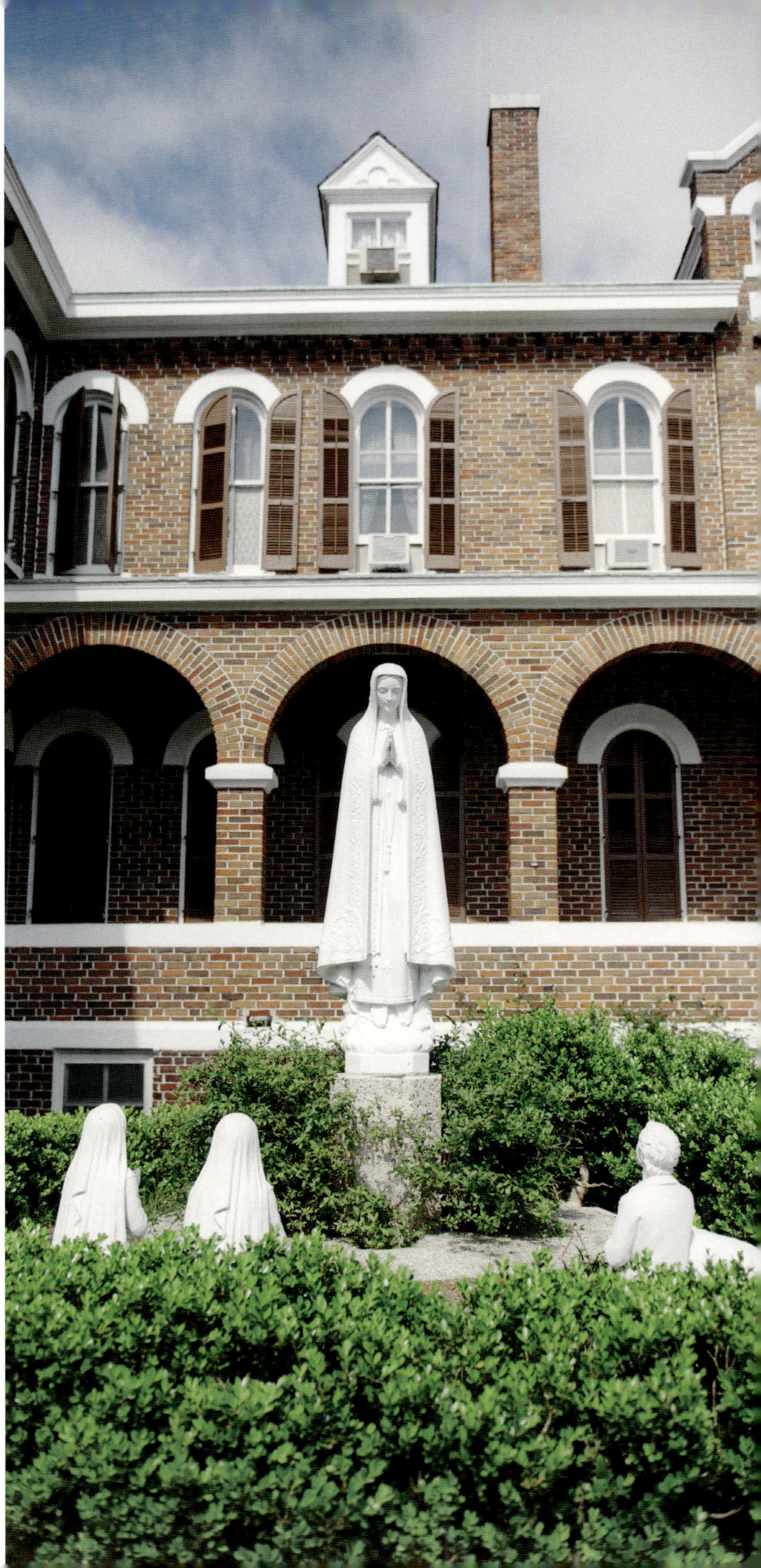

St. Clare's Monastery, home of the Poor Clares, on the corner of Henry Clay at Magazine.

Henry Clay, was completed in 1914.

Elaine Nicoll came from a family of six children and in the 1960s lived at the corner of Joseph and Chestnut in half of a big double house. Her cousin's family lived on the other side. Like many double houses all over Uptown New Orleans, this double has been converted into a single house.

"Every corner you went you had a grocery," remembered Mrs. Nicoll. There was a store every few blocks on Magazine, but, her family shopped at a store on Joseph at Camp that is now apartments. She also recalls Moullidoux's grocery at what is today a parking lot near Jefferson, and a second location owned by a Moullidoux brother at Magazine and Webster, where Cicero's was in the 1920s and '30s.

In the 1960s she said that Maurice Charles Sciortino Academy of Hair Styling was in the building where Uptown Delivery Pharmacy is today. Later the school moved to Napoleon at 4432 Magazine, where Ten Gallery is now located. From 1969 to 1971, Mrs. Nicoll worked at Mozer's Pharmacy on Magazine at State. She has fond memories of owner Bob Mozer. He would stay open late on Friday, and when the store closed for the evening, he would always buy shrimp sandwiches from Compagno's across Magazine for the "girls" who worked for him.

Mrs. Nicoll recalled that it was "wonderful living near Magazine." As a child she could go outside and play, and everybody knew everybody else on the block. It was like living in a small town. Until she grew to be a teenager, she was not allowed to go beyond Napoleon Avenue. The limit was the Napoleon Theater, which was a block off Magazine on Napoleon Avenue behind Laurence Square. In the other direction on Magazine, she could go to Audubon Park and go swimming in the old pool, as long as she went with her older sister.

For children in the neighborhood, a trip to the Audubon Zoo was an easy outing and one they often made unchaperoned by adults. Charles "Buddy" Drago, who lived in the neighborhood and was related to the family that owned Cicero's grocery, reminisced that in the 1950s, when he was about age ten, he would "disappear" on Saturday mornings to go to the zoo at 10:00 A.M. feeding time. When the zoo obtained giraffes during this same period, their feeding time was 7:00 A.M. On weekdays he would make it to the zoo in time to watch the giraffes get fed full loaves of French bread before heading to school. One morning the caretaker let Buddy feed a loaf to a giraffe. The giraffe wrapped his long black tongue around both the bread and Buddy's arm and started to pull. The caretaker intervened, but Buddy was frightened and never wanted to feed the giraffes again. Mr. Drago remembered that the caretaker of the zoo was Mr. Champagne, who lived across the street from his family in the 5200 block of Magazine, but Mr. Champagne later moved to a house on the zoo grounds in the early 1960s.

In the 1930s it was not just Uptown kids who could get easily to the park. At that time there were still half a dozen ferries crossing the river in the city, and one of these was between Westwego and Walnut Street, just above the park. One elderly gentleman remembered that as a boy in the summer, he would take a ferry ride with friends from Westwego and they would spend the day in the park. It was also not a long walk to the Magazine streetcar and a ride to Canal Street.

Just past the park, Magazine Street comes to a rather inauspicious end at the intersection with Leake Avenue and the high levee hiding the Mississippi River.

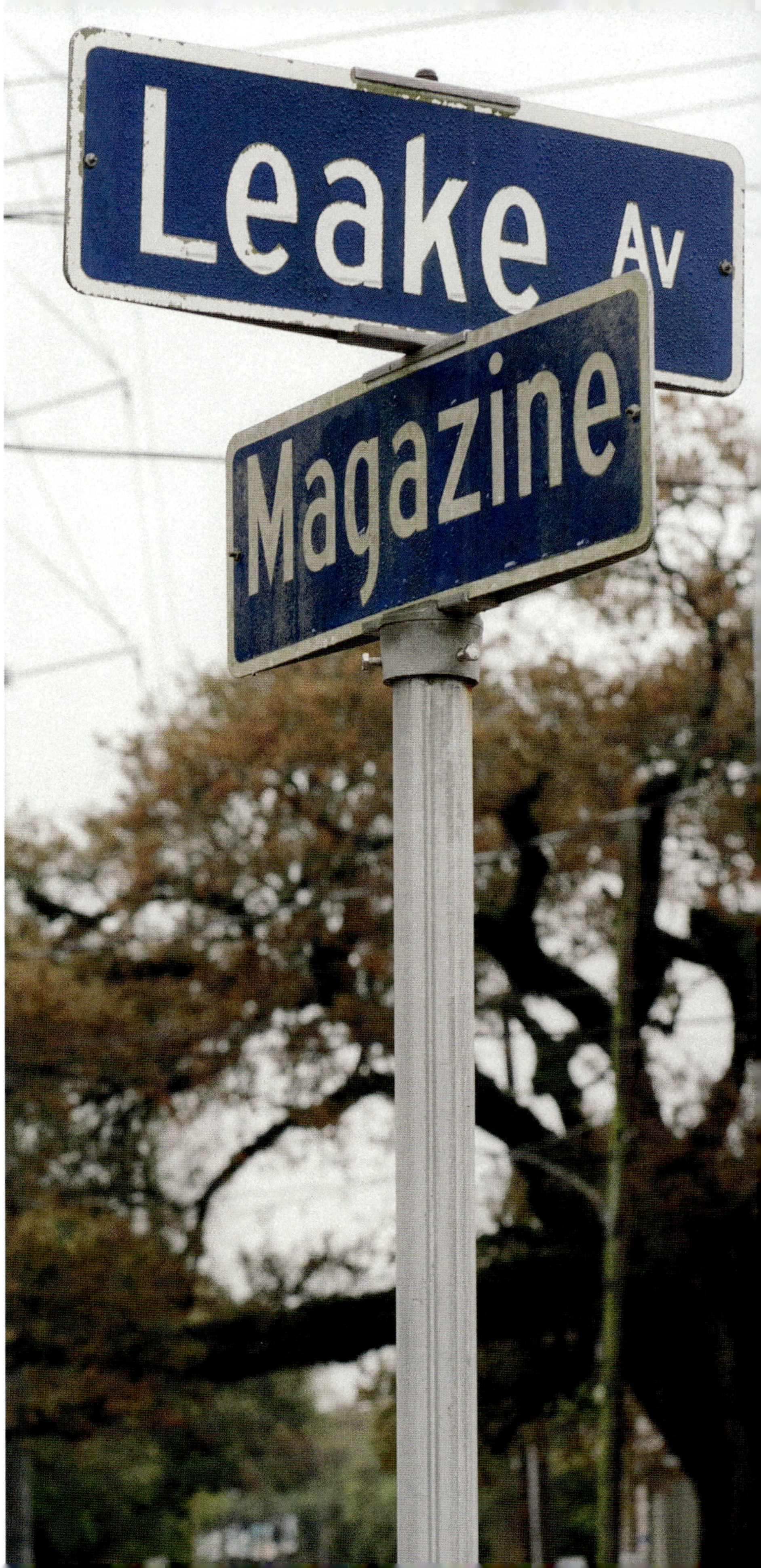

Magazine Street ends at the Mississippi River levee, where it meets Leake Avenue.

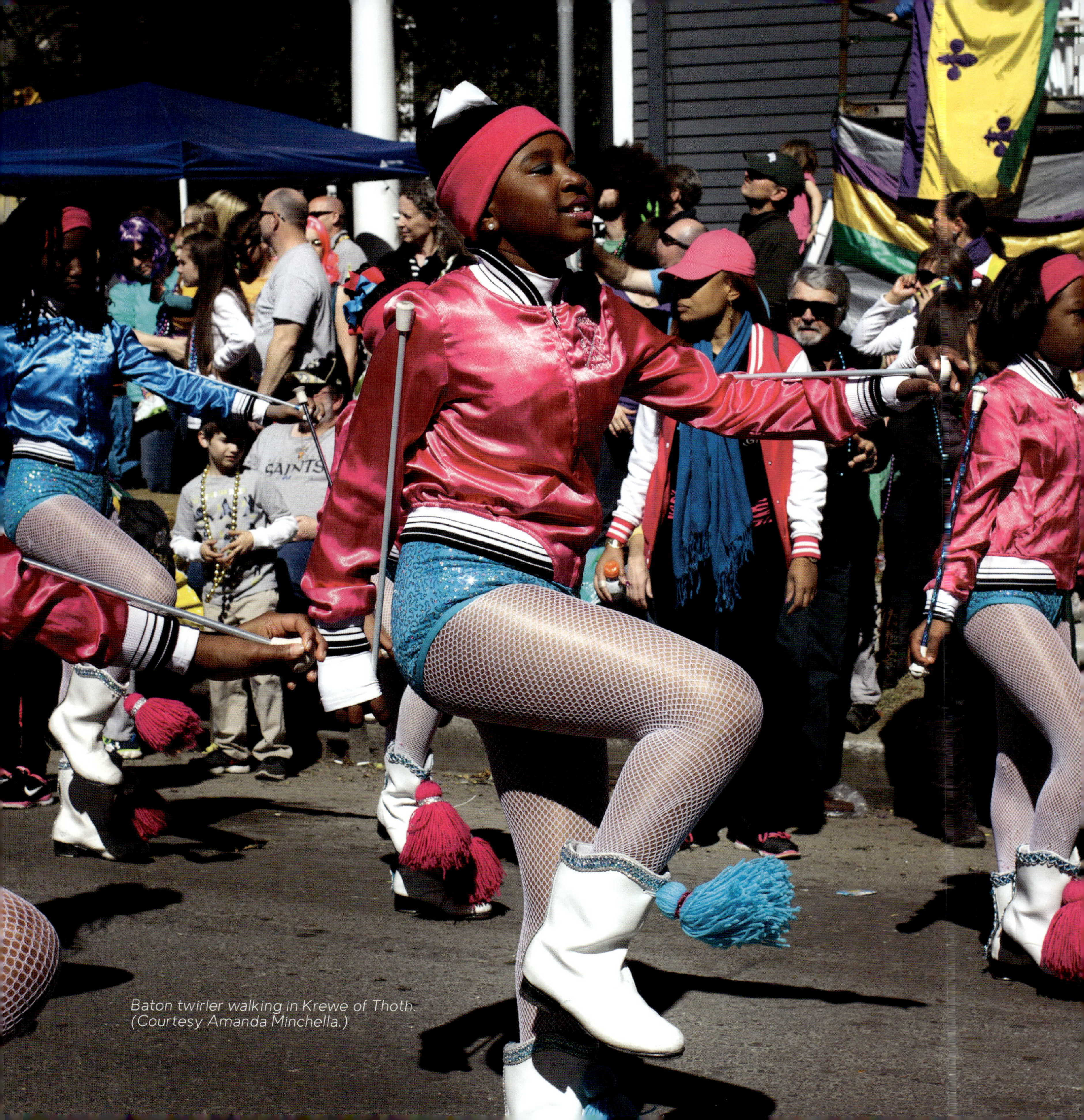

Baton twirler walking in Krewe of Thoth.
(Courtesy Amanda Minchella.)

Chapter Nine

Family and Festivities on Magazine

Part of Magazine Street's allure in the twenty-first century goes beyond locally owned businesses, dining, and night spots. For many people it has become the most popular destination for Carnival parades. While Magazine Street launched its evolution into an incomparable cultural and shopping destination with its "M" Day celebration in 1948, today the street draws cheerful crowds for its many Mardi Gras parades. Magazine may be pleasantly quiet on Fat Tuesday itself, when the revelry heads elsewhere, but for a week and a half it is lined with young and old parade-goers enjoying nightly and weekend parades. Unlike "M" Day there are plenty of throws being hurled through the air toward waving arms. Magazine is a Carnival parade destination not only for nearby residents who can walk to their favorite spots, but for parade aficionados from throughout the area who have to hunt for parking along side streets.

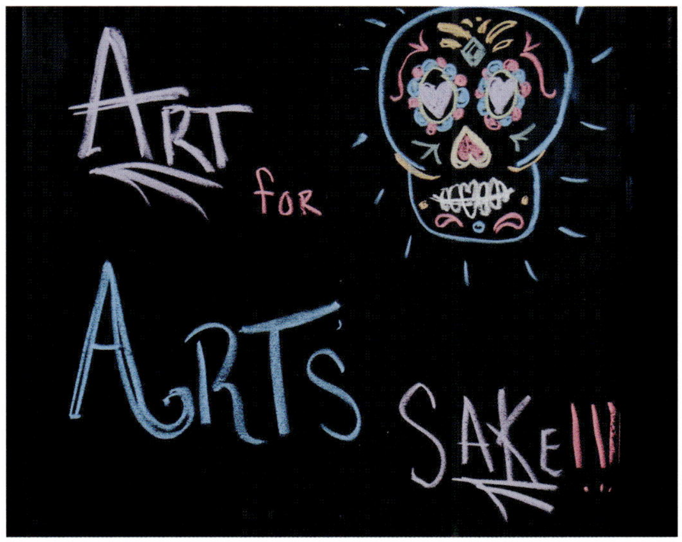

Sign promoting Art for Art's Sake on Magazine Street. (Courtesy Magazine Street Merchants Association.)

Magazine is a new parade

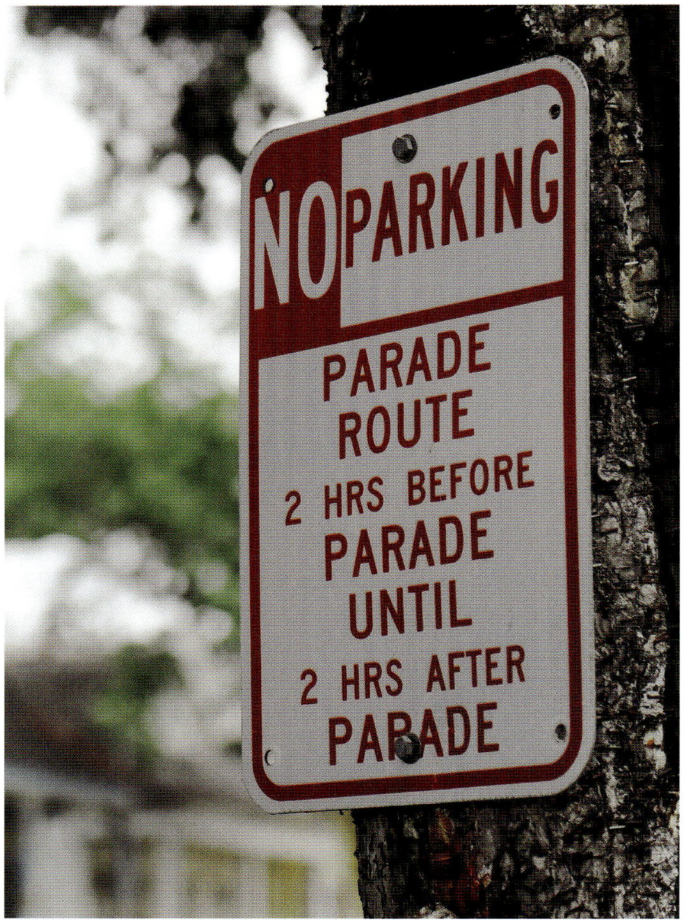

Magazine Street's status as a Carnival destination is evidenced throughout the year by street signs.

route, only dating to the start of the twenty-first century. To ease stress on the police department during Carnival parades, parade routes in New Orleans—except for Endymion on Canal Street—focus on Napoleon and St. Charles, ending near the foot of Canal Street downtown. Since Hurricane Katrina more and more parades are beginning at Jefferson Avenue and follow Magazine before turning onto Napoleon. Other parades start on Napoleon and cross Magazine. Altogether Carnival gives Magazine more than a week of bands, floats, throws, and spectacle. Year round, trees and fence posts are decorated with beads.

Carnival on Magazine starts the Friday a week before Fat Tuesday with the Krewe of Cleopatra and Pygmalion. Pontchartrain, Choctaw, Freret, Sparta, Femme Fatale, Carrollton, King Arthur, and Alla all follow throughout the weekend. Monday and Tuesday the week before Mardi Gras are quiet with no parades rolling, but beginning Wednesday, Magazine really comes alive. That evening Babylon crosses the street at Napoleon, while Druids and Nyx both begin at Jefferson. Thursday brings Chaos, which crosses at Napoleon, and Muses starts at Jefferson. Friday has Hermes crossing the street at Napoleon as both Le Krewe d'Etat and Morpheus start their march at Jefferson. Magazine is much quieter on Saturday with only Tucks crossing it at Napoleon.

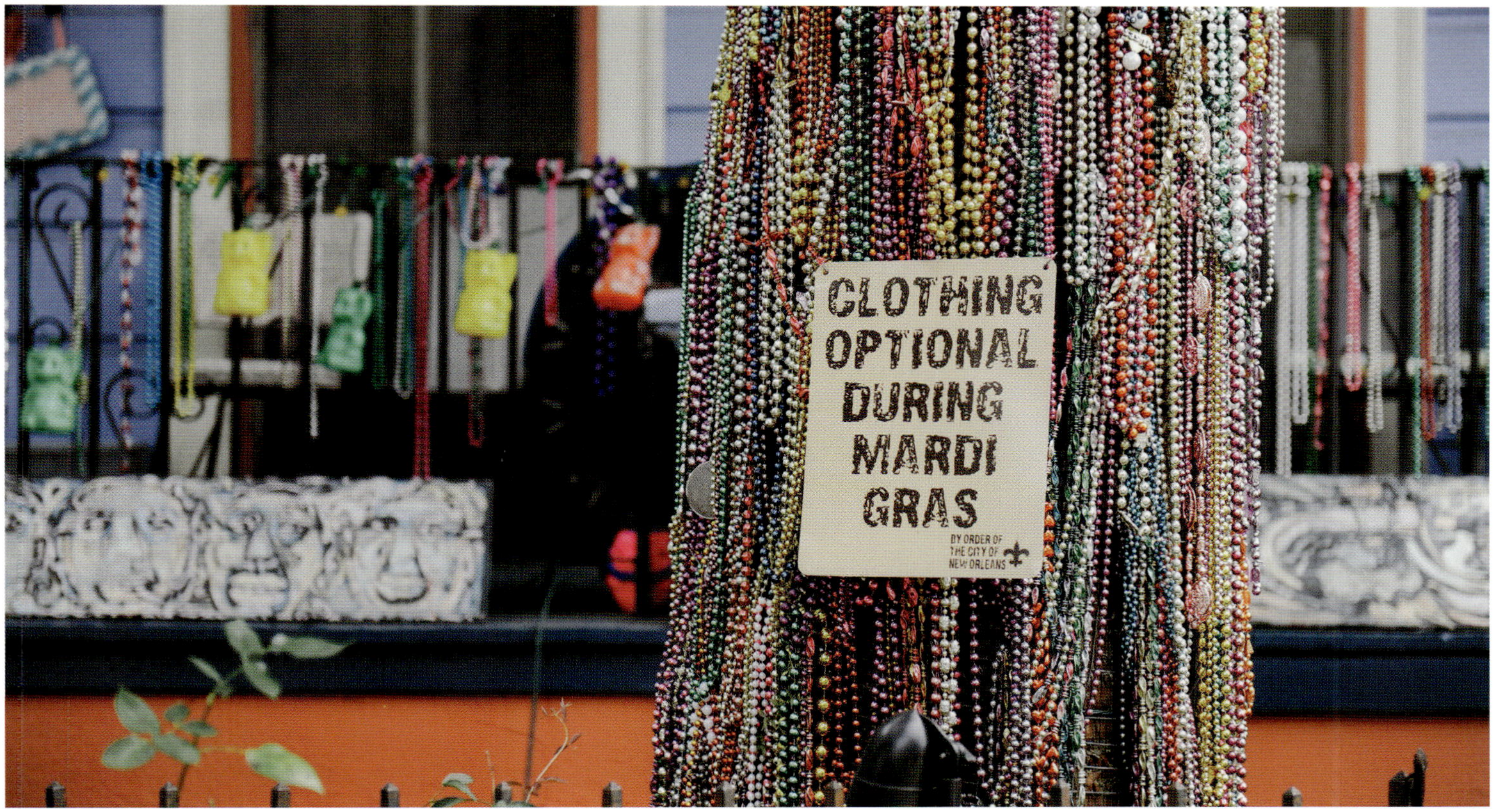

A Magazine Street resident's Mardi Gras bead tree and lighthearted sign.

The next day, the Sunday before Mardi Gras, has long been Magazine's biggest Carnival day. Okeanos and Mid-City both begin at Jefferson Avenue, while Thoth is the granddaddy of all Magazine parades. This day is commonly and lovingly called Thoth Sunday by anyone on or near the Magazine parade route. Thoth starts on Tchoupitoulas at State Street then turns onto Henry Clay Avenue to Magazine, marching then to Napoleon through excited throngs of people. On a beautiful day the crowds can extend from wall to wall, not to mention those partying on many house porches.

The Krewe of Thoth is the oldest Carnival parade along upper Magazine and for decades it was the only one. Named for the Egyptian god of wisdom, god of scribes, and measurer of time, the Thoth

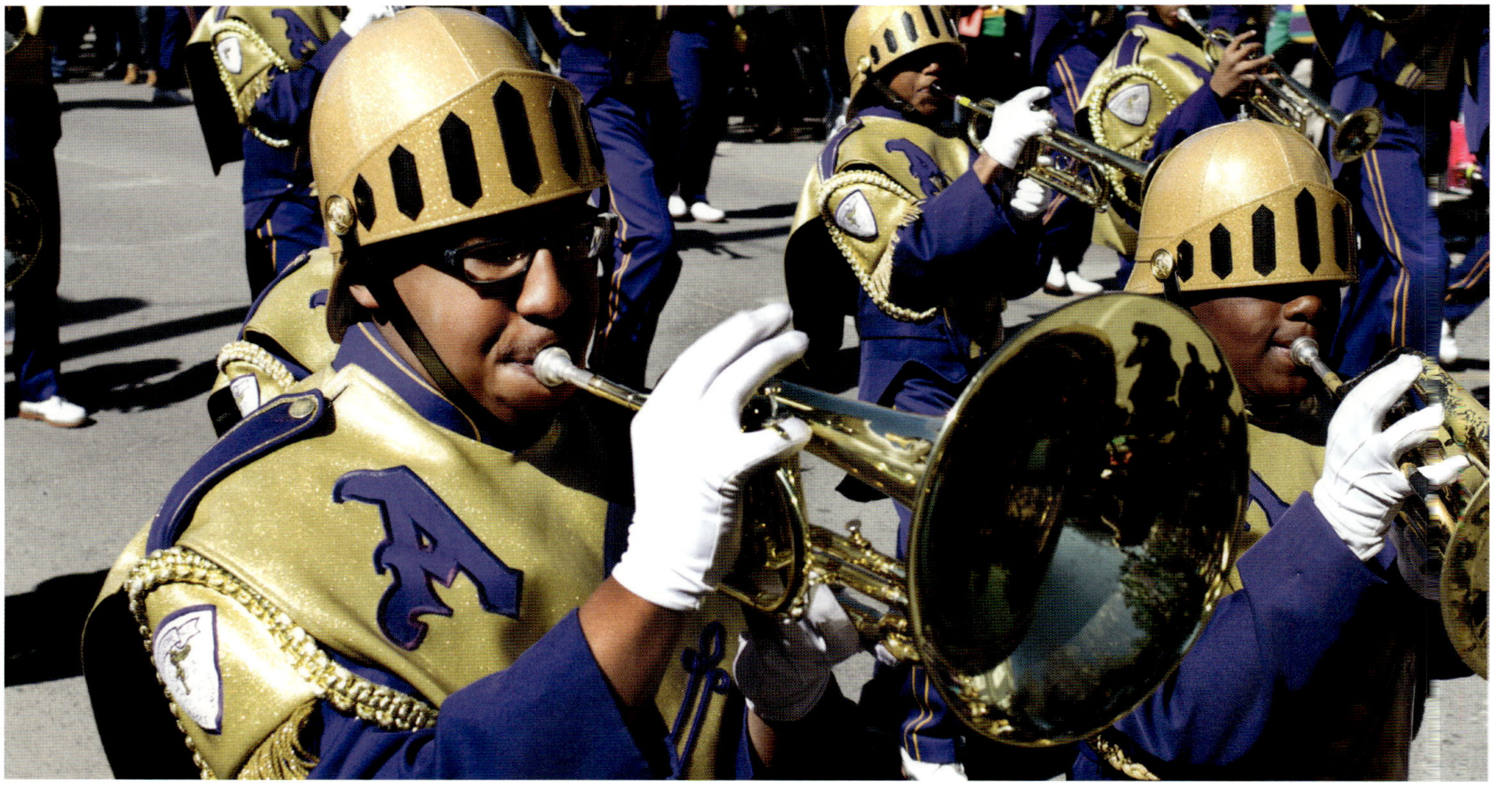

A trumpet player from St. Augustine's Purple Knights "Marching 100" passes during the Thoth parade. (Courtesy Amanda Minchella.)

Carnival and Social Club was founded by a group of civic-minded citizens in 1947. With fifty members, five floats, and the theme "A Succession of Mythological Divinities and Demigods," its first parade traversed Magazine and Prytania Streets on February 8, 1948. It was conceived as the parade for shut-ins since it passed orphanages, hospitals, sanitariums, and homes for the elderly. Meeting with great acclaim from the start, Thoth has grown considerably larger and longer and its route has changed, but just as in the 1940s it still passes near institutions like Children's

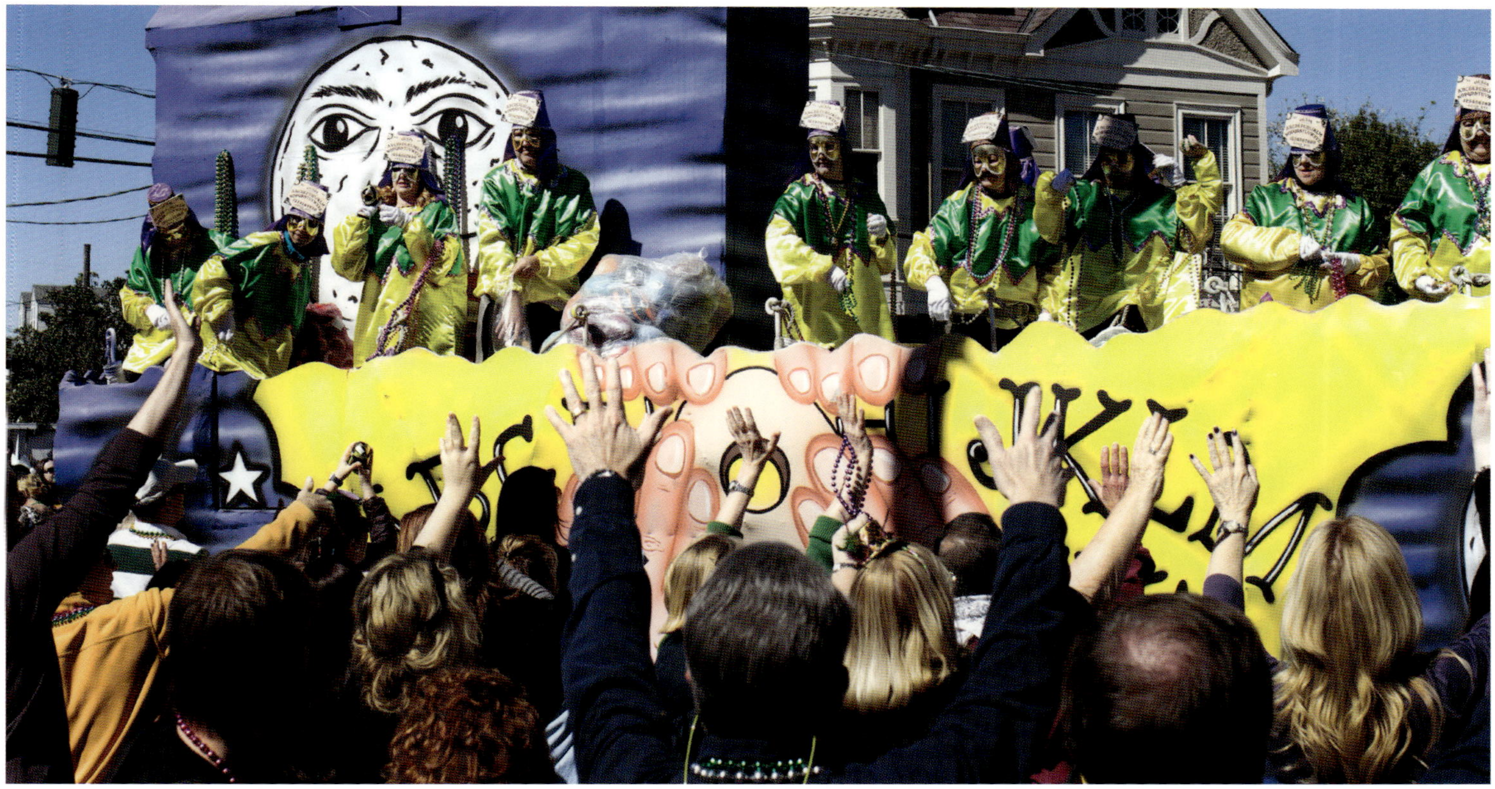

Reaching for throws from Krewe of Thoth. (Courtesy Amanda Minchella.)

Hospital of New Orleans and the Poydras Home.

Thoth Sunday has grown into one of the most anticipated days of the entire Carnival season. Between those hosting open houses and those looking for invitations, Magazine between Napoleon and Henry Clay is one big, family-friendly party. Nowadays, Thoth Sunday is bigger than ever, since Thoth no longer parades alone. Indeed, so many other parades start at Magazine and Jefferson throughout the season, it can be said that Magazine Street hosts a weeklong celebration.

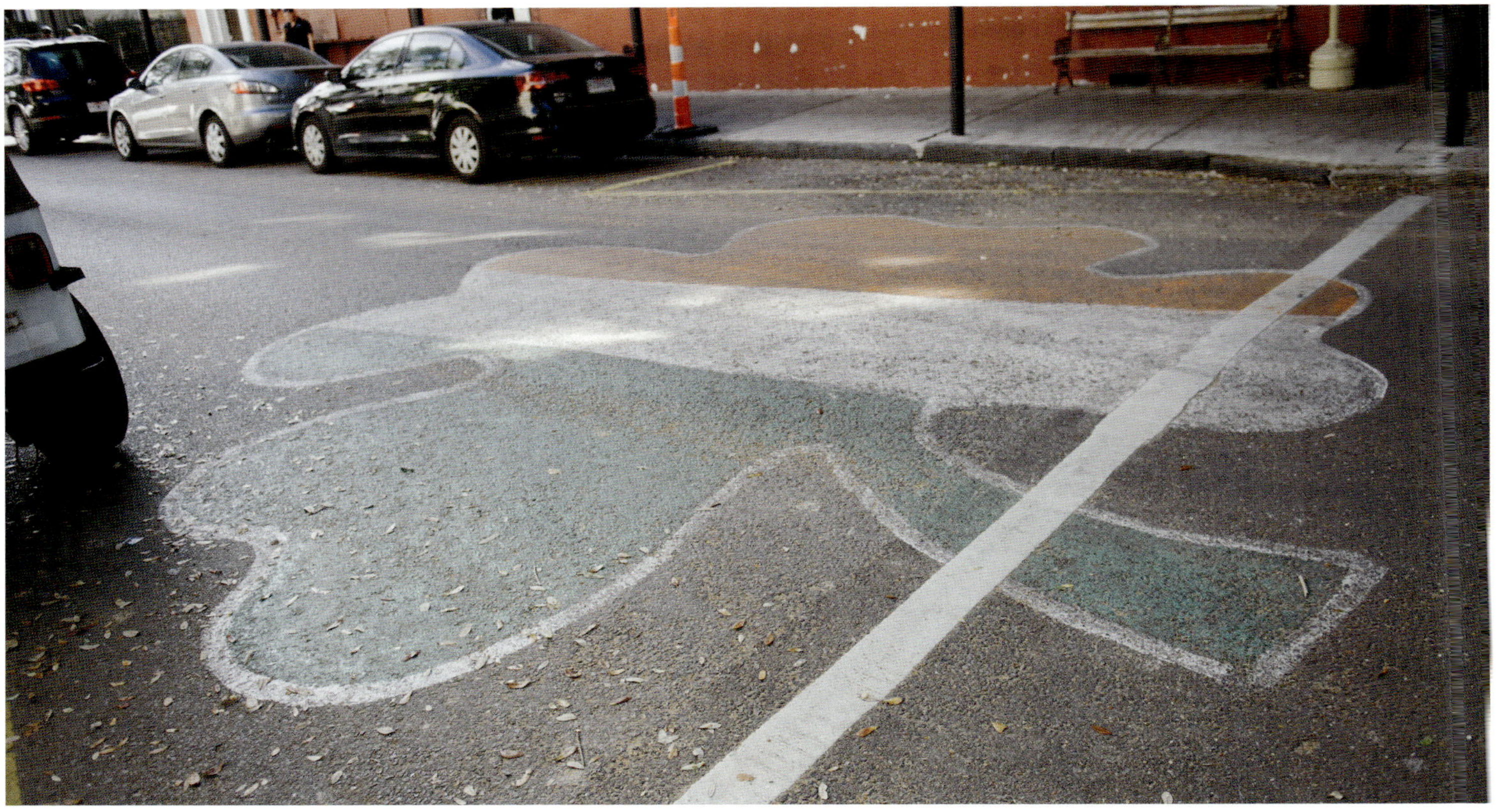

Shamrock at Tracey's Original Irish Channel Bar, a popular St. Patrick's Day spot.

For the thousands of revelers who are not quite finished with parades and partying after Mardi Gras, there is the Irish Channel Parade the Saturday before St. Patrick's Day, which extends into Magazine's Irish pubs, Parasol's and Tracey's.

While Carnival and St. Patrick's Day parades attract increasing numbers of parade-goers, the parades introduce visitors to other attractions and events along the street. At night taverns and restaurants are thronged with people. At some spots tables fill the sidewalk and patrons cluster along the street. Magazine Street is seen by many young adults as a popular and fun place to hang out with its trendy fashion and beauty shops, galleries, late-night restaurants, and taverns. For those so inclined there are several tattoo parlors.

While Magazine at night may be mostly

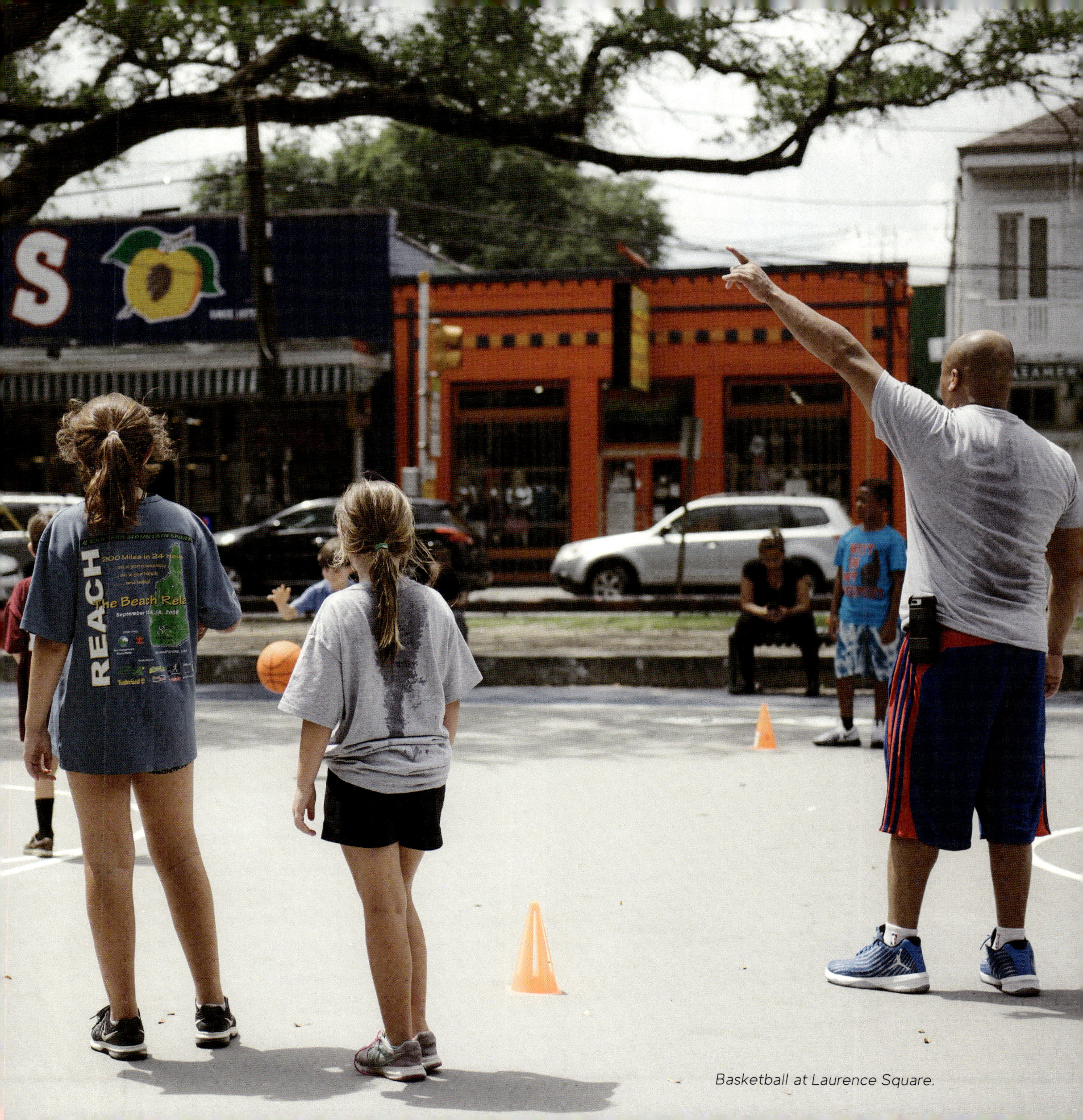

Basketball at Laurence Square.

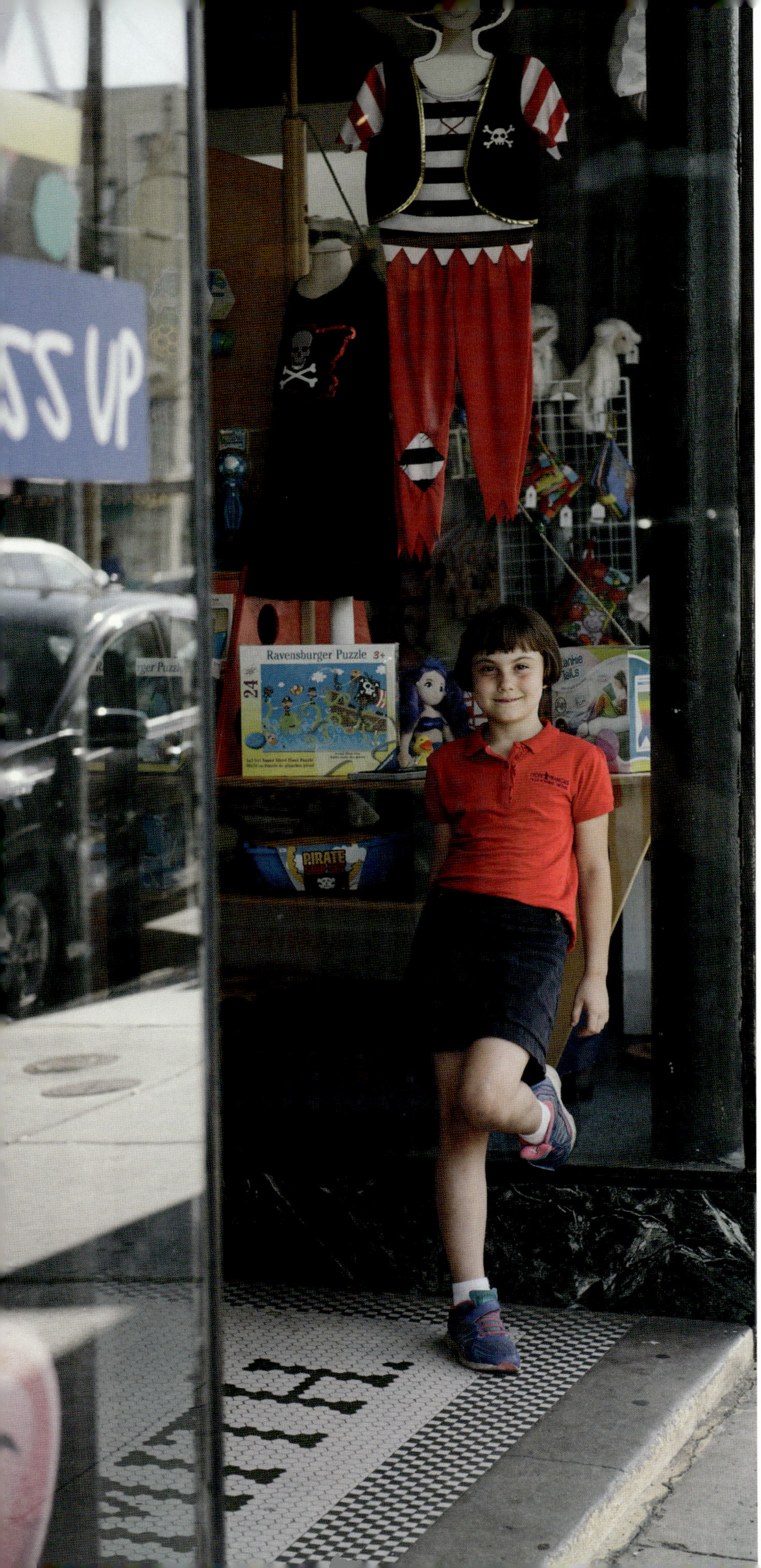

an adult world, during the day it is more than that. Throughout its six miles, Magazine is truly a family destination. It is anchored at either end by two of the most outstanding attractions in New Orleans—the National WWII Museum and the Audubon Zoo—and both are ideal for children. Special events at the museum include family workshops, special days for Scouts, and even an overnight pajama party. The zoo also has regular family-oriented events, including the annual Zoo-To-Do for the grownups on the first Friday in May and the Zoo-To-Do for Kids, on the last Friday in April. During Halloween season, families enjoy Audubon's always popular Boo at the Zoo.

All along Magazine on any day of the week, parents push children in strollers or walk with toddlers hand-in-hand taking in the sights. There are many places for children—even grownup children. Magic Box Toys welcomes children of all ages at 5508 Magazine, near Octavia. The building is much different than it was in the 1980s, when it was known as Top Cleaners.

Not far from Magic Box is Octavia Books, on Octavia Street near Laurel, where both kids and parents can browse specially selected books in the children's book

Magic Box Toys, 5508 Magazine.

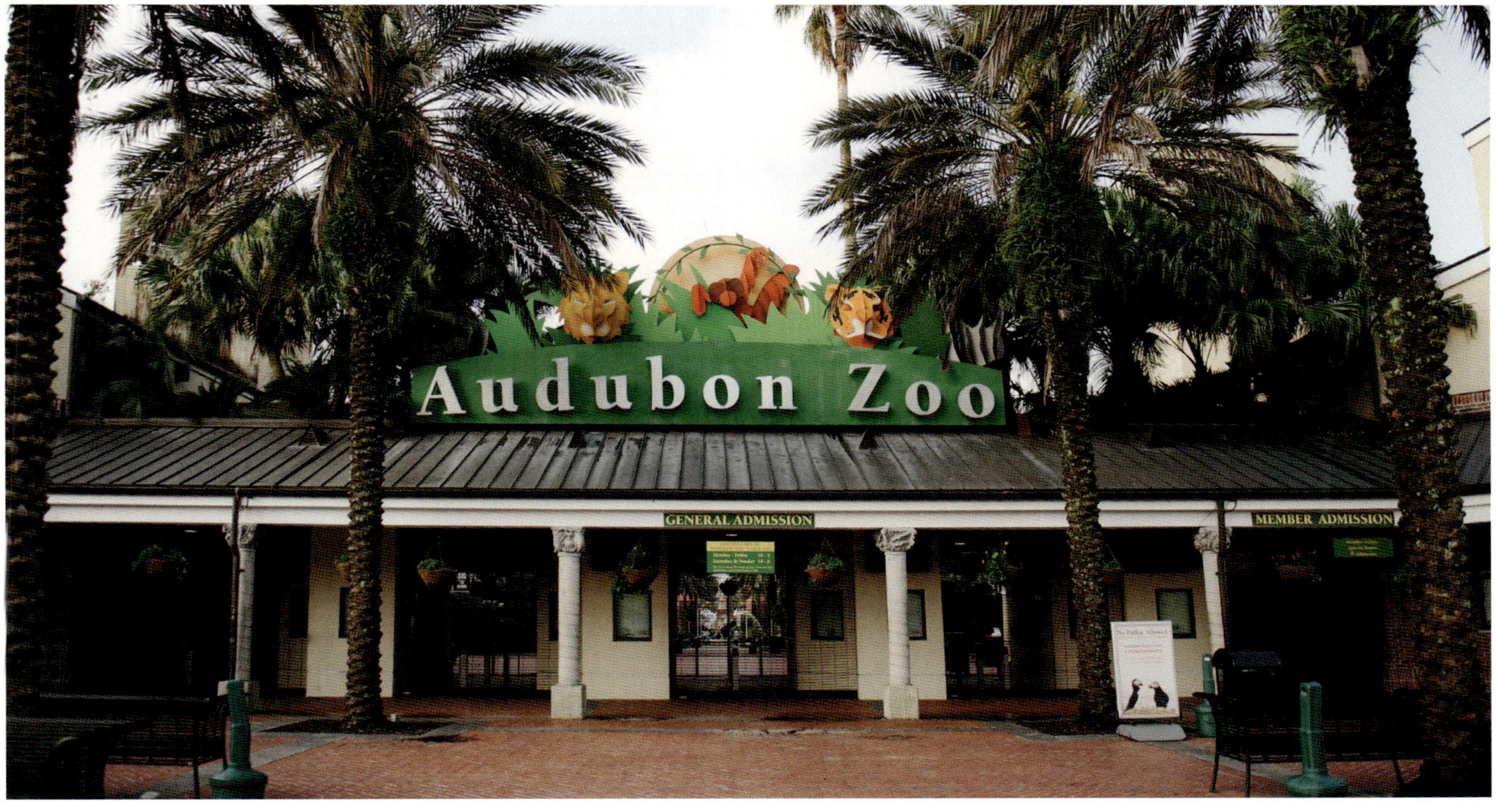

Entrance to Audubon Zoo.

section. Children's books can also be found at the French Library at 3811 Magazine. Specializing in French children's books, the store has frequent children's events including weekly story time for different age groups, even tots three years old and under.

With its many fashion stores, there are also outfitters for even the youngest. Pippen Lane at 2930 Magazine, on the corner of Seventh Street, specializes in luxury children's clothing, toys, and even furniture. It is a mother's fantasy that only Magazine Street can offer. Next door at 2928 is NOLA Couture, which might deal more in adult accessories but also includes kids' ties and bow ties. Orient Expressed, at 3446 offers embroidered and smocked children's clothing and gifts. Perlis, at 6070 Magazine and the corner

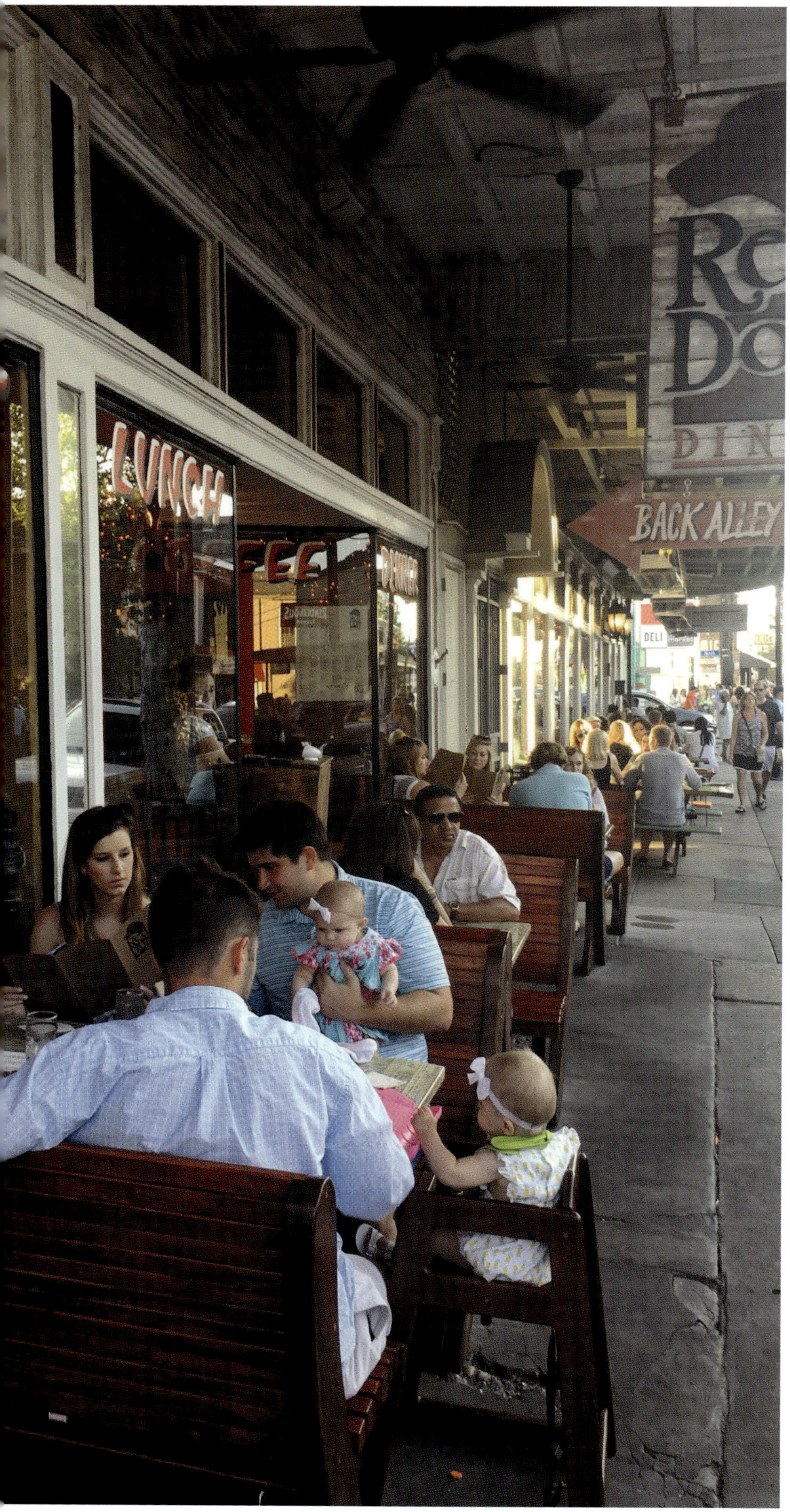

of Webster, has for generations provided young men with their first seersucker or white linen suit and later on a young man's first tuxedo and full-dress for Carnival balls. Aside from these, Magazine offers a world of gifts, toys, records, and art supplies that are part of the life of any family.

From school block parties to festivals promoting the city's food, art, and culture, Magazine also entertains those looking to spend a day outside the boutiques. *Fête Française*, benefiting *Ecole Bilingue de la Nouvelle-Orléans*, is held on the last Saturday in March and celebrates French heritage with food, music, art, dancing, and games. Xavier Prep Alumni Association hosts the Remember When music festival, which highlights some of the finest musicians in New Orleans, art works, and food from top restaurants.

The Magazine Street Merchants Association sponsors events that take place along the entire length of Magazine Street. Lauren Haydel, owner of Fleurty Girl, said that these festivals bring people out for a "fun experience," and they seem to attract more people every year. Mrs. Haydel said of the 2017 Champagne Stroll that it was the best one Fleurty Girl has

Families dining at Red Dog Diner, 3122 Magazine Street. (Courtesy Magazine Street Merchants Association.)

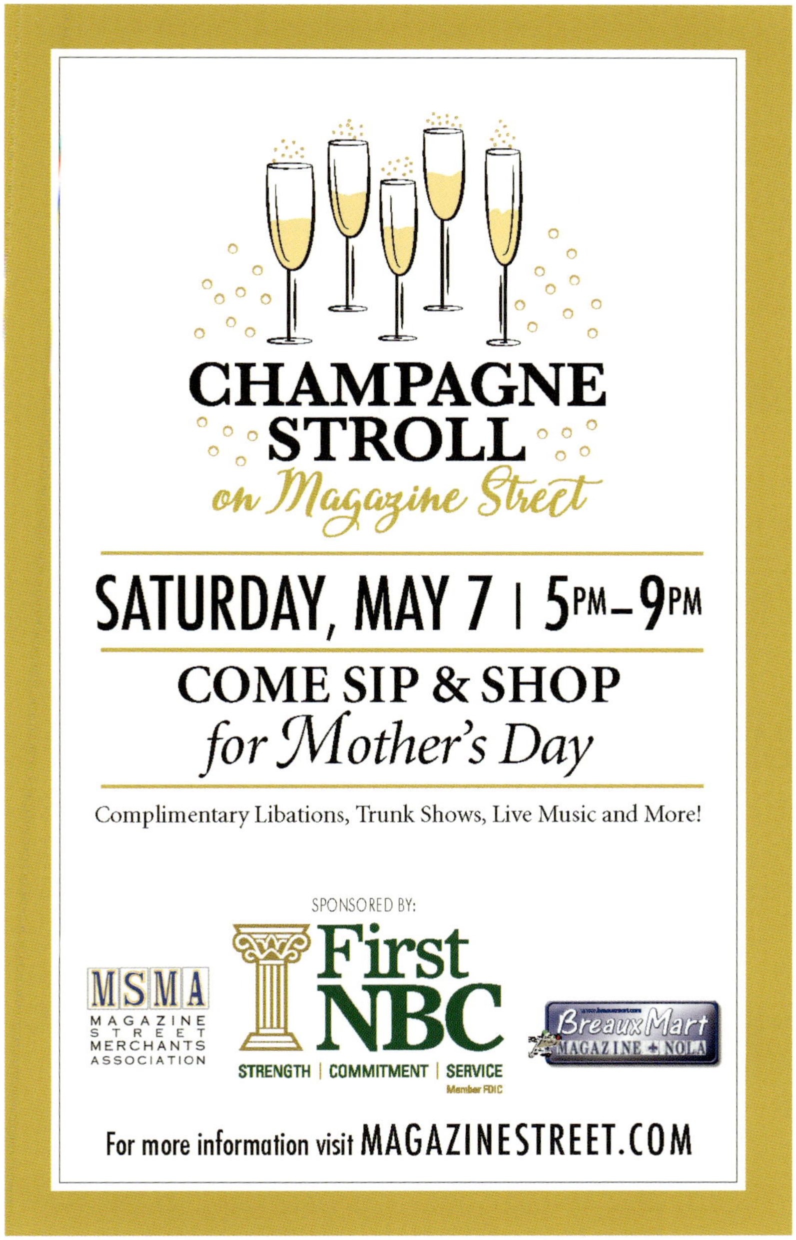

Poster for Champagne Stroll on Magazine Street. (Courtesy Magazine Street Merchants Association.)

ever experienced. Held the Saturday before Mother's Day, the Champagne Stroll is the first festival of the year sponsored by the Magazine Street Merchants Association. Shops keep their doors open late, and strollers can find special merchandise and sales, shopping to the accompaniment of music and, of course, bubbly.

Art for Art's Sake is the street's biggest annual event, attracting an estimated thirty thousand art enthusiasts, as well as those just looking for a good time. Held on the first Saturday in October, art galleries along the street, as well as in the Arts District, stay open until 9:00 P.M. This kicks off the city's arts season with new exhibits, wine, and food. It also helps welcome fall after a long Crescent City summer.

The last big event of the year on Magazine Street is Merriment on Magazine, a regional highlight of the holiday season. It kicks off the day after Thanksgiving with "Black Friday" sales followed the next day with "Small Business Saturday"—logical for Magazine with its many small,

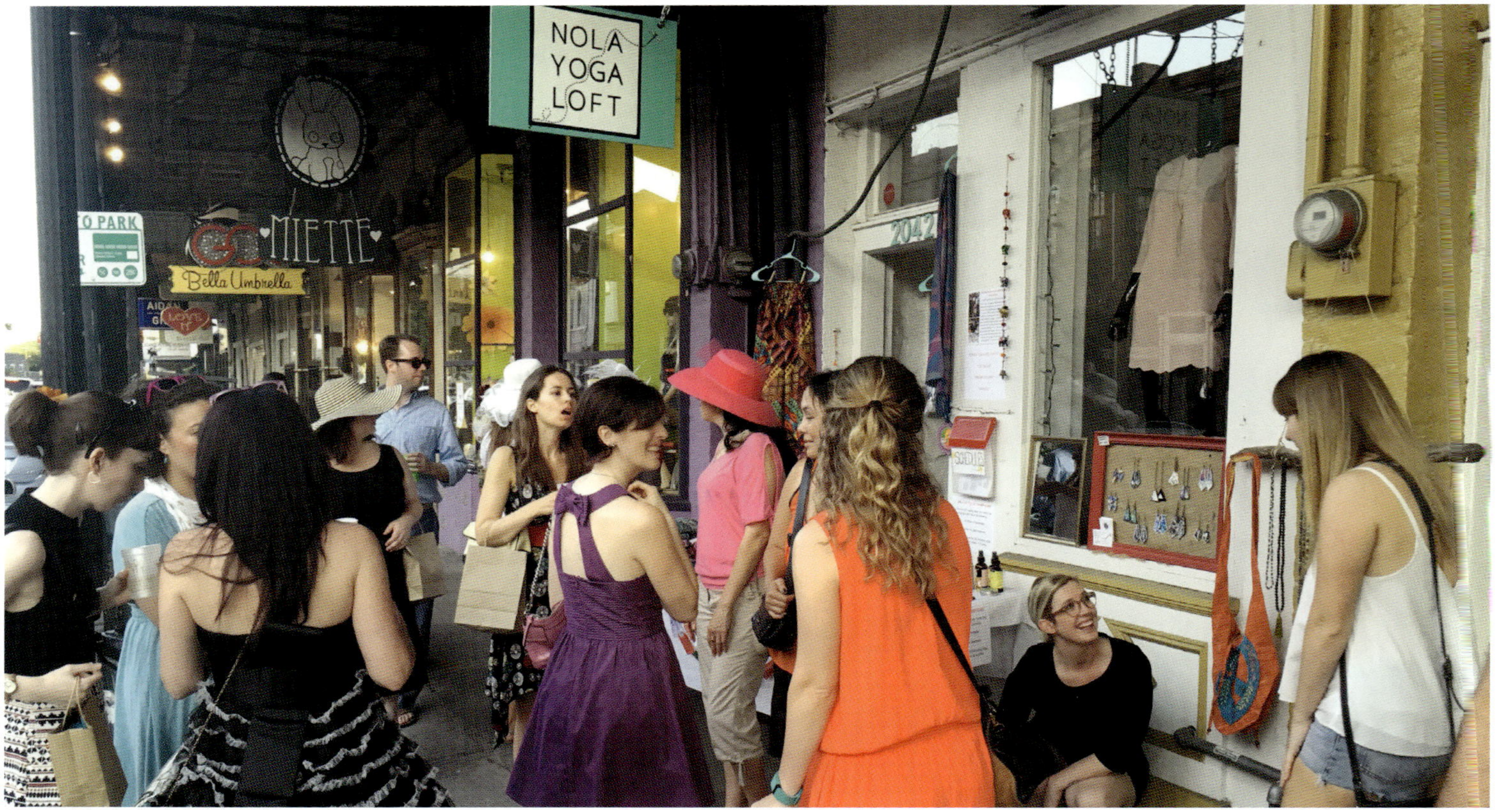

Shoppers and strollers at Champagne Stroll. (Courtesy Magazine Street Merchants Association.)

locally owned businesses. The slogan for Merriment on Magazine is "Shop, Eat, Drink & Be Merry," and it helps commemorate the holiday shopping season after Hurricane Katrina in 2005, when Magazine was one of the few shopping venues in town that had re-opened its doors.

From shopping to wining and dining, health and beauty to art galleries, Magazine truly does have something for everyone.

But the character of Magazine has not been lost in its transition from residential street to a shopping destination. While many residences on Magazine itself have been refashioned into businesses, just half a block off the street in every direction the cityscape becomes almost solidly residential, representing over two centuries of Uptown urban growth through several diverse neighborhoods, of which

Magazine is the main street. While these neighborhoods blend one into the other, each has its own personality, history, population, and architectural style. What they all have in common is that they are unified by a very trendy, yet old-fashioned Magazine Street, which itself is at once diverse and unified in character.

Previously considered shabby, out-of-date, and even dangerous, through its own evolution and perhaps simply luck, the "incomparable" Magazine Street has in its own singular way become an exciting, ever-changing gathering place. From its infancy in the late eighteenth and early nineteenth centuries, Magazine has evolved from little better than a country road into a countrified residential street with a series of neighborhood shopping districts into today's important business district. It has had its ups and downs and just as recently as the twentieth century it had declined into a gritty area some people felt best to avoid. But today it is a popular destination offering shopping, culture, entertainment, food, and history. It can be said that every city should have a Magazine Street. It is fun, it is exciting, and it is different, promising an experience unlike any other.

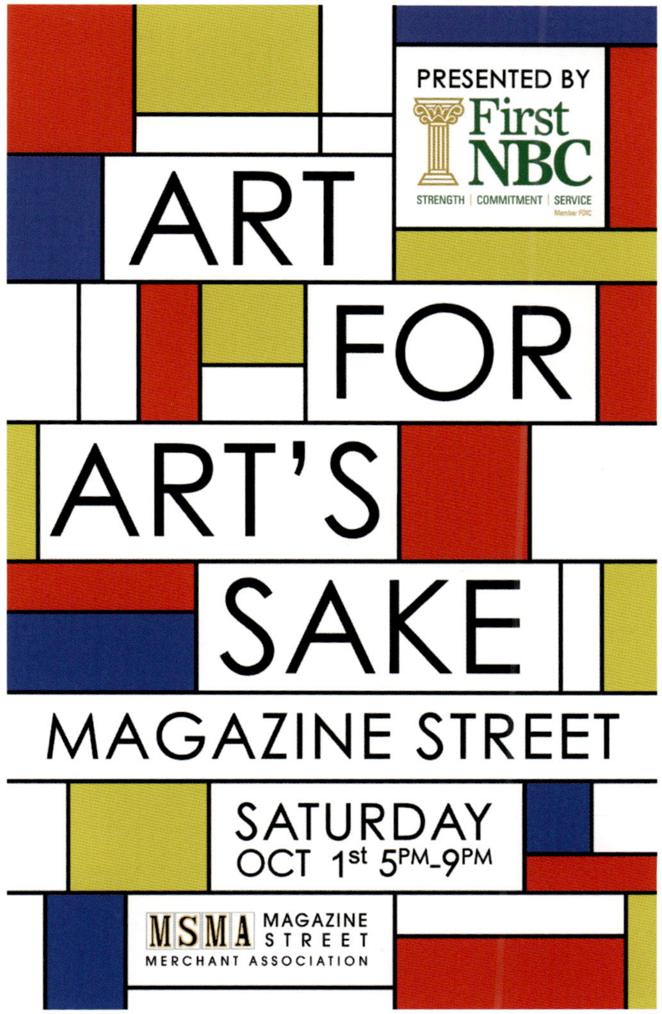

Art for Art's Sake poster.
(Courtesy Magazine Street Merchants Association.)

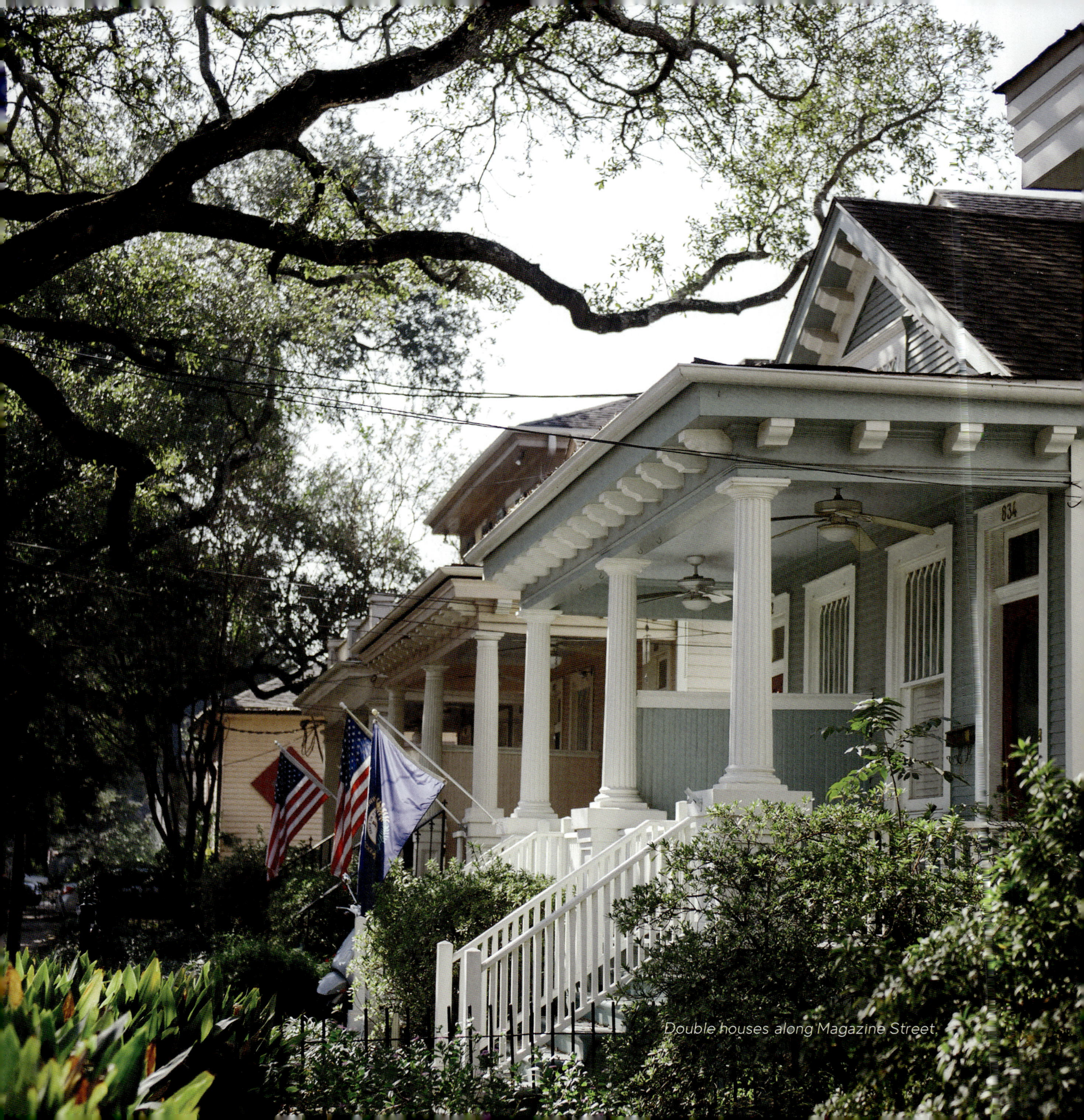
Double houses along Magazine Street.

Acknowledgments

The Incomparable Magazine Street grew out of a discussion with River Road Press publisher Scott Campbell at the Five Happiness Chinese Restaurant on Carrollton Avenue the day before Mardi Gras in 2015. I was soon to be retiring after thirty-three years with The Historic New Orleans Collection, and a book project seemed an interesting idea. After several of my suggestions fell flat, I suggested writing something about Magazine Street. The idea clicked.

The Incomparable Magazine Street not only tells how Magazine fits into the urban growth of the Crescent City, it also highlights what it has become: an enchanting combination of both elegance and the down-to-earth. The book is meant to be a jumping-off point to acquaint locals, newcomers, and visitors to a street that many love but frequently take for granted. It has long been a spine of Uptown New Orleans, but Magazine might now be regarded as New Orleans' new main street. Even so, there has never been a book written specifically about Magazine Street before.

It takes many people to help put together a book like this and put life into it, especially for a subject as untouched and as broad as more than two centuries of Magazine Street. It required personally interviewing a number of people who have lived, worked, or just spent time on Magazine. Some of the individuals I already knew as personal friends, while others were newly met—some we just ran into as we explored the street—and kindly allowed me to intrude on their memories and observations. Some had been brought up on or near the street and in most cases own businesses in the area. All were excited to tell his or her Magazine story.

There are several individuals who suggested sources that

helped lead me into a desired direction. Great friend and work colleague for over thirty years is Historic New Orleans Collection Senior Librarian/Rare Books Curator Pamela D. Arceneaux, who introduced me to the big, red booklet entitled *The "M" Day Celebration of the Improvement of Magazine Street*, which outlines the 1948 festivities when Magazine was repaved and trolleybuses replaced streetcars. Val Earhart kindly lent me a 1978 booklet entitled *New Orleans Underground Shopping: Magazine St. Volume,* compiled by his late wife Diana D. Earhart and Ann H. Earhart. My fellow reader of plays and short stories is Ivan Mandich, who led me to Ada Louise Huxtable's *Goodbye History, Hello Hamburger: An Anthology of Architectural Delights and Disasters* (Preservation Press, 1986), from which the title of this book was derived.

Individuals who provided insight and recollections of Magazine Street include Paul L. Arceneaux—husband of Pamela Arceneaux—and Charlotte Hoggatt, neither of whom lived on Magazine but remembered its second-hand furniture stores. Libby Bonner, as manager of British Antiques, has heard many Magazine stories. Uptown sisters Kate Robinson and Ann Trice shared their own tales. We met Mary Shelly sitting on her Magazine Street front porch, and we met Catherine "Cath" Wilson in an art gallery on Magazine. She had grown up in the 2000 block of Magazine. Leonard Palmisano knew Cath since they grew up on the same block. Elaine Nicoll grew up closer to Audubon Park. Stan Levy is a retired antiques dealer. I was also introduced by Missy Couhig, owner of The Conundrum bookstore in St. Francisville, Louisiana, to members of her family whose Magazine neighborhood roots go back to the early twentieth century. They included Rosalie Cefalu LeClere, Frances Drago Hymel, John Drago, and Charles "Buddy" Drago. Harold Cavillier, who lives in the front of the old Lee Harvey Oswald property, invited me into his home.

There are many merchants and businesspeople in the vicinity of Magazine Street, and while some of their businesses have been around for many years, others have more recently joined the ranks of Magazine Street. In alphabetical order, sincere thanks go to all those who are included herein: Keith Andrews, Apolline Restaurant and president of Magazine Street Merchants Association (MSMA); Bryan Batt, Hazelnut; Leon and Darren Clement, Clement's Hardware; Mignon Faget and Alexis Stahl, archivist and special projects coordinator, Mignon Faget Ltd.; Sam Farnet, Joey K's Restaurant and former president of MSMA; Ron Forman, CEO, and Frank Donze, communications specialist, Audubon Nature Institute; Aidan Gill, Aidan Gill for Men; Steve Gogreve, Henry's Bar; Katrina Greer, French Library; Peggy Gundlach, manager, Basics Underneath; Lauren Haydel, Fleurty Girl; Tierre Hazelwood, executive secretary, Second District Police Station; Simon Hardeveld, Simon's; Debbie Hughes, Edward Jones; Philip Jacobson, Joseph; Katherine Bullock Joyner, Pilot and Powell; Judge Mary Ann Vial Lemmon, Senior United States District Judge of the United States District Court for the Eastern District of Louisiana; Thomas Lowenburg, Octavia Books; Dr. Gordon "Nick" Mueller, CEO, Coleman Warner, communications assistant, and Alan Raphael, marketing outreach manager, National WWII Museum; Joshua Mann Pailet, A Gallery for Fine Photography; David George Perlis, Perlis; Dannal Perry, Plum; Virginia Saussy, consultant to MSMA; Stephen Rizzo, Uptown Delivery Pharmacy; George Saucier and Tim Hobbs, The Shops at 2011; Ben Rauch and Nat Ward Bergeron, National Art & Hobby; Alon Shaya, Shaya's Restaurant; Ben Tanet, Chez Nous; and Bonnie Wilson, Weinstein's.

Special thanks go to the individuals at the Williams Research Center of The Historic New Orleans Collection, 410 Chartres Street: Priscilla Lawrence, THNOC executive director; John H. Lawrence, THNOC director of Museum Programs; Alfred E. Lemmon, THNOC director of the Williams Research Center; and Michelle Gaynor, manager of Retail Operations.

For all the superlative assistance provided by the staff of the Reading Room, thanks go to Rebecca Smith, head of Reader Services, who generously provided permission for use of historic images from The Collection in the book; M.L. Eichhorn, senior reference associate; Jennifer Navarre, senior reference associate; Robert Ticknor, reference associate; Heather Green, reference assistant; and Heather Szafran, reference assistant.

Kudos to The Collection's photography department, whose scanned reproductions were described by the book's production director as "top notch, very impressive": Keely Merritt, head of Photography; Melissa Carrier, photographer; Tere Kirkland, associate photographer; and Emily Hindin, assistant photographer.

For always offering a happy welcome at the front reception desk, thanks go to Frances Salvaggio, Sally Stassi, and Albert Dumas, Jr.

Heartfelt thanks go to publisher Scott Campbell and Marci Schramm for creating an enjoyable work environment and of course to their little ones, Tallulah and Delilah, who were always unfailingly entertaining.

In bringing the book to print, thanks go to Development Editor Lindsey Reynolds, Production Director Terry Callaway, and Asia Alvarado for all her help. Of course Magazine Street would never have come to life as it is here without the breathtaking photographs of Margot Landen.

Final thanks go to those who graciously agreed—even called it a fun idea—to be part of the cover photograph of feet around the Magazine Street tile sign at the corner of Robert. Those in the image are Bryan Batt, Simon Hardeveld, Judge Mary Ann Vial Lemmon, Joshua Mann Pailet, and Tallulah and Delilah Campbell, as well as the author. Several other individuals had graciously agreed to be part of this photograph, but other commitments prevented them from taking part when the initial shoot date had to be postponed by torrential rain: Aidan Gill, Katrina Greer, Lauren Haydel, David George Perlis, and Alon Shaya.

Bibliography

Brunet, Rene, and Jack Stewart. *There's One in Your Neighborhood: The Lost Movie Theaters of New Orleans.* New Orleans: Arthur Hardy Enterprises, 2012.

Chase, John C. *Frenchmen, Desire, Good Children . . . and Other Streets of New Orleans.* New Orleans: Robert L. Crager & Co., 1949.

Christovich, Mary Louise, Roulhac Toledano, Betsy Swanson, and Pat Holden. *New Orleans Architecture, Volume II: The American Sector.* Gretna, LA: Pelican Publishing Co., 1972.

Cruise, Boyd Research Cards, The Historic New Orleans Collection, New Orleans, Louisiana.

The City of New Orleans: The Book of the Chamber of Commerce and Industry of Louisiana and Other Public Bodies of the Crescent City. New Orleans: George W. Engelhardt, 1894.

Earhart, Ann H. and Diana D. Earhart. *New Orleans Underground Shopping: Magazine St. Volume.* New Orleans: Les Freres D'Sol, Publisher, 1978.

Engelhardt, George W., and The Picayune. *New Orleans, Louisiana, the Crescent City: The book of the Picayune also of the public bodies and business interests of the Place.* New Orleans: George W. Engelhardt, 1903-1904.

Forman, L. Ronald, and Joseph Logsdon with John Wilds. *Audubon Park: An Urban Eden.* New Orleans: Audubon Park Press, 1985.

Friends of the Cabildo. *New Orleans Architecture, Volume VII: Jefferson City.* Gretna, LA: Pelican Publishing Co., 1989.

Friends of the Cabildo. *New Orleans Architecture, Volume VIII: The University Section.* Gretna, LA: Pelican Publishing Co., 2000.

Green, Alvah J., III. "Fighting Spirit: A History of St. Henry's Catholic Church New Orleans, 1871-1929." M.A. thesis, University of New Orleans, December 2015. UNO. scholarworks.uno.edu.

Hardy, Arthur. *Arthur Hardy's Mardi Gras in New Orleans.* New Orleans: Arthur Hardy Enterprises, 2001.

Hennick, Louis C., and E. Harper Charlton. *The Streetcars of New Orleans.* Gretna, LA: Pelican Publishing Co., 1975.

"H. Rault Locksmiths." In *A Guide to the Historic Shops and Restaurants of New Orleans.* New York: The Little Bookroom, 2004. Google Books, books.google.com?isbn=1892145278.

Huxtable, Ada Louise. *Goodbye History, Hello Hamburger: An Anthology of Architectural Delights and Disasters.* Landmark Reprint Series. Washington D.C.: Preservation Press, 1986.

LaCour, Arthur, and Stuart Landry. *New Orleans Masquerade: Chronicles of Carnival.* Gretna, LA: Pelican Publishing Co., 1957.

Lemmon, Alfred E., John T. Magill, and Jason R. Wiese, eds. *Charting Louisiana: Five Hundred Years of Maps.* New Orleans: The Historic New Orleans Collection, 2003.

Magazine Street Merchants Association. www.magazinestreet.com.

McCash, Doug. "The Geography of an Assassin, Seeking out Lee Harvey Oswald's New Orleans Homes." *New Orleans Times-Picayune,* November 13, 2013. http://www.nola.com/politics/index.ssf/2013/11/the_geography_of_an_assassin_s.html.

The "M" Day Celebration of the Improvement of Magazine Street and the Inauguration of Electric Trolley Coaches July 9, 1948 Sponsored by the Combined Magazine Business Men's Association. New Orleans: Prepared by New Orleans Public Service, Inc., 1948.

Robinson, E[lisha], and R[oger] H. Pidgeon. *Robinson's Atlas of the City of New Orleans, Louisiana.* New York: E. Robinson, 1883. Reproduced online as "The Robinson Atlas," by Clerk of Civil District Court for the Parish of Orleans. http://www.orleanscivilclerk.com/robinson.

Sanborn Map and Publishing Co. *New Orleans, Louisiana.* New York: Sanburn Map and Publishing Co., 1886, 1887, 1896, 1909 (updated to 1938), and 1973.

Sauder, Robert A. "The Origin and Spread of the Public Market System in New Orleans." *Louisiana History* 22, no. 3 (Summer 1981).

Soniat, Meloncy C. "The Faubourgs Forming the Upper Section of New Orleans." *The Louisiana Historical Quarterly* 20 (1937).

Southern Bell Telephone and Telegraph Co., New Orleans, La. Street Address Telephone Directory: Spring and Summer 1928 Issue. New Orleans: Southern Bell Telephone and Telegraph Co., 1928.

Southern Bell Telephone and Telegraph Co., New Orleans, La. Street Address Telephone Directory: Summer 1930 Issue. New Orleans: Southern Bell Telephone and Telegraph Co., 1930.

Starr, S. Frederick. *Southern Comfort: The Garden District of New Orleans.* The Flora Levy Humanities Series. Princeton, NJ: Princeton University Press, 1998.

Vermeulen, Perry. "Magazine St., New Orleans: Where Oswald Lived." Three Shots Were Fired. Posted September 27, 2013. http://threeshotswerefired.com/?p=1055.

Wilson, Samuel, Jr., and Bernard Lemann. *New Orleans Architecture, Volume I: The Lower Garden District.* Gretna, LA: Pelican Publishing Co., 1971.

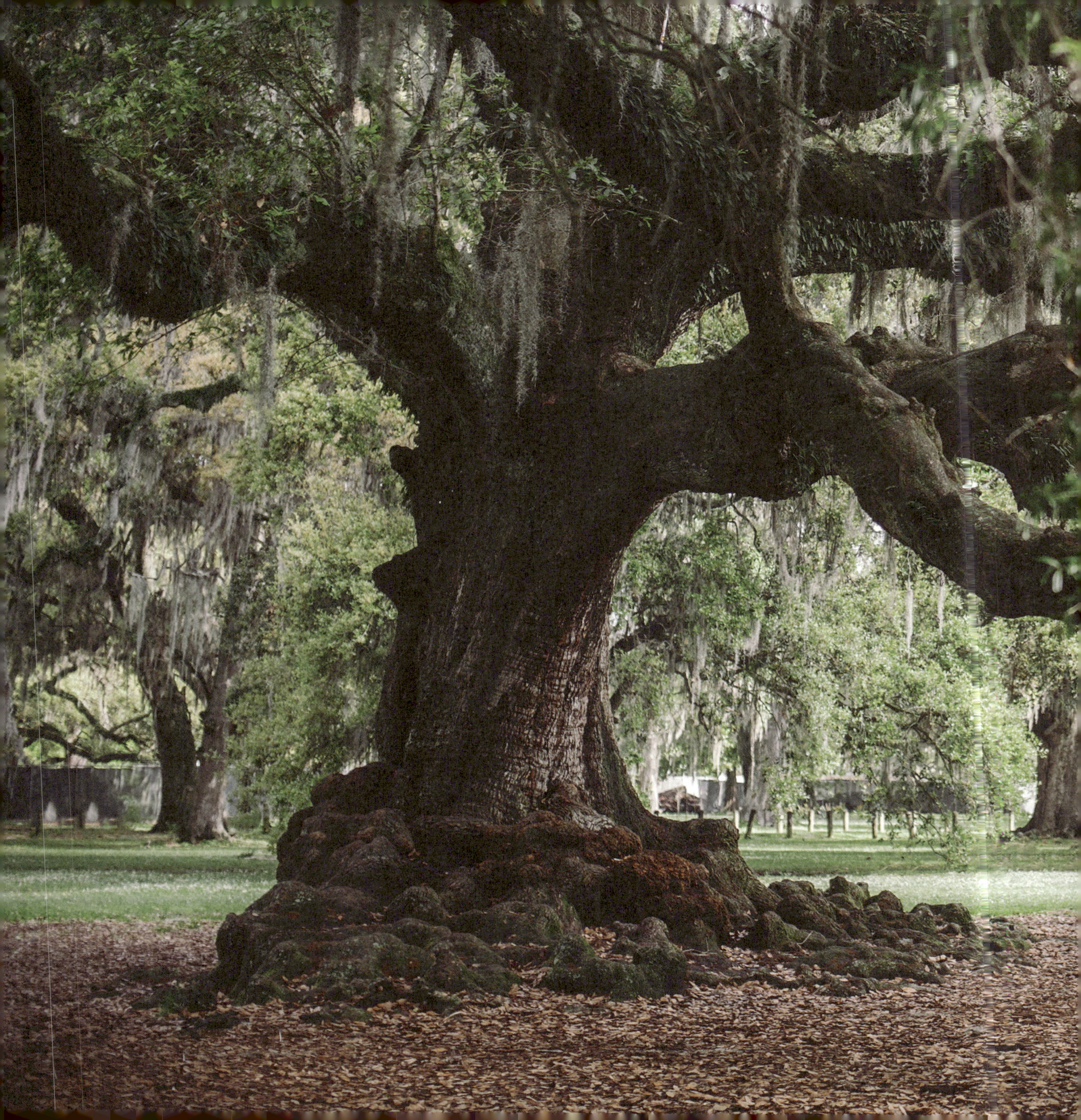